THE EXPERIENCE OF LITERATURE

A READER WITH COMMENTARIES

LIONEL TRILLING
Columbia University

Library of Congress Catalog Card Number: 67-15654

2628402

Printed in the United States of America

123456789

COPYRIGHT ACKNOWLEDGMENTS

CITY LIGHTS BOOKS

for Allen Ginsberg, "A Supermarket in California" from *HOWL and Other Poems,* copyright 1956, 1959 by Allen Ginsberg; and "To Aunt Rose" from *KADDISH and Other Poems,* copyright 1961 by Allen Ginsberg. Reprinted by permission of City Lights Books.

COLLINS-KNOWLTON-WING, INC.

for Robert Graves, "Warning to Children" and "To Juan at the Winter Solstice" from *Collected Poems of Robert Graves,* Doubleday and Company. Reprinted by permission of Collins-Knowlton-Wing, Inc., copyright © 1955 by International Authors, N.V.

J. M. DENT & SONS LTD.

for Dylan Thomas, "The Force that through the Green Fuse," "Do Not Go Gentle into that Good Night," "In My Craft or Sullen Art," and "Fern Hill" from *The Collected Poems of Dylan Thomas,* copyright 1953 by Dylan Thomas, published by New Directions, reprinted in Canada by the permission of J. M. Dent & Sons Ltd. and the Literary Executors of the Dylan Thomas Estate.

DOUBLEDAY & COMPANY, INC.

for Theodore Roethke, "Frau Bauman, Frau Schmidt, and Frau Schwartze," copyright 1952 by Theodore Roethke. From the book *Words for the Wind* by Theodore Roethke. Reprinted by permission of Doubleday & Company, Inc. And for Theodore Roethke, "The Far Field," copyright © 1963 by Beatrice Roethke as Administratrix of the Estate of Theodore Roethke; and "Light Listened," copyright © 1964 by Beatrice Roethke as Administratrix of the Estate of Theodore Roethke, from the book *The Far Field* by Theodore Roethke. Reprinted by permission of Doubleday & Company, Inc.

for Rudyard Kipling, "Recessional" and "Danny Deever" from *Rudyard Kipling's Verse:* Definitive Edition. Reprinted by permission of Mrs. George Bambridge and Doubleday & Company, Inc.

DUELL, SLOAN & PEARCE INC.

for E. E. Cummings, "anyone lived in a pretty how town," copyright 1939, 1940 by E. E. Cummings. From *50 Poems by E. E. Cummings,* reprinted by permission of Duell, Sloan & Pearce, Inc.

FABER AND FABER LTD.

for T. S. Eliot, "The Waste Land," "La Figlia Che Piange," "Sweeney Among the Nightingales," "Journey of the Magi," and "Animula," from *Collected Poems 1909–1962.* Permission to reprint in Canada granted by Faber and Faber Ltd.

for W. H. Auden, "In Memory of W. B. Yeats," "In Memory of Sigmund Freud," and "Musée des Beaux Arts" from *Collected Shorter Poems.* Reprinted in Canada by permission of Faber and Faber Ltd.

FARRAR, STRAUS AND GIROUX, INC.

for Robert Lowell, "For the Union Dead" from *For The Union Dead,* copyright 1960 by Robert Lowell. Reprinted by permission of Farrar, Straus and Giroux, Inc.

for John Berryman, "Conversation" from *The Dispossessed,* reprinted by permission of the author. Copyright 1948 by John Berryman. "Dream Song: 14," and "Dream Song: 18" from *77 Dream Songs* by John Berryman, copyright © 1963, 1964 by John Berryman. Reprinted by permission of Farrar, Straus and Giroux, Inc.

Harcourt, Brace & World, Inc.

for Robert Lowell, "The Quaker Graveyard in Nantucket" and "Mr. Edwards and the Spider" from *Lord Weary's Castle,* copyright 1944, 1946 by Robert Lowell. Reprinted by permission of Harcourt, Brace and World, Inc. And for "The Fat Man in the Mirror," copyright 1947 by Robert Lowell. Reprinted from his volume *The Mills of the Kavanaughs* by permission of Harcourt, Brace & World, Inc.

for T. S. Eliot, "The Waste Land," "La Figlia Che Piange," "Sweeney Among the Nightingales," "Journey of the Magi," and "Animula" from *Collected Poems 1909–1962* by T. S. Eliot, copyright 1936 by Harcourt, Brace & World, Inc.; copyright © 1963, 1964 by T. S. Eliot. Reprinted by permission of the publishers.

for E. E. Cummings, "My Father Moved Through Dooms of Love," and "i say no world," copyright 1940 by E. E. Cummings. Reprinted from his volume *Poems 1923–1954* by permission of Harcourt, Brace & World, Inc. And for "All in Green My Love Went Riding," copyright 1923, 1951 by E. E. Cummings. Reprinted from his volume *Poems 1923–1954* by permission of Harcourt, Brace & World, Inc. And for "My girl's tall with hard long eyes," copyright 1937 by E. E. Cummings. Reprinted from his volume *Poems 1923–1954* by permission of Harcourt, Brace & World, Inc.

Harvard University Press

for Emily Dickinson, "I taste a liquor never brewed," "A narrow fellow in the grass," "A clock stopped—not the mantels," "Because I could not stop for death," "There's a certain slant of light," "Heavenly Father, Take to Thee," "I've seen a dying eye," "Papa Above!" " 'Twas later when the summer went," and "Go Tell it—What a Message—" The poems of Emily Dickinson are reprinted by permission of the Publishers and Trustees of Amherst College from Thomas H. Johnson, Editor, *The Poems of Emily Dickinson,* The Belknap Press of Harvard University Press, Cambridge, Massachusetts, copyright 1951, 1955 by The President and Fellows of Harvard College.

Holt, Rinehart and Winston, Inc.

for Stanley Burnshaw, "Historical Song of Then and Now," "Modes of Belief," and "Poetry, the Art," from *Caged in an Animal's Mind* by Stanley Burnshaw. Copyright 1952, © 1958, 1961, 1963 by Stanley Burnshaw. Reprinted by permission of Holt, Rinehart and Winston, Inc.

for Robert Frost, "Neither Out Far Nor In Deep," "Home Burial," "Stopping by Woods on a Snowy Evening," "Design," "Provide, Provide," and "Directive," from *Complete Poems of Robert Frost.* Copyright 1923, 1930, 1939, 1947 by Holt, Rinehart and Winston, Inc. Copyright 1936, 1951, © 1958 by Robert Frost. Copyright © 1964, 1967 by Lesley Frost Ballantine. Reprinted by permission of Holt, Rinehart and Winston, Inc.

for A. E. Housman, "Loveliest of Trees, the Cherry Now," and "Be Still, My Soul, Be Still," from "A Shropshire Lad"—Authorised Edition—from *The Collected Poems of A. E. Housman.* Copyright 1939, 1940 © 1959 by Holt, Rinehart and Winston, Inc. Copyright © 1967 by Robert E. Symons. Reprinted by permission of Holt, Rinehart and Winston, Inc.

Houghton Mifflin Company

for Archibald MacLeish, "Ars Poetica," "End of the World," and "You, Andrew Marvell" from *The Collected Poems of Archibald MacLeish.* Reprinted by permission of the publisher, Houghton Mifflin Company.

Little, Brown and Company

for Stanley Kunitz, "Foreign Affairs" (originally in *The New Yorker*), and "For the Word is Flesh," copyright © 1958 by Stanley Kunitz, from *Selected Poems 1928–1958* by Stanley Kunitz, by permission of Atlantic-Little Brown and Co.

for Emily Dickinson, "Papa Above!" and "Heavenly Father, Take to Thee," copyright, 1914, 1942 by Martha Dickinson Bianchi, from *The Complete Poems of Emily Dickinson,* by permission of Little, Brown and Co.

Liveright Publishing Corporation

for Hart Crane, "Voyages II," and "At Melville's Tomb." Reprinted by permission of Liveright Publishers, New York from *The Collected Poems of Hart Crane,* © R 1961 by Liveright Publishing Corporation.

The Macmillan Company

for Marianne Moore, "Elephants," reprinted with permission of The Macmillan Company from *Nevertheless* by Marianne Moore. Copyright 1944 by Marianne Moore. And "Poetry," reprinted with permission of The Macmillan Company from *Collected Poems* by Marianne Moore. Copyright 1935 by Marianne Moore. Renewed 1963 by Marianne Moore and T. S. Eliot.

for Edwin Arlington Robinson, "Mr. Flood's Party." Reprinted with permission of

The Macmillan Company from *Collected Poems* by E. A. Robinson. Copyright 1921 by E. A. Robinson. Renewed 1949 by Ruth Nivison.

for William Butler Yeats, "Byzantium," reprinted with the permission of The Macmillan Company from *The Winding Stair* by William Butler Yeats. Copyright 1933 by The Macmillan Company. Renewed 1961 by Bertha Georgie Yeats. "Sailing to Byzantium" and "Leda and the Swan." Reprinted with permission of The Macmillan Company from *The Tower* by W. B. Yeats. Copyright 1928 by The Macmillan Company. Renewed 1956 by Georgie Yeats. "The Second Coming" and "A Prayer for My Daughter." Reprinted with permission of The Macmillan Company from *Later Poems from Michael Robartes and the Dancer* by W. B. Yeats. Copyright 1924 by The Macmillan Company. Renewed 1952 by Bertha Georgie Yeats.

for Thomas Hardy, "The Darkling Thrush," "The Subalterns," "Wives in the Sere," "The Lacking Sense," "The Voice," "The Five Students," "Who's in the Next Room?" and "Afterwards." Reprinted with permission of The Macmillan Company from *Collected Poems,* by Thomas Hardy. Copyright 1925 by The Macmillan Company.

New Directions Publishing Corporation

for Ezra Pound, "A Pact," "Ite," "Les Millwin," "Prayer for his Lady's Life," and "Come my Cantilations" from *Personae* by Ezra Pound. Copyright 1926, 1954 by Ezra Pound. Reprinted by permission of the publisher, New Directions Publishing Corporation.

for Delmore Schwartz, "In the Naked Bed, in Plato's Cave" and "The Heavy Bear" from *In Dreams Begin Responsibilities* by Delmore Schwartz, copyright 1938 by New Directions; © 1966 by Delmore Schwartz. Reprinted by permission of the publisher, New Directions Publishing Corporation.

for Dylan Thomas, "The force that through the green fuse," copyright 1938 by New Directions Publishing Corp.; "In My Craft or Sullen Art," "Fern Hill" and "Do Not Go Gentle into That Good Night," copyright 1953 by Dylan Thomas, from *Collected Poems* by Dylan Thomas. Reprinted by permission of the publisher, New Directions Publishing Corporation.

Oxford University Press

for Gerard Manley Hopkins, "Spring and Fall: To a Young Child," "The Leaden Echo and the Golden Echo," "Pied Beauty," "The Wind Hover," and "Carrion Comfort," from *Poems of Gerard Manley Hopkins,* Third Edition, edited by W. H. Gardner, copyright 1948 by Oxford University Press, Inc. Reprinted by permission.

Random House, Inc. Alfred A. Knopf, Inc.

for W. H. Auden, "In Memory of W. B. Yeats," "In Memory of Sigmund Freud," and "Musée des Beaux Arts," copyright 1940 by W. H. Auden. Reprinted from *The Collected Poetry of W. H. Auden* by permission of Random House, Inc. And for "The Shield of Achilles," copyright 1952 by W. H. Auden. Reprinted from *The Shield of Achilles* by W. H. Auden, by permission of Random House, Inc.

for Wallace Stevens, "Peter Quince," "Sunday Morning," "Anecdote of the Jar," and "Thirteen Ways of Looking at a Blackbird." Copyright 1923 and renewed 1951 by Wallace Stevens. Reprinted from *The Collected Poems of Wallace Stevens* by permission of Alfred A. Knopf, Inc. And for "Soldier, There is a War," copyright 1942 by Wallace Stevens. Reprinted from *Notes Toward a Supreme Fiction* by Wallace Stevens, by permission of Alfred A. Knopf, Inc.

for John Crowe Ransom, "Here Lies a Lady," "Bells for John Whiteside's Daughter," and "Blue Girls," copyright 1924 by Alfred A. Knopf, Inc. and renewed 1952 by John Crowe Ransom. Reprinted from *Selected Poems by John Crowe Ransom* by permission of the publisher.

for Robert Penn Warren, "Variation: Ode to Fear" from *Selected Poems 1923–1943* by Robert Penn Warren, copyright 1944 by Robert Penn Warren, reprinted by permission of Random House, Inc., and "Bearded Oaks" from *Selected Poems: Old and New, 1923–1966* by Robert Penn Warren, copyright © 1966 by Robert Penn Warren, reprinted by permission of Random House, Inc.

Charles Scribner's Sons

for Edwin Arlington Robinson, "Miniver Cheevy," copyright 1907, Charles Scribner's Sons; renewal copyright 1935, reprinted with the permission of Charles Scribner's Sons from *The Town Down the River* by Edwin Arlington Robinson. And for "Luke Havergal," reprinted with the permission of Charles Scribner's Sons from *The Children of the Night* by Edwin Arlington Robinson.

for Allen Tate, "Ode to the Confederate Dead," copyright 1932, Charles Scribner's Sons; renewal copyright © 1960, Allen Tate; and "The Mediterranean," reprinted with the permission of Charles Scribner's Sons from *Poems* by Allen Tate (1960).

The Society of Authors

for Walter de la Mare, "The Listeners." Permission has been granted by The Literary Trustees of Walter de la Mare and The Society of Authors as their representative. From the book *Rhymes and Verses* by Walter de la Mare.

THE VIKING PRESS, INC.

for D. H. Lawrence, "The Snake" from *The Complete Poems of D. H. Lawrence.* Edited by Vivian de Sola Pinto and F. Warren Roberts. Copyright 1923, 1950 by Frieda Lawrence. Reprinted by permission of The Viking Press, Inc. And "The Elephant Is Slow to Mate" from *The Complete Poems of D. H. Lawrence.* Copyright 1929 by Frieda Lawrence Ravagli. All rights reserved. Reprinted by permission of The Viking Press, Inc. And "Tortoise Shout" from the same volume, copyright 1923, 1950 by Frieda Lawrence. Reprinted by permission of The Viking Press, Inc.

A. P. WATT & SON

for Robert Graves, "The Climate of Thought," reprinted by permission of Robert Graves and Collins-Knowlton-Wing, Inc., together with A. P. Watt & Son, from *Collected Poems,* copyright © 1955 and 1965 by International Authors N. V. and published by Doubleday & Company, Inc., and Cassell & Co. Ltd.

for Rudyard Kipling, "Danny Deever" and "Recessional," reprinted in Canada by permission of Mrs. George Bambridge and The Macmillan Co. of Canada Ltd., together with A. P. Watt & Son. "Danny Deever" is from *Barrack Room Ballads* and "Recessional" from *The Five Nations.*

for W. B. Yeats, "Leda and the Swan," "The Second Coming," "Sailing to Byzantium," "Byzantium," and "A Prayer for My Daughter," reprinted in Canada by permission of Mr. M. B. Yeats and the Macmillan Company of Canada Ltd., together with A. P. Watt & Son, from *Collected Poems of W. B. Yeats.*

WESLEYAN UNIVERSITY PRESS

for James Dickey, "The Fiend," copyright © 1965 by James Dickey. Reprinted from *Buckdancer's Choice,* by James Dickey, by permission of Wesleyan University Press.

PREFACE

This is an anthology designed to be used in college courses that undertake the study of literature in general, often with a view to "introducing" the student to an art that he perhaps thinks of as remote from his interest. Such courses have had an established place in the curriculum for a considerable time, and for almost as long their convenience has been served by books that bring together notable examples of the chief literary genres, usually, like this one, drama, fiction, and poetry. In its purpose, then, and in most of its elements, the present volume is of a familiar kind. What will not be familiar from similar anthologies is the commentaries, in the form of brief essays, that follow each of the plays and stories and certain of the poems. They have only one end in view —to make it more likely that the student's act of reading will be an experience, having in mind what that word implies of an activity of consciousness and response. Their intention, that is to say, is no other than that of every teacher of literature as he works with his students in the classroom.

That there are classrooms in which literature is the subject of instruction testifies to our recognition that the reading of literature is not always and necessarily an experience. As every teacher of literature knows, a student can proceed with diligence from the beginning of a work to its end and yet give but little response to what he reads. We count on what takes place in the classroom to initiate a more appropriate degree of activity. By means of the discussion he institutes, the teacher brings his students to understand that the work before them is an object that may be freely touched and handled, picked up, turned over, looked at from this angle or that, and, at least in some sense, possessed. The commentaries in this book have been supplied in the belief that something has been gained for the classroom situation if the student has previously been led to think about what he will be asked to talk about.

It will readily be seen that no special theory of literature or method of criticism informs what I have written. In some of the commentaries the emphasis falls on formal matters, such as imagery, diction, versification, tone, point of view, and so on. But I have not thought it necessary to limit myself to such considerations as being more truly, or more purely, literary than others. I have felt free to enter into the overt or implicit meanings of a work and to pursue (sometimes to question) its moral, or social, or religious ideas. I have not hesitated to refer to critical theories or canons of taste of the past. If a biographical or historical circumstance seems to be to the point, I have adduced it. In short, I have availed myself of any of the usual elements of literary discourse that I thought relevant to the work and useful to the student.

I can scarcely fail to be aware of the opinion of some teachers that students should not read anything *about* a work of literature. It is held that coherent discourse in print interferes with the student's perception and feeling, making his response to the work less immediate and sincere, less his own. This is a view that must be taken seriously, especially at the present time, when it may sometimes seem that literature exists chiefly to provide occasions for its being explicated, expounded, and judged, and that, as a consequence of so much public to-do, the individual reader's experience of literature has an ever-diminishing chance of being private and autonomous.

Yet a jealous concern for the privacy and autonomy of the experience of literature must not obscure the truth that the literary experience is, of its very nature, communal—it asks to be shared in discourse. It is certainly possible for literary discourse to become excessive and intrusive, yet in any developed culture the impulse to say things about literature and to take account of what others say about it is no less natural than the creation and the enjoyment of the art. We find a pleasure that seems instinctual not only in the emotions that are aroused by what we read in private but also in communicating them to each other, in trying to understand why we feel as we do, in testing our emotions by those that others tell us they have, in discovering what we might possibly feel beyond what we do feel. And discourse leads to dialectic: we disagree with others in observation and response and in the general principles that we and they have insensibly been led to form. This activity, in itself interesting and pleasant, has the effect of increasing the interest and the pleasure of the private experience. The belief that this is so makes the ground upon which all instruction in literature proceeds. There is, indeed, no other ground. The activity of discourse and dialectic takes various forms and among them there is really no difference in the way they relate to the individual's privacy and autonomy. The discourse of an essay and the dialectic it initiates between itself and the reader are not different in kind from the discourse and the dialectic that go on in the free but directed discussion of the classroom. Neither the discussion nor the essay can be supposed to violate the student's privacy or limit his autonomy—unless on this score the whole process of education is to be impugned!

Nothing could be further from the intention of the commentaries than to usurp or circumscribe the teacher's function. They could hardly say all that is to be said about the works to which they address themselves, and they have tried to say no more than will bring the student into a more intimate and more active connection with what he has read. They obviously do not seek to impose themselves as anything like doctrine and they will not have failed of their purpose if they arouse either the student or the teacher, or both together, to disagreement.

The serviceability of a teaching anthology of this kind is judged by criteria that are obvious enough. Its selection of examples of the various genres should be sufficiently large to permit catholicity and variety. The critical standards by which it makes its choice should be uncompromising, yet applied with the awareness that, among the innumerable works that command our admiration, some are more accessible to students than others and some are more teachable than others. It should assume that literature is a continuous enterprise and include on an equal footing both the traditional and the new. I have had these considerations in mind and a few others as well. In making choice of the works to be included I have preferred those that I thought would prove memorable to the student by reason of momentousness of theme and force of dramatic or intellectual energy. That a work had already proved memorable to many was a special recommendation: not all the works I have chosen are "great" but I have, I think, made preponderant those to which the adjective may be applied.

The plays and stories have been drawn from several literatures. The poems, for obvious reasons, are all English and American. Although the selection of poems for further reading is large, it does not pretend to be canonical, and this is especially to be said of the selection of contemporary poets. It is perhaps here that I should remark that I have thought it best that the poets of our own time who are included in this section of the anthology should be read without footnotes.

The examples of each genre are arranged chronologically, although there are a few violations of this order for particular reasons. Historical considerations in themselves are naturally not paramount in introductory courses in literature, yet literary study cannot proceed without awareness of the fact that from one age to another changes take place in the meanings of words, in aesthetic conventions, in intellectual and moral assumptions, and in modes of behavior. The order of chronology is a first means to this necessary awareness.

* * *

I was peculiarly fortunate in the help I was given with this book and I am deeply grateful to those who gave it. The work on the footnotes was begun by Kent Hieatt, continued by David Thompson, and completed by Terry Schutz. Bernard Lionel Einbond of Hunter College kindly took in charge the task of checking the textual accuracy of the poems. Seeing the book through the press with Brian Heald was to me a revelation of what editorial intelligence, precision, and efficiency can be and I shall always remember our collaboration with pleasure. To Stanley Burnshaw I owe an especial debt of gratitude not only for his many valuable suggestions but also for his unfailing sympathy and his supernal patience.

New York, N.Y. L.T.
January 1967

which it makes its choice should be uncompromising, yet applied with the awareness that, among the innumerable works that command our admiration, some are more accessible to students than others and some are more teachable than others. It should assume that literature is a continuous enterprise and include on an equal footing both the traditional and the new. I have had these considerations in mind and a few others as well. In making choice of the works to be included I have preferred those that I thought would prove memorable to the student by reason of momentousness of theme and force of dramatic or intellectual energy. That a work had already proved memorable to many was a special recommendation: not all the works I have chosen are "great" but I have, I think, made preponderant those to which the adjective may be applied.

The plays and stories have been drawn from several literatures. The poems, for obvious reasons, are all English and American. Although the selection of poems for Further reading is large, it does not pretend to be canonical, and this is especially to be said of the selection of contemporary poets. It is perhaps here that I should remark that I have thought it best that the poets of our own time who are included in this section of the anthology should be read without footnotes.

The examples of each genre are arranged chronologically, although there are a few violations of this order for particular reasons. Historical considerations in themselves are naturally not paramount in introductory courses in literature, yet literary study cannot proceed without awareness of the fact that from one age to another changes take place in the meanings of words, in aesthetic conventions, in intellectual and moral assumptions, and in modes of behavior. The order of chronology is a first means to this necessary awareness.

I was peculiarly fortunate in the help I was given with this book and I am deeply grateful to those who gave it. The work on the footnotes was begun by Kent Hieatt, continued by David Thompson, and completed by Terry Schutz. Bernard Lionel Einbond of Hunter College kindly took in charge the task of checking the textual accuracy of the poems. Seeing the book through the press with Brian Heald was to me a revelation of what editorial intelligence, precision, and efficiency can be and I shall always remember our collaboration with pleasure. To Stanley Burnshaw I owe an especial debt of gratitude not only for his many valuable suggestions but also for his unfailing sympathy and his supernal patience.

L.T.

New York, N.Y.
January 1967

CONTENTS

PART 2: POETRY FOR FURTHER READING

PART 1 POETRY WITH COMMENTARIES

EDWARD

ANONYMOUS

"Why dois your brand[1] sae[2] drap wi bluid,
Edward, Edward?
Why dois your brand sae drap wi bluid,
And why sae sad gang[3] yee O?"
"O I hae killed my hauke[4] sae guid, 5
Mither, mither,
O I hae killed my hauke sae guid,
And I had nae mair bot[5] hee O."

Your haukis bluid was nevir sae reid,
Edward, Edward, 10
Your haukis bluid was nevir sae reid,
My deir son I tell thee O."
"O I hae killed my reid-roan steid,[6]
Mither, mither,
O I hae killed my reid-roan steid, 15
That erst[7] was sae fair and frie O."

"Your steid was auld, and ye hae gat mair,
Edward, Edward,
Your steid was auld, and ye hae gat mair,
Sum other dule[8] ye drie[9] O." 20
"O I hae killed my fadir[10] deir,
Mither, mither,
O I hae killed my fadir deir,
Alas, and wae is mee O!"

"And whatten penance wul ye drie for that, 25
Edward, Edward?
And whatten penance wul ye drie, for that?
My deir son, now tell me O."
"Ile set my feit in yonder boat,
Mither, mither 30

[1] Sword. [2] So. [3] Go. [4] Hawk. [5] But. [6] Steed. [7] Once. [8] Grief. [9] Suffer. [10] Father.

Ile set my feit in yonder boat,
And Ile fare ovir the sea O."

"And what wul ye doe wi your towirs and your ha,[11]
Edward, Edward?
And what wul ye doe wi your towirs and your ha, 35
That were sae fair to see O?"
"Ile let thame stand tul they doun fa,
Mither, mither,
Ile let thame stand tul they doun fa,
For here nevir mair maun[12] I bee O." 40

"And what wul ye leive to your bairns[13] and your wife,
Edward, Edward?
And what wul ye leive to your bairns and your wife,
Whan ye gang ovir the sea O?"
"The warldis room, late them beg thrae[14] life, 45
Mither, mither,
The warldis room, late them beg thrae life,
For thame nevir mair wul I see O."

"And what wul ye leive to your ain mither deir,
Edward, Edward? 50
And what wul ye leive to your ain mither deir?
My deir son, now tell me O."
"The curse of hell frae me sall ye beir,
Mither, mither,
The curse of hell frae me sall ye beir, 55
Sic[15] counseils ye gave to me O."

COMMENTARY

It is obvious that the extraordinary force of this poem depends largely on its element of surprise. There are two occasions of surprise, both intense, but the one that comes midway in the poem is less shocking than the one at the end because in some measure we have been led to anticipate it. We know that we can expect the disclosure of an especially terrible deed when, to the mother's question about the blood on his sword and the look on his face, the son returns the first of his two prevaricating answers, saying that he has killed his hawk. The substance of this lie is dismaying enough—in the days when hawking was a common sport of the nobility, there was felt to be a close

[11] Hall, house. [12] Must. [13] Children. [14] Through. [15] Such.

communion between the falcon and the falconer. For a man to kill his horse, as Edward then says he did, perhaps goes even further against natural feeling. And if Edward had in fact killed neither the hawk nor the horse, if the blood on his sword and the look on his face are to be explained by some other killing, we expect it to be yet more horrifying, and of course it is—Edward has killed his father. Shocking as this revelation is, we have been at least a little prepared for it. But we are wholly unprepared for the second revelation, that he has killed his father at the behest of his mother.

In the face of the enormity it sets forth, "Edward" maintains an entire imperturbability. *We* are taken aback, but the poem is not even startled. The violence of its subject does not disorder the strict formality of its pattern; its composure is never ruffled. And this decorum transfers itself to the two characters: the mother's first question, which is asked in a tone that is not especially agitated, is answered in kind by the son, and once the question-and-answer mode of dialogue is established, it is sustained up to the end of the poem, when all the accumulated restraint releases itself in the explosion of the son's last terrible answer. The son is certainly not without emotion from the beginning—he is "sad," he speaks of his father as "deir" to him and bewails the murder, and his reply to his mother's question about his life in the future is bitter. Yet his emotions can scarcely be considered sufficient to his deed, and they do not become so until his last utterance. Up to that point he has submitted to his mother's questioning with a kind of grim courtesy; when at last the curse is torn from him, it is that much the more terrible because it has been so long held back. Yet even when he does utter the curse, which reveals his mother's part in the murder, his utterance is in the strict form the poem has established. What I have called the imperturbability of the poem creates the quiet out of which the terrible surprise leaps at us.

Of a piece with the poem's manner is its objectivity of view, which is uncompromising. Just as "Edward" refuses to make any emotional response to its subject, it refuses to make any moral comment on it—it is wholly detached from what it represents. By employing the dialogue form without a single narrative phrase, it refuses to assume even such involvement as is implied by *telling* what has happened; it undertakes to do nothing more than record what two persons said to each other. We are left free to judge the persons of the dialogue as we will, or must, while the poem itself is silent.

Nor does it say anything by way of explaining the dire happening that it reports. It does not consent to tell us the "whole story." This would consist of many episodes, of which the confrontation of the mother and the son would be only the last. If the events that took place before the dialogue have a claim upon our interest, it is a claim the poem does not recognize. We shall never know what sort of man the dead husband and father was, nor why his wife wanted him dead, nor by what means she induced her son to serve her purpose.

This frustration of our curiosity is strangely pleasurable. We do not find ourselves at a loss because the antecedent events of the poem have not been given us; we willingly consent to the high-handed way in which the poem denies the past. Its actually represented time is a brief moment of the immediate present. Of the five questions and seven answers that occupy this moment of the present, four questions and their answers have to do with the future. But to the past there is no reference at all until the last line, when the past is loosed in all its retributive ferocity. It has, of course, been lying in wait all through the poem. Doubtless the force of that last line is in large part achieved by its effect upon our moral sense: the intensity of our surprise does indeed relate to our horror at the mother's wickedness. Yet it is not only, and perhaps not even chiefly, the moral enormity that so satisfyingly disturbs us: it is rather the sudden, inexorable—we might almost say vengeful—return of the past, which the poem had seemed determined to exclude from its purview.

It has been said of "Edward" that it is "one of the best of all the ballads," and it may enhance our sense of the poem to be reminded that its characteristics are not unique but are shared by many poems in the same tradition.

Ballads divide, roughly, into two categories, literary and traditional, the latter sometimes called "popular" or "folk" ballads. In the eighteenth century there developed a considerable interest in the traditional ballads—the genre, in England and Scotland, took its rise in the fifteenth century—and many poets began to write in imitation of them or under their inspiration. But none of the traditional ballads can be assigned to any known author. This is not to say that they were not first composed by individual poets—no credence is now given to the theory, so attractive to many scholars in the nineteenth century, that the ballads were communal creations, that "the people" or "the folk" made them up by some process of composition the nature of which was never explained. The ballads are "popular" in the sense that they were made for and loved by the people, that is to say, by those members of a society who do not belong to the nobility: the literature of the people is distinguished from the literature of the court. But though each ballad was composed by an individual poet, his name was not attached to it and it did not long remain peculiarly his, nor did it necessarily circulate in its original form. For the ballads were not composed in writing nor were they meant to be read. They were intended to be sung and they had their existence in the memories of the people who sang them. The tune of a ballad was more likely to stay constant than its words, which might be altered by the whim of the singer, or by his failure to recall accurately what he had learned, or by his inability to understand one or another detail, such as a custom or an idiom no longer familiar to him. As a consequence, most of the traditional ballads exist in a number of versions.[1]

What may be thought of as the hallmark of the traditional ballads, the trait common to all examples of the genre, is their way of telling a story. Usually the story concerns an act of violence; it consists of a single situation which is presented at its point of climax, as near as possible to its conclusion. The method of presentation is dramatic rather than narrative, in the sense that it proceeds largely by dialogue; descriptions of scene and the use of what might be called stage-directions are kept to a minimum and are always very simple (in "Edward" there are none). Although the action is violent, the manner in which it is recounted is restrained. No effort is made to achieve originality of diction—the ballad-maker uses simple language and relies upon phrases that are traditional, or even clichés of the tradition. Explanation of motives and comment on morality are rigorously suppressed, and the attitude is one of detachment. It will readily be seen that many of these characteristics derive from the fact that the ballads were sung.

[1] The taking down of the words of ballads from the lips of the singer began in the eighteenth century and still goes on.

In "Edward" two traditional devices of the ballad play a decisive part in the poem's dramatic effectiveness. One of these is called by scholars "incremental repetition," a parallelism of phrase and idea that is strictly maintained, often in the form of question and answer; in "Edward" the natural effectiveness of this device is pointed up by the reiteration of courteous vocatives: "Edward, Edward" and "Mither, mither." Incremental repetition often takes the form of the so-called "nuncupative testament"—*nuncupative* means oral, as distinguished from written, and the phrase refers to a series of questions and answers in which a person in an extreme and usually fatal situation is asked what, upon his death or exile, he will bequeath to each of his relatives. Characteristically the answers are bitter and ironic, and the answer to the last question is usually climactic in its fierceness.

Many of the traditional ballads came over to America and some of them are still sung in parts of the country. "Edward" is one of these, but the American version has none of the tragic import of the Scottish. The son explains the stain on his "shirt sleeve" first as the blood of his "little yellow dog," then as the blood of his "little yellow horse"; it is his brother, not his father, he has killed; the cause of the quarrel is fully explained; his mother is not implicated in the murder; he speaks of his departure not as exile but as escape, and he plans to take "Katie dear" with him "to bear [him] company."

THEY FLEE FROM ME

SIR THOMAS WYATT

1503–1542

They flee from me that sometime did me seek,
With naked foot stalking in my chamber.
I have seen them gentle, tame, and meek,
That now are wild, and do not remember
That some time they put themselves in danger 5
To take bread at my hand; and now they range,
Busily seeking with a continual change.

Thanked be fortune, it hath been otherwise
Twenty times better; but once, in special,
In thin array, after a pleasant guise,[1] 10
When her loose gown from her shoulders did fall,
And she caught me in her arms long and small.[2]
Therewith all sweetly did me kiss,
And softly said, Dear heart, how like you this?

It was no dream; I lay broad waking. 15
But all is turned, thorough[3] my gentleness,
Into a strange fashion of forsaking;
And I have leave to go of her goodness,
And she also to use newfangleness.
But since that I so kindely am served,[4] 20
I fain[5] would know what she hath deserved.

COMMENTARY

One of the things that are bound to strike us early in our acquaintance with this poem is the shift from the "they" of the first stanza to the "she" of the rest of the poem. In the first lines the poet seems to be recalling the high favor in which he stood with many women, or women in general. In the second stanza

[1] Looking pleasant. [2] Thin. [3] Through. [4] Dealt with. [5] Gladly, with pleasure.

he recalls one erotic occasion "in special," with a woman who is strongly particularized. And the emotions that follow upon this encounter occupy his bitter and bewildered thought in the third stanza.

Some interpretations of the poem tell us that we must not take the "they" literally, that from the beginning the poet is really talking about "she." There is an advantage in this view—if we accept it, we can suppose that the happening the poet remembers "in special" is not the first love-encounter with one mistress out of many, but one peculiarly memorable encounter out of many with the same woman; of the two possibilities, the latter is the more interesting. But if "they" is really "she," it is by no means clear why the poet pluralized and generalized his mistress. In any case, the visual effect that "they" makes in the first stanza cannot be easily obliterated—one has the delighted impression that all the women the poet may ever have made love to are present at the same time in his chamber, all "stalking" together, a little multitude of glimpsed presences, rather like a flock or herd. The adjectives used of them evoke the image of delicate and charming animals: the "naked foot" evokes their lightness of step; their graceful stealth is suggested by their "stalking." This word has more than one meaning—it can refer to the action of a hunter trying to approach an animal without being seen, heard, or scented; or it can describe a way of walking, of humans or animals, with stiff, high, measured steps, like a long-legged bird—but Wyatt probably intended the now obsolete use of the word, which means the soft, cautious tread of an animal. No doubt he wished to create the image of a little herd of light-stepping deer which, in the park of some great manor house, become tame enough to take food from human hands.

But in the conclusion of the stanza three words occur which, for Wyatt's contemporary audience, would tend to modify, even to dispel, the enchanting picture of the preceding lines. Hunting was the chief sport of the gentlemen and ladies of the sixteenth century and they were conversant with its elaborate technical vocabulary. "Range," "seek," and "change" are hunting terms, all referring to the behavior of dogs. "Range" was the word used to describe the action of dogs who rove and stray in search of game. " 'Seek!' " (or " 'Seek out!' ") was the command to a dog to begin the search, and "a seek" was a series of notes upon the hunting horn calling the hounds to begin a chase. A "change" was an animal which the hounds meet by chance and then hunt instead of the quarry. These technical meanings are certainly not exclusive of others, and of course they contradict the idea that the pleasing animals, once "gentle, tame, and meek," have become "wild"—hunting dogs and hounds, even when fierce, are not wild. Yet it is probably not an accident that Wyatt uses three words associated with the hunt. The vocabulary of the field suggests that "they" who might once have been hunted have taken on the character of hunters.

"They" were perhaps never without their predatory aspect, and certainly "she" was not. The charm of the remembered erotic scene of the second stanza lies in the mistress's boldness in seduction, her overt display of her erotic power over her lover. Her ever-remembered utterance on the occasion makes this plain, and to Wyatt's audience her way of addressing her lover, "Dear heart," would have brought the idea of a deer, a hart, the pun being then a common one, the easier to make because there was no established difference in the spelling of the two words.

The "specialness" of the episode is superbly conveyed by the first line of the last stanza, "It was no dream; I lay broad waking," of which the very sound suggests the lover's incredulity over the delight of the event at the same time that he insists on its actuality.

Wyatt's poem makes a particular appeal to modern taste because of the directness and colloquial simplicity of its diction: it avoids, as modern poetry characteristically does, any reliance on "poetical" language. Another claim upon modern admiration is the way it handles its metre. The basic pattern of the verse is iambic pentameter, a line of five feet, the foot being typically of two syllables with the stress on the second; for example, the first line of the poem, "They fleé from mé that sómetime díd me séek," conforms to this pattern. But many of the succeeding lines—"Busily seeking with a continual change"; "And she me caught in her arms long and small"; "It was no dream; I lay broad waking"—clearly violate this metrical scheme. The prevailing modern supposition is that Wyatt knew exactly what he was doing, that he broke the pattern to achieve the effects he desired. But according to older opinion, Wyatt wrote as he did out of ignorance or incompetence; he was thought to have a bad ear and no control over metrics.

This opinion was established, at least by implication, within a few years after Wyatt's death, in 1557, when Tottel's famous miscellany, *Songs and Sonnets,* was published. Although Wyatt would seem to have had a considerable reputation as a poet, his poems had never been printed in his lifetime, and the *Miscellany* was his first significant publication. To judge by the large space he gave to Wyatt's poems, the editor of the volume had a general admiration of the poet. But he took rather a dim view of Wyatt's skill as a metrist, revising the poems extensively to make them suit the taste of a period which esteemed verse that was "musical" in a mellifluous way. The text of the poem that I use in this book is that of Wyatt's manuscript, except that the spelling has been modernized. Here is the revised and "corrected" version as it appeared in the *Miscellany,* with the spelling modernized:

They flee from me, that sometime did me seek
With naked foot stalking within my chamber.
Once have I seen them gentle, tame, and meek,
That now are wild, and do not once remember
That sometime they have put themselves in danger,
To take bread at my hand; and now they range,
Busily seeking in continual change.

Thanked be fortune, it hath been otherwise
Twenty times better; but once especial,
In thin array, after a pleasant guise,
When her loose gown did from her shoulders fall,
And she me caught in her arms long and small,
And therewithal so sweetly did me kiss,
And softly said, "Dear heart, how like you this?"

It was no dream, for I lay broad awaking.
But all is turned now, through my gentleness,
Into a bitter fashion of forsaking;
And I have leave to go, of her goodness,
And she also to use newfangleness.
But since that I unkindly so am served,
How like you this? what hath she now deserved?

The emendations make a poem that is no doubt prettier than the original but, by that token, a poem less masculine and strong. They dispose of any questions about stress that the original version might present to us, but in doing this deprive the poem of a considerable part of its interest. When, for example, the two syllables are added to the line we have had occasion to notice and we read it as regular iambic pentameter, "It wás no dreám, for Í lay bróad awák-ing,"[1] it comes very smoothly off the tongue, but how much firmer, bolder, and more dramatic is the line as Wyatt actually wrote it. When we speak the original line aloud, our emphasis falls very decisively: once we are aware that it is not conforming to the pattern, we say, "It was nó dream," or perhaps, "It was no dréam," for either stress is possible and our freedom to choose between the two makes the phrase the more engaging. Then as we go on to the second half of the line, "I lay broad waking," our stress falls weightily on "broad" and we naturally tend to sustain the sound for a perceptible instant in order to accomplish the somewhat difficult transition to the stressed syllable that immediately follows, for in the line as Wyatt wrote it we naturally stress "waking" equally with "broad." The emended line, compared to the original, is light, easy, and relatively characterless, and the same judgment can be made on all the other editorial changes in the poem.

But aware as we may be of Wyatt's bold colloquialism and his roughness of metre, we must not leave out of account in our response to the poem the part played in it by formal strictness. The stanza that Wyatt uses is the so-called Rhyme Royal, which has a tradition going back to Chaucer and the Scottish poets; Shakespeare was later to use it for his *Rape of Lucrece*. The stanza moves with an energy that is at once vivacious and grave, and its inherent elegance makes a happy frame for the colloquial directness of the lines themselves.

There is one point at which we may regard the Tottel version with some degree of sympathy, in its revision of the last two lines of the poem. The editor's repetition of "How like you this?" would seem to express his sense that the stanza should be brought into a firmer relation with the rest of the poem, that it dissipates rather than discharges the energy that the first two stanzas have built up. Certainly the lover's plaint creates the effect of diffuseness, even of anticlimax. In fact, for many readers the meaning of these lines proves far too elusive, or, if discovered, inadequate to the earlier stanzas of the poem. It is not difficult to understand that the lover's "gentleness" should have been the cause of his mistress's indifference and infidelity. But why is the "fashion of forsaking" a "strange" one? (Although one would rather have it a "strange" than a "bitter" fashion, as in the revised version.) That the lover should have been given "leave to go" by the mistress's "goodness" is an irony which is either obscure or too simple, and it is certainly not clear why she has need of her own "goodness" to give her leave to "use newfangleness." Even if we have in mind the old meaning of "kindly"—that is, "naturally"—the irony of "But since that I so kindely am served" seems querulous (perhaps that is one reason why Tottel changes it to "unkindly") and the question about what the mistress "hath deserved" has the aspect of mere petulance.

Yet so great is the authority of what has gone before in the poem that many readers are not disposed to be severe upon the faults they find in the conclusion. Their love of the whole leads them to decide that the troubling part is not so much a failure as a puzzle.

[1] The concluding extra syllable does not make it irregular. Even a strict adherence to rule does not require only a series of five iambics to a line.

A VALEDICTION
Forbidding Mourning

JOHN DONNE

1573–1631

As virtuous men pass mildly away,
And whisper to their souls, to go
Whilst some of their sad friends do say,
The breath goes now, and some say, no:

So let us melt, and make no noise, 5
No tear-floods, nor sigh-tempests move,
'Twere profanation of our joys
To tell the laity our love.

Moving of th' earth brings harms and fears,
Men reckon what it did and meant, 10
But trepidation of the spheres,
Though greater far, is innocent.[1]

Dull sublunary[2] lovers' love
(Whose soul is sense[3]) cannot admit
Absence, because it does remove 15
Those things which elemented[4] it.

But we by a love, so much refin'd,
That our selves know not what it is,
Inter-assurèd of the mind,
Care less, eyes, lips, and hands to miss. 20

Our two souls therefore, which are one,
Though I must go, endure not yet

[1] "Trepidation," in Ptolemaic astronomy, referred to motion of the outermost of the nine transparent spheres that comprised the universe, which caused the "innocent" or harmless variation in the occurrence of the equinox. [2] Terrestrial, and hence, inferior. [3] Sensuality. [4] Constituted.

A breach, but an expansion,
Like gold to airy thinness beat.

If they be two, they are two so 25
As stiff twin compasses[5] are two,
Thy soul the fix'd foot, makes no show
To move, but doth, if th' other do.

And though it in the center sit,
Yet when the other far doth roam, 30
It leans, and hearkens after it,
And grows erect, as that comes home.

Such wilt thou be to me, who must
Like th' other foot, obliquely run;
Thy firmness makes my circle just,[6] 35
And makes me end, where I begun.

COMMENTARY

In 1912 the Oxford University Press published Professor H. J. C. Grierson's edition of the poems of John Donne, two handsomely printed volumes bound in the familiar Oxford dark-blue cloth. The first volume contained the poems, many of which had never before been printed; the second volume was devoted to notes which dealt with problems of the text and explicated the often obscure philosophical, scientific, and historical allusions. Perhaps no other work of English literary scholarship in our century is so famous or has had so much influence.

It would not be true to say that Donne had been unknown or unvalued in the nineteenth century and the first years of the twentieth. Edmund Gosse's biography in 1899 and three editions of the poetical works between 1872 and 1896 attest to a continuing awareness of the poet. But he was likely to be considered a minor figure, interesting chiefly for the vivacious idiosyncrasies of his style and for the discrepancy between the bold cynicism of his early poems and the passionate religious intensity of his later years when, after taking holy orders, he became one of the notable figures of the Church of England. Historians of literature were not disposed to study his work in any particularity and the criticism of the day scarcely took him into account. After Grierson's edition, however, Donne came to be seen as a pre-eminent figure not only of the seventeenth century but of the whole of English literature. The scholarly and critical studies of his work proliferated rapidly and are by now innumerable.

Yet Donne in his own time had been greatly admired; he had fallen into

[5] One pair of dividers. [6] Perfect.

disesteem only in the eighteenth century. The reasons for the decline were formulated in Dr. Samuel Johnson's essay on Cowley in *The Lives of the English Poets*. In a passage that has become a *locus classicus* of English criticism, Johnson dealt with the group of seventeenth-century poets whom he called "metaphysical." He used the word, in the fashion of his time, with the intention of reproach, to characterize a kind of poetry that he considered so abstruse, fine-drawn, and far-fetched as to be quite out of accord with good sense and even nature itself. Johnson's name for the group established itself and is still in use, although without any of its former pejorative meaning.[1]

The first characteristic of the metaphysical poets remarked on by Johnson was their learning and their desire to exhibit it. They took pleasure in deriving the elements of their poems from esoteric knowledge of all kinds and, in what to Johnson seemed an extravagant desire to be original and striking, they brought together facts and ideas which he thought incongruous and therefore unnatural; they filled their poems, he said, with "enormous and disgusting hyperboles," their figures of speech were often "grossly absurd" and sometimes "indelicate." They gave precedence to ingenuity over emotion, with the result that "their courtship was void of fondness and their lamentations of sorrow. Their wish was only to say what they hoped had never been said before."

By their excessive concern with minute particularities they transgressed against a chief tenet of eighteenth-century poetic theory, which held that poetry's most impressive effects were to be gained through spacious generalizations. "Great thoughts," said Johnson, "are always general, and consist in positions not limited by exceptions, and in descriptions not descending to minuteness." Dryden, while belittling Donne as a poet, had conceded that he was to be praised for his wit, but Johnson, defining wit "as a kind of *discordia concors,* a combination of dissimilar images or discovery of occult resemblances in things apparently unlike," concluded that "of wit thus defined" Donne and his fellows "have more than enough." The versification of the metaphysical poets won as little approval from Johnson as their diction and imagery—he judged it to be wholly contrived and inept. He does not deny these poets a measure of respect, but the praise it yields is small indeed: "Yet great labor, directed by great abilities is never wholly lost: if they frequently threw away their wit upon false conceits, they likewise sometimes struck out unexpected truth; if their conceits were far-fetched, they were often worth the carriage. To write on their plan, it was at least necessary to read and think."

But early in the nineteenth century the pendulum of taste began its swing to a more favorable view of the metaphysical school, especially Donne. Coleridge anticipated modern opinion when he spoke of Donne's "force" and observed that his "most fantastic out of the way thoughts" were expressed in "the most pure and genuine mother English." Still, that a sense of Donne as odd and eccentric and not in the line of succession of the great English poets qualified Coleridge's admiration is made clear in his much-quoted lines describing Donne's poetical mode:

> With Donne, whose muse on dromedary trots,
> Wreathe iron pokers into true-love knots;
> Rhyme's sturdy cripple, fancy's maze and clue,
> Wit's forge and fire-blast, meaning's press and screw.

[1] Although Dryden had earlier said that "Donne affects the metaphysics," it was Johnson who gave currency to the adjective as a way of characterizing a mode of writing.

Later in the century, two other poets, Browning and Hopkins, both of them antagonistic to the prevailing belief that English verse was at its best when it was harmonious and "smooth," found an affinity with Donne and his dromedary-mounted muse and Rosetti and Swinburne held him in esteem especially for his love-poetry. But no poet of the nineteenth century could speak of him with Yeats's intensity of praise, an intensity that actually comes close to nonsense—writing to thank Professor Grierson for the gift of his edition, Yeats says of Donne that "he who is but a man like us all has seen God."

The new enthusiasm for Donne is explained, of course, by the confirmation he gave to an important tendency of modern poetry. A celebrated statement of what the new poets found in him was made by T. S. Eliot in his review of an anthology of the metaphysical poets that Grierson published in 1921. For Eliot the characteristic virtue of the seventeenth-century poets was their ability to "feel their thought," to experience it as if it were a sensation, "as immediately as the odor of a rose." At some point later in the century, Eliot goes on to say, there occurred a "dissociation of sensibility," and thought and feeling in poetry became separated from each other. Eliot does not refer explicitly to Johnson's objection that metaphysical poetry was excessively intellectual at the cost of feeling, but when he says of Donne that to him "a thought was an experience, it modified his sensibility," it is obviously Johnson's view which he has in mind and means to contradict. Yeats had said much the same thing in his letter to Grierson: "Your notes tell me exactly what I want to know. Poems that I could not understand or could but understand are now clear and I notice that the more precise and learned the thought the greater the beauty, the passion; the intricacies and subtleties of his imagination are the length and depths of the furrows made by his passion."

It was not only Donne's power of conjoining thought and emotion that seemed so important to the modern poets but also his taking it for granted that any of the seemingly disparate elements of experience might be brought together with interesting and significant effect. The conjunction of things and ideas not usually believed to consort with each other had seemed to Dr. Johnson to be a poetical vice, a departure from nature. The modern poets, and after them the modern critics, held it to be a poetical virtue, and exactly because it was natural, at least for poets. "When a poet's mind is perfectly equipped for its work," Eliot said, "it is constantly amalgamating disparate experience; the ordinary man's experience is chaotic, irregular, fragmentary. The latter falls in love or reads Spinoza, and these two experiences can have nothing to do with each other, or with the noise of the typewriter or the smell of cooking; in the mind of the poet these experiences are always forming wholes." This well-known passage exemplifies the tendency of modern writers to reject the belief that there are orders of experience, distinct in themselves and separate from each other, of which some are appropriate to art, others inappropriate.

Donne's versification was no less important to the new poets than the quality of his thought and feeling. What Dr. Johnson and most eighteenth-century readers heard as "rugged" verse and therefore unpleasing, what Coleridge heard as powerful but ungraceful, the trot of the dromedary, the limp of the sturdy cripple, was heard by the poets of the twentieth century as the authoritative accent of actuality. They understood—as had the readers of the seventeenth century—that Donne did not fail in an attempt to conform to the demands of a metrical system but that he wrote a kind of verse in which the rhythms of the natural speaking voice assert themselves against, and modify, the strict pattern of the metre. It is worth noting that Yeats received the gift of Grierson's edition at the point in his development when, under the influence of Ezra Pound, his verse was moving steadily away from the relatively soft and "poetic" mode of his early work to the harder, more downright and forceful versification (and diction) of his great period.

In reading "A Valediction: Forbidding Mourning" it is the voice of the poem that first engages our attention. The opening line is audacious in its avoidance of the metre that is to be established in the following lines of the stanza and maintained through the rest of the poem, although not in a strict or mechanical way; no matter how we read it, we cannot scan that opening line, and its bold freedom leads us to feel that it is saying something "actual" rather than "poetic." The succeeding lines, although controlled by metre, sustain this feeling; they sound in the ear as the utterance of a present speaker. It is in the ambience of the speaker's voice that the metaphysical elements of the poem are presented to us. The comparison between the significance of earthquakes and the "trepidation of the spheres" and the brief simile of the beaten gold, the elaborated simile of the pair of compasses, are the less likely to seem merely ingenious, or studied, or out of the way, because they are suffused with the tones of the voice that proposes them, its directness and masculine vigor, its gravity and its serious humor.

Dr. Johnson took particular notice of the compass simile, introducing his quotation of the three stanzas in which it is developed with this sentence: "To the following comparison of a man that travels and his wife that stays at home, with a pair of compasses, it may be doubted whether absurdity or ingenuity has a better claim." For Johnson the absurdity lay in the fact that compasses seemed to him to be incongruous with the emotional circumstances they were meant to represent. A pair of compasses suggests what is mechanical and unfeeling: it is metallic and stiff, and an instrument of precision employed in, and emblematic of, the sternly rational and abstract discipline of geometry; it therefore stands at the furthest remove from the emotion of love. The simile of the compasses substantiated Johnson's opinion that metaphysical poetry cannot express emotion and is "void of fondness."

Although we will perceive as readily as Dr. Johnson that there is some measure of unlikelihood in the comparison, this will not prevent our having pleasure in it. On the contrary, we will tend to be pleased exactly because we are taken aback. For us, the figure's suggestion of cold rationality and abstractness is modified by the humor with which it is developed, a humor which does not in the least diminish the direct sincerity of the utterance. Isaac Walton, in his brief life of his friend, tells us that Donne composed the poem in 1611 while he was on a diplomatic mission to France and that it was addressed to his wife Anne. The marriage was a famous one in its day, both because of the tempestuous courtship that preceded it and the unbroken tender devotion of the husband and wife. Walton mentions the circumstance in which the poem was written and the person to whom it was addressed out of his sense that the poem, for all the ingenuity of its "conceits," is a direct, personal, and fully felt communication, wholly appropriate to its occasion. With this judgment the modern reader would find it hard to disagree.

LYCIDAS[1]

JOHN MILTON
1608–1674

In This Monody the Author Bewails a Learned Friend, Unfortunately Drowned in His Passage from Chester on the Irish Seas, 1637; and, by Occasion, Foretells the Ruin of Our Corrupted Clergy, Then in Their Height.

Yet once more, O ye laurels, and once more,
Ye myrtles brown,[2] with ivy never sere,
I come to pluck your berries harsh and crude,[3]
And with forced fingers rude
Shatter your leaves before the mellowing year. 5
Bitter constraint, and sad occasion dear[4]
Compels me to disturb your season due;
For Lycidas is dead, dead ere his prime,
Young Lycidas, and hath not left his peer.
Who would not sing for Lycidas? he knew 10
Himself to sing, and build the lofty rhyme.
He must not float upon his watery bier
Unwept, and welter to the parching wind,
Without the meed of some melodious tear.
Begin, then, Sisters of the sacred well[5] 15
That from beneath the seat of Jove doth spring;
Begin, and somewhat loudly sweep the string.
Hence with denial vain and coy excuse:
So may some gentle Muse[6]
With lucky words favour my destined urn, 20
And as he passes turn,
And bid fair peace be to my sable[7] shroud!
For we[8] were nursed upon the self-same hill,
Fed the same flock, by fountain, shade, and rill.
Together both, ere the high lawns appeared 25
Under the opening eyelids of the Morn,
We drove a-field, and both together heard

[1] Lycidas is the name of a shepherd in a poem by the Roman poet, Virgil. Milton's "Lycidas" was Edward King (1612–1637), a college friend who drowned in the Irish Sea. [2] Dark, dusky. [3] Unripe. Laurel, myrtle, and ivy are symbols of immortality that poets were crowned with in ancient Greece. [4] Keenly felt. [5] The Muses, Greek deities of the arts and sciences to whom all creative inspiration was attributed. [6] Here, poet, one inspired by a Muse. [7] Black. [8] Lycidas and the poet.

What time the gray-fly[9] winds[10] her sultry horn,
Battening[11] our flocks with the fresh dews of night,
Oft till the star that rose, at evening, bright 30
Toward heaven's descent had sloped his westering wheel.[12]
Meanwhile the rural ditties were not mute;
Tempered to[13] the oaten flute,
Rough Satyrs[14] danced, and Fauns[15] with cloven heel
From the glad sound would not be absent long; 35
And old Damaetas[16] loved to hear our song.

But, oh! the heavy change, now thou art gone,
Now thou art gone and never must return!
Thee, Shepherd, thee the woods and desert caves,
With wild thyme and the gadding[17] vine o'ergrown, 40
And all their echoes, mourn.
The willows, and the hazel copses green,
Shall now no more be seen
Fanning their joyous leaves to thy soft lays.[18]
As killing as the canker[19] to the rose, 45
Or taint-worm to the weanling herds that graze,
Or frost to flowers, that their gay wardrobe wear,
When first the white-thorn blows;
Such, Lycidas, thy loss to shepherd's ear.

Where were ye, Nymphs, when the remorseless deep 50
Closed o'er the head of your loved Lycidas?
For neither were ye playing on the steep
Where your old bards, the famous Druids,[20] lie,
Nor on the shaggy top of Mona[21] high,
Nor yet where Deva[22] spreads her wizard stream. 55
Ay me! I fondly dream
"Had ye been there"—for what could that have done?
What could the Muse herself that Orpheus bore,[23]
The Muse herself, for her enchanting son,
Whom universal nature did lament, 60
When, by the rout that made the hideous roar,
His gory visage down the stream was sent,
Down the swift Hebrus to the Lesbian shore?

Alas! what boots it[24] with uncessant care
To tend the homely, slighted, shepherd's trade, 65
And strictly meditate the thankless Muse?
Were it not better done, as others use,

[9] Insect that flies with a loud humming noise. [10] Blows. [11] Fattening, feeding. [12] Venus, the "evening star," appears in the western sky. [13] In time with. [14] In Greek mythology, goat-men who lived in the woodlands and spent much time in amorous pursuit of the nymphs. [15] Satyr-like beings. [16] Name for a herdsman that, like "Lycidas," comes from Virgil. [17] Spreading aimlessly. [18] Tunes, poems. [19] Cankerworm. [20] Priests and poets (bards), of ancient Britain. [21] The isle of Anglesey, off the coast of Wales; it was a Druidic center. [22] The river Dee, which runs through England and Wales. [23] Calliope, Muse of epic poetry, was the mother of Orpheus, who was torn to pieces by drunken worshippers of Bacchus. His head floated down the Hebrus to the island of Lesbos. [24] Of what advantage is it?

To sport with Amaryllis in the shade,
Or with the tangles of Neaera's hair?[25]
Fame is the spur that the clear spirit doth raise 70
(That last infirmity of noble mind)
To scorn delights, and live laborious days;
But the fair guerdon[26] when we hope to find,
And think to burst out into sudden blaze,
Comes the blind Fury[27] with the abhorrèd shears, 75
And slits the thin-spun life. "But not the praise,"
Phoebus[28] replied, and touched my trembling ears:
"Fame is no plant that grows on mortal soil,
Nor in the glistering foil[29]
Set off to the world, nor in broad rumour lies, 80
But lives and spreads aloft by those pure eyes,
And perfect witness of all-judging Jove;
As he pronounces lastly on each deed,
Of such fame in heaven expect thy meed."
O fountain Arethuse,[30] and thou honoured flood, 85
Smooth-sliding Mincius,[31] crowned with vocal reeds,
That strain I heard was of a higher mood.
But now my oat[32] proceeds,
And listens to the Herald of the Sea[33]
That came in Neptune's[34] plea. 90
He asked the waves, and asked the felon winds,
What hard mishap hath doomed this gentle swain?
And questioned every gust of rugged wings
That blows from off each beakèd promontory.
They knew not of his story; 95
And sage Hippotades[35] their answer brings;
That not a blast was from his dungeon strayed,
The air was calm, and on the level brine
Sleek Panope with all her sisters[36] played.
It was that fatal and perfidious bark, 100
Built in the eclipse, and rigged with curses dark,
That sunk so low that sacred head of thine.
Next, Camus,[37] reverend sire, went footing slow,
His mantle hairy, and his bonnet sedge,
Inwrought with figures dim, and on the edge 105
Like to that sanguine flower[38] inscribed with woe.

[25] Amaryllis and Neaera are traditional names for nymphs. [26] Reward. [27] Probably Atropos, the Fate who cuts the thread of life. (Milton, perhaps intentionally, confuses the Fates and the Furies here.) [28] Apollo, god of—among other things—poetic inspiration. [29] A thin metal leaf used as a background for a precious stone to increase its brilliance. [30] The traditional fountain of pastoral verse in Sicily. The nymph Arethusa, pursued by the river-god Alpheus (see line 132), was changed into a fountain by Diana. [31] A river in Lombardy, Italy, that Virgil once lived near. [32] Pastoral song (see "oaten flute," line 33 above). [33] Triton, a merman, who here pleads the innocence of the sea in causing Lycidas' death. [34] Neptune was the Roman god of the sea. [35] Aeolus, god of the winds. [36] Water nymphs. [37] The river Cam, representing Cambridge University, where Milton and King first knew each other. [38] The hyacinth, which is said to bear markings resembling the Greek word for "alas."

"Ah! who hath reft," quoth he, "my dearest pledge?"[39]
Last came, and last did go,
The Pilot of the Galilean Lake;[40]
Two massy keys he bore of metals twain 110
(The golden opes, the iron shuts amain).
He shook his mitred locks, and stern bespake:—
"How well could I have spared for thee, young swain,
Enow of such as, for their bellies' sake,
Creep, and intrude, and climb into the fold! 115
Of other care they little reckoning make
Than how to scramble at the shearers' feast,
And shove away the worthy bidden guest.
Blind mouths! that scarce themselves know how to hold
A sheep-hook, or have learnt aught else the least 120
That to the faithful herdman's art belongs!
What recks it them? What need they? They are sped;[41]
And, when they list,[42] their lean and flashy songs
Grate on their scrannel[43] pipes of wretched straw;
The hungry sheep look up, and are not fed, 125
But, swoln with wind and the rank mist they draw,
Rot inwardly, and foul contagion spread;
Besides what the grim wolf[44] with privy paw
Daily devours apace, and nothing said.
But that two-handed engine at the door 130
Stands ready to smite once, and smite no more."[45]
Return, Alpheus;[46] the dread voice is past
That shrunk thy streams; return, Sicilian Muse,[47]
And call the vales, and bid them hither cast
Their bells and flowerets of a thousand hues. 135
Ye valleys low, where the mild whispers use
Of shades, and wanton winds, and gushing brooks,
On whose fresh lap the swart star[48] sparely looks,
Throw hither all your quaint enamelled eyes,
That on the green turf suck the honeyed showers, 140
And purple all the ground with vernal flowers.
Bring the rathe[49] primrose that forsaken dies,
The tufted crow-toe, and pale jessamine,
The white pink, and the pansy freaked[50] with jet,
The glowing violet, 145

[39] "Who hath taken away my dearest child?" [40] St. Peter, wearing a bishop's miter (he was the first bishop of Rome) and carrying the keys of heaven. Edward King is mourned as a poet, as a scholar, and now as a churchman. [41] What does it matter to them? What do they need? They have fared well. [42] Want, desire. [43] Feeble. [44] Probably the Anglican Church. [45] That is, the corrupt clergy will be punished finally and absolutely. What the "two-handed engine" is has been much debated. "Not less than 34 different explanations have been traced in print" (Le Comte, *A Milton Dictionary*). The likeliest explanation is that it refers to the two-handled sword of the Archangel Michael. [46] The lover of Arethusa; they both symbolize pastoral poetry. He has fled from the "dread voice" of St. Peter. [47] The muse of Theocritus, a poet of ancient Greece, and others who wrote pastorals. [48] Sirius, the Dog Star. It is called "swart" because it rises in the late summer when heat scorches and darkens vegetation. [49] Early. [50] Spotted.

The musk rose, and the well-attired woodbine,
With cowslips wan that hang the pensive head,
And every flower that sad embroidery wears;
Bid amaranthus all his beauty shed,
And daffadillies fill their cups with tears, 150
To strew the laureate hearse where Lycid lies.
For so, to interpose a little ease,
Let our frail thoughts dally with false surmise.
Ay me! whilst thee the shores and sounding seas
Wash far away, where'er thy bones are hurled; 155
Whether beyond the stormy Hebrides,
Where thou perhaps under the whelming tide
Visit'st the bottom of the monstrous[51] world;
Or whether thou, to our moist vows denied,
Sleep'st by the fable of Bellerus[52] old, 160
Where the great Vision of the guarded mount[53]
Looks toward Namancos and Bayona's hold.
Look homeward, Angel, now, and melt with ruth:
And, O ye dolphins, waft[54] the hapless youth.[55]
Weep no more, woeful shepherds, weep no more, 165
For Lycidas, your sorrow, is not dead,
Sunk though he be beneath the watery floor.
So sinks the day-star[56] in the ocean bed,
And yet anon repairs his drooping head,
And tricks his beams, and with new-spangled ore 170
Flames in the forehead of the morning sky:
So Lycidas sunk low, but mounted high,
Through the dear might of Him that walked the waves,[57]
Where, other groves and other streams along,
With nectar pure his oozy locks he laves, 175
And hears the unexpressive[58] nuptial songs,
In the blest kingdoms meek of joy and love.
There entertain him all the Saints above,
In solemn troops, and sweet societies,
That sing, and singing in their glory move, 180
And wipe the tears for ever from his eyes.
Now, Lycidas, the shepherds weep no more;
Henceforth thou art the Genius[59] of the shore,
In thy large recompense, and shalt be good
To all that wander in that perilous flood. 185
Thus sang the uncouth swain to the oaks and rills,
While the still morn went out with sandals grey:
He touched the tender stops of various quills,[60]

[51] Full of sea monsters. [52] A mythical Cornish giant. [53] Off Land's End in Cornwall, a large rock, traditionally guarded by the archangel Michael, points towards Namancos (Nemancos) and Bayona in Spain. [54] Bear, carry (through water or air). [55] Dolphins rescued Arion, a semimythical poet who was attacked at sea by sailors who intended to rob him. [56] The sun. [57] Christ. [58] Inexpressible. [59] Protective spirit. [60] Holes in different reeds, or pipes of Pan.

With eager thought warbling his Doric[61] lay:
And now the sun had stretched out all the hills, 190
And now was dropt into the western bay;
At last he rose, and twitched his mantle blue:
To-morrow to fresh woods, and pastures new.

COMMENTARY

It is often said by critics and teachers of literature that "Lycidas" is the greatest lyric poem in the English language, and very likely it is. But the word "greatest" applied to a work of art is not always serviceable; the superlative judgment can immobilize a reader's response to a work, or arouse his skeptical resistance. It may be that we are given a more enlightening introduction to the poem by a critic who held it in low esteem—so far from thinking that "Lycidas" was superlatively great, Samuel Johnson thought it a very bad poem. Without doubt Dr. Johnson was wrong in this judgment and the grounds on which he bases it are quite mistaken. But his erroneous views, stated in his characteristically bold and unequivocal fashion, make plain how the poem ought to be regarded.

The sum of Dr. Johnson's objections is that "Lycidas" is insincere. It purports to be a poem of mourning; the poet is expressing grief over the death of a friend. But can we possibly believe in the truth of his emotion? Grief, Dr. Johnson says in effect, inclines to be silent or at least to be simple in its utterance. It does not express itself so elaborately, with as much artifice as Milton uses or with such a refinement of fancy and such a proliferation of reference to ancient legend and lore. "Passion plucks no berries from myrtle or ivy," Dr. Johnson said, "nor calls upon Arethuse and Mincius, nor tells of rough *satyrs* or *fauns with cloven heels*. Where there is leisure for fiction, there is little grief."

Of the poem's elaborateness of artifice, even of artificiality, there can be no question. The poet does not speak in his own person but in the guise of a "shepherd" or "swain." That is to say, he expresses his grief, such as it is, through the literary convention known as the pastoral, so called because all the persons represented in it are shepherds (the Latin word for shepherd is *pastor*). This convention of poetry has a long history. It goes back to the Greek poet Theocritus (c. 310–250 B.C.), who, in certain of his poems, pretended that he and his poet-friends were shepherds of his native Sicily. Far removed from the sophistication and corruption of cities, the fancied shepherds of Theocritus devoted themselves to the care of their flocks and to two innocent pursuits—song and the cultivation of love and friendship. Their only ambition was to be accomplished in song; their only source of unhappiness was a lost love or the death of a friend, the latter being rather more grievous than the former and making the occasion for an *elegy,* a poem of lament. Virgil brought the pastoral convention into Roman literature with his *Eclogues,* and it was largely through his influence that it became enormously popular in the Renaissance. This popularity continued through the eighteenth century, but the mechanical way

[61] Pastoral.

in which it came to be used in much of the verse of that period justifies Dr. Johnson in speaking of the pastoral mode as "easy, vulgar, and therefore disgusting." In the nineteenth century the convention lost its vogue, but even then it was used for two great elegies, Shelley's "Adonais" and Matthew Arnold's "Thyrsis." For the poets of our time it seems to have no interest.

The fictional nature of the pastoral was never in doubt. Nobody was supposed to believe and nobody did believe that the high-minded poetic herdsmen were real, in charge of actual flocks. Yet the fiction engaged men's imagination for so long a time because it fulfilled so real a desire of mankind—it speaks of simplicity and innocence, youth and beauty, love and art. And although the poets were far from claiming actuality for their pastoral fancies, they often used the convention to criticize actual conditions of life, either explicitly as Milton does in the passage on the English clergy (lines 108–131) or by implication.

The traditional and avowedly artificial nature of the pastoral was exactly suited to the occasion which produced "Lycidas." Milton could scarcely have felt at Edward King's death the "passion" that Dr. Johnson blames him for not expressing, for King, although a college mate, had not been a close friend. He composed "Lycidas" not on spontaneous impulse but at the invitation of a group of Cambridge men who were bringing out a volume of poems to commemorate King. For Milton to have pretended to an acute sense of personal loss would have been truly an insincerity. Yet he could not fail to respond to what we might call the general pathos of a former comrade's dying "ere his prime," and by means of the pastoral elegy he was able to do what was beautifully appropriate to the situation—he associated King's death with a long tradition in which the deaths of young men had been lamented. Ever since the dawn of literature the death of a young man has been felt to have an especial pathos—how often it is evoked in the *Iliad;* and few things in the Bible are more affecting than David's mourning for his young friend Jonathan and his young son Absolom. It is this traditional pathos that Milton evokes from the death of Edward King. Had he tried to achieve a more personal expression of feeling, we should have responded not more but less. What engages us is exactly the universality of the emotion.

The pastoral convention is also appropriate to King's commemoration in two other respects. One is the extent to which the pastoral elegy was known and cultivated by young men in the English universities of Milton's time, if only because in their study of the ancient languages they were assigned the task of composing verses in this genre. Milton's own earliest-known poems are such college exercises, and all the poets who are mentioned or referred to in "Lycidas"—Theocritus, Virgil, Ovid—were subjects of university study. And in Milton's age as in ours, the college days of a young man were thought to have something like a pastoral quality—from mature life men look back to that time as being more carefree, and to their relationships then as having been more generous, disinterested, and comradely than now: why else do college alumni return each spring to their old campuses? Our very word *alumnus* expresses what Milton means when he says that he and King were "nurs'd upon the self-same hill," for an *alumnus* is a foster child, a nursling of *alma mater,* the fostering mother.

Dr. Johnson did not make it an item in his charge of insincerity that

Milton, mourning a young man dead, is so preoccupied with a young man alive —himself. But we cannot fail to see that this is the case. Milton begins his poem with an unabashed self-reference, to his feeling about himself as a young poet who has not yet reached the point of his development when he is ready to appear before the public. One reason he gives for overcoming his reluctance and undertaking the poem in memory of King is his hope that this will make it the more likely that someone will write to commemorate him when he dies. When he speaks about the poetic career and about poetic fame in relation to death, it is manifestly his own career and fame and his own death that he has in mind —the thought arouses him to a proud avowal of his sense of his high calling. And as the poem concludes, it is again to himself that he refers. Having discharged his duty of mourning, he turns from death and sorrow back to life and his own purposes:

> At last he rose, and twitch'd his mantle blue:
> To-morrow to fresh woods, and pastures new.

These passages have led many readers to conclude that "Lycidas" is not about Edward King at all but about John Milton. They are quite content that this should be so. They take the view that though the poem may fail in its avowed intention, it succeeds in an intention that it does not avow—they point to the fact that the most memorable and affecting parts of the poem are those in which Milton is his own subject. But in weighing this opinion we might ask whether it is ever possible to grieve for a person to whom we feel akin without grieving for ourselves, and, too, whether the intensity with which we are led to imagine our own inevitable death is not a measure of the kinship we feel with the person who has already died. Certainly nothing in "Lycidas" more strongly enforces upon us the pathos of untimely death than that it puts the poet in mind of his own death—for what he says of himself we are bound to feel of ourselves. And how better represent the sadness of death than to put it beside the poet's imagination of the fulness of life?

It must also be observed that Milton speaks of the death of Edward King and of his own imagined death and actual life in a context that does not permit our mere ordinary sense of the personal to prevail. He brings them into conjunction not only with the traditional pathos of young men dead ere their prime but also with the traditional evocations of the death of young gods, and their resurrection. No religious ceremonies of the ancient peoples were more fervently performed than those in which the death of a young male deity—Osiris, Adonis, Atys, Thammuz—was mourned and his resurrection rejoiced in. The myths of these gods and the celebration of their death and rebirth represented the cycles of the vital forces; the dying and reborn god symbolized the sun in its annual course, the processes of vegetation, the sexual and procreative energy, and sometimes, as in the case of Orpheus, poetic genius. Once we are aware of this, Milton's concern with himself takes on a larger significance. It is not himself-the-person that Milton is meditating upon but himself-the-poet: that is, he is thinking about himself in the service not of his own interests but of the interests of the "divine" power that he bears within him.

In this service Milton is properly associated with Edward King, who was also a poet—it does not matter that King was not distinguished in his art. But there was yet another aspect of the service of divine power in the fact that King was a clergyman, a priest of the Church of England, which licenses the inclusion in the elegy of St. Peter's explosion of wrath against the negligent and corrupt clergy of the time. This famous passage constitutes only a small part of the poem, but the importance that Milton gave it is made plain by his extended reference to it in the "argument." Some readers will find a bitter condemnation of clerical corruption inappropriate to an elegy, and will be jarred and dismayed by the sudden introduction of Christian personages and considerations into a poem that has been, up to this point, consistently pagan. That Milton is himself quite aware that the passage will seem incongruous to the pastoral form is indicated in the lines in which he invokes the "return" of the "Sicilian Muse," who has been scared away by St. Peter's "dread voice." But in Milton's thought ancient pagan literature and mythology and the Judaeo-Christian religion were never really at odds with each other. It is a salient characteristic of his great and enormously learned mind that Milton gave allegiance to both, and used for Christian ideas the literary forms of paganism. In the pastoral convention he found a natural conjunction of the two: we can readily see that the poetic convention has affinity with the feelings attached to the pastoral life by Biblical Judaism and, more elaborately, by Christianity. The peaceable Abel was a shepherd and so was Abraham. So was David, and a poet-shepherd at that, one of whose psalms begins, "The Lord is my Shepherd, I shall not want." It was shepherds who saw the Star of Bethlehem rise; Jesus is both the Lamb of God and the Good Shepherd. *Pastor* is the name for the priest of a parish, the congregation being his flock, and the form of a bishop's crozier is the shepherd's crook.[1]

As the poem moves toward its conclusion the mingling of pagan and Christian elements is taken wholly for granted. This conjunction of the two traditions exemplifies yet another characteristic of the poem, its inclusiveness. "Lycidas" gathers up all the world, things the most disparate in space and time and kind, and concentrates them in one place and moment, brings them to bear upon one event, the death of the poet-priest. The poem's action is, as it were, summarized in the lines about "the great Vision" of St. Michael the Angel who, from Land's End, the southernmost tip of England, looks afar to Spain but is abjured to "look homeward." So the poem looks afar to the ancient world and also turns its gaze upon contemporary England. From "the bottom of the monstrous world" it turns to heaven, and from all the waters of the world to all the flowers of all the seasons of the Earth, and from the isolation of Lycidas in death to the "sweet societies" of his resurrection and everlasting life through the agency of Christ. It plays literary games with the most solemn sub-

[1] The affinity between the pagan and the Christian idealizations of the pastoral life was no doubt affirmed by the common belief that Virgil's fourth *Eclogue* was a prophecy of the birth of Christ. The Christian acceptance of the pagan convention imposed one small condition which it is amusing to note: Although I have referred throughout my comment to shepherds, the herdsmen of the Greek bucolic poets herded either sheep or goats, and, indeed, Milton took the name Lycidas from a character in a poem by Theocritus who was not a shepherd but a goatherd. But Christianity separates the sheep from the goats, regarding the latter with suspicion and even aversion—in fact, it assigns the physical attributes of the goat to the Devil himself—and does not permit their presence in pastoral poetry. When Spenser in *The Shepheardes Calender* mentions a "Goteheard," his anonymous pedantic contemporary who annotated the poems explains: "By Gotes in scrypture he represented the wicked and reprobate, whose pastour also must needes be such."

jects, and juxtaposes the gravest ideas with the smallest blossoms, using their most delicate or homely names (culminating in the daffadillies, which sound like the very essence of irresponsible frivolity). And then, when it has brought all the world together, and life out of death and faith out of despair, it has its "uncouth swain," the shepherd-poet, with the jauntiness of a task fully discharged, announce that the mourning is now at an end. Life calls the poet to other work and he must answer the call.

TO HIS COY MISTRESS

ANDREW MARVELL

1621–1678

Had we but world enough, and time,
This coyness, Lady, were no crime.
We would sit down and think which way
To walk and pass our long love's day.
Thou by the Indian Ganges' side   5
Shouldst rubies find;[1] I by the tide
Of Humber[2] would complain.[3] I would
Love you ten years before the Flood,
And you should, if you please, refuse
Till the conversion of the Jews.   10
My vegetable love should grow
Vaster than empires, and more slow;
An hundred years should go to praise
Thine eyes and on thy forehead gaze;
Two hundred to adore each breast,   15
But thirty thousand to the rest;
An age at least to every part,
And the last age should show your heart.
For, Lady, you deserve this state,
Nor would I love at lower rate.   20
    But at my back I always hear
Time's winged chariot[4] hurrying near;
And yonder all before us lie
Deserts of vast eternity.
Thy beauty shall no more be found,   25
Nor, in thy marble vault, shall sound
My echoing song; then worms shall try[5]
That long preserved virginity,
And your quaint honor turn to dust,
And into ashes all my lust: 30

[1] Most rubies now come from Burma, but they might once have been mined from the Ganges Delta. [2] An estuary in England. Marvell's town, Hull, is on it. [3] Lament. [4] Probably an allusion to the chariot driven by Helios, the sun god of ancient Greece. [5] Subject to a severe test.

The grave's a fine and private place,
But none, I think, do there embrace.
    Now therefore, while the youthful hue
Sits on thy skin like morning dew,
And while thy willing soul transpires 35
At every pore with instant fires,
Now let us sport us while we may,
And now, like amorous birds of prey,
Rather at once our time devour
Than languish in his slow-chapped[6] power. 40
Let us roll all our strength and all
Our sweetness up into one ball,
And tear our pleasures with rough strife
Thorough the iron gates of life:
Thus, though we cannot make our sun 45
Stand still, yet we will make him run.

COMMENTARY

In his essay on Andrew Marvell, T. S. Eliot remarks that Marvell's best poems, which are few in number, "must be well known from the *Golden Treasury* and the *Oxford Book of English Verse.*" Eliot regards "To His Coy Mistress" as one of the best of Marvell's poems and certainly it is quite the best known, occupying a special place not only in the awareness but in the affection of the readers of our time. And it is, to be sure, found in the *Oxford Book of English Verse*. But it does not appear, as Eliot supposed, in the *Golden Treasury*, the famous anthology of English lyrical poems which has been in print ever since it was first published in 1861. The editor of the *Golden Treasury*, F. T. Palgrave, was a man of excellent literary judgment. From among Marvell's poems he chose three very good ones for his volume. But he did not choose "To His Coy Mistress"—which tells us much about the Victorian age and the nature of taste and how it changes.

Its omission is particularly interesting in the light of what Palgrave tells us of the high esteem in which it was held by his close friend Tennyson, an esteem that Palgrave himself clearly shared. When the *Golden Treasury* was in the making, Palgrave often discussed the selections with Tennyson; in his account of their conversations, the only one of the poet's opinions that he records in detail is the one about "To His Coy Mistress," which, Palgrave says, Tennyson delighted to read aloud, "dwelling more than once on the magnificent hyperbole, the powerful union of pathos and humor." Yet despite the great authority his friend's judgment had for Palgrave, it did not induce him to include the poem in his collection.

It would seem that a poem for which two Victorian gentlemen might express great admiration in private conversation could, because of its unsuitable moral and emotional tone, be thought inappropriate for the general public. The

[6] Slowly devouring (*chap*, "jaw").

erotic content of the poem is of a quite explicit kind, and the intentions of the lover are not what the Victorian audience would have called "honorable," for it is not marriage that his urgency proposes to the lady. He speaks openly of his "lust" and slightingly of the lady's ideas of honor and virginity. Despite his preoccupation with time and mortality, he does not promise the lady that his love, after its consummation, will endure at least until death: he is concerned only with *now,* and in the last of the three movements of the poem the word occurs three times. Victorian morality put a great value upon chastity; it did not sanction the directly erotic impulse outside of marriage nor did it permit the literary representation of the erotic even in the married state. It could only have been offended by Marvell's frank naturalism, which takes no account of moral considerations and even suggests that they are set at naught by the inexorability of time and the inevitability of death.

The "powerful union of pathos and humor" to which Tennyson responded so warmly is undoubtedly the element of the poem that chiefly engages the present-day reader. But Palgrave had reason to suppose that the Victorian audience would be made uncomfortable by this very thing. The Victorian reader was certainly not unused to a union of pathos and humor, but he—perhaps more especially she—was not likely to be at ease with an instance of the union that issued in an irony at once gay and bitter, especially when the irony touched the subject of love. The double-mindedness of irony is alien to the tradition of Victorian love poetry, which cherished a direct singleness of emotion.

The humor of the poem begins, of course, in the "magnificent hyperbole" and it is directed both to the lady herself and to the conventions of courtly love, according to which the lover dedicates himself to the beloved, who accepts his adoration but holds out no hope that his wooing will ever be successful. The lover says that the lady deserves to be wooed according to this convention, virtually *ad infinitum,* and he goes into precise detail to explain how much time might properly be given to the contemplation and praise of each of her charms, were the couple to have, as we say, all the time in the world. In this gay absurdity we hear a note of solemnity, even of fear—the reference to *so much* time, to the long procession of centuries and ages which is to culminate in "the last age" that brings the world to an end, cannot fail to be awesome. Yet the awe is only lightly suggested; as yet it yields no more than a faint undertone to the humor with which the lover teases his lady.

The teasing breaks off, however, with dramatic suddenness when the lover brusquely evokes "Time's winged chariot" and the death it is bringing. The huge leisure of the first movement is instantly dispelled. The world has been seen as a Garden of Eden through which the couple, its Adam and Eve, wander at will; now, at the sound of the hurrying chariot of Time, the garden, fertilized by its rivers, the distant exotic Ganges and the homely Humber, is transformed into the "deserts of vast eternity," which are not to be traversed and which do not accommodate the unceasing growth of a "vegetable love." Now the tone of the lover's urging becomes brutally explicit in its reference to death, for it is not death in the abstract that the lady is asked to think about but the physical decay which makes a mockery of the scruples that keep her from putting her body to what her lover thinks is its right and natural use. But his bitter, desperate evocation of death modulates to the magnificent whimsicality with which the second movement concludes:

The grave's a fine and private place,
But none, I think, do there embrace.

It is as if the lover, having done all he could to frighten the lady into an awareness of the human situation, would now wish to lighten the imposed weight of reality by a humor that is at least as tender as it is grim.

The poem, we readily perceive, is an argument in quite strict logical form. Each of the three movements is a step in a syllogism: 1. If we had all time at our disposal. . . . 2. But we do not. . . . 3. Therefore. . . . What the "therefore" proposes is, of course, love upon the instant. The metaphors in which the proposal is made are curious and of great intensity. In the second movement Time had been given something of a divine character, for the "winged chariot" brings to mind the sun-god, Phoebus Apollo, who, in ancient Greek myth, was represented as a charioteer coursing through the heavens. But now Time, in a vague yet powerful image, is represented as a carnivorous beast, the more dreadful because it is not swift and fierce; and the lover speaks of himself and the lady as no less predatory than their foe—they are to be "amorous birds of prey," capable of devouring Time itself by the ferocity of their love. The image of the lovers as birds of prey, which inverts the old conventional image of the amorous dove, was intended to be startling. To the modern reader the phrase "birds of prey" will perhaps have unpleasant connotations, but to Marvell's contemporaries it would have brought to mind the falcon, which, in a day when hunting with the falcon was still a sport of the aristocracy, was thought to be a particularly noble and beautiful animal.

The conjunction of "strength" and "sweetness," in itself one of the striking details of the poem, naturally proceeds from the representation of Time as a carnivorous beast. When the young Samson killed a lion, he left the carcass in a thicket and a swarm of bees hived in it; returning to the spot, Samson ate some of the honey and this made the substance of the famous riddle he put to the Philistines: "Out of the eater came forth meat, and out of the strong came forth sweetness." The Philistines, unable to puzzle out the riddle by themselves, prevailed upon Samson's wife to find out the answer and were able to say, "What is sweeter than honey? and what is stronger than a lion?"[1]

The lover's suggestion that he and the lady should "roll" all their strength and all their sweetness "into one ball" is curious, even bizarre. The figure may possibly have its source in the scarab or beetle by which the Egyptians symbolized Horus, their god of the sun. It is characteristic of the scarab that it makes a ball of dung in which it lays its eggs; this ball appears in the innumerable representations of the scarab that the Egyptians made. It was thought of as the sun that the god propelled before him.

The "iron gates of life" through which the pleasures of the lovers are to be "torn" are difficult to visualize and to explain. Tennyson thought that the iron gates might better have been iron *grates,* as suggesting more directly the difficulty of tearing the pleasures through them, but this change would have destroyed the awesomeness of the great vague trope which, for Marvell's contemporary readers, would probably have brought to mind the two gates of Hades in Virgil's *Aeneid,* one of ivory through which the false dreams come, the other of horn through which come the true dreams. That the iron gates cannot easily

[1] See the Book of Judges, Chapter 14.

be visualized in relation to the pleasures will suggest that the force of a metaphor does not depend on its visual explicitness.

Certain words of the poem should perhaps be glossed to ensure that they are understood in the sense that Marvell intended. *Coy* means reluctant and hesitant, with implications of a certain self-consciousness or insincerity, but it does not have the overtone it later acquired, of vapidity or cuteness. In our modern usage, a man's *mistress* is a woman with whom he has an established sexual relationship, but in Marvell's day the word denotes the woman to whom a man has pledged his love. The *vegetable* quality of the love that the poet imagines if the lovers had all time at their disposal does not have the pejorative meaning we might now find in it, of being wholly dull, without sentience; it refers to the power of growth and implies the vitality or livingness of the growing thing. *Quaint* did not have its modern sense of something pleasantly old-fashioned but rather of something elegantly fanciful, with a touch of what we should call affectation.

AN ESSAY ON MAN
Epistle I

ALEXANDER POPE
1688–1744

ARGUMENT

Of the Nature and State of Man with respect to the Universe

Of *Man* in the abstract. I. That we can judge only with regard to our *own system,* being ignorant of the *relations* of systems and things. II. That Man is not to be deemed *imperfect,* but a Being suited to his *place* and *rank* in the creation, agreeable to the *general Order* of things, and conformable to *Ends* and *Relations* to him unknown. III. That it is partly upon his *ignorance* of *future* events, and partly upon the *hope* of a *future* state, that all his happiness in the present depends. IV. The *pride* of aiming at more knowledge, and pretending to more Perfection, the cause of Man's error and misery. The *impiety* of putting himself in the place of *God,* and judging of the fitness of unfitness, perfection or imperfection, justice or injustice of his dispensations. V. The *absurdity* of conceiting himself the *final cause* of the creation, or expecting that perfection in the *moral* world, which is not in the *natural.* VI. The *unreasonableness* of his complaints against *Providence,* while on the one hand he demands the Perfections of the Angels, and on the other the bodily qualifications of the Brutes; though, to possess any of the *sensitive faculties* in a higher degree, would render him miserable. VII. That throughout the whole visible world, an universal *order* and *gradation* in the sensual and mental faculties is observed, which causes a *subordination* of creature to creature, and of all creatures to Man. The gradations of *sense, instinct, thought, reflection, reason;* that Reason alone countervails all the other faculties. VIII. How much further this *order* and *subordination* of living creatures may extend, above and below us; were any part of which broken, not that part only, but the whole connected *creation* must be destroyed. IX. The *extravagance, madness,* and *pride* of such a desire. X. The consequence of all, the *absolute submission* due to Providence, both as to our *present* and *future* state.

Awake, my St. John![1] leave all meaner things
To low ambition, and the pride of Kings.
Let us (since Life can little more supply
Than just to look about us and to die)

[1] Henry St. John, Viscount Bolingbroke (1678–1751). His philosophical writings had some influence on Pope.

Expatiate free o'er all this scene of Man; 5
A mighty maze! but not without a plan;
A Wild, where weeds and flowers promiscuous shoot;
Or Garden, tempting with forbidden fruit.
Together let us beat this ample field,
Try what the open, what the covert yield; 10
The latent tracts, the giddy heights, explore
Of all who blindly creep, or sightless soar;
Eye Nature's walks, shoot Folly as it flies,
And catch the Manners living as they rise;
Laugh where we must, be candid where we can; 15
But vindicate the ways of God to Man.
I. Say first, of God above, or Man below,
What can we reason, but from what we know?[2]
Of Man, what see we but his station here,
From which to reason, or to which refer? 20
Through worlds unnumbered though the God be known,
'Tis ours to trace him only in our own.
He, who through vast immensity can pierce,
See worlds on worlds compose one universe,
Observe how system into system runs, 25
What other planets circle other suns,
What varied Being peoples every star,
May tell why Heaven has made us as we are.
But of this frame the bearings, and the ties,
The strong connexions, nice dependencies, 30
Gradations just, has thy pervading soul
Looked through? or can a part contain the whole?
Is the great chain,[3] that draws all to agree,
And drawn supports, upheld by God, or thee?
II. Presumptuous Man! the reason wouldst thou find, 35
Why formed so weak, so little, and so blind?
First, if thou canst, the harder reason guess,
Why formed no weaker, blinder, and no less?
Ask of thy mother earth, why oaks are made
Taller or stronger than the weeds they shade? 40
Or ask of yonder argent fields[4] above,
Why Jove's Satellites[5] are less than Jove?
Of systems possible, if 'tis confest
That Wisdom infinite must form the best,
Where all must full or not coherent be, 45
And all that rises, rise in due degree;
Then, in the scale of reasoning life,[6] 'tis plain,

[2] That is, how can we reason (about God or man) except on the basis of what we already know? [3] The "great chain of being," the conception of the structure of the universe put forth here, originated with the neoplatonist philosopher, Plotinus (third century), and was particularly influential in Europe in the seventeenth and early eighteenth centuries. [4] The heavens. *Argent,* silvery white. [5] The classical hierarchy of gods. [6] Life having the ability to reason.

There must be, somewhere, such a rank as Man:
And all the question (wrangle e'er so long)
Is only this, if God has placed him wrong? 50

Respecting Man, whatever wrong we call,
May, must be right, as relative to all.[7]
In human works, though laboured on with pain,
A thousand movements scarce one purpose gain;
In God's, one single can its end produce; 55
Yet serves to second too some other use.
So Man, who here seems principal alone,
Perhaps acts second to some sphere unknown,
Touches some wheel, or verges to some goal;
'Tis but a part we see, and not a whole. 60

When the proud steed shall know why Man restrains
His fiery course, or drives him o'er the plains;
When the dull Ox, why now he breaks the clod,[8]
Is now a victim, and now Egypt's God:
Then shall Man's pride and dulness comprehend 65
His actions', passions', being's, use and end;
Why doing, suffering, checked, impelled; and why
This hour a slave, the next a deity.

Then say not Man's imperfect, Heaven in fault;
Say rather, Man's as perfect as he ought: 70
His knowledge measured to his state and place;
His time a moment, and a point his space.
It to be perfect in a certain sphere,
What matter, soon or late, or here or there?
The blest to day is as completely so, 75
As who began a thousand years ago.

III. Heaven from all creatures hides the book of Fate,
All but the page prescribed, their present state:
From brutes what men, from men what spirits know:
Or who could suffer Being here below? 80
The lamb thy riot[9] dooms to bleed today,
Had he thy Reason, would he skip and play?
Pleased to the last, he crops the flowery food,
And licks the hand just raised to shed his blood.
Oh blindness to the future! kindly given, 85
That each may fill the circle marked by Heaven:
Who sees with equal eye, as God of all,
A hero perish, or a sparrow fall,
Atoms or systems into ruin hurled,
And now a bubble burst, and now a world. 90

Hope humbly then; with trembling pinions soar;
Wait the great teacher Death; and God adore.

[7] The entire universe. [8] That is, pulls a plow. The ox is a victim when it is used as meat, and Egypt's principal god, Osiris, was often represented as an ox. [9] Extravagance.

What future bliss, he gives not thee to know,
But gives that Hope to be thy blessing now.
Hope springs eternal in the human breast: 95
Man never Is, but always To be blest:
The soul, uneasy and confined from home,[10]
Rests and expatiates in a life to come.
Lo, the poor Indian! whose untutored mind
Sees God in clouds, or hears him in the wind; 100
His soul, proud Science never taught to stray
Far as the solar walk, or milky way;
Yet simple Nature to his hope has given,
Behind the cloud-topped hill, an humbler heaven;
Some safer world in depth of woods embraced, 105
Some happier island in the watery waste,
Where slaves once more their native land behold,
No fiends torment, no Christians thirst for gold.
To Be, contents his natural desire,
He asks no Angel's wing, no Seraph's fire;[11] 110
But thinks, admitted to that equal sky,
His faithful dog shall bear him company.
IV. Go, wiser thou! and, in thy scale of sense,
Weigh thy Opinion against Providence;
Call imperfection what thou fanciest such, 115
Say, here he gives too little, there too much:
Destroy all creatures for thy sport or gust,[12]
Yet cry, If Man's unhappy, God's unjust;
If Man alone engross not Heaven's high care,
Alone made perfect here, immortal there: 120
Snatch from his hand the balance[13] and the rod,
Re-judge his justice, be the GOD of GOD.
In Pride, in reasoning Pride, our error lies;
All quit their sphere, and rush into the skies.
Pride still is aiming at the blest abodes, 125
Men would be Angels, Angels would be Gods.
Aspiring to be Gods, if Angels fell,
Aspiring to be Angels, Men rebel:
And who but[14] wishes to invert the laws
Of Order, sins against th' Eternal Cause. 130
V. Ask for what end the heavenly bodies shine,
Earth for whose use? Pride answers, " 'Tis for mine:
For me kind Nature wakes her genial[15] power,
Suckles each herb, and spreads out every flower;
Annual for me, the grape, the rose renew 135
The juice nectareous, and the balmy dew;

[10] Heaven, or eternity. [11] The seraphim are the highest order of angels, especially distinguished by the ardor of their love. [12] Inclination, taste. [13] Scales. [14] Merely, only. [15] Generative.

For me, the mine a thousand treasures brings;
For me, health gushes from a thousand springs;
Seas roll to waft me, suns to light me rise;
My footstool earth, my canopy the skies." 140
But errs not Nature from this gracious end,
From burning suns when livid deaths[16] descend,
When earthquakes swallow, or when tempests sweep
Towns to one grave, whole nations to the deep?
"No" ('tis replied) "the first Almighty Cause 145
Acts not by partial, but by general laws;
Th' exceptions few; some change since all began:
And what created perfect?"—Why then Man?
If the great end be human Happiness,
The Nature deviates; and can Man do less? 150
As much that end a constant course requires
Of showers and sunshine, as of Man's desires;
As much eternal springs and cloudless skies,
As Men for ever temperate, calm, and wise.
If plagues or earthquakes break not Heaven's design, 155
Why then a Borgia,[17] or a Catiline?[18]
Who knows but he, whose hand the lightning forms,
Who heaves old Ocean, and who wings the storms;
Pours fierce Ambition in a Cæsar's mind,
Or turns young Ammon[19] loose to scourge mankind? 160
From pride, from pride, our very reasoning springs;
Account for moral, as for natural things:
Why charge we Heaven in those, in these acquit?
In both, to reason right is to submit.
Better for Us, perhaps, it might appear 165
Were there all harmony, all virtue here;
That never air or ocean felt the wind;
That never passion discomposed the mind.
But ALL subsists by elemental strife;
And Passions are the elements of Life. 170
The general ORDER, since the whole began,
Is kept in Nature, and is kept in Man.
VI. What would this Man? Now upward will he soar,
And little less than Angel, would be more;
Now looking downwards, just as grieved appears 175
To want the strength of bulls, the fur of bears.
Made for his use all creatures if he call,
Say what their use, had he the powers of all?
Nature to these, without profusion, kind,

[16] Plagues. [17] The Borgias rose to prominence in Italy during the Renaissance. Their name became a symbol of unbridled power, lust, and greed. [18] An unscrupulous Roman who conspired to overthrow the government by force. He was exposed by Cicero. [19] Alexander the Great, who was told by an oracle that he was the son of Ammon, an Egyptian deity.

The proper organs, proper powers assigned; 180
Each seeming want compensated of course,
Here with degrees of swiftness, there of force;[20]
All in exact proportion to the state;
Nothing to add, and nothing to abate.
Each beast, each insect, happy in its own: 185
Is Heaven unkind to Man, and Man alone?
Shall he alone, whom rational we call,
Be pleased with nothing, if not blessed with all?
The bliss of Man (could Pride that blessing find)
Is not to act or think beyond mankind; 190
No powers of body or of soul to share,
But what his nature and his state can bear.
Why has not Man a microscopic eye?
For this plain reason, Man is not a Fly.
Say what the use, where finer optics given, 195
T' inspect a mite, not comprehend the heaven?
Or touch, if tremblingly alive all o'er,
To smart and agonize at every pore?
Or quick effluvia[21] darting through the brain,
Die of a rose in aromatic pain? 200
If nature thundered in his opening ears,
And stunned him with the music of the spheres,[22]
How would he wish that Heaven had left him still
The whispering Zephyr,[23] and the purling rill?
Who finds not Providence all good and wise, 205
Alike in what it gives, and what denies?
VII. Far as Creation's ample range extends,
The scale of sensual,[24] mental powers ascends:
Mark how it mounts, to Man's imperial race,
From the green myriads in the peopled grass: 210
What modes of sight betwixt each wide extreme,
The mole's dim curtain, and the lynx's beam:
Of smell, the headlong lioness between,[25]
And hound sagacious on the tainted green:[26]
Of hearing, from the life that fills the flood,[27] 215

[20] It is a certain axiom in the anatomy of creatures, that in proportion as they are formed for strength, their swiftness is lessened; or as they are formed for swiftness, their strength is abated (Pope's note). [21] Exhalations affecting the sense of smell. [22] Spheres of ancient astronomy, according to which nine spheres of transparent material holding the planets and stars surrounded the earth. Pythagoras thought the planets must make sounds that corresponded to their different rates of motion and that, as all things in nature are harmoniously made, the different sounds must harmonize. [23] Gentle breeze. [24] Sensory. [25] The manner of the Lions hunting their prey in the deserts of Africa is this: At their first going out in the nighttime they set up a loud roar, and then listen to the noise made by the beasts in their flight, pursuing them by the ear, and not by the nostril. It is probable the story of the jackal's hunting for the lion was occasioned by observation of this defect of scent in that terrible animal (Pope's note). [26] Hunting grounds imbued with the scent of an animal. [27] Waterlife.

To that which warbles through the vernal wood:
The spider's touch, how exquisitely fine!
Feels at each thread, and lives along the line:
In the nice bee, what sense so subtly true
From poisonous herbs extracts the healing dew? 220
How Instinct varies in the groveling swine,
Compared, half-reasoning elephant, with thine!
Twixt that, and Reason, what a nice[28] barrier,
For ever separate, yet for ever near!
Remembrance and Reflection how allied; 225
What thin partitions Sense[29] from Thought divide:
And Middle natures, how they long to join,
Yet never pass th' insuperable line!
Without this just graduation, could they be
Subjected, these to those, or all to thee? 230
The powers of all subdued by thee alone,
Is not thy Reason all these powers in one?

VIII. See, through this air, this ocean, and this earth,
All matter quick,[30] and bursting into birth.
Above, how high, progressive life may go! 235
Around, how wide! how deep extend below!
Vast chain of Being! which from God began,
Natures ethereal, human, angel, man,
Beast, bird, fish, insect, what no eye can see,
No glass can reach; from Infinite to thee, 240
From thee to Nothing.—On superior powers
Were we to press, inferior might on ours:
Or in the full creation leave a void,
Where, one step broken, the great scale's destroyed:
From Nature's chain whatever link you strike, 245
Tenth or ten thousandth, breaks the chain alike.

And, if each system in gradation roll
Alike essential to th' amazing Whole,
The least confusion but in one, not all
That system only, but the Whole must fall. 250
Let Earth unbalanced from her orbit fly,
Planets and Suns run lawless through the sky;
Let ruling Angels from their spheres be hurled,
Being on Being wrecked, and world on world;
Heaven's whole foundations to their centre nod, 255
And Nature tremble to the throne of God.
All this dread ORDER break—for whom? for thee?
Vile worm!—Oh Madness! Pride! Impiety!

IX. What if the foot, ordained the dust to tread,
Or hand, to toil, aspired to be the head? 260
What if the head, the eye, or ear repined[31]
To serve mere engines to the ruling Mind?

[28] Fine, fragile. [29] Sensory perceptions. [30] Alive. [31] Complained, was discontented.

Just as absurd for any part to claim
To be another, in this general frame:
Just as absurd, to mourn the tasks or pains, 265
The great directing MIND of ALL ordains.

All are but parts of one stupendous whole,
Whose body Nature is, and God the soul;
That, changed through all, and yet in all the same;
Great in the earth, as in th' ethereal frame; 270
Warms in the sun, refreshes in the breeze,
Glows in the stars, and blossoms in the trees,
Lives through all life, extends through all extent,
Spreads undivided, operates unspent;
Breathes in our soul, informs our mortal part, 275
As full, as perfect, in a hair as heart;
As full, as perfect, in vile Man that mourns,
As the rapt Seraph that adores and burns:
To him no high, no low, no great, no small;
He fills, he bounds, connects, and equals all. 280

X. Cease then, nor ORDER Imperfection name:
Our proper bliss depends on what we blame.
Know thy own point: This kind, this due degree
Of blindness, weakness, Heaven bestows on thee.
Submit.—In this, or any other sphere, 285
Secure to be as blest as thou canst bear:
Safe in the hand of one disposing Power,
Or in the natal, or the mortal hour.
All Nature is but Art, unknown to thee;
All Chance, Direction, which thou canst not see; 290
All Discord, Harmony not understood;
All partial Evil, universal Good:
And, spite of Pride, in erring Reason's spite,
One truth is clear, WHATEVER IS, IS RIGHT.

COMMENTARY

Modern critics, even those who take the greatness of Pope for granted, are likely to use a tone of advocacy when they write about him. They are aware that the taste of most of their readers does not readily respond to the poet whose genius was universally acclaimed in his own time. Pope is the chief English poet of the eighteenth century and it is he who bore the brunt of the Romanticists' repudiation of the poetic standards of that age. To Wordsworth and Coleridge, he stood for everything in poetry that they contemned. They saw him as virtually an anti-poet, the corrupter of poetry's true essence. Only Byron among the Romanticists found it possible to admire him, and Byron's enthusiastic praise was thought by many to be a mere perversity. The nineteenth century's antagonism to Pope was brought to a climax and codified by Matthew Arnold in his famous essay, "The Study of Poetry." Speaking of the importance that poetry would have in the modern world and calling the roll of those English poets who were likely to be of the greatest spiritual value, Arnold explicitly excluded Pope and his great predecessor Dryden from the illustrious roster on the ground that they were really not poets at all. "Though they may write in verse," he said, "though they may in a certain sense be masters of the art of versification, Dryden and Pope are not classics of our poetry, they are classics of our prose."

In the early decades of the twentieth century the reputation of the two poets took a decided upward turn among serious students of literature: now no informed person would think it possible to say of either of them that he is not a classic of our poetry. The counter-revolution against nineteenth-century opinion as summed up by Arnold found its most notable agitator in T. S. Eliot, who, in his essays on Dryden, repelled "the reproach of the prosaic" that had so often been made and went on to question in a radical and telling way the whole nineteenth-century view of what was and what was not poetic.

Yet despite the thorough-going change in the estimate of Pope that has taken place among critics and scholars, it is still probably true that the great majority of readers who come to him for the first time and without critical indoctrination tend to resist him and to echo Arnold's judgment that he is not really a poet at all, that such virtues as are most salient in his work, those that Arnold identified as "regularity, uniformity, precision, and balance," are prose virtues; and perhaps they will go so far as to say that, of these virtues, not all pertain to the kind of prose that interests them most.

What probably makes the root of the difficulty is the verse form with which the genius of Pope is identified, the heroic couplet. It is likely to strike the unhabituated modern ear as limited, repetitive, and all too committed to syntax, justifying Keats's vehement charge that it was nothing but mechanical. The disaffected reader should know, however, that the better acquainted Keats became with the form, the more he admired it and admitted its influence upon his own verse.

Nothing could be simpler than the defining characteristics of the heroic couplet: two rhymed lines, each of five iambic feet, that is, feet of two syllables, the accent falling on the second. But as it came into wide use in the late seventeenth century and especially in the hands of Dryden, the simple form developed toward complexity and ever stricter demands were made upon it. It became the rule (which might, however, be broken now and then for the sake of variety) that each couplet be self-contained, its meaning complete. This tended to make for a sententious and even epigrammatic quality of utterance, which was much esteemed. Considerable attention was given to the caesura, a discernible pause in the progress of a line which is dictated not by the metre but by the natural rhythm of the language; variations in the placing of the caesura had the effect of helping the heroic couplet avoid its greatest danger, monotony. Rhetorical devices, such as parallelism and antithesis, were favored by the nature of the verse and came to be highly valued.

The chief advantage that Dryden ascribed to the heroic couplet will make it plain why the Romantic poets disliked the form and why many modern readers find it uncongenial. ". . . That benefit which I consider most in it," Dryden said, "is . . . that it bounds and circumscribes the fancy." And he goes on: "For imagination in a poet is a faculty so wild and lawless that, like an highranging spaniel, it must have clogs tied to it, lest it outrun the judgment.

The great easiness of blank verse renders the poet too luxuriant; he is tempted to say many things which might better be omitted, or at least shut up in fewer words; but when the difficulty of artful rhyming is interposed, where the poet commonly confines his sense to his couplet, and must contrive that sense into such words that the rhyme shall naturally follow them, not they the rhyme; the fancy then gives leisure to the judgment to come in. . . . That which most regulates the fancy, and gives the judgment its busiest employment, is like to bring forth the richest and clearest thoughts."

Nothing could be further from the nineteenth-century sense of how the poet should go about his work, of what poetry should be and do. And although modern poetry has in some measure responded to the influence of Dryden and Pope, there are few contemporary practitioners or theorists of poetry who would give their approval to a conception of poetry that was directed chiefly to bringing forth *thoughts,* no matter how rich and clear.

By Pope's time the advantages of the heroic couplet no longer seemed to be in need of reasoned defense; it was the accepted form for most poetic undertakings of importance.[1] If Pope ever thought of the limitations of the form, it was only as a challenge to his virtuosity. To him it was beyond doubt that the couplet in skilled hands—in hands made skilful as much by study and practice as by native endowment—was an instrument capable of producing the widest and most delightful range of effects. In an often-quoted passage of "An Essay on Criticism" he brilliantly demonstrated how various the "music" of the couplet may be and how precisely it could be related to the meaning that is being expressed. This correspondence of sense and sound, he says, is something to which the poet must give close attention—

> 'Tis not enough no harshness gives offence,
> The sound must seem an Echo to the sense:

He illustrates the precept by a couplet in which the sound of the verse is consonant with the "softness" of the action being referred to:

> Soft is the strain when Zephyr gently blows,
> And the smooth stream in smoother numbers flows.

There follows an example of a rough action expressed in a rough-sounding verse:

> But when loud surges lash the sounding shore,
> The hoarse, rough verse should like the torrent roar.

Then an example of laborious effort:

> When Ajax strives some rock's vast weight to throw,
> The line too labours, and the words move slow.

[1] But the taste of no period is monolithic and the dislike of the heroic couplet that was expressed by at least one considerable poet of the eighteenth century should be noted —Matthew Prior objected to it because it "produces too frequent an identity in the sound," moves too readily toward epigram, and is tiring to the reader.

And, in contrast to this, lightness and speed:

> Not so when swift Camilla scours the plain,
> Flies o'er the unbending corn, and skims along the main.

This famous display of virtuosity will suggest how large a part in Pope's art was played by the poet's sense that he was a performer, that it was his purpose to give pleasure to an audience whose right to judge his performance depended only upon a proper training of its faculty of judgment, its taste. The characteristic relation of later poets to their audiences will be very different: the idea of performance will come to be abhorrent to them and they will conceive it to be their purpose to serve not the pleasure of the reader but only the truth of their own feelings, which the reader is probably not competent to judge.

The poetry of exposition and argument, to which the heroic couplet so happily lends itself, has virtually no place in the modern tradition. In the eighteenth century the word "didactic" was used in a neutral descriptive sense when applied to poetry; early in the nineteenth century its meaning became opprobrious and has remained so. It means nothing more dreadful than "teaching," but, although we believe that much is to be learned from poetry, we now believe that it must not intend to instruct. To the poets of Pope's age, however, our adverse opinion of didactic poetry would have seemed arbitrary and pointless; they thought it nothing but natural that poetry should engage itself directly with ideas.[2]

But even if the modern reader should consent to give up his prejudice against didactic poetry in general, he is pretty sure to find that another barrier stands in the way of his coming to terms with "An Essay on Man." This is the poem's purpose of demonstrating that man has no justifiable complaint to make of the conditions of his life, that, if he truly comprehends the nature of the universe, he must see that his relation to it is wholly in accord with reason and be gratified that things are as they are and not otherwise.

Such a view can scarcely win assent in our day, when it has become virtually a commonplace of much of our influential literature that man's relation to the universe is so far out of accord with reason as to be absurd. Yet exactly the currency of this idea makes "An Essay on Man" of rather special interest to us, for the poem takes its impetus from the assumption that anyone who thinks about his relation to the universe will, as a first conclusion, judge it to be unreasonable to the point of absurdity. The Essay, of course, then undertakes to prove that the first conclusion is in error, but the arguments it advances in the demonstration are as desperate as they are ingenious. Where the ingenuity fails to convince us, the desperateness may yet succeed in moving us: there is something deeply affecting in the Essay's passionate defeated attempt to force the universe to be rational.

[2] But, again, the broad cultural generalization must be modified—in 1746, Joseph Warton, an important critic, protested the fashion of didactic poetry. And it should be said that in his preface to "An Essay on Man" Pope raised the question, perhaps only in a formal way, of whether he should not have treated his subject in prose, and he apologizes, again perhaps only in a formal way, for not having treated parts of his discourse "more *poetically*." It would seem to have been the abstruseness of the subject that raised doubts that had not existed in connection with the earlier "Essay on Criticism," which was no less didactic but considerably easier.

When it is said that man's relation to the universe is not in accord with reason, what is primarily meant is that there is no discernible answer to the question of why man suffers or why there is an overplus of pain as against pleasure in human existence. That the question should be asked at all implies the belief that the universe is controlled by principles that are analogous with those more or less rational principles that man has evolved for the control of his own behavior. It is expected, that is, that the answer will be given in terms of man's own reason in its various social aspects—the reason of the father in the family, of the judge in the court of law, of the king in the city or nation. And when the question about the reason of the universe is posed in the Judaeo-Christian tradition, it takes the form of asking why the perfect Father, Judge, and King, the God who is believed to be both omnipotent and wholly beneficent, should have ordained man's suffering. The terms of the question being what they are, the answer is not hard to make—it is possible to "justify the ways of God to man," as Milton expressed his intention in writing *Paradise Lost,* by telling the story of a man's fall from innocence through his disobedience to the divine command and of God's consequent anger. The pain of human life is explained as a punishment for sin, mitigated by the permitted hope of an eventual redemption. Such rationality as is thought to inhere in the human concept of morality and justice is proposed as the controlling principle of the universe.

This answer is in many ways satisfactory so long as the imagination is disposed to accept its terms and to sustain the belief in a God who is Father, Judge, and King, and who is susceptible to the emotions that are appropriate to each of his functions. But in the eighteenth century the imagination of educated men was not so disposed. "An Essay on Man" undertakes to "vindicate the ways of God to man," and the conscious echo of Milton's line informs us that Pope wanted to connect the purpose of his poem with that of *Paradise Lost.* Yet the elements out of which Pope constructed his argument were very different from those available to Milton. The God of the Essay is not personal except insofar as wisdom and beneficence may be attributed to him. Having once ordained his universe in perfection, he does not intervene in its processes. Where Milton, in the traditional way of religion, frames his explanation of man's destiny in terms of man's own thought and feeling, showing that God's ways are essentially in accord with man's ways taken at their best, Pope vindicates God's ways by demonstrating the difference—which does not, however, imply the discontinuity—between the divine and the human. The famous conclusion, "Whatever is, is right," asserts the rationality and perfection of the universe as God has created it, a rationality and perfection of which man's suffering—so runs the terrible line of reasoning!—is a necessary element.

At no point in "An Essay on Man" is the actuality of human suffering denied. Indeed, the poem is charged throughout with an awareness of pain, as well it might be, considering how much of it its author had endured. The opening lines are explicit about the unsatisfactoriness of life, which "can little more supply / Than just to look about us and to die." It is this acceptance of the fact of suffering that gives the poem its desperate tragic force, for the essence of its position is not merely that human suffering is inevitable but that without it the universe would be less rational and perfect than in fact it is. The argument is based on a conception of a universal order in which all created things stand on a scale of perfection from the lowest to the highest. On this scale there may be no gaps; the gradation from the lowest to the highest is continuous, constituting a "vast Chain of Being." From this premise of the order of Nature two conclusions follow. (1) Man has his place or "station" in this order of perfection, above the animals and below the angels, and if he did not occupy this place, there would be a link missing in the chain of being, a circumstance which, if it were thinkable, would be a diminution of the perfection of the universal order. (2) Situated where he is on the scale, or in the chain, man must be understood to have been endowed in a way that makes all his attributes appropriate to his station; both his power and his weakness are exactly right for that place. Which is to say that, in relation to the universal order, man himself is perfect.

More than once the point is made that nothing would be gained for man's well-being if his powers were greater than they are. It is said, in fact, that the contrary is so. If, for example, man were better able to foretell the future, he would have a greater apprehension of the calamities that are destined to befall him and he would therefore be the less able to bear his existence. But such considerations, adduced for what comfort they may give, are of no more than secondary importance to the argument; its primary intention is to demonstrate that the perfection of the universal order depends upon man's suffering.

It is generally said that Pope derived his general position and the particularities by which he expounded it from his friend Lord Bolingbroke, the St. John to whom all four epistles of the Essay are addressed, but an educated man of the time could scarcely have read any philosophy without gaining knowledge of a doctrine that was fashionable and received. Yet it was not everywhere received; Dr. Johnson, for one, would have none of it. Johnson had the highest admiration for Pope as a poet and he said of "An Essay on Man" that it "affords an egregious instance of the predominance of genius, the dazzling splendour of imagery, and the seductive powers of eloquence." But the praise he gives to the poet is the measure of his scorn of the philosopher. "Never," he goes on, "was penury of knowledge and vulgarity of sentiment so happily disguised," and he proceeds to show that the doctrine of the Essay may be reduced to a series of truisms and platitudes. "Surely," he says when the demolition is complete, "a man of no very comprehensive search may venture to say that he has heard all this before. . . ." And then, his antagonism to the philosopher having been given full vent, he is free to return to his praise of the poet: ". . . But it was never till now recommended by such a blaze of embellishments, or such sweetness of melody. The vigorous contraction of thoughts, the luxuriant amplification of others, the incidental illustrations, and sometimes the dignity, sometimes the softness of the verses, enchain philosophy, suspend criticism, and oppress judgment by overpowering pleasure." The double opinion recommends itself.

TYGER! TYGER!

WILLIAM BLAKE

1757–1827

Tyger! Tyger! burning bright
In the forests of the night,
What immortal hand or eye
Could frame thy fearful symmetry?

In what distant deeps or skies 5
Burnt the fire of thine eyes?
On what wings dare he aspire?
What the hand dare seize the fire?

And what shoulder, & what art,
Could twist the sinews of thy heart? 10
And when thy heart began to beat,
What dread hand? & what dread feet?[1]

What the hammer? what the chain?
In what furnace was thy brain?
What the anvil? what dread grasp 15
Dare its deadly terrors clasp?

When the stars threw down their spears,
And water'd heaven with their tears,
Did he smile his work to see?
Did he who made the Lamb make thee? 20

Tyger! Tyger! burning bright
In the forests of the night,
What immortal hand or eye,
Dare frame thy fearful symmetry?

[1] In revising the poem, Blake deleted a line that might seem necessary to the thought. He originally wrote:

What dread hand and what dread feet
Could fetch it from the furnace deep?

COMMENTARY

The reader who comes to "Tyger! Tyger!" for the first time will have no trouble understanding what a Tyger is. But he will want to know why it is spelled in this, rather than in the usual, way. In Blake's time the spelling of the word was the same as now; Dr. Johnson, in his great dictionary, which set the standard of correctness for the period, noted *tyger* as an alternative form of *tiger,* but he did not expect anyone to use it. Yet Blake's error, if such it is, is perpetuated: most modern editors, when they reprint the poem, conscientiously maintain the poet's spelling. They feel that to make the Tyger into a tiger would alter the nature of the beast and of the poem that celebrates him.

One reason for this feeling lies in the circumstances of the poem's original publication. The book in which "Tyger! Tyger!" appeared, *Songs of Experience* (1794), was not printed in the common way, from type. Blake was an engraver by trade and also an artist of considerable stature, and he made the whole book himself, designing each page as an elaborate picture in which the text of the poem was part of the design and the elements of the picture wove themselves in and out of the lines of the text. He engraved the texts and the outlines of the pictures on copper plates from which he printed the pages; he then colored by hand each page of each copy of the book. It is a tendency of modern criticism and scholarship to pay heed to every detail of a poet's work, even such "mechanical" matters as punctuation and spelling; if one of the older poets wrote *speke* where we would now write *speak,* or *sovran* where we would now write *sovereign,* many editors think that the very look of the words is an essential quality of the poem and should be preserved. How much more is this idea likely to prevail when the poet presents his poems, as Blake did, as actual visual objects, to be looked at as well as read.[1]

And certainly the spelling has its effect, if only that of being curious and therefore of making the animal which the word denotes the more remarkable—a Tyger is surely more interesting than a tiger. It startles our habitual expectations, it jolts our settled imagination of the beast and prepares us to see it as we never saw it before, as Blake saw it. Then, too, the *y* is a stronger, as it is a larger, letter than *i*; it suggests a longer-held sound and therefore supports the idea of an animal even fiercer than the tiger. (Conversely, the little boy in A. A. Milne's stories calls one of his animal friends Tigger, and by the shortening of the *i* wipes out all possibility of the creature's being dangerous.)

The dominant, the single, emotion of the poem is amazement, and perhaps no poem has ever expressed an emotion so fully—it is as if the poem were amazement itself. The means by which it achieves this effect is in part very simple: in the course of twenty-four lines it asks fourteen astonished questions. Up through Stanza IV the tempo of the questions is in continuous acceleration, generating an intense excitement. At Stanza V the speed of the questions diminishes and the excited wonder modulates to meditative awe.

But not only does the tempo of the poem change at the fifth stanza; its point of reference, its very subject, alters. Up to Stanza V the poem has undertaken to define the nature of the Tyger by the nature of God—such is the beauty and strength and wildness of the Tyger that he must be thought to

[1] Although I would give at least a qualified assent to the principle evoked, for obvious reasons I have not followed it in choosing the texts of this volume.

have been created by God's greatest exercise of power, a power put forth against resistance and even with some risk of failure. But at the fifth stanza the Tyger is no longer defined by the nature of God; now, in the two remaining stanzas, it is God who is defined by the nature of the Tyger. The amazement first evoked by the Tyger is now directed to God, as God reveals himself through his wonderful and terrible creature. And what the poem finds most amazing about God is not his power but his audacity—not the fact that God *could* (as in the first stanza) but that he *dared* (as in the last stanza) create the Tyger!

To ask a question about the audacity of God is in itself an act of inordinate audacity. For to dare to do a thing implies the possibility of fearing to do it, and what can God conceivably fear? The very idea of God, since it implies omnipotence, denies the possibility of his fearing anything at all. And yet there is one thing which, at least in a formal sense, God may be imagined to fear—the violation of his own nature by himself. The import of the last question of the poem, "What immortal hand or eye / Dare frame thy fearful symmetry?" is that, in creating the Tyger, God has perhaps committed just such a violation, that he has contradicted the self-imposed laws of his own being.[2]

This idea is quite explicitly proposed in the fifth stanza:

> When the stars threw down their spears,
> And water'd heaven with their tears,
> Did he smile his work to see?
> Did he who made the Lamb make thee?

The scholars tell us that for Blake the stars are the symbols and agents of reason, law, and order. If this is so, we must understand that the stars threw down their spears in token of defeat and watered heaven with their tears in chagrin because they disapproved of God's having created the Tyger. It seemed to them a controversion of that very order which God himself had instituted and which he had enjoined them to enforce.

What chiefly makes it possible to think of God as being inconsistent with himself is his having created the Lamb before the Tyger. Just as "Tyger! Tyger!" is the central poem of *Songs of Experience,* so the poem called "The Lamb" is central to the volume called *Songs of Innocence,* which Blake had published five years before, in 1789. In the established symbolism of Western culture, the

[2] That Blake thought the distinction between *could* and *dare* to be of great importance is made plain by the way he revised the poem. In the early drafts of "Tyger! Tyger!" the first stanza was exactly the same as the last; in both stanzas the question read, "What immortal hand or eye / Dare frame thy fearful symmetry?" But as Blake worked over the poem and understood better what it was trying to say, he perceived the striking—we might say shocking—effect that would be achieved by changing the phrase in the first stanza to the neutral "Could frame," reserving *dare* as a startling climax in the last stanza. To be sure, this is not the only use of the word *dare* in the poem, for it occurs twice in Stanza II and once in Stanza IV. We might wish that it did not, that it occurred uniquely and therefore the more startlingly in the last line. Yet the word as it is used in Stanzas II and IV may be said to differ in meaning from the word as it is used in Stanza VI. The questions in Stanzas II and IV all have to do with the executive part of creation, with physical acts, with power. Who would venture to put his power to the test of undertaking to create the Tyger? The answer implied by the question is that God alone would take this risk; but because God is all-powerful, there really is no risk—the word *dare* therefore comes to mean no more than *could.* But in the last stanza *dare* refers to the conceptual part of creation, to the idea of the Tyger as conceived by the mind of God. And because this idea may possibly be thought a contradiction of God's nature, the word has its full dramatic force.

Lamb stands for harmlessness, gentleness, and defenselessness; in Christian iconography, it stands for Jesus—for the Jesus who said, "Resist not evil," and who offered himself as a sacrifice for mankind. In "The Lamb" it is a child who asks of the Lamb the same question that the poet, speaking in his own voice as a mature man, asks of the Tyger: *Who made you?* The little questioner is in no doubt about the answer:

> Little Lamb, I'll tell thee;
> Little Lamb, I'll tell thee:
> He is callèd by thy name,
> For he calls himself a Lamb.
> He is meek, & he is mild:
> He became a little child,
> I a child, & thou a lamb,
> We are callèd by his name.

That God, who had created the Lamb and had incarnated himself in Jesus who *is* the Lamb, should also have created the Tyger as another aspect of his being—this seems to the stars, who are the agents of divine law, to be a clear contradiction by God of his own nature as he had declared it to them, and as the negation of the terms of their commission to maintain reason and order.

The poem, however, does not substantiate the view of the matter that is held by the reasonable stars. Rather, it would seem to present the opinions of these guardians of order with considerable irony, as being limited, even stupid, as failing to comprehend the wonderful complexity of God's nature. In the opinion of the poem—although this is not made fully explicit—the Tyger is not the negation or contradiction of the Lamb. He is by no means the Anti-Christ. The Jesus who is meek and mild, who speaks of turning the other cheek, and who is symbolized by the animal commonly used in ancient sacrifices, is the Jesus most frequently represented to the religious imagination, but this does not mean that he is the only Jesus. There is also the Jesus who said, "I bring not peace but a sword," who undertook to disrupt the habitual respectable lives of men, commanding them to leave their fathers and mothers and to follow him, who questioned and denied the established Law, who—so he is represented by Dostoevski in "The Grand Inquisitor" (*Fiction*, pages 45 ff.)—offered men a freedom too terrible for most to accept. This is the Jesus whom T. S. Eliot, in "Gerontion," could precisely call "Christ the tiger."

When Blake brought together his *Songs of Innocence* and his *Songs of Experience* in a single volume, he called it *Songs of Innocence and Experience, Shewing the Two Contrary States of the Human Soul,* and the title makes it sufficiently plain that in Blake's view a "state" which is "contrary" to another state is not necessarily a negation of it or antagonistic to it. The contrary of Innocence is not Wickedness or Evil but Experience, which is the condition in which a human being comes to realize and exercise his vital energies and in which he knows both the joy and the sorrow that follow upon their use. Both the state of the Lamb and the state of the Tyger are appropriate to mankind; both are sanctioned by the nature of God.

But although Blake is so nearly explicit in making the Tyger stand for one of the two aspects of Christ, or one of the two states of man, his symbolic intention is not limited to this alone. The Tyger, in its fierceness and beauty, can be regarded as that manifestation of the human mind which we call genius. (It is interesting to compare this representation of genius with that of Babel's story, "Di Grasso" [*Fiction,* pages 286 ff.].) And it can be thought to stand for the ruthless ferocity of political revolution, specifically of the French Revolution, with which Blake was much preoccupied.

RESOLUTION AND INDEPENDENCE

WILLIAM WORDSWORTH

1770–1850

I

There was a roaring in the wind all night;
The rain came heavily and fell in floods;
But now the sun is rising calm and bright;
The birds are singing in the distant woods;
Over his own sweet voice the Stock-dove broods; 5
The Jay makes answer as the Magpie chatters;
And all the air is filled with pleasant noise of waters.

II

All things that love the sun are out of doors;
The sky rejoices in the morning's birth;
The grass is bright with rain-drops;—on the moors 10
The hare is running races in her mirth;
And with her feet she from the plashy earth
Raises a mist; that, glittering in the sun,
Runs with her all the way, wherever she doth run.

III

I was a Traveller then upon the moor; 15
I saw the hare that raced about with joy;
I heard the woods and distant waters roar;
Or heard them not, as happy as a boy:
The pleasant season did my heart employ:
My old remembrances went from me wholly; 20
And all the ways of men, so vain and melancholy.

IV

But, as it sometimes chanceth, from the might
Of joy in minds that can no further go,

As high as we have mounted in delight
In our dejection do we sink as low; 25
To me that morning did it happen so;
And fears and fancies thick upon me came;
Dim sadness—and blind thoughts, I knew not, nor could name

V

I heard the sky-lark warbling in the sky;
And I bethought me of the playful hare: 30
Even such a happy Child of earth am I;
Even as these blissful creatures do I fare;
Far from the world I walk, and from all care;
But there may come another day to me—
Solitude, pain of heart, distress, and poverty. 35

VI

My whole life I have lived in pleasant thought,
As if life's business were a summer mood;
As if all needful things would come unsought
To genial faith, still rich in genial good;
But how can He expect that others should 40
Build for him, sow for him, and at his call
Love him, who for himself will take no heed at all?

VII

I thought of Chatterton,[1] the marvellous Boy,
The sleepless Soul that perished in his pride;
Of Him[2] who walked in glory and in joy 45
Following his plough, along the mountain-side:
By our own spirits are we deified:
We Poets in our youth begin in gladness;
But thereof come in the end despondency and madness.

VIII

Now, whether it were by peculiar grace, 50
A leading from above, a something given,
Yet it befell that, in this lonely place,
When I with these untoward thoughts had striven,
Beside a pool bare to the eye of heaven
I saw a Man before me unawares: 55
The oldest man he seemed that ever wore grey hairs.

[1] Thomas Chatterton (1752–1770), a promising poet who committed suicide at the age of 17. [2] Robert Burns (1759–1796), the Scottish poet, who had a difficult life and died early.

IX

As a huge stone is sometimes seen to lie
Couched on the bald top of an eminence;
Wonder to all who do the same espy,
By what means it could thither come, and whence; 60
So that it seems a thing endued with sense:
Like a sea-beast crawled forth, that on a shelf
Of rock or sand reposeth, there to sun itself;

X

Such seemed this Man, not all alive nor dead,
Nor all asleep—in his extreme old age: 65
His body was bent double, feet and head
Coming together in life's pilgrimage;
As if some dire constraint of pain, or rage
Of sickness felt by him in times long past,
A more than human weight upon his frame had cast. 70

XI

Himself he propped, limbs, body, and pale face,
Upon a long grey staff of shaven wood:
And, still as I drew near with gentle pace,
Upon the margin of that moorish[3] flood
Motionless as a cloud the old Man stood, 75
That heareth not the loud winds when they call;
And moveth all together, if it move at all.

XII

At length, himself unsettling, he the pond
Stirred with his staff, and fixedly did look
Upon the muddy water, which he conned, 80
As if he had been reading in a book:
And now a stranger's privilege I took;
And, drawing to his side, to him did say,
"This morning gives us promise of a glorious day."

XIII

A gentle answer did the old Man make, 85
In courteous speech which forth he slowly drew:
And him with further words I thus bespake,
"What occupation do you there pursue?
This is a lonesome place for one like you."

[3] On a moor.

Ere he replied, a flash of mild surprise 90
Broke from the stable orbs of his yet-vivid eyes.

XIV

His words came feebly, from a feeble chest,
But each in solemn order followed each,
With something of a lofty utterance drest—
Choice word and measured phrase, above the reach 95
Of ordinary men; a stately speech;
Such as grave Livers do in Scotland use,
Religious men, who give to God and man their dues.

XV

He told, that to these waters he had come
To gather leeches,[4] being old and poor: 100
Employment hazardous and wearisome!
And he had many hardships to endure:
From pond to pond he roamed, from moor to moor;
Housing, with God's good help, by choice or chance;
And in this way he gained an honest maintenance. 105

XVI

The old Man still stood talking by my side;
But now his voice to me was like a stream
Scarce heard; nor word from word could I divide;
And the whole body of the Man did seem
Like one whom I had met with in a dream; 110
Or like a man from some far region sent,
To give me human strength, by apt admonishment.

XVII

My former thoughts returned: the fear that kills;
And hope that is unwilling to be fed;
Cold, pain, and labour, and all fleshly ills; 115
And mighty Poets in their misery dead.
—Perplexed, and longing to be comforted,
My question eagerly did I renew,
"How is it that you live, and what is it you do?"

XVIII

He with a smile did then his words repeat; 120
And said that, gathering leeches, far and wide

[4] Bloodsucking worms formerly used by physicians to reduce what was thought to be an excess of blood.

He travelled; stirring thus about his feet
The waters of the pools where they abide.
"Once I could meet with them on every side;
But they have dwindled long by slow decay; 125
Yet still I persevere, and find them where I may."

XIX

While he was talking thus, the lonely place,
The old Man's shape, and speech—all troubled me:
In my mind's eye I seemed to see him pace
About the weary moors continually, 130
Wandering about alone and silently.
While I these thoughts within myself pursued,
He, having made a pause, the same discourse renewed.

XX

And soon with this he other matter blended,
Cheerfully uttered, with demeanour kind, 135
But stately in the main; and, when he ended,
I could have laughed myself to scorn to find
In that decrepit Man so firm a mind.
"God," said I, "be my help and stay secure;
I'll think of the Leech-gatherer on the lonely moor!" 140

COMMENTARY

Let us suppose that someone who had never read "Resolution and Independence" were to ask us what it is about and we were to comply with his request. Would there be much likelihood of his believing that this could make the material of one of the finest poems in the English language? I use the phrase "what it is about" in the simple and quite natural sense in which we employ it when we inquire about some story or play with which we have no acquaintance, expecting to be answered with a summary account of its chief happenings. We do not of course think we have been told much when we have been told only this, yet we do feel we have been supplied some ground for estimating the interest the story or play will have for us; we assume some relation between even a scant *résumé* and the real nature of a work. And in general we are right in this assumption. But not always, and not, surely, in the instance of "Resolution and Independence."

What is the poem about? It is about the poet's meeting with a very old man and the beneficent effect that this encounter has upon him. On a fine spring morning, the poet, who is a young or youngish man, is walking on the moors. He is in a happy frame of mind, but suddenly his spirits fall, and he is overcome by an intense anxiety about his future; he thinks about the disastrous fates that have befallen other poets and that might befall him. As he walks on in his painful state of depression and fear, he comes across a solitary decrepit figure standing in a shallow pool. To the poet's questions about his way of life, the old man replies with simple dignity. He makes a bare living by gathering leeches; the work grows ever more difficult for him; he is quite alone in the world. He is so old that it seems scarcely possible that he should go on living; and he has, as we say, nothing to live for; yet he utters no complaint and shows no self-pity. The poet is moved to shame for having been so much distressed by the mere imagination of misfortune; he resolves to make the old leech-gatherer his example of fortitude.

If this is a fair statement of what happens in "Resolution and Independence," it is certainly reasonable to conclude that the content of the poem is rather trivial and dull. What is more, it has the unpleasing quality of moral didacticism; it seems to have the intention of teaching a lesson in simple morality, or even something more boring than that, a lesson in mental hygiene: "Do not allow your imagination to bedevil you with thoughts of personal disaster. Confront the chances of life with a firm and equal mind." What, then, are the elements of the poem that make for its great quality?

The first of these is the idea of greatness itself. The chief characteristic of the old man is his dignity. The simile by which he is first described compares him to a "huge stone," a massive boulder such as we sometimes see "couched on the bald top of an eminence," which raises in our minds the question of how it came there. If we do not think rationally of the glacier or flood that transported the boulder to its present unlikely place but suppose that it had moved of its own volition, its imagined movement is wonderful and awesome, and no less so is the movement of the old man. He leans on a staff because he is feeble, but his posture is majestic; his staff is an attribute of his majesty. The difficulty with which he moves appears as a sign not of weakness but of firmness, of a nature that is not easily moved by circumstance.

> Motionless as a cloud the old Man stood,
> That heareth not the loud winds when they call;
> And moveth all together, if it move at all.

In all cultures the quality of majesty is associated with weightiness and a degree of immobility, or at least slowness of movement—a king in a hurry seems a contradiction in terms. The ceremonial robes of the king express the idea that he has no need to be active. And the impression of the old man's kingliness is borne out by his "stately" speech and the imperious "flash" of his "yet vivid eyes."

In addition to this majesty, the old man has for the poet something like a supernatural authority. He seems "like one whom I had met with in a dream"—

> Or like a man from some far region sent,
> To give me human strength, by apt admonishment.

The "far region" suggests a divine region; to the poet the Leech-gatherer is an agent or messenger of God, an angel in disguise. This idea is sustained as the poet speculates on how it came about that he met the old man at this particular moment, when the meeting is of such momentous significance to him. He wonders if the encounter takes place "by peculiar grace, / A leading from above, a something given." These are theological terms having reference to divine intervention in the lives of individual persons.

But if the old man, despite his actual feebleness, is a figure of majesty, so, in his way, is the poet, who speaks not merely in his own person but as the representative of all poets. For him the sorrow of poets in misfortune is the sorrow of kings in misfortune—he speaks of "mighty Poets in their misery dead." The characteristic attributes of poets are not only "joy" but "pride" and "glory." They are, indeed, even greater than kings, for their divine right is from themselves: "By our own spirits are we deified."

Yet it is by their own spirits that they are cast down—no sooner has the poet made his proud boast than he confronts the tragic fate that threatens the possessors of the poetic power. His words are shocking in their explicitness:

> We Poets in our youth begin in gladness;
> But thereof come in the end despondency and madness.

The life of poets, our poet is saying, follows the course of his own feelings of that very morning: his despondency had succeeded his high spirits as if caused by them. His joy and its evanescence have their visual counterpart in the hare he described in Stanza II:

> All things that love the sun are out of doors;
> The sky rejoices in the morning's birth;
> The grass is bright with rain-drops;—on the moors
> The hare is running races in her mirth;
> And with her feet she from the plashy earth
> Raises a mist; that, glittering in the sun,
> Runs with her all the way, wherever she doth run.

Wherever she doth run—but not for as long as she runs. For the earth will dry and the mist that enhaloes her will vanish. We know from other of his poems that Wordsworth feared the loss of his poetic gift, which he associated with his youth and which he often represented in terms of some effect of light.

The poem, we can say, is organized by an opposition between what is suggested, on the one hand, by the hare racing in its luminous mist, and, on the other hand, by the "huge stone" to which the Leech-gatherer is compared—on the one hand, movement, speed, brightness, but also evanescence; on the other hand, immobility and lack of sentience, but also endurance. The poetic temperament, which is characterized by its quick responsiveness, Wordsworth associates with the quick-moving hare. To this he opposes—what? What name are we to give to the other temperament?

We are tempted to call it religious because one of the salient facts about the old Leech-gatherer is that he belongs to a Scottish religious sect. And religion may indeed, and often does, play a part in what we seek to name. But it need not. And then, even apart from the fact that there have been many religious poets, religion and poetry have too much in common to permit us to set up any simple opposition between them. What stands here in contrast to the poetic temperament is the temperament that finds its fulfilment in strictness of control, in what we have come to call "character." The nature of the poet, at least in the modern view, is defined by sensitivity and free responsiveness. These traits no doubt have their connection with morality as well as creativity, yet a strict moral training will undertake to limit them in the interests of character. This is exemplified in a striking way by the statement of the famous physician Sir William Osler, who, in one of his lectures to medical students, spoke of the physician's need for the quality which he called "imperturbability." He also called it "immobility" and "impassiveness" and even went so far as to call it "callousness." He admitted that this quality might appear to patients and their friends as hardness of heart, an indifference to the suffering of others that verged upon the inhuman, but he went on to say how disconcerted the patient and his family would be if the physician lacked this quality, for upon his ability to shut off his sensitivity depend his "firmness and courage," his ability to make difficult decisions and carry them out.

The poem, then, may be said to ask this question: Must the poet, for the sake of his survival, take to himself some measure of imperturbability, of rock-like fortitude, even at the cost of surrendering some of the sensitivity and responsiveness which constitute the essence of his poetic power? The question has an intrinsic psychological interest. But what gives it its peculiar force in the poem is the circumstance in which it is posed, the aura of tragic destiny which attends this confrontation of two modes of human self-realization.

Considered from the point of view of prosodic technique, "Resolution and Independence" is a most remarkable achievement. We begin our understanding of how the poem "works" by taking note of the punctuation, the sheer amount and weight of it: in the first three stanzas almost every line has a strong stop at its end. This has the effect of making each line a decisive and dramatic statement. The energy of one line is not continuous with that of the next; each line initiates its own movement, of which we become the more conscious as it discharges its energy upon the semi-colon, colon, or period that stops it; the effect is like that of watching breaker after breaker rising up to hurl itself upon a cliff. After the first three stanzas, the punctuation becomes lighter, although it is still decisive, and now we become aware of the stanza rather than the line as the unit of energy. Each stanza is as discrete as, at the beginning of the poem, each line had been, for the lengthened last line of the stanza acts as a full stop. The poem is thus a series of initiations of energy and of resistances to it, an equal display of movement and solidity.

Many readers are disturbed, even distressed, by the concluding couplet. And with some reason, for there is no doubt that

> "God," said I, "be my help and stay secure;
> I'll think of the Leech-gatherer on the lonely moor!"

is in all ways an anticlimax. It is emotionally insufficient and its tone is downright jaunty, so that it almost seems to dismiss the great episode which it brings to an end. The casual appeal to God seems merely conventional and a negation of the powerful if vague reference to the divine "far region." To these objections an admirer of the poem can offer no defence, except to say that, although cogent, they do not much matter.

KUBLA KHAN
OR
A VISION IN A DREAM
A Fragment

SAMUEL TAYLOR COLERIDGE

1772–1834

In Xanadu did Kubla Khan[1]
A stately pleasure-dome decree:
Where Alph, the sacred river, ran
  Through caverns measureless to man
    Down to a sunless sea. 5
So twice five miles of fertile ground
With walls and towers were girdled round:
And here were gardens bright with sinuous rills,
Where blossomed many an incense-bearing tree;
And here were forests ancient as the hills, 10
Enfolding sunny spots of greenery.

But oh! that deep romantic chasm which slanted
Down the green hill athwart[2] a cedarn cover!
A savage place! as holy and enchanted
As e'er beneath a waning moon was haunted 15
By woman wailing for her demon-lover!
And from this chasm, with ceaseless turmoil seething,
As if this earth in fast thick pants were breathing,
A mighty fountain momently[3] was forced:
Amid whose swift half-intermitted burst 20
Huge fragments vaulted like rebounding hail,
Or chaffy grain beneath the thresher's flail:
And 'mid these dancing rocks at once and ever
It flung up momently the sacred river.

[1] Kubla Khan was founder of the Mongol dynasty in China. His court, in reality, was at Yenching, near Peking. [2] Across. [3] Every moment, continuously.

Five miles meandering with a mazy motion 25
Through wood and dale the sacred river ran,
Then reached the caverns measureless to man,
And sank in tumult to a lifeless ocean:
And 'mid this tumult Kubla heard from far
Ancestral voices prophesying war! 30
The shadow of the dome of pleasure
Floated midway on the waves;
Where was heard the mingled measure
From the fountain and the caves.
It was a miracle of rare device, 35
A sunny pleasure-dome with caves of ice!

A damsel with a dulcimer
In a vision once I saw:
It was an Abyssinian maid,
And on her dulcimer she played, 40
Singing of Mount Abora.
Could I revive within me,
Her symphony and song,
To such a deep delight 'twould win me,
That with music loud and long, 45
I would build that dome in air,
That sunny dome! those caves of ice!
And all who heard should see them there,
And all should cry, Beware! Beware!
His flashing eyes, his floating hair! 50
Weave a circle round him thrice,
And close your eyes with holy dread,
For he on honey-dew hath fed,
And drunk the milk of Paradise.

COMMENTARY

Although the intrinsic qualities of "Kubla Khan" justify the admiration that has been given to it, some part of its great fame must surely be attributed to the prefatory note in which, upon its first publication in 1816, Coleridge told his readers how the poem came to be composed, some eighteen years before. The circumstances that Coleridge relates have so engaged the interest of the world that we can scarcely think of the poem without having them in mind—they have become virtually an element of the poem itself.

"In the summer of the year 1797," Coleridge writes,[1] "the Author, then in ill health, had retired to a lonely farm-house between Porlock and Linton. . . .

[1] But his memory played him false. All evidence points to the impossibility of his having written the poem in that year. It was probably written in 1798, but 1799 and 1800 also fall within the possible range.

In consequence of a slight indisposition, an anodyne [it was opium] had been prescribed, from the effects of which he fell asleep in his chair at the moment that he was reading the following sentence, or words of the same substance, in 'Purchas's Pilgrimage': 'Here the Khan Kubla commanded a palace to be built, and a stately garden thereunto. And thus ten miles of fertile ground were enclosed with a wall.' The author continued for about three hours in a profound sleep, at least of the external senses, during which time he has the most vivid confidence, that he could not have composed less than from two to three hundred lines; if that indeed can be called composition in which all the images rose up before him as *things,* with a parallel production of the correspondent expressions, without any sensation or consciousness of effort. On awaking he appeared to himself to have a distinct recollection of the whole, and taking his pen, ink, and paper, instantly and eagerly wrote down the lines that are here preserved. At this moment he was unfortunately called out by a person on business from Porlock, and detained by him above an hour, and on his return to his room, found, to his no small surprise and mortification, that though he still retained some vague and dim recollection of the general purport of the vision, yet, with the exception of some eight or ten scattered lines and images, all the rest had passed away like the images on the surface of a stream into which a stone has been cast. . . ."

This account of how "Kubla Khan" was written was for a long time accepted without question. But the researches of an American scholar, Professor Elisabeth Schneider, have brought the literal truth of the story into serious question; they suggest that these circumstances of composition were as much the product of the poet's imagination as the poem itself. Yet in some sense the truthfulness of Coleridge's account does not matter—the important thing is that the poet believed that it was possible, if singular, to compose a poem in his sleep, without the aid of his conscious mind, without, as he puts it, "any sensation or consciousness of effort," and also that a particular virtue might be assigned to such a mode of composition.

We must not exaggerate the novelty of this proposition. Ever since literature has been the object of thoughtful curiosity, men have supposed that the composition of poetry may be other than a willed and conscious process. This has been commonly explained by the concept of "inspiration," the idea that a spirit—of the Muse or some other nonhuman being—enters the poet, takes possession of his mind, and speaks through him.[1] Plato, not in order to disparage poets but to explain them, said that they were "mad," and the idea of the poet's being "possessed," out of his own control, as an insane person is, became part of the popular conception of the poetic character—everybody in Shakespeare's audience knew what Theseus was talking about when he equated the lunatic and the poet and spoke of "the poet's eye, in a fine frenzy rolling." This notion of poetic composition persisted even into the era of rationalism; Dryden paid tribute to it in his famous couplet about the close alliance between great wit—by which he meant poetic genius—and madness.

Yet the rationalism of the late seventeenth and eighteenth centuries put its critical emphasis less upon the uncontrolled processes of composition than upon those that were conscious and reasoned, less upon the poet's inspired vision than

[1] For a superb exemplification of this idea, see Shelley's "Ode to the West Wind," pp. 74 ff.

upon his careful revision. Pope, like Dryden, admitted the primacy of inspiration, but the chief direction of both his precept and example was toward correctness, polish, and good taste. If nonrational inspiration was to be acknowledged in the composition of great poems, it was to be admired only if it submitted to the rule of good judgment, which might be defined as the codified knowledge of what will please men of good sense.

The preface to "Kubla Khan" constitutes, therefore, a radical denial of the character of the poet that had prevailed in the eighteenth century. We cannot read Pope's brilliant "Essay on Criticism" without understanding that it regards the poet as primarily a performer, and, as such, committed to pleasing an audience and submissive to the judgment of his audience's taste. This view of the poet was not supposed to diminish his dignity—his position can fairly be compared with that of a great performing musician or dancer of our own time. Pope assumes that in general the audience's taste is correct and to be relied upon in much the same way we now assume the authority of people who love music and the dance—if a performer can consistently meet the requirements of persons with a highly developed sensibility in his art, we by and large take it for granted that he is good. And as for the performer, he assumes that if he meets his own standard of what makes a good performance, he will be liked and praised; his standard of judgment and that of his audience are much the same.

But Coleridge's preface quite negates the idea of the poet as performer and of the poem as an artistic commodity offered to the audience for its approval. Indeed, "Kubla Khan" was so little a performance that it was not even finished. (Actually, of course, even though the poet calls it "a fragment," the poem is felt by most readers to be complete in the sense of being an aesthetic whole. But the preface inevitably tempts us to imagine how it would have continued if the person on business from Porlock had not paid his visit.) It is not something that the poet wrote with the intention of interesting or pleasing or edifying his audience. It came into being as if by its own necessity and by its own will—it is a fact in nature as much as in art, a psychological fact as much as a poetic fact. It would seem, that is, that the mind quite naturally makes poems, as it makes dreams, without intention, without effort, without thought, without revision or any awareness of the rules of literature.

Coleridge's preface is to be read, however, not only as a kind of manifesto on the working of the poetic mind but also as an explanation of how this particular poem is to be responded to. When it first appeared, there would still have been many readers whom it would have troubled and puzzled; they would have thought that Coleridge was not being unduly or falsely modest when he said that he was publishing it "rather as a psychological curiosity, than on the ground of any supposed *poetic* merits." Such readers were no doubt fewer than if the poem had appeared in the year of its composition, for in the intervening time other poets had begun to habituate the public to certain of its poetic qualities—its exoticism, its fantasy, its indifference to rational considerations. Yet there were still many who would have been at a loss to know what the poem was trying to "say" or "do," and for these the preface was, in effect, a guide. It suggested that "Kubla Khan" was not to be judged by the criteria which in its day were conventionally applied to poetry and that the reader was thus free to respond to it in new terms, the terms of the poem itself.

The modern reader is surely less likely to resist making this kind of response than was the reader of Coleridge's time. This is not to imply that we today are more sensitive to poetry and more intelligent about it than our forebears were, but only that the tendency of literary criticism and education has changed. In our time the poet's personal fantasy is given large license and authority. Less and less do we think it possible to ask that a poem conform to some preconception of what a poem should be; we even believe that we should have no such preconception. We tend to think that every poem suggests its own aesthetic criteria and that it should be judged by our sense of its being an authentic representation of the poet's state of feeling—so long, at least, as we have reason to suppose that this state of feeling is significant. We may even incline to the belief that the more alien from our own state of feeling a poem is, the more authentically it represents the poet's feelings and the more authority it has. For readers today it neither constitutes the failure of a poem nor a deficiency in our aesthetic perception if we are not readily able to say what the work means in all its various parts or as a whole. After all, we have never understood music in the sense of being able to explain its meaning, and nowadays we are surrounded by pictures which give us pleasure although (as the painters themselves are the first to say) we have no way to "understand" them rationally and articulately. We admit the possibility that a work of art can exist in its own right, without reference to us, like a tree, or a mountain, or an animal; it need have no relation to us except as we elect to have a relation to it, by finding interest and pleasure in it. We think of the work as a meaningful expression of its creator's mind but not, in any usual definition of the word, a communication.

"Kubla Khan" offers no literal difficulty to the reader—its statements, taken by themselves, are perfectly clear. Yet most readers, however strong their response to it, feel that they would be incapable of formulating what the poem as a whole is *really* saying. The concluding sentence of Coleridge's prefatory note may help us to become conscious of what it is that we respond to. "As a contrast to this vision," Coleridge says, "I have annexed a fragment of a very different character, describing with equal fidelity the dream of pain and disease." He is referring to his poem, "The Pains of Sleep," which describes in a very direct way the distress which opium and physical and mental ill-health introduced into his repose, the horrors of—as the poem calls them—"life-stifling fear, life-stifling shame." What "Kubla Khan" represents is indeed a contrast; it is the very opposite of whatever might be life-stifling—the vision is of life at its most intense. Life's power is announced in the decree of the great Khan, the mere utterance of which brought the "pleasure-dome" into being, by the ejaculative force of the "mighty fountain," by the passion of the "woman wailing for her demon-lover," by—finally—the great image of the poet in the transcendent strength of his magical art. Here, surely, is nothing "life-stifling." Nor does the war prophesied by the "ancestral voices" bring any fear: for the Khan, war is the very business of life. The woman who wails for her demon-lover utters her cry without any possibility of shame, and the poet envisages his dangerous strength ("Beware! Beware!") without compunction. To be sure, the meandering course of the "sacred river" comes to its end in a "sunless sea," a "lifeless ocean"; but the river is perpetual, having its source in the mighty fountain which is "momently" forced from the earth. The "caves of ice" beneath the "sunny pleasure-dome" contradict the fertility of the gardens and the forests, yet if they, like the sunless sea and the lifeless ocean, evoke the idea of death, they suggest the idea of a holy mystery rather than a denial of life; the fear or awe they generate is consonant with the sacredness of Alph, the sacred river; and when the poet says that with the power of his music he will "build" these caves of ice, he is as enraptured by this prospect as by the thought of building "that sunny dome" itself. The poem and what it implies of the nature of poetry celebrate pleasure but even more they celebrate life in its might and in its mystery of contradictions.

DON JUAN
An Episode from Canto II

GEORGE GORDON, LORD BYRON
1788–1824

Headnote

There are two things that the reader ought to know about Byron's Don Juan. The first is that his name is not pronounced in the Spanish fashion (*hwan*), but as if it were an English name spoken phonetically: Byron rimes it with "new one" and "true one." The second is that he has only the faintest connection with the Don Juan of legend. It is true that all his adventures involve love affairs of one kind or another, but he is nothing like the universal seducer of Molière's play or Mozart's opera. Indeed, he is a rather modest and virtuous young man whose love affairs either happen to him or are forced upon him by women. A native of Seville, he has been very strictly brought up by his extravagantly prudish and intellectual mother. When he is sixteen, his mother's friend, Donna Julia, "married, charming, chaste, and twenty-three," falls in love with him and he with her. Their liaison is discovered by Donna Julia's husband, a great scandal results, Donna Julia is packed off to a convent, and Juan is hustled out of the country by his mother. He takes ship at Cadiz; before his departure he has received from Julia a very touching letter of farewell and has been greatly moved by it.

*   *   *

1

Oh ye! who teach the ingenuous youth of nations,
    Holland, France, England, Germany, or Spain,
I pray ye flog them upon all occasions,
    It mends their morals, never mind the pain:
The best of mothers and of educations   5
    In Juan's case were but employ'd in vain,
Since, in a way that's rather of the oddest, he
Became divested of his native modesty.

2

Had he but been placed at a public school,
    In the third form, or even in the fourth,[1]   10

[1] Grade in a British secondary school. A "public school" in England is an endowed institution at which rather high fees are charged. It prepares for the public service or for the university.

His daily task had kept his fancy cool,
At least, had he been nurtured in the north;
Spain may prove an exception to the rule,
But then exceptions always prove its worth—
A lad of sixteen causing a divorce 15
Puzzled his tutors very much, of course.

3

I can't say that it puzzles me at all,
If all things be consider'd; first, there was
His lady-mother, mathematical,
A——never mind;—his tutor, an old ass; 20
A pretty woman—(that's quite natural,
Or else the thing had hardly come to pass)
A husband rather old, not much in unity
With his young wife—a time, and opportunity.

4

Well—well; the world must turn upon its axis, 25
And all mankind turn with it, heads or tails,
And live and die, make love and pay our taxes,
And as the veering wind shifts, shift our sails;
The king commands us, and the doctor quacks us,
The priest instructs, and so our life exhales, 30
A little breath, love, wine, ambition, fame,
Fighting, devotion, dust,—perhaps a name.

5

I said, that Juan had been sent to Cadiz—
A pretty town, I recollect it well—
'Tis there the mart of the colonial trade is, 35
(Or was, before Peru learn'd to rebel,)
And such sweet girls—I mean, such graceful ladies,
Their very walk would make your bosom swell;
I can't describe it, though so much it strike,
Nor liken it—I never saw the like: 40

6

An Arab horse, a stately stag, a barb[2]
New-broke, a cameleopard,[3] a gazelle,
No—none of these will do—and then their garb,
Their veil and petticoat—Alas! to dwell
Upon such things would very near absorb 45

[2] A Barbary horse, one of a breed noted for speed and endurance. [3] Giraffe.

A canto—then their feet and ankles,—well,
Thank Heaven I've got no metaphor quite ready,
(And so, my sober Muse—come, let's be steady—

7

Chaste Muse!—well, if you must, you must)—the veil
Thrown back a moment with the glancing hand, 50
While the o'erpowering eye, that turns you pale,
Flashes into the heart:—All sunny land
Of love! when I forget you, may I fail
To——say my prayers—but never was there plann'd
A dress through which the eyes give such a volley, 55
Excepting the Venetian Fazzioli.[4]

8

But to our tale: the Donna Inez sent
Her son to Cadiz only to embark;
To stay there had not answer'd her intent,
But why?—we leave the reader in the dark— 60
'Twas for a voyage the young man was meant,
As if a Spanish ship were Noah's ark,
To wean him from the wickedness of earth,
And send him like a dove of promise forth.[5]

9

Don Juan bade his valet pack his things 65
According to direction, then received
A lecture and some money: for four springs
He was to travel; and though Inez grieved
(As every kind of parting has its stings),
She hoped he would improve—perhaps believed: 70
A letter, too, she gave (he never read it)
Of good advice—and two or three of credit.

10

In the mean time, to pass her hours away,
Brave Inez now set up a Sunday school
For naughty children, who would rather play 75
(Like truant rogues) the devil, or the fool;
Infants of three years old were taught that day,
Dunces were whipt, or set upon a stool:
The great success of Juan's education
Spurr'd her to teach another generation. 80

[4] A dress worn in Venice in Byron's time. [5] After the flood, Noah repeatedly sent out a dove from the ark. When the bird failed to return, Noah knew that the land was dry and that it was safe to leave the ark (Genesis 8:8–13).

11

Juan embark'd—the ship got under way,
The wind was fair, the water passing rough;
A devil of a sea rolls in that bay,
As I, who've cross'd it oft, know well enough;
And, standing upon deck, the dashing spray 85
Flies in one's face, and makes it weather-tough:
And there he stood to take, and take again,
His first—perhaps his last—farewell of Spain.

12

I can't but say it is an awkward sight
To see one's native land receding through 90
The growing waters; it unmans one quite,
Especially when life is rather new:
I recollect Great Britain's coast looks white,
But almost every other country's blue,
When gazing on them, mystified by distance, 95
We enter on our nautical existence.

13

So Juan stood, bewilder'd on the deck:
The wind sung, cordage strain'd, and sailors swore,
And the ship creak'd, the town became a speck,
From which away so fair and fast they bore. 100
The best of remedies is a beef-steak
Against sea-sickness; try it, sir, before
You sneer, and I assure you this is true,
For I have found it answer—so may you.

14

Don Juan stood, and, gazing from the stern, 105
Beheld his native Spain receding far:
First partings form a lesson hard to learn,
Even nations feel this when they go to war;
There is a sort of unexprest concern,
A kind of shock that sets one's heart ajar: 110
At leaving even the most unpleasant people
And places, one keeps looking at the steeple.

15

But Juan had got many things to leave,
His mother, and a mistress, and no wife,
So that he had much better cause to grieve 115
Than many persons more advanced in life;
And if we now and then a sigh must heave

At quitting even those we quit in strife,
No doubt we weep for those the heart endears—
That is, till deeper griefs congeal our tears. 120

16

So Juan wept, as wept the captive Jews
By Babel's waters, still remembering Sion:[6]
I'd weep,—but mine is not a weeping Muse,
And such light griefs are not a thing to die on;
Young men should travel, if but to amuse 125
Themselves; and the next time their servants tie on
Behind their carriages their new portmanteau,
Perhaps it may be lined with this my canto.[7]

17

And Juan wept, and much he sigh'd and thought,
While his salt tears dropp'd into the salt sea, 130
"Sweets to the sweet";[8] (I like so much to quote;
You must excuse this extract,—'t is where she,
The Queen of Denmark, for Ophelia brought
Flowers to the grave;) and, sobbing often, he
Reflected on his present situation, 135
And seriously resolved on reformation.

18

"Farewell, my Spain! a long farewell!" he cried,
"Perhaps I may revisit thee no more,
But die, as many an exiled heart hath died,
Of its own thirst to see again thy shore: 140
Farewell, where Guadalquivir's waters glide!
Farewell, my mother! and, since all is o'er,
Farewell, too, dearest Julia!—(here he drew
Her letter out again, and read it through.)

19

"And oh! if e'er I should forget, I swear— 145
But that's impossible, and cannot be—
Sooner shall this blue ocean melt to air,
Sooner shall earth resolve itself to sea,
Than I resign thine image, oh, my fair!
Or think of anything, excepting thee; 150

[6] Zion, or Jerusalem; Babel, Babylon. [7] A division of a long poem. A canto, or song, was originally as much of a poem as a minstrel might recite without a break. [8] So says the queen, Gertrude, in *Hamlet* (Act V, Scene 1) as she scatters flowers over the grave of Ophelia, who, after the death of her father, Polonius, loses her sanity and then drowns.

A mind diseased no remedy can physic—
(Here the ship gave a lurch, and he grew sea-sick.)

20

"Sooner shall heaven kiss earth—(here he fell sicker)
Oh, Julia! what is every other woe?—
(For God's sake let me have a glass of liquor; 155
Pedro, Battista, help me down below.)
Julia, my love—(you rascal, Pedro, quicker)—
Oh, Julia!—(this curst vessel pitches so)—
Beloved Julia, hear me still beseeching!"
(Here he grew inarticulate with retching.) 160

21

He felt that chilling heaviness of heart,
Or rather stomach, which, alas! attends,
Beyond the best apothecary's art,
The loss of love, the treachery of friends,
Or death of those we dote on, when a part 165
Of us dies with them as each fond hope ends:
No doubt he would have been much more pathetic,
But the sea acted as a strong emetic.

22

Love's a capricious power: I've known it hold
Out through a fever caused by its own heat, 170
But be much puzzled by a cough and cold,
And find a quinsy[9] very hard to treat;
Against all noble maladies he's bold,
But vulgar illnesses don't like to meet,
Nor that a sneeze should interrupt his sigh, 175
Nor inflammations redden his blind eye.

23

But worst of all is nausea, or a pain
About the lower region of the bowels;
Love, who heroically breathes a vein,[10]
Shrinks from the application of hot towels, 180
And purgatives are dangerous to his reign,
Sea-sickness death: his love was perfect, how else
Could Juan's passion, while the billows roar,
Resist his stomach, ne'er at sea before?

[9] Sore throat. [10] Allows a vein to be lanced so as to let blood.

COMMENTARY

Don Juan is one of the celebrated books of the nineteenth century, and the odds are that it is quite the gayest. It is a very long poem, consisting of sixteen cantos ranging in length from 60 to 160 stanzas. It breaks off in the middle of a lively erotic adventure which the hero has embarked upon, brought to an end not by the poet's intention but by his death, and that it should stop rather than conclude is entirely appropriate to its nature. The poem has been called formless, and in some sense this is true—at least it can be said that Byron intended it to have no more form than is supplied by a single hero whose adventures and sexual escapades the poet follows, having first contrived them. Byron said that he planned to have Juan die on the guillotine during the French Revolution. But before reaching this grim consummation, he could have carried Juan through as many adventures as it pleased him to write. He intended that the chief interest of the poem should not be in the hero's living his life and dying his death but in the poet's writing the poem. Yet it would be wrong to think of Juan as a "mere puppet"—he is too engaging a figure to be regarded so; we come to have too much affection for his innocence and sweetness and readiness; and this is not to mention Byron's affection for him, as being—although of course not literally—a representation of his own youth. Nevertheless, Juan is not meant to create the illusion of being an autonomous person, like many characters in literature. His dependent status is announced in the poem's opening stanza:

> I want a hero: an uncommon want,
>   When every year and month sends forth a new one,
> Till, after cloying the gazettes with cant,
>   The age discovers he is not the true one:
> Of such as these I should not care to vaunt,
>   I'll therefore take our ancient friend Don Juan—
> We all have seen him in the pantomime.
> Sent to the devil somewhat ere his time.[1]

Having announced his selection of a hero, Byron goes on to tell us what his literary methods are going to be. Most epic poets, he says, start in the middle of the story—he quotes the famous phrase from Horace's *Art of Poetry*—and then, by some device, give the reader an account of what has gone before:

> Most epic poets plunge "in medias res"
>   (Horace makes this the heroic turnpike road),
> And then your hero tells, whene'er you please,
>   What went before—by way of episode,
> While seated after dinner at his ease,
>   Beside his mistress in some soft abode,
> Palace, or garden, paradise, or cavern,
> Which serves the happy couple for a tavern.

"Most epic poets"—does *Don Juan,* then, presume to think of itself as an epic poem? It does fulfill one requirement of an epic: it is very long. But what epic poem ever spoke in a voice so colloquial and casual, so downright careless,

[1] As I remarked in the headnote, Byron's hero has in fact very little in common with the legendary Don Juan.

so lacking in high seriousness? And what epic poem was ever at such pains to destroy all possibility of illusion, to make sure that the reader will not give the usual credence to the story he is being told? This epic poem—if that is what it is—mocks the very idea of epic poetry.

Don Juan is, in short, what we call a burlesque. The meaning of that word has been largely lost to a kind of theatrical entertainment which is devoted to rowdy humor, chiefly of a sexual kind, and to female nudity. But the modern burlesque show had its beginnings in actual burlesque—in, that is, the mockery of a serious play that was well known to the audience. Burlesque is a very old form of art—it was highly developed by the ancient Greeks—and many notable and even great works have been conceived in its spirit. Cervantes began *Don Quixote* as a burlesque of the elaborate prose romances of the sixteenth century. Fielding's *Joseph Andrews* is a burlesque of the moralism of Richardson's *Pamela,* and his *Tom Jones* teases the literary conventions of classical antiquity. Jane Austen's *Northanger Abbey* affectionately mocks the terror-novels of the day.

Burlesque is usually directed against a particular literary work or kind of work, with the intention of showing that it is false or foolish. But it may also be directed against the whole enterprise of literature, which it represents as an institution licensed to traduce reality. Parts of Flaubert's *Bouvard and Pécuchet* take this direction, as do parts of the great modern instance of burlesque, Joyce's *Ulysses.* And this is true also of *Don Juan.* The poet's ceaseless intrusion into his story, his avowed manipulation of it, his "asides," which must surely occupy more space than the narrative, his open references to himself, all enforce the idea that he is much too sensible a man to be taken in by the conventions of poetry, that he knows literature for what it really is, an elaborate game. He is perfectly willing to play the game, being the best-natured of men, but he will not pretend, or ask the reader to believe, that it is reality.

But although the episode of Juan struggling to maintain his high-minded sorrow against the assaults of the rising nausea of his seasickness is a notable example of burlesque, it quite transcends its genre. It goes beyond the mockery of a literary tradition, that of the faithful grieving lover, to raise radically subversive questions about the dignity of human nature and the autonomy of the human mind.

In any culture we are pretty sure to find two opposing views of man's nature. According to one view, man is at least potentially a being of great dignity, a spiritual being in the sense that he is not wholly or finally conditioned by material considerations. His dignity, spirituality, and freedom derive from his power and courage. In simpler societies power and courage are thought to belong almost exclusively to socially dominant figures, to the king, the warrior, and the priest. All these personages express by their mode of dress and by their bearing and manner of speech the dignity they claim for themselves. (The comments on the "kingliness" of Wordsworth's old Leech-gatherer [page 53] are relevant here—one of the tendencies of the literature of the late eighteenth and early nineteenth centuries was to assert the dignity of people not of the dominant classes.) The other view concentrates upon man as an animal creature, who provokes not respect but laughter. Contrary to a common assumption, even quite primitive peoples do not take their animal functions wholly for granted; in every culture sexuality and defecation are thought to be funny—

they are "accepted" as "natural" but they are thought to derogate from human dignity; they are always joked about. The same is true of the impulse to self-preservation: cowardice is thought to be "natural"—and funny.

Among the Greeks these two views of man's nature were expressed in two distinct literary forms. The view of man as a dignified, free, and spiritual being was represented by tragedy, with its persons of royal or noble birth, its grave and exalted language, its conscious suppression of all petty and sordid considerations. Comedy represented the view that man was bound by his animal nature; in the frankest possible way it took account of all the exigencies of animality, all the "low" conditions of human existence.

Aristotle said that tragedy showed men as better than they really are and that comedy showed men as worse than they really are. And of course he is right in suggesting that neither the bias of tragedy nor that of comedy tells the whole truth. But in defiance of Aristotle, as it were, comedy does claim truth for itself. If tragedy denies the comic view of man, it does so implicitly and silently; but comedy is quite often explicit in its opposition to tragedy—again and again it says straight out that the form and manner of tragedy are false and highfalutin. It claims reality for itself, insisting that reality is what is comprised by the "facts of life," by man's need and greed for food and drink, by his running away from danger, and by his copulation and defecation.

In general it can be said of the Greeks that they were able to hold the two views of man's nature in balance. They gave as much sanction to the subversive view of comedy as to the ideal view of tragedy. Yet at least one Greek, Plato, was distressed by man's double nature; his philosophy makes a strong commitment to the belief that man is most truly himself when he is free of the animal conditions of life. Christianity followed Plato in this—the essence of Christian morality lies in the wish to overcome the bondage of flesh. The way in which Christianity describes this bondage varies with the changes in the secular culture. The seventeenth century, for example, was a period of great intellectual achievement, and Christian thought at that time undertook to check intellectual pride by reminding man how conditioned by physical things his intellect was. It did this, we may say, in the manner of burlesque. The Christian poet John Donne took wry note of the fact that at a moment when his thoughts were fixed on God in prayer and meditation, a fly buzzing around his head could distract his attention from its great object and that no effort of will could restore his rapt concentration until the fly was silenced. And Pascal, one of the great mathematicians of all times as well as a profound psychologist of the religious emotions, based his whole sense of the religious life upon similar observations, upon the discrepancy between man's "greatness" and his "littleness," reminding us that, powerful as the human intellect is, a man is never in full control of the right exercise of his mind, which is always at the mercy of the most trivial material circumstances.

The early nineteenth century was an age that took pride not so much in intellectual as in emotional power; it looked upon love and passion as an indication of human freedom and dignity, and perhaps no one had done more to establish this idea than Byron himself. Whatever else Byron is burlesquing in *Don Juan* he is burlesquing his own early work, in which love and passion asserted themselves without regard to the facts of animal existence. He did indeed represent love and passion as meeting with opposition from the world and as ensuing often in pain and defeat, but this of course constitutes anything but a skeptical comment upon them—in literature the pain and defeat of a person who lives according to his belief in his spiritual nature are taken to be the affirmation of spirit itself. What Byron is now saying, however, is reductive enough; he is proposing that it is not by the great catastrophes that the life of spirit is brought into question but by the small ones. Man's sense of his autonomy and dignity is not limited by his tragic sufferings but by those that are traditionally thought to be comic—the cold in the head and the passing afflictions of the stomach.

ODE TO THE WEST WIND

PERCY BYSSHE SHELLEY

1792–1822

1

O wild West Wind, thou breath of Autumn's being,
Thou, from whose unseen presence the leaves dead
Are driven, like ghosts from an enchanter fleeing,

Yellow, and black, and pale, and hectic red,
Pestilence-stricken multitudes: O thou, 5
Who chariotest to their dark wintry bed

The wingèd seeds, where they lie cold and low,
Each like a corpse within its grave, until
Thine azure sister of the spring shall blow

Her clarion o'er the dreaming earth, and fill 10
(Driving sweet buds like flocks to feed in air)
With living hues and odors plain and hill:

Wild spirit, which art moving everywhere;
Destroyer and preserver;[1] hear, oh hear!

2

Thou on whose stream, 'mid the steep sky's commotion, 15
Loose clouds like earth's decaying leaves are shed,
Shook from the tangled boughs of Heaven and Ocean,

[1] The seemingly opposed powers of destruction and preservation were frequently attributed to a single god in ancient times.

Angels of rain and lightning: there are spread
On the blue surface of thine airy surge,
Like the bright hair uplifted from the head 20

Of some fierce Maenad,[2] even from the dim verge
Of the horizon to the zenith's height
The locks of the approaching storm. Thou dirge

Of the dying year, to which this closing night
Will be the dome of a vast sepulchre, 25
Vaulted with all thy congregated might

Of vapours, from whose solid atmosphere
Black rain, and fire, and hail will burst: O, hear!

3

Thou who didst waken from his summer dreams
The blue Mediterranean, where he lay, 30
Lulled by the coil of his crystalline streams,

Beside a pumice[3] isle in Baiæ's bay,[4]
And saw in sleep old palaces and towers
Quivering within the wave's intenser day,

All overgrown with azure moss and flowers 35
So sweet, the sense faints picturing them! Thou
For whose path the Atlantic's level powers

Cleave themselves into chasms, while far below
The sea-blooms and the oozy woods which wear
The sapless foliage of the ocean, know 40

Thy voice, and suddenly grow gray with fear,
And tremble and despoil themselves: O hear!

[2] In Greek mythology, mad or frenzied women who attended the god Dionysus, or Bacchus. [3] Obsidian. [4] Bay of Naples. Baiae is a town on an inlet of the bay.

4

If I were a dead leaf thou mightest bear;
If I were a swift cloud to fly with thee;
A wave to pant beneath thy power, and share 45

The impulse of thy strength, only less free
Than thou, O, uncontrollable! If even
I were as in my boyhood, and could be

The comrade of thy wanderings over heaven,
As then, when to outstrip thy skiey speed 50
Scarce seemed a vision; I would ne'er have striven

As thus with thee in prayer in my sore need,
Oh! lift me as a wave, a leaf, a cloud!
I fall upon the thorns of life! I bleed!

A heavy weight of hours has chained and bowed 55
One too like thee: tameless, and swift, and proud.

5

Make me thy lyre, even as the forest is:
What if my leaves are falling like its own!
The tumult of thy mighty harmonies

Will take from both a deep, autumnal tone, 60
Sweet though in sadness. Be thou, Spirit fierce,
My spirit! Be thou me, impetuous one!

Drive my dead thoughts over the universe
Like withered leaves to quicken a new birth!
And, by the incantation of this verse, 65

Scatter, as from an unextinguished hearth
Ashes and sparks, my words among mankind!
Be through my lips to unawakened earth

The trumpet of a prophecy, O, Wind,
If Winter comes, can Spring be far behind? 70

COMMENTARY

This is a strangely primitive poem to have been written in the nineteenth century. Not that its language and form are primitive—they are anything but that. The primitive quality of the poem is found in certain of its modes of thought. To a very considerable extent the "Ode to the West Wind" deals with the world as men of early pagan cultures dealt with it.

The poet represents himself as experiencing a crisis of the spirit; he is at the point of despair, and in his extremity he invokes the aid of the autumn wind, asking that it give him its wild energy—"Be thou, Spirit fierce, / My spirit!" We know, certainly, that a wind cannot in actual fact do for a man what Shelley asks it to do for him. Nothing is more likely than that the poet's asking help of the wind should seem to be a mere conceit, a play of poetical fancy, and that we should satisfy our sense of actuality by explaining to ourselves that the wind "is of course only a symbol." Yet in fact we do not think of the West Wind as functioning in the poem in a merely symbolic way. We find ourselves believing that it really is the spiritual and moral force Shelley represents it as being, that, indeed, it is just what he calls it, a spirit, and that it might perfectly well enter a man and restore the power he has lost. We believe this because the poem believes it—the Ode is based on the primitive identification of spirit and wind, for the word *spirit* comes from the Latin *spiritus,* meaning breath, which in turn comes from *spirare* meaning "to blow." Shelley is entirely literal in making such an identification. Dispirited, he asks to be again inspirited, to have the breath of life blown into him.

And he goes about getting what he wants in primitive fashion. The people of an earlier time believed that words had power over things and over the unseen forces of the universe; poetry and magic were once closely allied, virtually interchangeable. The Ode assumes this old connection; Shelley would seem to have been conscious of his magician's role, for in line 65 he speaks of "the incantation of this verse." *Incantation,* although derived from the Latin word which means simply to sing or chant, always means the singing or chanting of magic spells. Another form of the word is, of course, enchantment.

Shelley's method of incantation or enchantment is in the orthodox tradition of magic. Each of the first three stanzas is an invocation—literally, a "calling" in the sense of "summoning"—of the spirit. All the three invocations follow the same form: each opens with an address to the Spirit; each ends with the plea—or is it a command?—"Oh, hear!"; in each the Spirit is characterized by his powers, and each characterization has two parts, the second beginning with the reiteration of the pronoun "Thou." The repetitiveness of this form is quite in keeping with the lore of magic, which gives great importance to the precise repetition of a fixed form of words. The order of the words is as important as the words themselves. A spell has to be exactly right or it will not work. (In this connection, it is interesting to note that our word *glamour,* in its sense of enchantment, comes from *grammar*—the modest art of using words correctly, according to rule, comes to be thought of as a magical power.)

The device by which the Spirit is summoned is also quite in accord with established magical practice. Primitive people believe that there is an integral connection between a person and a representation of him, and that by means of the representation it is possible to control him. One can, for instance, injure or destroy a human enemy by making a figure of him and mistreating it in appropriate ways; the spirit of a god is supposed to enter an image of him set up before his shrine. It is an analogous belief that the name of a person or god is integral with him and that, like an image, it can be used to control him. For that reason, in some societies, people keep their real names secret, and in the ancient Jewish ritual the name of God was permitted to be uttered only once a year, by the High Priest, and in great solemnity and fear. In the light of these primitive beliefs, we can see what the first three stanzas of the Ode are doing—they are making a verbal image of the Spirit; they are naming him as completely as possible by detailed description of his attributes, his power over the earth, over the sky, and over the sea. To define him is to circumscribe him. To know him is to have the power to influence his behavior.

The process of control by representation extends to the very structure of the verse in which the West Wind is described. *Terza rima* is a form which has an unusually urgent forward movement—such is the arrangement of the rimes (a b a, b c b, c d c, etc.) that scarcely have we begun one tercet than the rime-sound of the next is announced. In the three invocation stanzas this forward impulse is given the greatest possible freedom, for the sense of the line does not require the voice to pause at the end, but, on the contrary, carries it rapidly over to the next line. (In this respect the verse is at an opposite extreme from the opening of Wordsworth's "Resolution and Independence" [pages 50, 57].) And the syntax is as open and unchecked, as onward moving, as the verse.

In the first stanza the Spirit is addressed in a striking epithet—he is called "destroyer and preserver." This has led some readers to believe that the West Wind represents the continuing spirit of the French Revolution, for revolution, ideally conceived, may be said to destroy in order to preserve; it destroys the old and outworn elements of society in order to allow the new to develop. The interpretation is entirely consonant with what we know of Shelley's temperament and political beliefs and it does seem to be sustained by details of the poem. Thus, the line "Wild Spirit, which art moving everywhere" suggests that the Spirit moves not only over earth, sky, and sea, but also in the hearts, councils, and cities of men. And the identification might seem to be made virtually explicit by lines 63–69, in which the phrases "quicken a new birth," "my words among mankind," "the trumpet of a prophecy," all point to the poet's hope of a great social and political redemption.

We do well to have this possible meaning of the West Wind in mind. But we must be careful not to allow it to make the concluding part of the poem simpler, or more simply optimistic, than in fact it is. It may be the poet has been led beyond his personal despair by the thought that the autumnal destruction of what is bad in society will bring a springtime of happiness to mankind and that in this renovation his own ideas and suffering will have had some part. And this may permit him to feel that his autumnal despair, the devastation of his own life, is but a state in the process of life in general, and that he may hope for a personal renewal; he draws this hope from the analogy of the cycle of the seasons, for the death of the year is the augury of its rebirth—

O, Wind,
If Winter comes, can Spring be far behind?

So the poem ends. The terms of the poem, however, do not really allow us to assume that the concluding line expresses, though with pathetic interrogation, the emergence of the poet from despair to some degree of optimism. Actually they do not permit Shelley to rest in hope, for if his vision of the human fate, and of his own fate, must be in accord with everything to be inferred from the cycle of the seasons, it requires little skepticism, and no cynicism at all, to understand that if spring follows winter, so too does winter follow spring. Renovation may indeed come to society and to individual man but if we derive this hopeful thought from contemplation of the cycle of the seasons, we must recognize that the coming of spring portends the eventual autumnal decay. Perhaps it is the poet's repressed consciousness of this sad irony that accounts for the memorable poignancy of the triumphant cry at the end of the poem, in which there is almost as much despair as there is comfort.

Almost, but not quite. The cycle of the seasons must always have its import of despair, but its import of hope seems to be more insistent. Men have always celebrated the shortest day of the year as the time when the year turns and the days begin to grow longer, and we hang the baubles on our Christmas trees in token of our happy expectation of the blossoms of spring and the fruits of summer.

ODE TO A NIGHTINGALE

JOHN KEATS

1795–1821

My heart aches, and a drowsy numbness pains
My sense, as though of hemlock[1] I had drunk,
Or emptied some dull opiate to the drains
One minute past, and Lethe-wards[2] had sunk.
'Tis not through envy of thy happy lot, 5
But being too happy in thine happiness—
That thou, light wingèd Dryad[3] of the trees,
In some melodious plot
Of beechen green, and shadows numberless,
Singest of summer in full-throated ease. 10

O, for a draught of vintage! that hath been
Cooled a long age in the deep-delvèd earth,
Tasting of Flora[4] and the country green,
Dance, and Provençal song,[5] and sunburnt mirth!
O for a beaker full of the warm South, 15
Full of the true, the blushful Hippocrene,[6]
With beaded bubbles winking at the brim,
And purple-stainèd mouth;
That I might drink, and leave the world unseen,
And with thee fade away into the forest dim: 20

Fade far away, dissolve, and quite forget
What thou among the leaves hast never known,
The weariness, the fever, and the fret
Here, where men sit and hear each other groan;

[1] A poisonous potion obtained from the hemlock. [2] Lethe, in Greek mythology, was the river of oblivion from which all dead souls drank as they passed into Hades. [3] Tree nymph. [4] The Roman goddess of flowers and gardens. [5] Song of Provence, a region in the south of France noted, during the Middle Ages, for its troubadours, or lyric poets. [6] Water of the Hippocrene, the fountain of the Muses in Greek mythology; hence, poetic inspiration.

Where palsy shakes a few, sad, last gray hairs, 25
Where youth grows pale, and specter-thin, and dies;
Where but to think is to be full of sorrow
And leaden-eyed despairs,
Where Beauty cannot keep her lustrous eyes,
Or new Love pine at them beyond tomorrow. 30

Away! away! for I will fly to thee,
Not charioted by Bacchus and his pards,[7]
But on the viewless[8] wings of Poesy,
Though the dull brain perplexes and retards:
Already with thee! tender is the night, 35
And haply the Queen-Moon is on her throne,
Clustered around by all her starry Fays;[9]
But here there is no light,
Save what from heaven is with the breezes blown
Through verdurous glooms and winding mossy ways. 40

I cannot see what flowers are at my feet,
Nor what soft incense hangs upon the boughs,
But, in embalmèd[10] darkness, guess each sweet
Wherewith the seasonable month endows
The grass, the thicket, and the fruit-tree wild; 45
White hawthorn, and the pastoral eglantine;
Fast fading violets covered up in leaves;
And mid-May's eldest child.
The coming musk-rose, full of dewy wine,
The murmurous haunt of flies on summer eves. 50

Darkling[11] I listen; and, for many a time,
I have been half in love with easeful Death,
Called him soft names in many a musèd rime,
To take into the air my quiet breath;
Now more than ever seems it rich to die, 55
To cease upon the midnight with no pain,
While thou art pouring forth thy soul abroad
In such an ecstasy!
Still wouldst thou sing, and I have ears in vain—
To thy high requiem become a sod. 60

Thou wast not born for death, immortal Bird!
No hungry generations tread thee down;

[7] Leopards or panthers. Bacchus, or Dionysus, the god of wine, is frequently represented in a chariot drawn by tigers. [8] Invisible. [9] Fairies. [10] Aromatic, balmy. [11] In the dark.

The voice I hear this passing night was heard
    In ancient days by emperor and clown:
Perhaps the self-same song that found a path 65
    Through the sad heart of Ruth, when, sick for home,
        She stood in tears amid the alien corn;[12]
            The same that oft-times hath
    Charmed magic casements, opening on the foam
        Of perilous seas, in faery lands forlorn. 70

Forlorn! the very word is like a bell
    To toll me back from thee to my sole self,
Adieu! the fancy cannot cheat so well
    As she is famed to do, deceiving elf.
Adieu! adieu! thy plaintive anthem fades 75
    Past the near meadows, over the still stream,
        Up the hillside; and now 'tis buried deep
            In the next valley glades:
    Was it a vision, or a waking dream?
        Fled is that music—Do I wake or sleep? 80

COMMENTARY

The nightingale, which is a species of thrush known in Europe and Asia although not in America, has haunted the imagination of poets for centuries because of the beauty of its song and the strangeness of its nocturnal habit, for the nightingale sings only in darkness. Actually it is the male bird that sings, and medieval poetry conformed to this fact. But ancient Greek legend makes the singing bird female. Keats, in the first stanza of his Ode, follows the Greek mythological tradition; he addresses the nightingale as a dryad, a tree-nymph. But in the rest of the poem we can have no doubt that he means us to think of the bird as male. The song of the nightingale is of course erotic; the male bird sings only in the mating season and this knowledge was adhered to in medieval poetry. Keats's nightingale, however, does not sing of love. And when Keats speaks of the bird as "happy," as singing in "full-throated ease," he quite controverts both the Greek and the medieval view that the song is sorrowful. The Greek nightingale lamented the terrible wrongs done to her as a woman, before her metamorphosis into a bird. The medieval nightingale was believed to sing out of the pain of unfulfilled desire, although there was a charming fancy that he pressed his breast against a thorn to induce the pain that he uttered so beautifully. But it is exactly the point of Keats's poem that the nightingale sings in spontaneous and unremitting joy.

An ode has no very exact definition in the usage of English poets, but in general it may be said to be a poem on a lofty theme, of no prescribed length but long enough to allow for considerable elaborateness of development. The

[12] See the Book of Ruth, Chapter 2.

subject to be dealt with must be worthy of great praise, and we expect of an ode that it will reach a high point in intensity in bestowing this praise. In Greek *ode* is the word for "song"; the Greek odes were sung. The English poets did not write their odes to be set to music but they nevertheless had the ancient practice in mind and sought to approximate a musical immediacy and passionateness.

Few odes achieve this goal as fully as the Nightingale Ode. The poem does more than celebrate the song of the bird, it emulates and rivals it. Although the mode of feeling of the poem is different from that of the song it describes, for the song is said to be happy whereas the poem is sad, the poem affects the reader much as the nightingale's song does the poet—to the point indeed, where many readers are so entranced by its lyric charm that they are content with only a limited sense of what, precisely, is being said. This is unfortunate since our delight in the Ode is bound to increase in the degree that we comprehend its complexity. The general purport of the Ode is clear enough. The poet feels the burden of mortality, not only death itself but illness and pain, the passing of youth, fatigue at the consciousness of the human condition. The nightingale's song suggests, and is, the opposite of all this; it is immortal and it is not subject to adverse circumstance. We understand, of course, that in actuality a nightingale is as surely destined for death as the poet himself. But it is not this particular bird that is the object of the poet's emotions, rather the generic nightingale, which is what it is by reason of its song—it is as if Keats were saying that the immortal and unchanging song creates new generations of actual birds to utter it.

In some degree the poem is dramatic; its action consists of the attempts which the poet makes in his imagination to achieve or approximate the existence of the nightingale. All these attempts fail. The first of them is represented in the opening stanza. The poet speaks of the painful depression of spirit—it seems to him the very threshold of death—into which he has fallen when his intense response to the nightingale's song has reached its climax. The human mind would seem not to be capable of sustaining the joy it can momentarily know; as Wordsworth says in "Resolution and Independence":

> . . . from the might
> Of joy in minds that can no further go,
> As high as we have mounted in delight
> In our dejection do we sink as low.

This cycle of feeling, from intensity or ecstasy to obliviousness or dissolution and pain, appears three more times in the course of the Ode. The second dissolution is achieved through wine. It is real wine that the poet asks for, even though the name that he gives it is not that of any known vintage but of a well-known water—the Hippocrene is the fountain of the Muses on Mount Helicon; a draft of its water was supposed to give poetic inspiration. Between the song of the nightingale and the wine which bears the name of the inspiring water there is a close association; the bird sings "of summer in full-throated ease" and the wine is said to be summer itself—the beaker that the poet longs for is to be "full of the warm South." The delight of the imagined intoxication turns out, however, to be only mediate, a step on the way to a desired extinction. This extinction, to be sure, is pleasurable, consisting as it does of fading, dissolving, forgetting, and it is meant to be redemptive, the means by which the poet frees himself from the burdens of his mortal condition. But the imagination of an ecstasy which will lead to extinction, and of an extinction which shall be an escape, ends in the vivid realization of what is being escaped—"the weariness, the fever, and the fret," all the frustrations of human existence as they are set forth in Stanza III.

In Stanza IV wine is rejected in favor of poetry as a means of escape. But the imagined flight of poetry toward the light ends in the darkness of Stanzas IV and V, which suggests the idea of liberation from the burden of life through death, as do also, perhaps, the ephemeral flowers and the short-lived May flies of the exquisite fifth stanza. It is not a new idea for the poet; he has, he says, "many a time / . . . been half in love with easeful Death"—the epithet "easeful" recalls the "full-throated ease" of the nightingale's song—and "now more than ever" he thinks of death as a "rich" experience. In some degree death is comparable to the nightingale's ecstasy: the image of Death taking "into the air my quiet breath" may not be equal in intensity to that of the nightingale "pouring [its] soul abroad" but there is a general likeness between them.

It is not uncommon for poetry to represent death as a positive and pleasurable experience. Death and dying seem naturally to associate themselves with love—the words are used to express the ultimate degree of erotic pleasure, and all great love stories end in death, as if this were the sign and validation of the lovers' passion. Even in casual speech, we express the force of a desire by the locution, "I am dying to . . ." or "I am dying for . . ." We think only of grace and charm when we speak of music "dying away," or when we see a dancer perform "The Dying Swan." This association with agreeable things indicates something of the nature of Keats's imagination of death as it is first expressed in the poem. But if the words "die" and "death" can suggest a pleasurable and even a voluptuous experience,[1] the word "dead" cannot; it is a harsh, grim word, meaning all that we can conceive of insentience. Although Keats first thinks of dying as an experience of ecstasy equivalent to the nightingale's song, his awareness of reality supervenes to tell him that dying leads to *being dead*—the fancy of the "richness" of dying yields to this brute fact, best communicated in a brutal word: he speaks of himself as becoming a "sod," a mere inanimate piece of earth such as that under which we are buried.

But it is the seventh stanza which is for many readers the most memorable part of the poem, presenting us with a curious and deeply moving paradox. The poet speaks of the long-dead persons who have heard the voice of the nightingale; it is his purpose to contrast the joyous immortality of the song with the sad evanescence of human life. We understand this intention; yet we are not wholly willing to accept the validity of the contrast that is being proposed. The sadness of Ruth amid the alien corn, the peril of the seas, the forlornness of the faery lands, so far from being incongruous with the nightingale's song, seem to us to be at one with it in beauty and immortality, and we may even suppose that they are what the song is *about,* for it can often seem that the pain of human life is the subject of our most beautiful poetic utterances. In "The Solitary Reaper," a poem that Keats would have known, Wordsworth finds the charm of the girl's song in what she is singing about:

> . . . old, unhappy, far-off things,
> And battles long ago . . .

[1] See the commentary on Whitman's "Out of the Cradle Endlessly Rocking," p. 97.

But although Keats, by the nature of his poetic imagination, may have been momentarily seduced into suggesting that human mortality and sorrow, seen through the veils of time and art, are more beautiful than painful, he cannot rest with this idea. His sense of reality once more enforces upon his imagination an admission of the actuality of the pain of human life.

It is with this in mind that Keats opens the eighth stanza with a repetition of the word "forlorn" which ends the seventh, pointing to it with the phrase, "the very word." And he describes its effect upon him in terms which suggest that whereas in the seventh stanza he had been speaking as one whose concern was only with beauty, now it is actuality that is his main concern—his affinity with the nightingale is at an end, now he must exist as a "sole self." In Stanza VII he had used the word "forlorn" for its charm, which derives from its lovely sound and from its possible connotation of a sadness that is distant and unreal. Now the full literal import of the word breaks upon him—it really means abandoned, lost, without hope, desperate[2]—and he is moved to a critical examination of himself as a poet; he speaks slightingly of one of a poet's faculties, the fancy. (We could wish he had called it almost anything but a "deceiving elf"!) Up to now the vanishing song of the nightingale had been only joyous; at this point it becomes "plaintive," as if the poet's certitude of the bird's joy were being denied. Still, at the same time it is called an "anthem," which is a song of joyful praise.

In sharp contrast with the lyricism which sustains itself through the whole poem and which is quite as apparent in the expressions of sadness or despair as in the expressions of ecstasy, the question with which the poem concludes—"Do I wake or sleep?"—shocks us with its sudden flatness and harshness of tone. That question was both explicated and answered by Shelley in "Adonais," his great elegy for Keats:

> Peace, peace! he is not dead, he doth not sleep—
> He hath awakened from the dream of life.

[2] It is possible that Keats knew that "the forlorn" was the old name for the call on the hunting-horn that brought back the hunters from the chase.

DOVER BEACH

MATTHEW ARNOLD

1822–1888

The sea is calm to-night.
The tide is full, the moon lies fair
Upon the straits; on the French coast the light
Gleams and is gone;[1] the cliffs of England stand,
Glimmering and vast, out in the tranquil bay. 5
Come to the window, sweet is the night-air!
Only, from the long line of spray
Where the sea meets the moon-blanched land,
Listen! you hear the grating roar
Of pebbles which the waves draw back, and fling, 10
At their return, up the high strand,
Begin, and cease, and then again begin,
With tremulous cadence slow, and bring
The eternal note of sadness in.

Sophocles long ago 15
Heard it on the Ægæan, and it brought
Into his mind the turbid ebb and flow
Of human misery; we
Find also in the sound a thought,
Hearing it by this distant northern sea. 20

The Sea of Faith
Was once, too, at the full, and round earth's shore
Lay like the folds of a bright girdle furled.
But now I only hear
Its melancholy, long, withdrawing roar, 25
Retreating, to the breath
Of the night-wind, down the vast edges drear
And naked shingles[2] of the world.

[1] Lights on the French coast are visible from Dover, the closest point in England (about 20 miles) to the continent. The cliffs near Dover are white and quite high.
[2] Coarse beach gravel.

Ah, love, let us be true
To one another! for the world, which seems 30
To lie before us like a land of dreams,
So various, so beautiful, so new,
Hath really neither joy, nor love, nor light,
Nor certitude, nor peace, nor help for pain;
And we are here as on a darkling plain 35
Swept with confused alarms of struggle and flight,
Where ignorant armies clash by night.

COMMENTARY

Matthew Arnold occupies a rather strange place in the community of English poets. Few people, I think, would include him among the great poets of England. The body of his work is not large, certainly not in comparison with the production of other poets of the Victorian age, and of this relatively small canon only a handful of poems are wholly successful. Yet Arnold is generally ranked as one of the three most important poets of his time, the other two being Tennyson and Browning. Indeed, despite his manifest faults, Arnold as a poet makes an appeal to the reader of today which is likely to be greater than that of either of his two imposing contemporaries.

A phrase I have just used, "Arnold as a poet," will perhaps seem odd and need explanation. We do not speak of "Tennyson *as* a poet" or of "Browning *as* a poet"—they *were* poets, we know them as nothing else. But Arnold, having begun his literary life in poetry, gave up what we might call the professional practice of the art at about the age of thirty. It was not possible for him to make an adequate living by writing alone and he therefore accepted an appointment as an inspector of elementary schools; he served in this capacity until a few years before his death. The work was fatiguing and depressing, and he could command neither the leisure nor the emotional energy that poetry requires. He did, however, find it possible to write prose, and, working in that medium, he became one of the leading intellectual figures of England. He was the most admired literary critic of his day, and, indeed, is generally accounted one of the great critics of the world. He was a very notable theorist of politics, and his writings on religion played an important part in the crisis of faith which so deeply distressed many of his contemporaries. Perhaps more than any other man of his time and nation he perceived the changes that were taking place in the conditions of life and in the minds of men to bring into being the world we now know—in certain respects he was, of all the intellectual figures of his period, the most modern.

The sensitivity to the cultural circumstances of his day which Arnold showed in his prose does much to explain his interest as a poet. Both in his early poems, which make up the larger body of his canon, and in the infrequent later poems, some of which are among his best, Arnold showed an awareness of the emotional conditions of modern life which far exceeds that of any other poet of his time. He spoke with great explicitness and directness of the alienation, isolation, and excess of consciousness leading to doubt which are, as so much of later literature testifies, the lot of modern man. And it is plain that he speaks from an unabashedly personal experience of pain, fatigue, and thwarted hope—his poetry has for us the authority of authenticity even when it lacks a high poetic grace.

"Dover Beach," however, can scarcely be said to be lacking in grace. It is one of the handful of Arnold's wholly successful poems and among these it is pre-eminent. For many readers it is the single most memorable poem of the Victorian age. In it the authenticity that is in general the characteristic note of Arnold's poetry achieves a peculiar pathos. The diction is perfect in its lightness and simplicity. The verse, moving in a delicate crescendo of lyricism from the muted beginning to the full-voiced desperate conclusion, is superbly managed. Not the least of the elements of its success is that a poem so modest in tone and in apparent scope should contain within it such magnificent vistas of space and time.

The poem is dramatic in the sense that, although there is only one speaker, there are two characters, the speaker and the woman he addresses as his love, presumably his wife. The setting of the dramatic scene is of central importance; the American reader might not recognize what an English reader would know at once, that the couple are staying at a hotel, for Dover is one of the two English ports from which one takes ship to cross the English Channel to France. The circumstance that the couple are setting out on a journey abroad makes it all the more likely that they should be inclined to think of the world as being "so various, so beautiful, so new."

The window through which the speaker is gazing and to which he invites his companion might well bring to mind the "magic casements" of the "Ode to a Nightingale" (page 82). Like the window in Keats's poem, it opens "on the foam / Of perilous seas," and on forlorn lands, although not faery lands. It has the effect of framing the view and of emphasizing the sense of vista that plays so material a part in the poem. The immediate view—the great white chalk cliffs of Dover, the French coast twenty miles off, indicated by the momentary light, the moonlit waters of the Channel between—is in itself sufficiently impressive. But it opens out both in space and time to reach across Europe to the Aegean Sea and ancient Greece. It is worth noting that several of Arnold's poems depend for their most moving effects upon similar representations of great vistas both of geography and history and that in one of his early sonnets Arnold refers to Europe as "The Wide Prospect," deriving the phrase from a possible translation of the Greek name, and seeming to suggest that it was the essential quality of the European mind that it could encompass great reaches of space and time. Although in general Arnold's distances imply liberation and even joy, in "Dover Beach," when the imagination goes beyond the Aegean, it proceeds in darkness to the "vast edges drear / And naked shingles of the world."

The emptiness and despair of the vision bring the speaker back to the place from which his imagination had started, to the room from whose window he looks out, and he turns in despairing sadness to his companion, at that moment seemingly the only other person in the world, to offer her, and ask from her, loyalty in love. Perhaps literature does not know a love avowal and a love plea so sad as these—perhaps never before in literature has a lover given a *reason* for love, and a reason which, while asserting its necessity, denies its delight. It is believed by all lovers that love has the power not only of making the world various and beautiful and new, but also of maintaining it in variety, beauty, and novelty. But the lover of "Dover Beach" denies love's efficacy in this respect. Of all that love may be presumed to give, he asks only loyalty in a world that promises neither joy nor peace.

It is to this pass that the lover has been brought by his sense of modern life, which has seen the ebbing of the sea of faith. We assume that he means religious faith, and this assumption is borne out by other of Arnold's poems in which the diminution of religious faith is a reason for melancholy. But Arnold felt that the lessening of religious faith went hand in hand with the lessening of personal energy, vitality, and confidence, of that happy, unquestioning attachment to life which William James called "animal faith." When Arnold speaks of Sophocles hearing the roar of the pebbles on the beach under the receding wave and of its having brought "into his mind the turbid ebb and flow / Of human misery," he is almost certainly making reference to the opening of the third chorus of Sophocles' *Antigone*. Here is the passage in the translation of R. J. Jebb: "Blest are they whose days have not tasted of evil. For when a house hath once been shaken from heaven, there the curse fails nevermore, passing from life to life of the race [i.e., family]; even as, when the surge is driven over the darkness of the deep by the fierce breath of Thracian sea-winds, it rolls up the black sand from the depths, and there is a sullen roar from the wind-vexed headlands that front the blows of the storm." The chorus ostensibly speaks of the misery of the members of certain families living under a curse, and not of "human misery" in general. But the generalization can of course be made, and we may readily believe that Arnold had in mind the contrast between the passage from the third chorus to which he refers and the more famous second chorus of *Antigone,* which begins "Wonders are many, and none is more wonderful than man," and goes on to sing with joy of man's triumphs. It is the faith in man and his destiny so proudly expressed by the second chorus that has ebbed, leaving the world to bleakness.

The great grim simile with which the poem ends has attracted much attention, and efforts have been made to find the inspiration for it in Arnold's reading. The likeliest possibility is the account of the battle of Epipolae given by Thucydides in his *History of the Peloponnesian War* (Book VII, Chapters 43–44); this guess is encouraged by the circumstance that Arnold's father, Thomas Arnold, had published a well-known edition of the *History*. A striking quality of the simile is its unexpectedness. Up to this point the lovers have looked out on a world of wind and water, quite empty of people; now the scene is a plain filled with armies in strife. The suddenness of the shift reinforces the violence of the dark image of deteriorated existence.

OUT OF THE CRADLE ENDLESSLY ROCKING

WALT WHITMAN

1819–1892

Out of the cradle endlessly rocking,
Out of the mocking-bird's throat, the musical shuttle,
Out of the Ninth-month midnight,
Over the sterile sands and the fields beyond, where the child leaving his bed wander'd alone, bareheaded, barefoot,
Down from the shower'd halo, 5
Up from the mystic play of shadows twining and twisting as if they were alive,
Out from the patches of briers and blackberries,
From the memories of the bird that chanted to me,
From your memories sad brother, from the fitful risings and fallings I heard,
From under that yellow half-moon late-risen and swollen as if with tears, 10
From those beginning notes of yearning and love there in the mist,
From the thousand responses of my heart never to cease,
From the myriad thence-arous'd words,
From the word stronger and more delicious than any,
From such as now they start the scene revisiting, 15
As a flock, twittering, rising, or overhead passing,
Borne hither, ere all eludes me, hurriedly,
A man, yet by these tears a little boy again,
Throwing myself on the sand, confronting the waves,
I, chanter of pains and joys, uniter of here and hereafter, 20
Taking all hints to use them, but swiftly leaping beyond them,
A reminiscence sing.

Once Paumanok,[1]
When the lilac-scent was in the air and Fifth-month grass was growing,
Up this seashore in some briers, 25
Two feather'd guests from Alabama, two together,
And their nest, and four light-green eggs spotted with brown,
And every day the he-bird to and fro near at hand,
And every day the she-bird crouch'd on her nest, silent, with bright
eyes,
And every day I, a curious boy, never too close, never disturbing them, 30
Cautiously peering, absorbing, translating.

Shine! shine! shine!
Pour down your warmth, great sun!
While we bask, we two together.

Two together! 35
Winds blow south, or winds blow north,
Day come white, or night come black,
Home, or rivers and mountains from home,
Singing all time, minding no time,
While we two keep together. 40

Till of a sudden,
May-be kill'd, unknown to her mate,
One forenoon the she-bird crouch'd not on the nest,
Nor return'd that afternoon, nor the next,
Nor ever appear'd again. 45

And thenceforward all summer in the sound of the sea,
And at night under the full of the moon in calmer weather,
Over the hoarse surging of the sea,
Or flitting from brier to brier by day,
I saw, I heard at intervals the remaining one, the he-bird, 50
The solitary guest from Alabama.

Blow! blow blow!
Blow up sea-winds along Paumanok's shore;
I wait and I wait till you blow my mate to me.

Yes, when the stars glisten'd, 55
All night long on the prong of a moss-scallop'd stake,

[1] Indian name for Long Island.

Down almost amid the slapping waves,
Sat the lone singer wonderful causing tears.

He call'd on his mate,
He pour'd forth the meanings which I of all men know. 60

Yes my brother I know,
The rest might not, but I have treasur'd every note,
For more than once dimly down to the beach gliding,
Silent, avoiding the moonbeams, blending myself with the shadows,
Recalling now the obscure shapes, the echoes, the sounds and sights after their
sorts, 65
The white arms out in the breakers tirelessly tossing,
I, with bare feet, a child, the wind wafting my hair,
Listen'd long and long.

Listen'd to keep, to sing, now translating the notes,
Following you my brother. 70

Soothe! soothe! soothe!
Close on its wave soothes the wave behind,
And again another behind, embracing and lapping, every one close,
But my love soothes not me, not me.

Low hangs the moon, it rose late, 75
It is lagging—O I think it is heavy with love, with love.

O madly the sea pushes upon the land,
With love, with love.

O night! do I not see my love fluttering out among the breakers?
What is that little black thing I see there in the white? 80

Loud! loud! loud!
Loud I call to you, my love!
High and clear I shoot my voice over the waves,
Surely you must know who is here, is here,
You must know who I am, my love. 85

Low-hanging moon!
What is that dusky spot in your brown yellow?

O it is the shape, the shape of my mate!
O moon do not keep her from me any longer.

Land! land! O land! 90
Whichever way I turn, O I think you could give me my mate back again if you only would,
For I am almost sure I see her dimly whichever way I look.

O rising stars!
Perhaps the one I want so much will rise, will rise with some of you.

O throat! O trembling throat! 95
Sound clearer through the atmosphere!
Pierce the woods, the earth,
Somewhere listening to catch you must be the one I want.

Shake out carols!
Solitary here, the night's carols! 100
Carols of lonesome love! death's carols!
Carols under the lagging, yellow, waning moon!
O under that moon where she droops almost down into the sea!
O reckless despairing carols.

But soft! sink low! 105
Soft! let me just murmur,
And do you wait a moment you husky-nois'd sea,
For somewhere I believe I heard my mate responding to me,
So faint, I must be still, be still to listen,
But not altogether still, for then she might not come immediately to me. 110

Hither my love!
Here I am! here!
With this just-sustain'd note I announce myself to you,
This gentle call is for you my love, for you.

Do not be decoy'd elsewhere, 115
That is the whistle of the wind, it is not my voice,
That is the fluttering, the fluttering of the spray,
Those are the shadows of leaves.

O darkness! O in vain!
O I am sick and sorrowful. 120

O brown halo in the sky near the moon, dropping upon the sea!
O troubled reflection in the sea!

O throat! O throbbing heart!
And I singing uselessly, uselessly all the night.

O past! O happy life! O songs of joy! 125
In the air, in the woods, over fields,
Loved! loved! loved! loved! loved!
But my mate no more, no more with me!
We two together no more.

The aria sinking, 130
All else continuing, the stars shining,
The winds blowing, the notes of the bird continuous echoing,
With angry moans the fierce old mother incessantly moaning,
On the sands of Paumanok's shore gray and rustling,
The yellow half-moon enlarged, sagging down, drooping, the face of the sea almost touching, 135
The boy ecstatic, with his bare feet the waves, with his hair the atmosphere dallying,
The love in the heart long pent, now loose, now at last tumultuously bursting,
The aria's meaning, the ears, the soul, swiftly depositing,
The strange tears down the cheeks coursing,
The colloquy there, the trio, each uttering, 140
The undertone, the savage old mother incessantly crying,
To the boy's soul's questions sullenly timing, some drown'd secret hissing,
To the outsetting bard.

Demon or bard! (said the boy's soul,)
Is it indeed toward your mate you sing? or is it really to me? 145
For I, that was a child, my tongue's use sleeping, now I have heard you,
Now in a moment I know what I am for, I awake,
And already a thousand singers, a thousand songs, clearer, louder and more sorrowful than yours,
A thousand warbling echoes have started to life within me, never to die.

O you singer solitary, singing by yourself, projecting me, 150
O solitary me listening, never more shall I cease perpetuating you,
Never more shall I escape, never more the reverberations,
Never more the cries of unsatisfied love be absent from me,
Never again leave me to be the peaceful child I was before what there in the night,

By the sea under the yellow and sagging moon, 155
The messenger there arous'd, the fire, the sweet hell within,
The unknown want, the destiny of me.

O give me the clew! (it lurks in the night here somewhere,)
O if I am to have so much, let me have more!

A word then, (for I will conquer it,) 160
The word final, superior to all,
Subtle, sent up—what is it?—I listen;
Are you whispering it, and have all the time, you sea waves?
Is that it from your liquid rims and wet sands?

Whereto answering, the sea, 165
Delaying not, hurrying not,
Whisper'd me through the night, and very plainly before daybreak,
Lisp'd to me the low and delicious word death,
And again, death, death, death, death,
Hissing melodious, neither like the bird nor like my arous'd child's heart, 170
But edging near as privately for me rustling at my feet,
Creeping thence steadily up to my ears and laving me softly all over,
Death, death, death, death, death.

Which I do not forget,
But fuse the song of my dusky demon and brother, 175
That he sang to me in the moonlight on Paumanok's gray beach,
With the thousand responsive songs at random,
My own songs awaked from that hour,
And with them the key, the word up from the waves,
The word of the sweetest song and all songs, 180
That strong and delicious word which, creeping to my feet,
(Or like some old crone rocking the cradle, swathed in sweet garments, bending aside,)
The sea whisper'd me.

COMMENTARY

Historians of American literature often speak of Walt Whitman and Henry James as virtually symbolic representatives of two opposed tendencies in our national culture. Whitman in his lifetime undertook to make himself a symbolic figure—he wanted, both in his person and his art, to stand for all that was "democratic" in American life, by which he meant whatever was free, impulsive, and accepting; he spoke of himself as "one of the roughs," and described his poetry as "a barbaric yawp." James had no conscious wish to put himself before the world in a symbolic light, but it was almost inevitable that he should be seen in this way. He came of a patrician family and he had as strong a feeling for elegance and decorum as Whitman had for looseness and the free-and-easy. He lived his mature years away from his native land because of his liking for the complexity of English society and his strong commitment to the artistic traditions of Europe. By reason of his style of life, he has been taken—often all too simply—to stand for conservatism, propriety, and gentility; and by reason of the nature of his art he has come to be regarded as the very spirit of consciousness, control, and precision.

The extreme differences between the two men make the dramatic point of a famous anecdote which Edith Wharton relates in her autobiography. Mrs. Wharton was a close friend and great admirer of Henry James and she tells of an evening party at her country home at which, in the course of conversation, "someone spoke of Whitman, and it was a joy to me to discover that James thought him, as I did, the greatest of American poets." James, Mrs. Wharton tells us, read poetry aloud in a very beautiful way, and now the discussion led to his being asked to read from Whitman's *Leaves of Grass,* "and all that evening we sat rapt while he wandered from 'The Song of Myself' to 'When Lilacs Last in the Door-yard Bloomed' (when we read 'Lovely and soothing Death' his voice filled the hushed room like an organ adagio), and then let himself be lured on to the mysterious music of 'Out of the Cradle' reading, or rather crooning it in a mood of subdued ecstasy till the fivefold invocation to Death tolled out like the knocks in the opening bars of [Beethoven's] Fifth Symphony."

Mrs. Wharton concludes her story by saying that James's admiration of Whitman, "his immediate response to that mighty appeal, was a new proof of the way in which, above a certain level, the most divergent intelligences walk together like gods." The generalization is not true. We can be fairly certain that Whitman would not have given James's work the same respect that James gave his. And James himself, fine critic though he was, was incapable of responding to certain "divergent intelligences" of his time, Thomas Hardy, for example, or the young D. H. Lawrence. But it is greatly to his credit that, with so much that might stand in the way of his sympathy, he did respond to Whitman. What might have intervened was the erroneous belief, which prevailed at the time and is sometimes met with even now, that Whitman wrote on mere free impulse, without the consciousness and self-criticism that normally go into poetic composition. James, whose feeling for conscious artistry was almost a religion with him, was happily not deceived into any such false notion.

Whitman himself did much to foster the misconception of his poetry when he spoke of it as a "barbaric yawp" and in general insisted on his radical difference from all preceding poets. And the mistake is likely to be confirmed by wrong ideas about the kind of verse he wrote, whose very name, "free verse," is misleading. In point of fact, Whitman was a consummate craftsman. No poems were ever more carefully composed than those which James chose to read aloud that evening at Mrs. Wharton's; we know from Whitman's manuscripts how extensively they were revised and worked over.[1] Whitman's verse-form, so far

[1] It is a fact worth noting that even Whitman's letters, which are marked by an extreme simplicity of style, were very fully revised and recopied before they were mailed.

from being prosaic because it does not use meter and rime, is supremely musical, as James made plain by the manner in which he read it. James was a man not given to public display, yet when he read "Out of the Cradle Endlessly Rocking," he surrendered wholly to the demands it made upon him and, as Mrs. Wharton tells us, "crooned it in a mood of subdued ecstasy."

"Out of the Cradle Endlessly Rocking" is not the first poem in this volume in which the ecstatic song of a bird is involved with thoughts of death, and in which death is regarded in an ambiguous way—the similarity of this poem to Keats's "Ode to a Nightingale" (page 84) will be readily apparent. In both poems the poet makes an identification between the singing bird and himself in his character of poet. In both poems, although in different ways, death is the source not only of sorrow but also of the hope of transcendence.

Yet the more we are aware of the affinity which the two poems have with each other, the more striking their differences become. Certain of these differences arise from the fact that one is an English and the other an American poem. The birds they celebrate are nationally distinct: there are no American nightingales and no English mocking-birds. And Whitman, as if to emphasize his bird's American habitat, tells us the name of its native state, Alabama. It is almost as if he had Keats's nightingale in mind—its identification with the poetic traditions of Europe, its place in Greek mythology—and as if he were saying, "*That* is the bird of the Old World, *mine* is the bird of the New."

The very names of the birds—"nightingale" with its euphonic, remote loveliness, "mocking-bird" with its hard immediacy and explicitness—suggest a national difference in the language of the two poems. It was part of Whitman's conception of his poetic mission to write in the American mode of the English tongue, both in order to express the American temperament and to make his poetry readily accessible to American readers. To these ends, he used the vocabulary, syntax, and rhythms of colloquial speech, and what literary models he did turn to were such as Americans would know without special education, the oration and the Bible. But we must not suppose that Whitman was unique in his use of everyday speech. It is one of the recurrent concerns of poetry to seek to reduce the distance between the speech of the people and the special language that any tradition of poetry tends to evolve. Dante said that he wanted a language for his poetry that would be comprehensible to housewives; and Wordsworth undertook to purge poetry of artificiality by using "the real language of real men." And a comparison of the language of Whitman with that of Keats must proceed with caution, for Keats too was concerned to free himself from the linguistic conventions of poetry; his realization that he must no longer submit to the influence of Milton's elaborate diction made a crisis in his poetic life. To the first readers of the "Ode to a Nightingale" the diction might very well have seemed too relaxed and insufficiently "literary." Still, in the use of the common speech for poetry that yet aims at a beautiful exaltation of tone, there is no doubt that Whitman went further than Keats—further, indeed, than anyone before him had gone. The following lines will suggest how bold was his use of colloquialism and to what an exquisite effect:

> Oh night! do I not see my love fluttering out
> among the breakers?
> What is that little black thing I see there in the white?

Or again:

> Whichever way I turn, O I think you could give me my
> mate back again if you only would . . .

And quite apart from the colloquialisms of lines like these, we are aware—an English reader would be still more aware—that their rhythm and idiom are American rather than English. Keats said of Milton's majestic style, "It is magnificent but it is not English." In effect, Whitman said of all English poetry from Shakespeare down, "It is magnificent but it is not American."

In one of his essays, W. H. Auden tries to account for the differences between English and American poetry by reference to the dissimilar landscape and climate of the two countries and their influence on temperament and feeling. Certainly nothing could be less alike than the settings of "Ode to a Nightingale" and "Out of the Cradle Endlessly Rocking," especially the sense of geography which each poem conveys. The topography of Keats's Ode is comprised of glades, dells, and valleys, of enclosed, discrete places. Even the darkness encloses. Indeed, the dominant emotion of the Ode can be described as a response to limitation. The one great vista in the poem is that of time rather than of space, the view back to the "ancient days" in which the nightingale's song was heard. When the poet expresses the wish to "fade far away," the furthest destination he can imagine is "the forest dim," which seems to be quite near at hand and where he is again enclosed. And even the description of the bird's flight, which carries its song out of hearing, does not propose the idea of great distance:

> . . . thy plaintive anthem fades
> Past the near meadows, over the still stream,
> Up the hillside; and now 'tis buried deep
> In the next valley glades . . .

But the spaces of "Out of the Cradle" seem limitless—the unending stretch of Long Island beach, the dunes behind, the sea in front, the sky unobstructed. And we are mindful of the thousand miles the mocking-bird has flown to come to Long Island from Alabama. There are no demarcations of place, no dells and valleys. Nor are there any trees—lilacs somewhere, but not near the great scene, and certainly none of the luxurious blossoms that blow in the fifth stanza of the Ode, only briars and blackberries. Although it is true that no human habitation is referred to in the Ode, yet the fertile landscape permits the possibility of it, and nothing in the poem contradicts our extraneous knowledge of the fact that Keats heard the nightingale and wrote his poem in the garden of his pleasant house at Hampstead, near London. The scene of "Out of the Cradle" is far less genial, and in it there is only one sign of human life, the single stake in the water upon which the mourning bird sits, the one vertical object in the poem, the one fixed thing upon which the eye may focus:

> All night long on the prong of a moss-scallop'd stake,
> Down almost amid the slapping waves,
> Sat the lone singer wonderful causing tears.

But even more divergent are the ways in which the two poems respond to death. Although Keats is able to conceive of death as a purging of life into pure being, and although, almost against his will, he represents mortality as the source of beauty, these are only momentary fancies. They give him no real consolation in the face of his knowledge that death is insentience and extinction. The ideas that Keats rejects are intensely affirmed by Whitman. For him passion itself arises from death, and it was his having heard and understood the mocking-bird's song of sorrow that changed him from a boy into a man—and into a poet. Nor is it passion only, but life itself, that arises from death: death is "the word" which the sea, the mother of all life, "lisps" and "hisses" and "whispers" to him in response to his plea for the "clew"; and that word, the poet says, is even "more" than the mocking-bird's song: it is the word "of the sweetest song and all songs."

We can scarcely think of these differing attitudes to death as in any way national. And yet Whitman himself thought that the celebration of the beauty of death was appropriate to America and pertinent to the health of the republic. In 1871 he published a great embittered essay, *Democratic Vistas,* in which he indicts America for its failure to fulfill its true moral and political destiny and speaks of the redemption that may yet come, in part from the good effects of an appropriate national poetry. "In the future of these States," he says, "must arise poets immenser far, and make great poems of death. The poems of life are great, but there must be poems of the purports of life, not only in itself, but beyond itself." The great poem of death, he says in sum, will check the growing American vulgarity by bringing faith and large-mindedness. "Then will man indeed confront Nature, and confront time and space . . . and take his right place, prepared for fortune and misfortune. And then that which was long wanted will be supplied, and the ship that had it not before in all her voyages, will have an anchor."

Perhaps Henry James had in his own way a not dissimilar conception of death. Mrs. Wharton tells us in her autobiography that when James suffered the first of the series of strokes that were to end his life, "in the very act of falling . . . he heard in the room a voice which was distinctly, it seemed, not his own, saying: 'So here it is at last, the distinguished thing.' "

THE LEADEN ECHO AND THE GOLDEN ECHO (Maidens' song from St. Winefred's Well[1])

GERARD MANLEY HOPKINS

1844–1889

THE LEADEN ECHO

How to kéep[2]—is there ány any, is there none such, nowhere known some, bow
or brooch or braid or brace, láce, latch or catch or key to keep
Back beauty, keep it, beauty, beauty, beauty, . . . from vanishing away?
Ó is there no frowning of these wrinkles, rankèd wrinkles deep,
Dówn? no waving off of these most mournful messengers, still messengers, sad
and stealing messengers of grey?
No there's none, there's none, O no there's none, 5
Nor can you long be, what you now are, called fair,
Do what you may do, what, do what you may,
And wisdom is early to despair:
Be beginning; since, no, nothing can be done
To keep at bay 10
Age and age's evils, hoar hair,
Ruck[3] and wrinkle, drooping, dying, death's worst, winding sheets, tombs and
worms and tumbling to decay;
So be beginning, be beginning to despair.
O there's none; no no no there's none:
Be beginning to despair, to despair, 15
Despair, despair, despair, despair.

[1] St. Winefred was murdered by her would-be ravisher, the chieftain Caradoc. The water of her well, which gushed spontaneously out of the ground after her death, is believed to have curative powers. [2] Hopkins made a practice of indicating with accent marks which syllables were to receive the strongest stress. [3] Crease.

Spare![4]
There ís one, yes I have one (Hush there!);
Only not within seeing of the sun,
Not within the singeing of the strong sun, 20
Tall sun's tingeing, or treacherous the tainting of the earth's air,
Somewhere elsewhere there is ah well where! one,
Ońe. Yes I cán tell such a key, I dó know such a place,
Where whatever's prized and passes of us, everything that's fresh and fast flying of us, seems to us sweet of us and swiftly away with, done away with, undone,
Undone, done with, soon done with, and yet dearly and dangerously sweet
Of us, the wimpled[5]-water-dimpled, not-by-morning-matchèd face, 26
The flower of beauty, fleece of beauty, too too apt to, ah! to fleet,
Never fleets móre, fastened with the tenderest truth
To its own best being and its loveliness of youth: it is an everlastingness of, O it is an all youth!
Come then, your ways and airs and looks, locks, maiden gear, gallantry and gaiety and grace, 30
Winning ways, airs innocent, maiden manners, sweet looks, loose locks, long locks, lovelocks, gaygear, going gallant, girlgrace—
Resign them, sign them, seal them, send them, motion them with breath,
And with sighs soaring, soaring síghs deliver
Them; beauty-in-the-ghost,[6] deliver it, early now, long before death
Give beauty back, beauty, beauty, beauty, back to God, beauty's self and beauty's giver. 35
See; not a hair is, not an eyelash, not the least lash lost; every hair
Is, hair of the head, numbered.
Nay, what we had lighthanded left in surly[7] the mere mould[8]
Will have waked and have waxed and have walked with the wind what while we slept,
This side, that side hurling a heavyheaded hundredfold 40
What while we, while we slumbered.
O then, weary then whý should we tread? O why are we so haggard at the heart, so care-coiled, care-killed, so fagged, so fashed,[9] so cogged,[10] so cumbered,
When the thing we freely fórfeit is kept with fonder a care,
Fonder a care kept than we could have kept it, kept
Far with fonder a care (and we, we should have lost it) finer, fonder 45
A care kept.—Where kept? Do but tell us where kept, where.—
Yonder.—What high as that! We follow, now we follow.—Yonder, yes yonder, yonder,
Yonder.

[4] Forbear. [5] Rippled. [6] Spiritual beauty. [7] Sullenly. [8] Earth. [9] Troubled. [10] Deceived.

COMMENTARY

The poems of Gerard Manley Hopkins were first published in 1918, nearly thirty years after the poet's death, and to their early readers they seemed difficult and odd. They now stand in very high repute, but even a half century of habituation has not made them exactly easy for us. As for their oddness, this the poet himself was ready enough to concede; on one occasion he described himself as being taken aback by it. In a letter to his friend and future editor, Robert Bridges, Hopkins said that the oddness of his poems "may make them repulsive at first" and told how shocked he was when he read one of them that a friend had borrowed and sent back to him. ". . . I opened and read some lines, as one commonly reads whether prose or verse, with the eyes, so to say, only, and it struck me aghast with a kind of raw nakedness and unmitigated violence I was unprepared for. . . ." It needed a perceptible moment for Hopkins to perceive the true nature of his own poem. ". . . But take breath," he went on, "and read it with your ears, as I always wish to be read, and my verse becomes all right."

To take breath and read with the ears is what we must learn to do with any poem of Hopkins. "Read Hopkins aloud," says his latest editor, W. H. Gardner, "and you will find that his obscurity is never entirely opaque. . . ."

Hopkins was born in 1844, of a gifted family of the comfortable middle class. An excellent student, he devoted himself at Oxford to the study of Greek and Latin, in which he distinguished himself. In his Oxford days he came under the influence of John Henry Newman, later Cardinal Newman, and converted to the Roman Catholic Church in 1866; two years later he entered the Society of Jesus. The duties of that exigent order were arduous and sometimes personally uncongenial to Hopkins, but he discharged them with exemplary assiduity and still found time to speculate profoundly upon the nature of prosody, to develop his theory of English verse, and to write the poems which were to establish his posthumous fame. If the poems seemed odd in 1918, when literary experiment in England began to be the order of the day, they would have seemed far odder in the poet's lifetime, yet Hopkins might have risked publication had not the Jesuit discipline prevented it.

Many elements contribute to the radical novelty of Hopkins' style, but his chief theoretical statement, his preface to the manuscript volume of his mature poems, deals with one subject only, that of rhythm. The preface is not polemical: it says nothing adverse about the practice of other poets. But the implication of Hopkins' theory is that English verse had curtailed its strength by submitting to the rule of metre, by conforming, even though not with mechanical exactitude, to fixed line-patterns. His conception of the course that English verse should take has a considerable affinity with Wyatt's practice (see page 10), although of the two poets Hopkins is much the more radical. Hopkins would have stood in opposition to the "correct" taste that had contrived the version of "They Flee from Me" which appeared in Tottel's *Miscellany* and that would have led Victorian readers to prefer this revised version to the original. He would have defended the rightness of Wyatt's departures from the pattern of the iambic pentameter line and of all the roughnesses and irregularities by which the poet exploited the actuality of the speaking voice. But in his preface Hopkins confined himself to explaining his own practice; he did not advance the idea which he obviously held, that the established system of English verse seemed to its practitioners to be the only possible one merely because of long habit. For his own prosody, he drew upon the verse systems of Welsh and Greek poetry and upon the tradition of English alliterative verse which had prevailed before the Renaissance.

He also drew upon music, of which he was an accomplished amateur, and for the better understanding of his rhythmic effects he devised a system of marks, analogous to the directive marks on a musical score, which he placed over syllables, words, and groups of words in order to show the reader how to read the poem with his ears. But on the manuscript of "The Leaden Echo and the Golden Echo" he wrote this note: "I have marked the stronger stresses, but with the degree of the stress so perpetually varying no marking is satisfactory. Do you think all had best be left to the reader?" He seems to have answered his own question affirmatively; and any reader who deals with the poem as a singer deals with a new song, "running through" it experimentally a few times to see how the voice should proceed, may reasonably feel that he is not betraying Hopkins' trust in him.

Although rhythm is Hopkins' chief aural concern, it is by no means the only one. He uses alliteration to an extent that no poet has ever ventured; and internal rhyme; and assonance; and subtle, planned progressions and modulations of vowel sounds. The following portion of the first line of "The Leaden Echo and the Golden Echo" illustrates all these effects: ". . . is there none such, nowhere known some, bow or brooch or braid or brace, láce, latch or catch or key to keep." The elaborate devices of Hopkins' prosody are especially in evidence throughout the poem because of its avowed vocal nature. It is not a "lyric" in the sense of being a poem to be set to music for singing and therefore kept simple and modest so that the music may have its way. It is a lyric in the sense of being the whole song itself, words and music together, the vocal line and the accompaniment, both of considerable complexity and virtuosity.

But no doubt because it is so much a song, two characteristics of Hopkins' verse are not strongly apparent in this particular poem. One is the intense visuality that Hopkins usually sought after, the rendering of the specificity of beauty that he called "inscape," though we do have an example of it in the lines descriptive of beautiful girlhood:

> Come then, your ways and airs and looks, locks, maiden gear,
>   gallantry and gaiety and grace,
> Winning ways, airs innocent, maiden manners, sweet looks,
>   loose locks, long locks, lovelocks, gaygear, going gallant,
>   girlgrace—

The other is Hopkins' idiosyncratic rhetoric, which often, but not here, makes for difficult or delayed comprehension. In the passage

> Not within the singeing of the strong sun,
> Tall sun's tingeing, or treacherous the tainting of the earth's
>   air . . .

the last phrase offers only a momentary resistance—we quickly see that "treacherous the tainting" is to be understood as "the treacherous tainting." Nor are we much puzzled by the charming rhetorical idiosyncrasy of "it is an everlasting of, O it is an all youth!"

In common with the rest of Hopkins' poems, "The Leaden Echo and the Golden Echo" is suffused with religious feeling, which, as in many of the poems, is aroused (and colored) by the perception of beauty, frequently human beauty, and, as in this case, by the recognition of its transience. The passing of youth is of course one of poetry's oldest-established and most frequently recurrent themes; sadness or despair are the emotions which generally accompany its statement, and Hopkins, taking these to be the natural first response to transience, proposes the comfort that will be given by the resignation of youthful beauty into God's keeping. The recommendation is perhaps less a serious religious idea than a tender religious conceit; as such, it has an appealing sweetness of intention and but little power to hold grievous feelings at bay. It does, however, serve as the occasion for a peculiarly fresh and poignant celebration of the passing physical beauty for which it seeks a spiritual permanence.

"GO TELL IT"— WHAT A MESSAGE—

EMILY DICKINSON
1830–1886

"Go tell it"—What a Message—
To whom—is specified—
Not murmur—not endearment—
But simply—we—obeyed—
Obeyed—a Lure—a Longing? 5
Oh Nature—none of this—
To Law—said sweet Thermopylae
I give my dying Kiss—

COMMENTARY

One of the tenets of modern literary criticism is that a poem is a self-contained entity, that it must be regarded as wholly independent of all considerations that are not proposed by its own elements. For example, any knowledge of the personal life of the poet, even of the circumstances that led to the writing of the poem, is considered irrelevant—it may be interesting in itself but it cannot tell us anything we need to know in order for the poem to have its right effect upon us. There are critics who go so far as to say that an interest in the personal existence of the poet interferes with our direct response to the poem.

This idea must be granted the merit of its intention. When we read "Resolution and Independence," it is not necessary to know that Wordsworth, shortly before he wrote the poem, actually did meet an old man such as he describes, or that he was soon to be married and might therefore be expected to feel anxiety over the future. For a precise response to "Ode to a Nightingale" we do not have to know that it was written not many weeks after Keats had witnessed the death of his younger brother. And if we felt it necessary to seek out such information, the poem could of course be thought by that much the less complete in itself, for in part it would then depend for its effect upon something outside itself.

But the truth is that extrinsic information, whether we wish it or not, and whether the critics in their strictness like it or not, often does impinge upon our awareness of a particular poem and become an element in our relation to it which we cannot ignore. When we read "Lycidas," we cannot dismiss from our minds the fact that the young poet who speaks so proudly of the profession of poetry and of his noble desire for fame is to become one of the world's great poets, as famous as ever he could have wished. How different our response to "Lycidas" would be if Milton had died not long after its composition! We should then not take the poem to be, among other things, the superb prelude to a triumphant career, but a vaunt which had been made pathetic and ironic by circumstance. In this instance, the mere awareness of Milton's reputation is an extraneous knowledge that inevitably plays some part in our reading of the poem, and it would be a strict critic indeed who would say that it should not.

Another kind of information which properly has its share in our response to a poem comes from our familiarity with other poems from the same pen. Anyone acquainted with the canon of Wordsworth's work knows that the poet conceived of his creative power as being dependent upon the emotions of his childhood and early youth and that he believed that the passing years would diminish it. Whoever has read even a few of Keats's poems is aware that the poet was preoccupied with the antithesis between what is eternal and "pure" and what is transient and mundane. Such awarenesses constitute some knowledge of the poets as persons, and this knowledge cannot fail to have its effect upon our way of responding to a single one of their poems, nor does there seem to be any good reason for supposing that this effect is anything but natural. It is a positive advantage in our reading of "Resolution and Independence" to know that Wordsworth's fear of losing his creative powers is not a momentary fancy but an emotion that conditioned his whole life. It can scarcely confuse our response to "Ode to a Nightingale" to know that Keats is *again* moved to a passionate consideration of the eternal and the transitory.

And in the case of Emily Dickinson's striking little poem, there is at least one personal fact about the author which it is essential we bring to our reading —that the poet is a woman. If we were not aware of this, we might well be made uncomfortable by the poem, for its tone and diction seem appropriate to a woman but not to a man, and we would surely be ill at ease if we thought a man had been the writer.

The poem is, as it were, based upon the femininity of the poet. The word femininity is never used in a neutral sense but always with the intention of praise; it connotes charm, delicacy, tenderness. These qualities are no doubt readily seen, or heard, in the poem, but they will be the more quickly perceived by the reader who has some previous acquaintance with Emily Dickinson's work and knows the extent to which the poet represents herself in the postures of femininity, as a young woman, or girl, of high sensitivity, delicate, fastidious, quick to be apprehensive yet courageous and even daring, standing in a daughterly relation to God, whom, on one occasion, with the licensed audacity of rebelliousness characteristic of her manner, she addresses as "Papa above" (page 382). The rules of the world are laid down by masculine beings and the point of many of her poems lies, as in the present one, in the opposition of the feminine creature to the masculine authority, which usually delights her even though she addresses it in irony or protest.

There are two speakers in the poem. They are of opposite sexes and they are half a world and some twenty-five centuries apart. When Emily Dickinson wrote, she could count on a prompt appreciation of what "message" it is that begins "Go tell it . . ." Most readers of the nineteenth century knew the story of the Spartans at Thermopylae—how the huge Persian army under the great king Xerxes moved to conquer Greece; how the small Greek army took its stand at Thermopylae, where, between the precipitous mountain on the one side and the sea on the other, there was a pass so narrow that only a few soldiers could enter it abreast; how, when the Greek position was betrayed, the greater part of the Greek forces withdrew, leaving only the Spartans under their king Leonidas to hold the pass; and how the Spartans, some three hundred in number, were exterminated. Upon the spot a monument was erected which bore this inscription: "Go, stranger, and tell Sparta that here, obeying her commands, we fell." What a message indeed!

The feminine voice—and perhaps we should say the modern feminine voice—questions the basis of the Spartans' act even though the message says unmistakably what that is: obedience. The feminine mind wishes to understand the heroism as an impulse, specifically as an impulse of love. The language used is that of erotic attraction—the poet speaks of the heroic deed as having been a response to "a Lure—a Longing"; she sees it as instinctual, rising out of Nature. And across the centuries the men of Thermopylae refuse her interpretation of their act. They address her by the name of the principle she has invoked, speaking to her as if she were Nature itself, and, brushing aside the idea of their having responded to a "Lure" or a "Longing," assert that it was not Love but Law that moved them.

Yet the feminine voice is not to be silenced. In the very act of reporting how it is refuted and rebuked, it asserts itself in the peculiarly feminine epithet by which it characterizes the great event—"sweet Thermopylae," it says. And the men of Thermopylae seem suddenly to assent to the feminine understanding of their sacrifice—the salute which they send to Law is a kiss. The striking inappropriateness of applying the adjective *sweet* to the grim heroic battle is matched by the inappropriateness—almost comic—of the men of Thermopylae sending a kiss to the Law of Sparta, the most rigorous the world has known. The imperturbable soldiers have been beguiled into taking the feminine view of their action, and Law and Love are made one.

The text of " 'Go tell it'—" that I have used is the one established by Professor Thomas H. Johnson; it reproduces exactly the punctuation of the manuscript. The numerous dashes are characteristic of the poet's practice; Professor Edith Stamm has advanced the theory (in *The Saturday Review,* March 30, 1963) that they are intended to guide the voice in reading.

SAILING TO BYZANTIUM[1]

WILLIAM BUTLER YEATS

1865–1939

That is no country for old men. The young
In one another's arms, birds in the trees,
—Those dying generations—at their song,
The salmon-falls, the mackerel-crowded seas,
Fish, flesh, or fowl, commend all summer long 5
Whatever is begotten, born, and dies.
Caught in that sensual music all neglect
Monuments of unaging intellect.

An aged man is but a paltry thing,
A tattered coat upon a stick, unless 10
Soul clap its hands and sing, and louder sing
For every tatter in its mortal dress,
Nor is there singing school but studying
Monuments of its own magnificence;
And therefore I have sailed the seas and come 15
To the holy city of Byzantium.

O sages standing in God's holy fire
As in the gold mosaic of a wall,
Come from the holy fire, perne[2] in a gyre,
And be the singing-masters of my soul. 20
Consume my heart away, sick with desire
And fastened to a dying animal
It knows not what it is; and gather me
Into the artifice of eternity.

Once out of nature I shall never take 25
My bodily form from any natural thing.
But such a form as Grecian goldsmiths make

[1] An ancient great city, the holy city of eastern Christendom. [2] Turn, spin.

Of hammered gold and gold enamelling
To keep a drowsy Emperor awake;
Or set upon a golden bough to sing 30
To lords and ladies of Byzantium
Of what is past, or passing, or to come.[3]

COMMENTARY

One of Hans Christian Andersen's best-known stories tells of an Emperor of China in whose garden lived a small brown bird. It was a nightingale, and the beauty of its song was a chief delight of the Emperor's life. But one day the court jewelers presented their master with an artificial bird which they had contrived with great artistry and ingenuity. It was made of gold and set with gems, and by means of a clockwork mechanism it was able to sing. The Emperor was captivated by the wonderful toy and quite forgot the nightingale of flesh and blood, who, in sorrow over his neglect, flew away. Time passed, the unvarying song of the nightingale of artifice palled on the Emperor, who was now old and near death, and one day the clockwork gave out. The Emperor, lonely on his deathbed, longed for the comfort of the real nightingale's singing. He spoke his longing aloud, the bird appeared at his window and sang for him, and the Emperor died happy.

We cannot be sure that Yeats knew Andersen's story, although anyone who had been a child in a literate home in the late nineteenth century was likely to have been acquainted with it.[1] But whether he did or not, the story is pertinent to "Sailing to Byzantium" because it gives simple and memorable expression to an attitude which the poem controverts. For most people the word "artifice" and the adjective derived from it carry an adverse connotation. They imply something false; "nature" and "natural" suggest the real and true. Much of the force of "Sailing to Byzantium" derives from the heresy, as we might call it, of its preference for "artifice" as against "nature." The poet expresses the wish to be "out of nature," to be, exactly, a golden nightingale, a work of artifice.

The shock that the expression of this desire is calculated to produce is made the more intense by the reputation of the city that Yeats makes the comprehensive symbol of the non-natural or even of the anti-natural. Byzantium—later known as Constantinople, now as Istanbul—was the chief city of the Roman empire of the East. Eventually it became the administrative and cultural center of the whole Roman world in its long Christianized phase and, in its luxury and magnificence, it surpassed the city of Rome itself. Its architecture, which drew upon a highly developed engineering skill, has never lacked for admiration. But the pictures with which the churches, monasteries, and palaces were decorated fell into disrepute in Western Europe after the early days of the Renaissance. The chief ground for the unfavorable judgment was the indiffer-

[3] I have read somewhere that in the Emperor's palace at Byzantium was a tree made of gold and silver, and artificial birds that sang. (Yeats's note)

[1] His footnote to line 32 permits the conjecture that Yeats may indeed have known the story and that, for his own poetic purposes, he had unconsciously transformed the Chinese emperor into a Byzantine emperor.

ence that the Byzantine artists showed to naturalistic representation, especially of the human form. The personages in Byzantine pictures are always clothed, and their voluminous robes give no indication of the body beneath. Their postures are static, and we have the impression that although these people are accessible to certain religious emotions, they have no capacity either for worldly feelings or for physical movement. The personal inspiration of the artist is subordinated to the control of tradition and convention; his indifference to naturalistic considerations can by no means be ascribed to a deficiency of skill in representation but to a complex aesthetic, derived from an elaborate theology, which repudiated the body in favor of the soul.

To the taste of the present time, Byzantine painting makes a strong appeal. The development of modern painting has been away from naturalistic representation and we take pleasure in the very abstractness that once was thought uninteresting and even repellent. But this revision of judgment is relatively recent, and up through the early years of the twentieth century, Byzantine painting was not likely to be admired except by scholars and connoisseurs of unconventional taste. Byzantium figured in most people's minds as the very type of a formalized "lifeless" culture.

Yeats's interest in Byzantium began when he was advanced in middle age. This was far from being the first time that a past culture had seemed to him of momentous relevance to his own life—indeed, nothing is so characteristic of Yeats, from the start of his career, as his preoccupation with the quality of life of some epoch of the past. It was thus that he expressed his passionately adverse sense of the modern world, which he thought ignoble in its rationalism, materialism, and calculating self-interest. As an Irishman, he was especially inclined to ascribe the modern ignobility to England although he also directed his scorn upon his own countrymen for betraying their heritage of romantic magnanimity. Against the dull prudence of modern life, he set the irrational heroic passions of the legendary Irish past; against the vulgarity and disorder of the present he evoked the recollection of a past era closer at hand, that of the eighteenth century, when the proud elegance of an assured aristocracy and the rich intuitiveness of an uncorrupted peasantry made the conditions of a good life. Such were the historical-cultural fantasies of the young poet who believed that the culture in which he had his actual existence stood in the way of his desire for fullness of life. Advancing years made a very different past culture seem desirable—to the aging poet Byzantium spoke of immortality.

The established and scarcely debatable view of Yeats's development is that, although he was a gifted and interesting poet from his early youth, he did not become a great one until his middle age. He was nearly fifty before he began to write the poems that won him his high place in modern literature. A special interest of his later work derives from the new diction he taught himself to use: hard, downright, fierce in its directness, and, as we say, "unpoetic." It is a manner consonant with the characteristic matter of the later poems, which is an aging man's harsh resentment of an ineluctable circumstance of human life, that we grow old.

This matter, which is to be distinguished from a concern with the transience of youth or of all of life, is new not only to the poet but to poetry. Yeats may well be the first writer ever to make his own representation of himself as an aging man a chief element of his creation. The general human importance of this cannot be underestimated—it might even be said that Yeats added a whole stage of life to man's existence: by his impassioned resentment of it, he made the world know that old age may be as sentient and significant a period in a man's life as his youth. Hitherto old age had been represented wholly from the outside: the aged or aging person was made the *object* of understanding or sympathy; it is someone else, not the poet, who experiences the aging process.[2] But Yeats, perhaps because he so feared and hated his old age, refused to let it make him into a mere object; he claimed it and proclaimed it as his experience, he imposed his imagination upon it—and thus remained a subject.

It is, then, as an aging man, with the prospect of actual old age before him, that Yeats takes leave of "nature" and seeks refuge in the permanence of "artifice"—of art, not as it refers to life in its shifting cycles of joy or pain, but as it suggests fixity and timelessness. His hope is much the same as that of Professor Cornelius, the historian of Thomas Mann's "Disorder and Early Sorrow" (*Fiction,* pages 261 ff.), who sees in the unchanging orderliness of the past a means of escaping from the pain of the living present of youthful desire. But one need not be a man of middle age, like Professor Cornelius, or a man on the threshold of old age, like Yeats, to entertain the imagination of beautiful permanence. Keats was only twenty-four when he wrote "Ode to a Nightingale" (pages 80 ff.), the theme of which is not unlike that of "Sailing to Byzantium"; his "Ode on a Grecian Urn" (pages 312 f.) is yet closer to Yeats's poem in the complex opposition it makes between beauty in nature, with its susceptibility to mutability and deterioration, and beauty in the permanence of art.

But we cannot read the first stanza of "Sailing to Byzantium" without being made aware of the poet's ambivalence toward nature, of how deeply Yeats loves what he says he has rejected. The beings that "commend" the natural cycle of existence, the life of generation, birth, and death, win from the poet the commendation of his scarcely disguised envy. And when he imagines his existence in "artifice," as the golden bird, it is not of timeless abstractions that he tells us he will sing but of nature and time, or nature *in* time—the triad which describes the burden of his song, "what is past, or passing, or to come," echoes the triad of rejected things in the first stanza, "Whatever is begotten, born, and dies." This has to be seen as a contradiction, and a moving one. And perhaps equally moving is Yeats's choice of the form of artifice in which the poet would wish to have his existence—not a great, still monument of the soul's magnificence but a miniscule creature of gold and enamel, a little toy of a bird.

[2] See, for example, the Leech-gatherer of "Resolution and Independence" (pp. 50 ff.), the greatest of Wordsworth's many representations of old men.

THE WASTE LAND

THOMAS STEARNS ELIOT

1888–1965

> *"Nam Sibyllam quidem Cumis ego ipse oculis meis vidi in ampulla pendere, et cum illi pueri dicerent: Σίβυλλα τί θέλεις; respondebat illa: ἀποθανεῖν θέλω."*[1]

For Ezra Pound
il miglior fabbro.[2]

I. THE BURIAL OF THE DEAD

April is the cruelest month, breeding
Lilacs out of the dead land, mixing
Memory and desire, stirring
Dull roots with spring rain.
Winter kept us warm, covering 5
Earth in forgetful snow, feeding
A little life with dried tubers.
Summer surprised us, coming over the Starnbergersee
With a shower of rain; we stopped in the colonnade,
And went on in sunlight, into the Hofgarten, 10
And drank coffee, and talked for an hour.
Bin gar keine Russin, stamm' aus Litauen, echt deutsch.[3]
And when we were children, staying at the arch-duke's,
My cousin's, he took me out on a sled,
And I was frightened. He said, Marie, 15
Marie, hold on tight. And down we went.
In the mountains, there you feel free.
I read, much of the night, and go south in the winter.

[1] For with my own eyes I saw the Sibyl of Cumae hanging in a cage, and when the boys cried to her, "Sibyl, what do you want?" she answered, "I want to die" (from Petronius' *Satyricon*). The Sibyl, a prophetic old woman, was about a thousand years old at this time. [2] The superior artificer, maker. [3] I'm by no means a Russian, I come from Lithuania—real German.

What are the roots that clutch, what branches grow
Out of this stony rubbish? Son of man, 20
You cannot say, or guess, for you know only
A heap of broken images, where the sun beats,
And the dead tree gives no shelter, the cricket no relief,
And the dry stone no sound of water. Only
There is shadow under this red rock 25
(Come in under the shadow of this red rock),
And I will show you something different from either
Your shadow at morning striding behind you
Or your shadow at evening rising to meet you;
I will show you fear in a handful of dust. 30

Frisch weht der Wind
Der Heimat zu
Mein Irisch Kind,
Wo weilest du?[4]

"You gave me hyacinths first a year ago; 35
"They called me the hyacinth girl."
—Yet when we came back, late, from the Hyacinth garden,
Your arms full, and your hair wet, I could not
Speak, and my eyes failed, I was neither
Living or dead, and I knew nothing, 40
Looking into the heart of light, the silence.
Oed' und leer das Meer.[5]

Madame Sosostris, famous clairvoyante,
Had a bad cold, nevertheless
Is known to be the wisest woman in Europe, 45
With a wicked pack of cards. Here, said she,
Is your card, the drowned Phoenician Sailor,
(Those are pearls that were his eyes. Look!)
Here is Belladonna, the Lady of the Rocks,
The lady of situations. 50
Here is the man with three staves, and here the Wheel
And here is the one-eyed merchant, and this card,
Which is blank, is something he carries on his back,
Which I am forbidden to see. I do not find
The Hanged Man. Fear death by water. 55
I see crowds of people, walking round in a ring.
Thank you. If you see dear Mrs. Equitone,
Tell her I bring the horoscope myself:
One must be so careful these days.

Unreal City, 60
Under the brown fog of a winter dawn,
A crowd flowed over London Bridge, so many,

[4] A fresh wind blows toward the homeland; my Irish child, where are you lingering? (See Eliot's note to line 31.) [5] Wide and empty is the sea. (See Eliot's note to this line.)

I had not thought death had undone so many.
Sighs, short and infrequent, were exhaled,
And each man fixed his eyes before his feet. 65
Flowed up the hill and down King William Street,
To where Saint Mary Woolnoth kept the hours
With a dead sound on the final stroke of nine.
There I saw one I knew, and stopped him, crying: "Stetson!
"You who were with me in the ships at Mylae! 70
"That corpse you planted last year in your garden,
"Has it begun to sprout? Will it bloom this year?
"Or has the sudden frost disturbed its bed?
"Oh keep the Dog far hence, that's friend to men,
"Or with his nails he'll dig it up again! 75
"You! hypocrite lecteur!—mon semblable,—mon frère!"[6]

II. A GAME OF CHESS

The Chair she sat in, like a burnished throne,
Glowed on the marble, where the glass
Held up by standards wrought with fruited vines
From which a golden Cupidon peeped out 80
(Another hid his eyes behind his wing)
Doubled the flames of sevenbranched candelabra
Reflecting light upon the table as
The glitter of her jewels rose to meet it,
From satin cases poured in rich profusion; 85
In vials of ivory and coloured glass
Unstoppered, lurked her strange synthetic perfumes,
Unguent, powdered, or liquid—troubled, confused
And drowned the sense in odours; stirred by the air
That freshened from the window, these ascended 90
In fattening the prolonged candle-flames,
Flung their smoke into the laquearia,
Stirring the pattern on the coffered ceiling.
Huge sea-wood fed with copper
Burned green and orange, framed by the coloured stone, 95
In which sad light a carvèd dolphin swam.
Above the antique mantel was displayed
As though a window gave upon the sylvan scene
The change of Philomel, by the barbarous king
So rudely forced; yet there the nightingale 100
Filled all the desert with inviolable voice
And still she cried, and still the world pursues,
"Jug Jug" to dirty ears.
And other withered stumps of time
Were told upon the walls; staring forms 105
Leaned out, leaning, hushing the room enclosed.
Footsteps shuffled on the stair.

[6] Hypocritical reader!—my likeness,—my brother! (See Eliot's note to this line.)

Under the firelight, under the brush, her hair
Spread out in fiery points
Glowed into words, then would be savagely still. 110

"My nerves are bad to-night. Yes, bad. Stay with me.
"Speak to me. Why do you never speak. Speak.
"What are you thinking of? What thinking? What?
"I never know what you are thinking. Think."

I think we are in rats' alley 115
Where the dead men lost their bones.

"What is that noise?"
The wind under the door.
"What is that noise now? What is the wind doing?"
Nothing again nothing. 120
"Do
"You know nothing? Do you see nothing? Do you remember
"Nothing?"
I remember
Those are pearls that were his eyes. 125
"Are you alive, or not? Is there nothing in your head?"
But

O O O O that Shakespeherian Rag—
It's so elegant
So intelligent 130
"What shall I do now? What shall I do?"
"I shall rush out as I am, and walk the street
"With my hair down, so. What shall we do tomorrow?
"What shall we ever do?"
The hot water at ten. 135
And if it rains, a closed car at four.
And we shall play a game of chess,
Pressing lidless eyes and waiting for a knock upon the door.

When Lil's husband got demobbed, I said—
I didn't mince my words, I said to her myself, 140
HURRY UP PLEASE ITS TIME
Now Albert's coming back, make yourself a bit smart.
He'll want to know what you done with that money he gave you
To get yourself some teeth. He did, I was there.
You have them all out, Lil, and get a nice set, 145
He said, I swear, I can't bear to look at you.
And no more can't I, I said, and think of poor Albert,
He's been in the army four years, he wants a good time,
And if you don't give it him, there's others will, I said.
Oh is there, she said. Something o' that, I said. 150
Then I'll know who to thank, she said, and gave me a straight look.

HURRY UP PLEASE ITS TIME
If you don't like it you can get on with it, I said.
Others can pick and choose if you can't.
But if Albert makes off, it won't be for lack of telling. 155
You ought to be ashamed, I said, to look so antique.
(And her only thirty-one.)
I can't help it, she said, pulling a long face,
It's them pills I took, to bring it off, she said.
(She's had five already, and nearly died of young George.) 160
The chemist said it would be all right, but I've never been the same.
You *are* a proper fool, I said.
Well, if Albert won't leave you alone, there it is, I said,
What you get married for if you don't want children?
HURRY UP PLEASE ITS TIME 165
Well, that Sunday Albert was home, they had a hot gammon,
And they asked me in to dinner, to get the beauty of it hot—
HURRY UP PLEASE ITS TIME
HURRY UP PLEASE ITS TIME
Goonight Bill. Goonight Lou. Goonight May. Goonight. 170
Ta ta. Goonight. Goonight.
Good night, ladies, good night, sweet ladies, good night, good night.

III. THE FIRE SERMON

The river's tent is broken: the last fingers of leaf
Clutch and sink into the wet bank. The wind
Crosses the brown land, unheard. The nymphs are departed. 175
Sweet Thames, run softly, till I end my song.
The river bears no empty bottles, sandwich papers,
Silk handkerchiefs, cardboard boxes, cigarette ends
Or other testimony of summer nights. The nymphs are departed.
And their friends, the loitering heirs of city directors— 180
Departed, have left no addresses.
By the waters of Leman I sat down and wept . . .
Sweet Thames, run softly till I end my song,
Sweet Thames, run softly, for I speak not loud or long.
But at my back in a cold blast I hear 185
The rattle of the bones, and chuckle spread from ear to ear.
A rat crept softly through the vegetation
Dragging its slimy belly on the bank
While I was fishing in the dull canal
On a winter evening behind the gashouse 190
Musing upon the king my brother's wreck
And on the king my father's death before him.
White bodies naked on the low damp ground
And bones cast in a little low dry garret,
Rattled by the rat's foot only, year to year. 195
But at my back from time to time I hear
The sound of horns and motors, which shall bring

Sweeney to Mrs. Porter in the spring.
O the moon shone bright on Mrs. Porter
And on her daughter 200
They wash their feet in soda water
Et O ces voix d'enfants, chantant dans la coupole![7]
Twit twit twit
Jug jug jug jug jug jug
So rudely forc'd. 205

Tereu

Unreal City
Under the brown fog of a winter noon
Mr. Eugenides, the Smyrna merchant
Unshaven, with a pocket full of currants 210
C.i.f. London: documents at sight,
Asked me in demotic French
To luncheon at the Cannon Street Hotel
Followed by a weekend at the Metropole.

At the violet hour, when the eyes and back 215
Turn upward from the desk, when the human engine waits
Like a taxi throbbing waiting,
I Tiresias, though blind, throbbing between two lives,
Old man with wrinkled female breasts, can see
At the violet hour, the evening hour that strives 220
Homeward, and brings the sailor home from sea,
The typist home at teatime, clears her breakfast, lights
Her stove, and lays out food in tins.
Out of the window perilously spread
Her drying combinations touched by the sun's last rays, 225
On the divan are piled (at night her bed)
Stockings, slippers, camisoles, and stays.
I Tiresias, old man with wrinkled dugs
Perceived the scene, and foretold the rest—
I too awaited the expected guest. 230
He, the young man carbuncular, arrives,
A small house agent's clerk, with one bold stare,
One of the low on whom assurance sits
As a silk hat on a Bradford millionaire.
The time is now propitious, as he guesses, 235
The meal is ended, she is bored and tired,
Endeavours to engage her in caresses
Which still are unreproved, if undesired.
Flushed and decided, he assaults at once;
Exploring hands encounter no defence; 240
His vanity requires no response,

[7] And oh these children's voices, singing in the cupola. (See Eliot's note to this line.)

And makes a welcome of indifference.
(And I Tiresias have foresuffered all
Enacted on this same divan or bed;
I who have sat by Thebes below the wall 245
And walked among the lowest of the dead.)
Bestows one final patronising kiss,
And gropes his way, finding the stairs unlit . . .

She turns and looks a moment in the glass,
Hardly aware of her departed lover; 250
Her brain allows one half-formed thought to pass:
"Well now that's done: and I'm glad it's over."
When lovely woman stoops to folly and
Paces about her room again, alone,
She smoothes her hair with automatic hand, 255
And puts a record on the gramophone.

"This music crept by me upon the waters"
And along the Strand, up Queen Victoria Street.
O City city, I can sometimes hear
Beside a public bar in Lower Thames Street, 260
The pleasant whining of a mandoline
And a clatter and a chatter from within
Where fishmen lounge at noon: where the walls
Of Magnus Martyr hold
Inexplicable splendour of Ionian white and gold. 265

The river sweats
Oil and tar
The barges drift
With the turning tide
Red sails 270
Wide
To leeward, swing on the heavy spar.
The barges wash
Drifting logs
Down Greenwich reach 275
Past the Isle of Dogs.
Weialala leia
Wallala leialala
Elizabeth and Leicester
Beating oars 280
The stern was formed
A gilded shell
Red and gold
The brisk swell
Rippled both shores 285
Southwest wind
Carried down stream

The peal of bells
White towers
        Weialala leia   290
        Wallala leialala

"Trams and dusty trees.
Highbury bore me. Richmond and Kew
Undid me. By Richmond I raised my knees
Supine on the floor of a narrow canoe."   295
"My feet are at Moorgate, and my heart
Under my feet. After the event
He wept. He promised 'a new start.'
I made no comment. What should I resent?"

"On Margate Sands.   300
I can connect
Nothing with nothing.
The broken fingernails of dirty hands.
My people humble people who expect
Nothing."   305
            la la
To Carthage then I came

Burning burning burning burning
Oh Lord Thou pluckest me out
O Lord Thou pluckest   310

burning

IV. DEATH BY WATER

Phlebas the Phoenician, a fortnight dead,
Forgot the cry of gulls, and the deep sea swell
And the profit and loss.   315
                A current under sea
Picked his bones in whispers. As he rose and fell
He passed the stages of his age and youth
Entering the whirlpool.
                Gentile or Jew   320
O you who turn the wheel and look to windward,
Consider Phlebas, who was once handsome and tall as you.

V. WHAT THE THUNDER SAID

After the torchlight red on sweaty faces
After the frosty silence in the gardens
After the agony in stony places   325
The shouting and the crying
Prison and palace and reverberation

Of thunder of spring over distant mountains
He who was living is now dead
We who were living are now dying
With a little patience 330

Here is no water but only rock
Rock and no water and the sandy road
The road winding above among the mountains
Which are mountains of rock without water
If there were water we should stop and drink 335
Amongst the rock one cannot stop or think
Sweat is dry and feet are in the sand
If there were only water amongst the rock
Dead mountain mouth of carious teeth that cannot spit
Here one can neither stand nor lie nor sit 340
There is not even silence in the mountains
But dry sterile thunder without rain
There is not even solitude in the mountains
But red sullen faces sneer and snarl
From doors of mudcracked houses 345
If there were water
And no rock
If there were rock
And also water
And water 350
A spring
A pool among the rock
If there were the sound of water only
Not the cicada
And dry grass singing 355
But sound of water over a rock
Where the hermit-thrush sings in the pine trees
Drip drop drip drop drop drop drop
But there is no water

Who is the third who walks always beside you? 360
When I count, there are only you and I together
But when I look ahead up the white road
There is always another one walking beside you
Gliding wrapt in a brown mantle, hooded
I do not know whether a man or a woman 365
—But who is that on the other side of you?

What is that sound high in the air
Murmur of maternal lamentation
Who are those hooded hordes swarming
Over endless plains, stumbling in cracked earth 370
Ringed by the flat horizon only
What is the city over the mountains

Cracks and reforms and bursts in the violet air
Falling towers
Jerusalem Athens Alexandria 375
Vienna London
Unreal

A woman drew her long black hair out tight
And fiddled whisper music on those strings
And bats with baby faces in the violet light 380
Whistled, and beat their wings
And crawled head downward down a blackened wall
And upside down in air were towers
Tolling reminiscent bells, that kept the hours
And voices singing out of empty cisterns and exhausted wells. 385

In this decayed hole among the mountains
In the faint moonlight, the glass is singing
Over the tumbled graves, about the chapel
There is the empty chapel, only the wind's home.
It has no windows, and the door swings, 390
Dry bones can harm no one.
Only a cock stood on the rooftree
Co co rico co co rico
In a flash of lightning. Then a damp gust
Bringing rain 395
Ganga was sunken, and the limp leaves
Waited for rain, while the black clouds
Gathered far distant, over Himavant.
The jungle crouched, humped in silence.
Then spoke the thunder 400
Da
Datta: what have we given?
My friend, blood shaking my heart
The awful daring of a moment's surrender
Which an age of prudence can never retract 405
By this, and this only, we have existed
Which is not to be found in our obituaries
Or in memories draped by the beneficent spider
Or under seals broken by the lean solicitor
In our empty rooms 410
Da
Dayadhvam: I have heard the key
Turn in the door once and turn once only
We think of the key, each in his prison
Thinking of the key, each confirms a prison 415
Only at nightfall, aethereal rumours
Revive for a moment a broken Coriolanus
Da
Damyata: The boat responded

Gaily, to the hand expert with sail and oar 420
The sea was calm, your heart would have responded
Gaily, when invited, beating obedient
To controlling hands

I sat upon the shore
Fishing, with the arid plain behind me 425
Shall I at least set my lands in order?
London Bridge is falling down falling down falling down
Poi s'ascose nel foco che gli affina
Quando fiam uti chelidon[8]—O swallow swallow
Le Prince d'Aquitaine à la tour abolie[9] 430
These fragments I have shored against my ruins
Why then Ile fit you. Hieronymo's mad againe.
Datta. Dayadhvam. Damyata.

Shantih shantih shantih

NOTES ON "THE WASTE LAND"

[*T. S. Eliot*]

Not only the title, but the plan and a good deal of the incidental symbolism of the poem were suggested by Miss Jessie L. Weston's book on the Grail legend: *From Ritual to Romance* (Cambridge). Indeed, so deeply am I indebted, Miss Weston's book will elucidate the difficulties of the poem much better than my notes can do; and I recommend it (apart from the great interest of the book itself) to any who think much elucidation of the poem worth the trouble. To another work of anthropology I am indebted in general, one which has influenced our generation profoundly; I mean *The Golden Bough;* I have used especially the two volumes *Adonis, Attis, Osiris*. Anyone who is acquainted with these works will immediately recognise in the poem certain references to vegetation ceremonies.

I. THE BURIAL OF THE DEAD

LINE 20. Cf. Ezekiel II, i.
23. Cf. Ecclesiastes XII, v.
31. V. Tristan und Isolde, I, verses 5–8.
42. Id. III, verse 24.
46. I am not familiar with the exact constitution of the Tarot pack of cards, from which I have obviously departed to suit my own convenience. The Hanged Man, a member of the traditional pack, fits my purpose in two ways: because he is associated in my mind with the Hanged God of Frazer, and because I associate him with the hooded figure in the passage of the disciples to Emmaus in Part V. The Phoenician Sailor and the Merchant appear later; also the "crowd of people," and Death by Water is executed in Part IV. The Man with Three Staves (an authentic member of the Tarot pack) I associate, quite arbitrarily, with the Fisher King himself.
60. Cf. Baudelaire:

[8] Then he hid him in the flame that refines them / When shall I become as the swallow? (See Eliot's notes to lines 428 and 429.) The anonymous Latin poem from which Eliot has taken part of line 429 celebrates the spring festival in honor of Venus, goddess of love and increase. [9] The Prince of Aquitaine at the ruined tower. (See Eliot's note to this line.)

"Fourmillante cité, cité pleine de rêves,
"Où le spectre en plein jour raccroche le passant."[10]

63. Cf. Inferno III, 55–57:

"si lunga tratta
di gente, ch'io non avrei mai creduto
che morte tanta n'avesse disfatta."[11]

64. Cf. Inferno IV, 25–27:

"Quivi, secondo che per ascolatare,
"non avea pianto, ma' che di sospiri,
"che l'aura eterna facevan tremare."[12]

68. A phenomenon which I have often noticed.
74. Cf. the Dirge in Webster's *White Devil.*
76. V. Baudelaire, Preface to *Fleurs du Mal.*

II. A GAME OF CHESS

77. Cf. *Antony and Cleopatra,* II ii, l. 190.
92. Laquearia. V. *Aeneid,* I, 726:

dependent lychni laquearibus aureis incensi, et noctem flammis funalia vincunt.[13]

98. Sylvan scene. V. Milton, *Paradise Lost,* IV, 140.
99. V. Ovid, *Metamorphoses,* VI, Philomela.
100. Cf. Part III, l. 204.
115. Cf. Part III, l. 195.
118. Cf. Webster: "Is the wind in that door still?"
126. Cf. Part I, l. 37, 48.
138. Cf. the game of chess in Middleton's *Women Beware Women.*

III. THE FIRE SERMON

176. V. Spenser, *Prothalamion.*
192. Cf. *The Tempest,* I, ii.
196. Cf. Marvell, *To His Coy Mistress.*
197. Cf. Day, *Parliament of Bees:*

"When of the sudden, listening, you shall hear,
"A noise of horns and hunting, which shall bring
"Actaeon to Diana in the spring,
"Where all shall see her naked skin . . ."

199. I do not know the origin of the ballad from which these lines are taken: it was reported to me from Sydney, Australia.
202. V. Verlaine, *Parsifal.*
210. The currants were quoted at a price "carriage and insurance free to London" and the Bill of Lading etc. were to be handed to the buyer upon payment of the sight draft.
218. Tiresias, although a mere spectator and not indeed a "character," is yet the most important personage in the poem, uniting all the rest. Just as the one-eyed merchant seller of currants, melts into the Phoenician Sailor, and the latter is not wholly distinct from Ferdinand Prince of Naples, so all the women are one woman, and the two sexes met in Tiresias. What Tiresias *sees,* in fact, is the substance of the poem. The whole passage from Ovid is of great anthropological interest:

[10] Swarming city, full of dreams, where ghosts in broad daylight accost passers-by. [11] So long a train of people, I had not ever believed that death had undone so many. [12] Here there was no plaint that could be heard, except of signs, which made the eternal air to tremble. [13] Lighted lamps hang down from the fretted roof of gold, and flaming torches drive out the night.

". . . Cum Iunone iocos et maior vestra profecto est
Quam, quae contingit maribus," dixisse, "voluptas."
Illa negat; placuit quae sit sententia docti
Quaerere Tiresiae: venus huic erat utraque nota.
Nam duo magnorum viridi coeuntia silva
Corpora serpentum baculi violaverat ictu
Deque viro factus, mirabile, femina septem
Egerat autumnos; octavo rursus eosdem
Vidit et "est vestrae si tanta potentia plagae,"
Dixit "ut auctoris sortem in contraria mutet,
Nunc quoque vos feriam!" percussis anguibus isdem
Forma prior rediit genetivaque venit imago.
Arbiter hic igitur sumptus de lite iocosa
Dicta Iovis firmat; gravius Saturnia iusto
Nec pro materia fertur doluisse suique
Iudicis aeterna demnavit lumina nocte,
At pater omnipotens (neque enim licet inrita cuiquam
Facta dei fecisse deo) pro lumine adempto
Scire futura dedit poenamque levavit honore.[14]

221. This may not appear as exact as Sappho's lines, but I had in mind the "longshore" or "dory" fisherman, who returns at nightfall.
253. V. Goldsmith, the song in *The Vicar of Wakefield.*
257. V. *The Tempest,* as above.
264. The interior of St. Magnus Martyr is to my mind one of the finest among Wren's interiors. See *The Proposed Demolition of Nineteen City Churches:* (P. S. King & Son, Ltd.).
266. The Song of the (three) Thames-daughters begins here. From line 292 to 306 inclusive they speak in turn. V. *Gotterdammerung,* III, i: the Rhine-daughters.
279. V. Froude, *Elizabeth,* Vol. I, ch. iv, letter of De Quadra to Philip of Spain: "In the afternoon we were in a barge, watching the games on the river. (The queen) was alone with Lord Robert and myself on the poop, when they began to talk nonsense, and went so far that Lord Robert at last said, as I was on the spot there was no reason why they should not be married if the queen pleased."
293. Cf. *Purgatorio,* V, 133:

"Ricorditi di me, che son la Pia;
"Siena mi fe', disfecemi Maremma."[15]

307. V. St. Augustine's *Confessions:* "to Carthage then I came, where a cauldron of unholy loves sang all about mine ears."
308. The complete text of the Buddha's Fire Sermon (which corresponds in importance to the Sermon on the Mount) from which these words are taken, will be found translated in the late Henry Clarke Warren's *Buddhism in Translation* (Harvard Oriental Series). Mr. Warren was one of the great pioneers of Buddhist studies in the Occident.

[14] It chanced that Jove (as the story goes), while warmed with wine, put care aside and bandied good-humored jests with Juno in an idle hour. "I maintain," said he, "that your pleasure in love is greater than that which we [the male gods] enjoy." She held the opposite view. And so they decided to ask the judgment of the wise Tiresias. He knew both sides of love. For once, with a blow of his staff, he had outraged two huge serpents mating in the green forest; and, wonderful to relate, from man he was changed into a woman, and in that form spent seven years. In the eighth year he saw the same serpents again and said: "Since in striking you there is such magic power as to change the nature of the giver of the blow, now will I strike you once again." So saying, he struck the serpents, and his former state was restored, and he became as he had been born. He, therefore, being asked to arbitrate the playful dispute of the gods, took sides with Jove. Saturnia [Juno], they said, grieved more deeply than she should and than the issue warranted, and condemned the arbitrator to perpetual blindness. But the Almighty Father (for no god may undo what another god has done) in return for his loss of sight gave Tiresias the power to know the future, lightening the penalty by the honor" (*Metamorphoses,* III, 318–338, translated by Frank J. Miller in the Loeb Classical Library). [15] Remember me, who am La Pia; Siena made me, Maremma unmade me.

309. From St. Augustine's *Confessions* again. The collocation of these two representatives of eastern and western asceticism, as the culmination of this part of the poem, is not an accident.

V. WHAT THE THUNDER SAID

In the first part of Part V three themes are employed: the journey to Emmaus, the approach to the Chapel Perilous (see Miss Weston's book) and the present decay of eastern Europe.

357. This is *Turdus aonalaschkae pallasii,* the hermit-thrush which I have heard in Quebec Province. Chapman says (*Handbook of Birds of Eastern North America*) "it is most at home in secluded woodland and thickety retreats. . . . Its notes are not remarkable for variety or volume, but in purity and sweetness of tone and exquisite modulation they are unequalled." Its "water-dripping song" is justly celebrated.

360. The following lines were stimulated by the account of one of the Antarctic expeditions (I forget which, but I think one of Shackleton's); it was related that the party of explorers, at the extremity of their strength, had the constant delusion that there was *one more member* than could actually be counted.

366–77. Cf. Hermann Hesse, *Blick ins Chaos:* "Schon ist halb Europa, schon ist zumindest der halbe Osten Europas auf dem Wege Chaos, fährt betrunken im heiligem Wahn am Abgrund entlang und singt dazu, singt betrunken und hymnisch wie Dmitri Karamasoff sang. Ueber diese Lieder lacht der Bürger beleidigt, der Heilige und Seher hört sie mit Tränen."[16]

402. "Data, dayadhvam, damyata" (Give, sympathise, control). The fable of the meaning of the Thunder is found in the *Brihadaranyaka—Upanishad,* 5, 1. A translation is found in Deussen's *Sechzig Upanishads des Veda,* p. 489.

408. Cf. Webster, *The White Devil,* V, vi:

> ". . . they'll remarry
> Ere the worm pierce your winding-sheet, ere the spider
> Make a thin curtain for your epitaphs."

412. Cf. *Inferno,* XXXIII, 46:

> "ed io sentii chiavar l'uscio di sotto
> all'orribile torre."[17]

Also F. H. Bradley, *Appearance and Reality,* p. 346.
"My external sensations are no less private to myself than are my thoughts or my feelings. In either case my experience falls within my own circle, a circle closed on the outside; and, with all its elements alike, every sphere is opaque to the others which surround it. . . . In brief, regarded as an existence which appears in a soul, the whole world for each is peculiar and private to that soul."

425. V. Weston: *From Ritual to Romance;* chapter on the Fisher King.

428. V. *Purgatorio,* XXVI, 148.

> " 'Ara vos prec per aquella valor
> 'que vos guida al som de l'escalina,
> 'sovegna vos a temps dê ma dolor.'
> Poi s'ascose nel foco che gli affina."[18]

429. V. *Pervigilium Veneris.* Cf. Philomela in Parts II and III.

430. V. Gerard de Nerval, Sonnet *El Desdichado.*

432. V. Kyd's *Spanish Tragedy.*

434. Shantih. Repeated as here, a formal ending to an Upanishad. "The Peace which passeth understanding" is our equivalent to this word.

[16] Already half Europe, at least half of Eastern Europe, is on the way to chaos, driving drunken in sacred folly along the edge of the abyss and, drunken, singing hymnlike songs as Dmitri Karamazov sang. Offended by these songs the burgher laughs, while the saint and seer listen to them with tears" (translated by Agnes Eisenberger). [17] And below I heard the outlet of the horrible tower locked up. [18] Now I pray you that goodness that guides you to the top of the stairs, be mindful at times of my pain. Then he hid him in the fire that refines them.

COMMENTARY

"The Waste Land" is the most famous and influential English poem of our time, the most elaborate and highly wrought, and the most ambitious in its scope, for its subject is nothing less than the nature of modern life, which it represents as the ground of personal desperation. There is no question but that it is a difficult poem. As such, it has engaged the study of many scholars and critics. Their work, and the passage of time, which to some extent domesticates all that is strange and unapproachable in art, have considerably reduced the resistance which "The Waste Land" offered to our understanding when it first appeared in 1922. But it still remains difficult, it still demands a more than usual effort of comprehension. It requires a knowledge of its conventions and assumptions and a degree of familiarity with the recondite lore to which it refers.

The difficulty of the poem and the necessity of dealing with it in a rather special way were recognized by the poet himself. After its first publication, Eliot —perhaps with some irony—provided a series of notes to help set the reader on the right path. These notes appear at the end of the poem.

Yet acquaintance with "The Waste Land" is best begun, not with the confrontation of any of the poem's manifest difficulties, but rather with a response to that element of the poem which is not at all difficult to appreciate, its music. "The Waste Land" is a poem in which the voice plays a definitive part. This is not to underestimate the importance of its visual imagery, but if we can speak of the order in which our impressions of the poem are gained it is its voice—or voices—that we are soonest aware of. Our first experience of "The Waste Land" should be that of hearing it, whether by listening to a recorded reading or by saying it aloud, and quite without any special effort to discover the precise significance of what we hear.

This is not an evasion of what the poem communicates but a first happy step toward it, and the poet himself has given us ground for believing that it is the right first step to take. In one of his later critical essays, "The Social Function of Poetry," Eliot speaks of his pleasure in reading poems in a language he does not know well, so that he is more aware of the sound of the poem than of its exact meanings; and in another essay, "The Music of Poetry," he tells us that when he composes a poem what often comes first to his mind is a certain rhythm or tune which later, as it were, acquires words. The first experience of "The Waste Land" might well be likened to an experience of actual music—what we hear has meaning for us (although not in a denotative way), we know that the meaning of one passage or movement is different from that of another, we perhaps find one *more* meaningful than another, and yet we cannot say *what* the meaning is. If a particular piece of music initially seems difficult to "follow" or "understand," greater familiarity will lead us to a sense of more thorough comprehension. A reader will have much the same experience of "The Waste Land" if he merely listens to it, without questioning the intention of any one line, or figure of speech, or allusion.

This is by no means to say that close study of the poem is not profitable. The opposite is true. But studious reading should come only after one has responded to the poem in those of its elements—they are many—that are to be apprehended readily. My sense that this is so has led me to decide not to supplement the poet's own notes with explicatory footnotes such as are provided for other poems in this book. (An exception is made of phrases and passages in foreign languages, which have been translated.)

And it is well to know from the outset that even when all the details of the poem will eventually have been mastered, when the recondite references are understood, and all the subtle interrelations of the pattern are traced, the poem still will not be mastered: it will always have some measure of mystery; it will hold back from us some secret of its existence. This element of mystery or secrecy—as I have said of other poems less difficult than this—is not a negative but a positive quality of "The Waste Land" and of our response to it. The poem's continued resistance to our best efforts of comprehension is a sign of its vitality and an invitation to our continued interest.

If we are introduced to "The Waste Land" by listening to it, inevitably we are struck by the large variety of its vocal modes, its many different kinds of utterance—we hear speech that is sometimes grave and simple, sometimes lyric and tender, sometimes hysterical, sometimes toneless, sometimes querulous, sometimes awed; and the utterance may be song, or exhortation, or prayer. From whom do these various utterances come? The answer—or at least a first answer—is simple enough. The poem is largely dramatic in form, in the sense that it is not one voice that is heard but many voices, of many persons or characters, some of whom are in relation to one another. It is confusing that some of these utterances are set off by quotation marks and some are not. We are inclined to suppose that the passages that are not punctuated in this way are spoken by the poet himself. But we soon perceive that this is not possible, that of the several speakers in such passages the poet himself is only one and that although now and then he speaks in a manner which does seem to refer to his actual personal existence and emotions—as, for example, in the opening lines and in the passage about the Hyacinth garden—his voice is often merely that of a narrator or of a puppet-master introducing his characters. And at all times the voice of the poet is likely to change without warning into the voice of someone else.

And even our sense that we have now and then heard the poet speak in his own person is challenged by Eliot's note (to line 218) about Tiresias, who, we are told, "although a mere spectator and not indeed a 'character,' is yet a most important personage, uniting all the rest. . . . What Tiresias *sees,* in fact, is the whole substance of the poem." But Tiresias does not see as other men see—this most famous of the ancient Greek seers is blind. Of his legend the note tells us only the circumstances of his having for a time been transformed into a woman, and of how he came to be blind and a prophet; Eliot relies on the reader to remember his role in the *Odyssey* (Odysseus descends into Hades to consult his prophetic wisdom) and in two of Sophocles' plays, *Antigone,* which is about the burial of the dead, and *Oedipus Rex* (*Drama,* pages 1 ff.), in which Thebes is a land made waste, deprived of fertility of every kind. No human figure in Greek literature was regarded with as much awed respect as Tiresias, and his presence in the poem gives rise to large conceptions—of the distant past which in some form is still alive in the present; of the future which, by Tiresias' fore-knowledge, also exists in the present; of the dark powers in control of human life which are inaccessible to human reason although not to the prophetic mind. If the poem is difficult, if its matter is often inscrutable, if its order is not in accord with the expectations of the ordinary human mind, this is because its "whole substance" is contained in the mind of Tiresias.

Tiresias does not identify himself until the third section of the poem, but the theme of ancient prophecy has been announced well before that, and, in fact, before the poem actually begins—in the epigraph, which refers to the Sibyl of Cumae, one of the most famous of the ancient prophetesses. The epigraph is integral to the poem and a summary of its import. The great Sibyl hung up for show in a cage epitomizes the idea of degeneration and deterioration which informs "The Waste Land," just as the horror of her fate epitomizes its chief emotion—the dread of a life that is no life, that is a life-in-death. And no less significant is the nature of the person who tells of having seen the Sibyl in her cage. He is Trimalchio, one of the characters of Petronius' great novel of Roman life in the time of Nero, *The Satyricon*. Trimalchio is a millionaire, ignorant, ostentatious, boastful. His ascendancy in contrast to the degradation of the once great Sibyl points to another leading theme of "The Waste Land," that in modern life vulgarity has triumphed over the ancient pieties.

These pieties are religious, but of no specific creed. Eliot was later to become a devout Christian of the Anglican communion, and certain elements of "The Waste Land" make this not surprising. But at the time of writing the poem he had not made his religious decision. "The Waste Land" draws upon the traditions of Jewish, Christian, and Indian religion, especially as these faiths conceive of despair and the possibility of salvation. Christianity is indeed salient, but Buddhism is of almost equal authority, and for the climax of the poem Eliot uses a Brahmanic devotional text.[1] Even more important than the part played by the highly developed religions is that of primitive religion. Eliot makes this plain in the first and most general of his notes in which he speaks of his indebtedness to Jessie Weston's book, *From Ritual to Romance,* and to the more famous and comprehensive work of Sir James Frazer, *The Golden Bough* (see page 112).

The concerns of primitive religion were not spiritual, in our meaning of the word, but utilitarian. The purpose of ritual was to secure the good will of a deity who was in control of one or another of the material circumstances of life; the fertility of the earth, upon which human life depends, was a matter of especial religious anxiety. The highly developed religions preserve the vestiges of this concern in their language about the spiritual life—religion as we know it has much to say about hunger and thirst, about water and green pastures, about bread and wine. But what is now metaphorical was once literal. The elaborate rituals to which Miss Weston and Frazer refer had once the practical intention of insuring the success of the crops and the fecundity of the flocks and herds, and also, what is of central importance in "The Waste Land," human fertility.

To many men, from the nineteenth century on, this primitive relation of human beings to the processes of nature has come to seem increasingly desirable, in itself a source of life. They feel that the rational processes of the intellect, which have grown in authority in recent centuries, have resulted in a dryness and deadness of feeling, in a loss of the vital power of the primitive imagination.

[1] In his first version of the note on the word with which the poem closes, the thrice-repeated "Shantih," Eliot could write, " 'The Peace which passeth understanding' is a feeble translation of the content of this word."

Of the poems commented on in this volume, "The Waste Land" has its closest historical affinity with "Dover Beach"—what Eliot says through complex dramatic symbolism, Arnold says in a single explicit utterance. When Arnold speaks of the ebbing of the sea of faith, he has in mind not primarily faith in a doctrinal religion but "animal faith," the sense that the energies of men are continuous with and supported by the energies of the world, which are in some way divine. It is true that the conceptions of doctrinal religion are always in the offing of "The Waste Land," but Eliot too is primarily concerned with the cultural circumstances that are the cause—and the result—of man's loss of belief in his old organic relation to the world. This connection is made by the imagination rather than by the intellect and provides a basis for the ability to experience life immediately and intensely, and, as we say, with meaning.

Miss Weston's book deals with the legend of the Holy Grail, the subject of numerous medieval romances in the cycle of stories about the Arthurian knights. The Grail itself was the cup in which the blood of Christ was received at the Crucifixion; the bleeding lance that figures in the story is the weapon that wounded Christ upon the Cross. The legend tells of a Fisher King—one of the symbols of Christ is a fish—who has received a wound that will not heal, by which he has been made sexually impotent. His condition has its effect upon the land over which he rules, so that it has lost all its fertility and lies sere and waste. The cure of the King and the consequent redemption of the land depend upon the right action of a perfect knight, usually Parsifal, who, led to the Waste Land by a vision of the Grail, which is in the possession of the King, must overcome certain trials of temptation and then ask certain questions about the Grail and the Lance which he beholds carried in ceremonial procession. We can scarcely fail to see that the Christian elements of the story are combined with those that are manifestly pagan, and it is Miss Weston's theory that the story is derived from the vegetation mysteries of India, and that the Cup and the Lance were originally sexual symbols in these rituals. The Wounded King brings the story into obvious connection with the many ancient stories of young men or young gods dying, often of a wound that is sexual in nature, and of being restored to life. Such stories formed the basis of the cults which Frazer deals with in *The Golden Bough*. To these ritual myths, many of which associate the dying and resurrected god with a tree and some of which represent him as being hanged on a tree, the story of the crucified and resurrected Christ has its manifest analogy.

Although Miss Weston's speculations on the origins of the Grail cycle were so important in the conception of Eliot's poem, the specific elements of the story are by no means obvious. The Fisher King is referred to in a shadowy way in line 189, and it would seem that in Part V the long passage beginning with line 331 refers to Parsifal's journey through the Waste Land to the so-called Chapel Perilous that figures in the story (the "empty chapel" of line 389). But Parsifal himself appears only once and by rather recondite reference (see line 202 and Eliot's note on it), and there is no overt reference to the Grail or the Lance. The Waste Land itself appears chiefly as an emotional condition, especially as this is demonstrated by the failure of love which most of the characters of the poem experience and acknowledge.

The theme of sexual failure is proposed first, and rather gently, in the opening of Part I, "The Burial of the Dead," in the speech of the aristocratic

German lady who can recall the joy of her girlhood but whose maturity or middle age is exiled and solitary. The song of the sailor quoted from the first act of Wagner's *Tristan and Isolde,* fresh, gay, and impudent, suggests the love-passion which the opera represents and celebrates, but it is echoed by the deathly negation of the line from the last act of the opera, which speaks of the vacant desolate sea. The poignant words spoken by the "hyacinth girl" are addressed to a lover who does not—cannot—respond, being "neither / Living nor dead." In Part II, "A Game of Chess," the failure of love is presented dramatically, almost sensationally, first in the scene of luxurious and elegant life, then in the scene, in a pub, of lower-class life; in both instances the failure of love has led to despair and boredom. Part III, "The Fire Sermon," is largely given over to the representation of loveless love-making, and also of homosexuality. The description of the Thames on a holiday makes use of the refrain from Spenser's "Prothalamion," in which the poet celebrates his approaching marriage and the beauty of the idea of married love; its presence here is obviously ironic—it brings to mind the deterioration both of the ideal of love and of the beauty of the river which was invoked by the poet in the famous refrain of his marriage song. Also serving the purpose of irony is the reference to Elizabeth and Leicester on the royal barge, symbolic of a vanished age of energy and glory; the irony is compounded by the unfulfilled and tragic sexual relation of the two great personages. The concluding passage, a quotation from *The Confessions of St. Augustine,* refers to the saint's unregenerate days and his conversion, and by implication—in reference to "Carthage" and "burning"—to the funeral pyre of Dido, the legendary queen of Carthage who slew herself when she was deserted by Aeneas.

With Part III the direct representation of sexual defeat ends. The brief fourth part, "Death by Water," speaks perhaps not only of death but of baptism and regeneration. Throughout the poem, water figures as the life-giving element, fire as the destructive element. Phlebas, the drowned Phoenician sailor, is commemorated in a brief elegy which may be intended to bring to mind the cool, sad commemorative verses of the *Greek Anthology,* perhaps also the drowning of Lycidas and the elegist's affirmation (see page 21) that Lycidas is not dead, "Sunk though he be beneath the watery floor," for he is "mounted high, / Through the dear might of Him that walked the waves." There is also striking reference to *The Tempest* in the second and third parts of the poem; its themes of the rightful lord dispossessed and restored, of rescue from the sea, of repentance, purging, and reconciliation, are much to the poem's purpose.

The scene of Part V is an actual waste land, stony and sun-parched, and since Eliot tells us in his note that the journey of the two disciples to Emmaus is one of the themes of the beginning of this part, we may bring to the aid of our visual imagination what we know of the harsh landscape of Palestine. ". . . The third who walks always beside you," may well be the resurrected Jesus, who (as the story is told in Chapter 24 of The Gospel According to St. Luke) joined the two disciples on the road and spoke with them without being recognized until he identified himself. The "murmur of maternal lamentation" may be the mourning of Mary but more likely it refers to the prophecy of catastrophe that Jesus utters in Chapter 23 of Luke, which tells of his condemnation and crucifixion: "And there followed him a great company of people, and of women, which also bewailed and lamented him. But Jesus turning unto them said, Daughters of Jerusalem, weep not for me, but weep for yourselves and for your children. For, behold, the days are coming, in which they shall say, Blessed are the barren, and the wombs that never bare, and the paps which never gave suck. Then shall they begin to say to the mountains, Fall on us; and to the hills, Cover us." It is a vision which manifestly accords with the poet's vision of the cultural and political decay of Europe, which in his notes he documents by a quotation from Hermann Hesse.

In the Vedic text known as the *Brihadaranyaka Upanishad,* the god Pragapati speaks in the voice of the thunder, uttering three times the sound "Da," the initial syllable of the Sanskrit words "*Datta, Dayadhvam, Damyata,*" which mean, as Eliot's note tells us, "give, sympathise, control." He who has given, sympathized, and controlled may achieve regeneration, a new birth of the spirit. With the utterances of the thunder, which promises the relief and renewal of fertilizing rain, the sexual theme comes again to the fore. The lines following *Datta* and *Dayadhvam* are ambiguous, they may or may not refer to sexual conduct. But those following *Damyata* are plain enough—the control that is meant is not, as we might at first expect, self-control, but the lover's beneficent control of his beloved in the act of love. Perhaps nothing in the poem is more directly affecting than the lines that begin "The sea was calm," with its perhaps conscious reminiscence of the opening lines of Matthew Arnold's "Dover Beach" (see page 86), and that go on: "your heart would have responded / Gaily, when invited, beating obedient / To controlling hands"; the comparison of the beloved's heart to a boat well managed is consummated in the word "beating," which applies not only to the action of the heart but to the progress of a boat by tacking into the wind. The heart that would have responded gaily when invited had not been invited, and that word "gaily" emerges from the passage with a terrible pathos, suggesting how simple —how "human," as we say—is the quality of life that this elaborate poem mourns for.

The last passage of the poem, after a recapitulating reference to the Fisher King, proceeds to the conscious incoherence of a desperate mind. But even in its desperation it cannot refrain from repeating the thunder's three words of regeneration and from uttering, as a "formal ending," the word that means "The Peace which passeth understanding."

Perhaps something should be said about the quotations, direct or indirect, that figure so prominently in "The Waste Land." Some readers are offended by them and regard their presence as an affectation, even a pedantry. A sympathetic view might take them as additional "voices" that haunt the poem, or the poet's mind in his making of the poem.

NEITHER OUT FAR NOR IN DEEP

ROBERT FROST

1874–1963

The people along the sand
All turn and look one way.
They turn their back on the land.
They look at the sea all day.

As long as it takes to pass 5
A ship keeps raising its hull;
The wetter ground like glass
Reflects a standing gull.

The land may vary more;
But wherever the truth may be— 10
The water comes ashore,
And the people look at the sea.

They cannot look out far.
They cannot look in deep.
But when was that ever a bar 15
To any watch they keep?

COMMENTARY

The power and charm of this poem lie in the discrepancy between, on the one hand, its tone and ostensible subject, and, on the other hand, its actual subject. The tone can be described as minimal, flat, even pinched, and perhaps as fatigued. The ostensible subject, an observation of the behavior of people at the seashore, is scarcely of great consequence and might even be thought rather trifling. The actual subject is the response of mankind to the empty immensity of the universe.

The discrepancy becomes manifest in the last line of the poem. Up to that point what "the people" do by the seashore is denoted by the word "look." This is perhaps our most commonplace and neutral verb for the act of seeing. It is the verb that least *dignifies* the act, for in itself it carries no implication of purpose or of any intensity, as do, for example, such verbs as "gaze," "view," "stare," or even "see." In everyday speech it is often linked with the minimizing or depreciating word "just"—"I'm just looking," or "I'm just looking at . . ." Of course, linguistic circumstances can endow the word with one or another degree of force. Used by itself in the imperative—"Look!"—it is intense indeed. To "look for" something is very purposeful; but to "look at" something may or may not convey the idea of intention, and it may even, as I have suggested, indicate an entire lack of purpose, a mere idleness, as it seems to do in the first stanza of the poem.

Yet as the word is reiterated through the poem, it grows in meaning and force. It is used five times, and the mere repetition is somehow impressive, as if the poet were obsessed by the idea of mere looking. The first time it is used, "the people" simply "look one way"—we are not even told that they are looking *at* anything. There is a degree of intensity implied by the phrase, "They look at the sea all day," but the looking is still idle enough. By the third stanza, however, the word becomes very intense indeed. This is partly because the looking is suddenly—startlingly—associated with a very large question, "Wherever the truth may be," and partly because "the people" seem forever fixed in their looking: the last two lines of the stanza seem to say that just as it is a fact of nature that the water comes ashore and will come forever, so it is a fact of nature that "the people" look at the sea and will look forever. The last two uses of the word, in the last stanza, deny or limit the effectuality of the looking—

> They cannot look out far,
> They cannot look in deep—

but by doing so they suggest that the looking, which first seemed idle and then seemed almost a trance, was after all not without some purpose. And this suggestion is fully and forcefully confirmed in the concluding two lines:

> They cannot look out far.
> They cannot look in deep.
> But when was that ever a bar
> To any watch they keep?

The word "look" has suddenly yielded to the "watch they keep"—the minimal word is replaced, and explained, by a phrase of great dignity and richness of meaning. It implies a strong intention, and the activity of the mind as well as of the eye. And the activity of the heart as well as of the mind. It is a phrase that may suggest the idea of danger, or of hope, or of solicitude, or of loyalty. What is more, it has an archaic character; it is not a phrase that we use casually or lightly in ordinary speech, and its effect in the poem, the language of which is in general colloquial and flat, is solemn and ceremonial. The people who keep the watch are doing what soldiers do, warders of the coast, or what the shepherds at Bethlehem did. They await some significant event.

The small observation which is the poem's ostensible subject first presents itself to our minds as a speculation in psychology or aesthetics. If the land varies more than the sea and is therefore presumably more interesting, why do the people at the shore turn their backs upon the land to look at the sea? Why do the solitary objects that break the monotony of the sea—the nearing ship, the gull reflected in the wet sand—hold the attention so firmly? But the psychological or aesthetic speculation gives place to another of a more momentous kind. Partly because of the word "truth" in the third stanza, but not only because of that, we come to know that "the people" are looking, and waiting, for *something*. We are not told what they hope to descry on the vacant immensity of the sea, and they themselves seem not to know, but we do not doubt that the object of their silent expectation is of transcendent importance.

We are often told that poetry deals with the particular and the concrete, that this is its very essence. If this is so, how shall we account for the peculiar effectiveness of the word "people"? Surely it is the most general and abstract word possible, yet it has, as used here, a strange pathos. Is it because its generality proposes to us the ultimate generality of mankind: all people, all over the world, at all times ("When was that *ever* a bar . . .?")? For some readers, it will have a reminiscence of the effect of naive simplicity with which the word is used in the Bible, as, for example, "Where there is no vision, the people perish." The word imputes a kind of humility: "the people" all "look at the sea" at the behest of something instinctual or innate, not at the behest of intellectual curiosity; there is something dumb, something of the animal, in the accord with which they turn their gaze in the one direction and keep it there. This imputation of an animal-like humility before the power of instinct is anything but contemptuous; on the contrary, it is tender. And the quiet anonymity which is suggested by the phrase "the people" is matched by the unnamedness of the thing they watch for.

The poem does not affirm that what is watched for will appear. It says no more than that it is the nature of "the people" to keep watch, whether or not there is anything to appear.

MY FATHER MOVED THROUGH DOOMS OF LOVE

E. E. CUMMINGS
1894–1962

my father moved through dooms of love
through sames of am through haves of give,
singing each morning out of each night
my father moved through depths of height

this motionless forgetful where 5
turned at his glance to shining here;
that if (so timid air is firm)
under his eyes would stir and squirm

newly as from unburied which
floats the first who, his april touch 10
drove sleeping selves to swarm their fates
woke dreamers to their ghostly roots

and should some why completely weep
my father's fingers brought her sleep:
vainly no smallest voice might cry 15
for he could feel the mountains grow.

Lifting the valleys of the sea
my father moved through griefs of joy;
praising a forehead called the moon
singing desire into begin 20

joy was his song and joy so pure
a heart of star by him could steer

and pure so now and now so yes
the wrists of twilight would rejoice

keen as midsummer's keen beyond 25
conceiving mind of sun will stand,
so strictly (over utmost him
so hugely) stood my father's dream

his flesh was flesh his blood was blood:
no hungry man but wished him food; 30
No cripple wouldn't creep one mile
uphill to only see him smile.

Scorning the pomp of must and shall
my father moved through dooms of feel;
his anger was as right as rain 35
his pity was as green as grain

septembering arms of year extend
less humbly wealth to foe and friend
than he to foolish and to wise
offered immeasurable is 40

proudly and (by octobering flame
beckoned) as earth will downward climb,
so naked for immortal work
his shoulders marched against the dark

his sorrow was as true as bread: 45
no liar looked him in the head;
if every friend became his foe
he'd laugh and build a world with snow.

My father moved through theys of we,
singing each new leaf out of each tree 50
(and every child was sure that spring
danced when she heard my father sing)

then let men kill which cannot share,
let blood and flesh be mud and mire,
scheming imagine, passion willed, 55
freedom a drug that's bought and sold

giving to steal and cruel kind,
a heart to fear, to doubt a mind,
to differ a disease of same,
conform the pinnacle of am 60

though dull were all we taste as bright,
bitter all utterly things sweet,
maggoty minus and dumb death
all we inherit, all bequeath

and nothing quite so least as truth 65
—i say though hate were why men breathe—
because my father lived his soul
love is the whole and more than all

COMMENTARY

In our elementary schooling we are—or used to be—taught the "parts of speech" and how to distinguish one from another, only to discover that they all incline to be interchangeable, their nature being protean, and determined not by definition but by use. *Walk* is a verb until we take a walk, when it is a noun. *Clear* is an adjective until we clear the snow from the sidewalk, when it is a verb. *Further* is an adverb, but we further our sense of how English works when we confront the fact that nothing requires this word to be permanently adverbial. *Beyond* is a mere preposition, but we have no trouble in understanding that in The Great Beyond it arises to the substantive status of a noun.

The tendency to this kind of interchange among the parts of speech is very strong in English and seems to accelerate. But it does not make its way without resistance; we respond to some instances of it with more dubiety or surprise than we do to others. *Yonder* is an adjective—"Yonder peasant, who is he?"—or an adverb—"You can easily find out by walking yonder a way and asking him." And it can, under light duress, be made to serve as a noun; as in the Air Force song "The Wild Blue Yonder." But the phrase startles us a little; we recognize it as a more or less successful effort to manipulate the language in an interesting—a poetic—way, and as such we accept it, but it is not possible that any of us will make the same use of the word in ordinary speech. We are more startled, and likely to be pleased, when Gerard Manley Hopkins exclaims over a falcon in flight, "the achieve of, the mastery of the thing!" The phrase has much more energy and verve than if it had read "the achievement of, the mastery of the thing!" Yet there is but little chance that *achieve* will replace *achievement* in common usage.

A considerable part of the interest of E. E. Cummings' poem comes from our surprise over its use of parts of speech in ways that we are not accustomed to and are scarcely likely to adopt, although we can understand the mode of their use if we make the effort to do so. To say of the father that he moved "through sames of am" is to speak of the integrity of his being; he was always, as we say, himself. "Haves of give" recalls the statement of Jesus that "it is more blessed to give than to receive"; it says that for the father this was true in the most literal sense possible: for him to give was to have. His relationship to people is exemplified by the effect he has on three of them, a where, an if, and a why—the "motionless forgetful where" who turned at the father's glance "to shining here" is, we may suppose, a young man who, until touched into activity, had been lost in a passive self-absorption, not easily to be reached by actuality, not even his own, since that had not yet come into being. The "if (so timid . . .)" would seem to be another young man, distrustful of life and of his own powers, who under the father's vivifying influence undergoes metamorphosis and is transformed from a nonpersonal being, a "which," into an actual personal self, a "who," like a butterfly emerging from its chrysalis. The weeping "why" of the next stanza is manifestly a woman or a girl whose being, at the moment, is defined by her bewilderment or resentment at some pain inflicted upon her.

"Most poetry," a critic has said, "is on commonplace themes, and the freshness, what the poet supplies, is in the language." Cummings' theme may be said to be commonplace enough—how often have we heard the praise of integrity and sincerity, how often have we been asked to be aware of the beneficent power of sympathy and unselfishness! Often enough, surely, to make the virtuous qualities that are praised seem as dull, abstract, and imprecise as the words that are used to denote them. But when the old words are translated in ways that startle us and that require some little effort of energy on our part to perceive the equivalence, the virtues being praised shed their commonplaceness and shine with the freshness of invention.

Yet the novelty of Cummings' language cannot claim all the credit for the poem's engagingness, which in some part comes from the poet's conception of the best kind of goodness, that which is spontaneous, natural, and arises from and moves toward joy. The father is represented as being virtuous rather than moral or ethical, which suggest a state of being arrived at by intention and effort. His virtue is to be understood in the old sense of the word, which meant power—he has a natural power of goodness that makes its effect less through what he does than through what he is. And this power is represented as being analogous with the beneficent workings of Nature; the instances and images that Cummings finds appropriate to his father, who was a Unitarian clergyman, might serve as well for some pagan fertility god. The poet touches upon the existence of his father in each season of the cycle of the year, but he makes spring his characteristic time, his characteristic action being, in Lucretius' phrase, to bring living things into the borders of light.

In Memory of SIGMUND FREUD[1] (d. Sept. 1939)

W. H. AUDEN

1907–

(1940)

When there are so many we shall have to mourn,
When grief has been made so public, and exposed
To the critique of a whole epoch
The frailty of our conscience and anguish,

Of whom shall we speak? For every day they die 5
Among us, those who were doing us some good,
And knew it was never enough but
Hoped to improve a little by living.

Such was this doctor: still at eighty he wished
To think of our life, from whose unruliness 10
So many plausible young futures
With threats or flattery ask obedience.

But his wish was denied him; he closed his eyes
Upon that last picture common to us all,
Of problems like relatives standing 15
Puzzled and jealous about our dying.

For about him at the very end were still
Those he had studied, the nervous and the nights,

[1] Sigmund Freud (1856–1939) was the originator of psychoanalysis. As a Jew living in Austria, he was forced to flee the Nazis in 1938. He went to London, where he remained until he died.

And shades that still waited to enter
The bright circle of his recognition 20

Turned elsewhere with their disappointment as he
Was taken away from his old interest
To go back to the earth in London,
An important Jew who died in exile.

Only Hate was happy, hoping to augment 25
His practice now, and his shabby clientèle
Who think they can be cured by killing
And covering the gardens with ashes.

They are still alive but in a world he changed
Simply by looking back with no false regrets; 30
All that he did was to remember
Like the old and be honest like children.

He wasn't clever at all: he merely told
The unhappy Present to recite the Past
Like a poetry lesson till sooner 35
Or later it faltered at the line where

Long ago the accusations had begun,
And suddenly knew by whom it had been judged,
How rich life had been and how silly,
And was life-forgiven and most humble. 40

Able to approach the Future as a friend
Without a wardrobe of excuses, without
A set mask of rectitude or an
Embarrassing over-familiar gesture.

No wonder the ancient cultures of conceit 45
In his technique of unsettlement foresaw
The fall of princes, the collapse of
Their lucrative patterns of frustration.

If he succeeded, why, the Generalised Life
Would become impossible, the monolith 50
Of State be broken and prevented
The co-operation of avengers.

Of course they called on God: but he went his way,
Down among the Lost People like Dante, down
To the stinking fosse[2] where the injured 55
Lead the ugly life of the rejected.

And showed us what evil is: not as we thought
Deeds that must be punished, but our lack of faith,
Our dishonest mood of denial,
The concupiscence of the oppressor. 60

And if something of the autocratic pose,
The paternal strictness he distrusted, still
Clung to his utterance and features,
It was a protective imitation

For one who lived among enemies so long; 65
If often he was wrong and at times absurd,
To us he is no more a person
Now but a whole climate of opinion,

Under whom we conduct our differing lives:
Like weather he can only hinder or help, 70
The proud can still be proud but find it
A little harder, and the tyrant tries

To make him do but doesn't care for him much.
He quietly surrounds all our habits of growth;
He extends, till the tired in even 75
The remotest most miserable duchy

Have felt the change in their bones and are cheered,
And the child unlucky in his little State,
Some hearth where freedom is excluded,
A hive whose honey is fear and worry, 80

Feels calmer now and somehow assured of escape;
While as they lie in the grass of our neglect,
So many long-forgotten objects
Revealed by his undiscouraged shining

[2] Ditch. There are several malodorous ditches full of lost souls in Dante's representation of Hell, the *Inferno*.

Are returned to us and made precious again; 85
Games we had thought we must drop as we grew up,
Little noises we dared not laugh at,
Faces we made when no one was looking.

But he wishes us more than this: to be free
Is often to be lonely; he would unite 90
The unequal moieties fractured
By our own well-meaning sense of justice.

Would restore to the larger the wit and will
The smaller possesses but can only use
For arid disputes, would give back to 95
The son the mother's richness of feeling.

But he would have us remember most of all
To be enthusiastic over the night
Not only for the sense of wonder
It alone has to offer, but also 100

Because it needs our love: for with sad eyes
Its delectable creatures look up and beg
Us dumbly to ask them to follow;
They are exiles who long for the future

That lies in our power. They too would rejoice 105
If allowed to serve enlightenment like him,
Even to bear our cry of "Judas,"
As he did and all must bear who serve it.

One rational voice is dumb: over a grave
The household of Impulse mourns one dearly loved. 110
Sad is Eros, builder of cities,
And weeping anarchic Aphrodite.[3]

[3] Eros, the Greek god of love, was the son of Aphrodite, the goddess of beauty and love. Both are symbols of libidinous energy, but Eros is perhaps more often constructive or creative, whereas Aphrodite can be the cause of destruction.

COMMENTARY

Among the first acts of the Nazi party after it came to power in Germany in 1933 was the suppression of the teaching of psychoanalysis in the medical schools and a ceremonial burning of the works of Sigmund Freud. This was in part a response to the fact that the founder of psychoanalysis was a Jew, for one of the axioms of the Nazi ideology was that the Jews were the cause of all the misfortunes of the German people and the source of all that was bad in the Western world. It was also a response to the actual content of psychoanalysis, especially to its theory that many disorders of the personality have a sexual etiology and can be traced to the patient's experience of the family situation in early infancy.

Freud, living in Vienna, was naturally much distressed over the turn of events, but he persuaded himself that the hostility of the Nazis would not come closer home. He was, of course, mistaken—in 1938 Hitler sent his troops into Austria and united that nation with Germany under his rule. Freud was forbidden to carry on his work and he and his family lived under the threat of the concentration camp. Before the invasion actually took place, he had resisted all suggestions that he leave Vienna, and even now he was reluctant to think of leaving the city in which he had lived all but two of his eighty-two years. Eventually, however, the counsels of his friends and colleagues prevailed and he consented to emigrate, but it was only after prolonged negotiations with the Nazi officials and the payment by his friends abroad of a large sum of money in ransom that Freud was permitted to leave Austria and, with his family, was brought to England, a country which he had held in affectionate admiration since boyhood and which now received him with great honor. He settled in London, and, although much enfeebled by the illness which had made existence a torture for many years—cancer of the jaw, necessitating innumerable operations—he resumed his habits of arduous work, seeing patients and pupils and carrying forward the composition of a new book. He died a year later, three weeks after the beginning of the Second World War.

Freud had never concerned himself directly with politics but the therapeutic psychology of which he was the inventor had social and ultimately political implications of great moment. If these had ever been obscure, they became manifest upon the violent Nazi opposition to psychoanalysis and they constitute the informing theme of Auden's commemoration of Freud.

The theory of psychoanalysis is enormously complex, but at its heart is the quite simple idea that the individual human personality is formed, and in all too many instances malformed, by the interaction of the biological impulses or "drives" with the controlling authority of the family, which is continuous with the authority of society and the state. The individual in the course of his development incorporates this authority into his emotional system, in both its conscious and its unconscious parts. If the authority thus internalized is excessively strict—as it may be either because it mirrors the actual repressiveness of the parental control or because the individual for some reason imagines the external authority to be more exigent than it actually is—there will result a malfunction of the instinctual life, inhibiting the healthy development of the personality and causing great emotional pain. The malfunction begins in earliest childhood, though it may not manifest itself until a later time, and Freud's method of therapy is to lead the patient to bring into the light of consciousness the particular circumstances, actual or fancied, that may serve to explain where his emotional life went wrong, why the "internalized authority" is devoted to causing pain. As Auden's poem puts it, Freud

> . . . told
> The unhappy Present to recite the Past
> Like a poetry lesson till sooner
> Or later it faltered at the line where
>
> Long ago the accusations had begun,
> And suddenly knew by whom it had been judged . . .

"Accusations" and "judged" are the crucial words—neurotic suffering may be ascribed to the patient's having instituted in his unconscious mind a juridical process in which the prosecuting attorney accuses too fiercely, the judge condemns too readily and sentences too sternly, and the jailer carries out the imposed punishment too eagerly.

By the time the Nazis banned it in Germany and Austria, psychoanalysis had won a considerable degree of acceptance, but only against a stubborn and often bitter resistance. The physicians who criticized its theory seldom did so in a spirit of disinterested scientific objectivity; they were likely to share the moralizing fervor of the many laymen who denounced it as a threat to society. The therapeutic goal of psychoanalysis is scarcely subversive and nowadays it is even said by some to err in the direction of social conformity, for it undertakes to make it possible for the patient to live in reasonable accord not only with himself but with his society. Yet even from the little that has been said here about the basic theory of psychoanalysis, it will be plain that it is antagonistic to authoritarianism, though not to rational authority. What Auden's poem aptly speaks of as Freud's "technique of unsettlement" cannot really be said to have overtly and explicitly foreseen "the fall of princes," but it nevertheless did bring the very idea of arbitrary rule into question. It is therefore not surprising that it should have incurred the hatred of "the ancient cultures of conceit."

At the present time the judgment on psychoanalysis is divided. Many still regard it uneasily or hostilely, yet it has established itself as part of the substance of modern thought. Its influence is especially strong in the United States, where its premises and conclusions are taken for granted by many who have never read any of the works in which its theory is expounded. For many Freud is indeed

> . . . no more a person
> Now but a whole climate of opinion . . .

Writing not long after Freud's death, Auden naturally made the large public aspects of Freud's thought salient in his commemoration. With totalitarianism in the ascendant, the aspects of psychoanalysis that might well seem of first importance were those that bore upon politics, such as the opposition it offers to "the Generalised Life" and "the monolith / Of State." But the poem does not fail to take account of the effects that the technique of unsettlement may have upon the personal and private life, and not only in situations of extreme pathology, among "the Lost People," "the injured" who "Lead the ugly life of the rejected," but also among those who are not so grossly afflicted and who yet live less freely than they might, immobilizing themselves behind "a set mask of rectitude," having less courage, simplicity, and power of responsive emotion than it is within their capacity to have.

The last quatrain brilliantly expresses the paradoxical nature of Freud's thought. By ancient convention, rationality and impulse are believed to be at hopeless odds with each other. But Freud put his "rational voice" at the service of impulse, seeking its liberation. It may be questioned, however, whether the last two lines, fine as they are, represent Freud's thought with entire accuracy. It is certainly true that Freud was in avowed alliance with "Eros, builder of cities," the love that makes the family, society, and civilization. But nothing in his work affirms the beneficence of "anarchic Aphrodite," the irresistible, heedless love that we call passion.

The poem claims much for the intention of Freud's science, much for its achievement. Yet this large optimism is qualified by the tone in which it is asserted. One may hear a note of reserve in the large positive statements as though the recognition of Freud's purpose and achievement went along with the sense of how much is still to be accomplished for human happiness and with the awareness that any celebration of human advance must be of a muted kind when uttered at the beginning of a war that promises to be long and terrible. The restrained, slightly dry tone is in part an effect of the diction, which is determinedly plain. It is also, and perhaps to an even greater extent, an effect of the stanzaic form, which seems to have been consciously modelled on the so-called Alcaic strophe of Greek and Latin poetry. In this strophe the first two lines are of eleven syllables, the third of nine, the fourth of ten, and Auden conforms quite strictly to the pattern; there are only a very few quite minor departures. Unlike the Alcaic strophe, Auden's form has no set metrical pattern within the fixed number of syllables for each line, nor, indeed, any metrical pattern at all; but the rhythm of each line is controlled and made more or less homogeneous with that of its matching lines by the fixed number of syllables. One has the sense of prose that is always at the point of becoming metrical, or at least markedly cadenced, and always being prevented, falling back to its prose tone. And this effect of an energy continually checked, even if continually asserting itself, is supported by the interplay between the lengths of the lines of which the stanzas consist, the ranging first two lines with which each stanza begins, the sharply curtailed third, the fourth that a little recoups what its predecessor had lost.

FOR THE UNION DEAD

ROBERT LOWELL

1917–

"Relinquunt Omnia Servare Rem Publicam."

The old South Boston Aquarium stands
in a Sahara of snow now. Its broken windows are boarded.
The bronze weathervane cod has lost half its scales.
The airy tanks are dry.

Once my nose crawled like a snail on the glass; 5
my hand tingled
to burst the bubbles
drifting from the noses of the cowed, compliant fish.

My hand draws back. I often sigh still
for the dark downward and vegetating kingdom 10
of the fish and reptile. One morning last March,
I pressed against the new barbed and galvanized

fence on the Boston Common. Behind their cage,
yellow dinosaur steamshovels were grunting
as they cropped up tons of mush and grass 15
to gouge their underworld garage.

Parking spaces luxuriate like civic
sandpiles in the heart of Boston.
A girdle of orange, Puritan-pumpkin colored girders
braces the tingling Statehouse, 20

shaking over the excavations, as it faces Colonel Shaw
and his bell-cheeked Negro infantry

on St. Gaudens' shaking Civil War relief,
propped by a plank splint against the garage's earthquake.

Two months after marching through Boston, 25
half the regiment was dead;
at the dedication,
William James could almost hear the bronze Negroes breathe.

Their monument sticks like a fishbone
in the city's throat. 30
Its Colonel is as lean
as a compass-needle.

He has an angry wrenlike vigilance,
a greyhound's gentle tautness;
he seems to wince at pleasure, 35
and suffocate for privacy.

He is out of bounds now. He rejoices in man's lovely,
peculiar power to choose life and die—
when he leads his black soldiers to death,
he cannot bend his back. 40

On a thousand small town New England greens,
the old white churches hold their air
of sparse, sincere rebellion; frayed flags
quilt the graveyards of the Grand Army of the Republic.

The stone statues of the abstract Union Soldier 45
grow slimmer and younger each year—
wasp-waisted, they doze over muskets
and muse through their sideburns . . .

Shaw's father wanted no monument
except the ditch, 50
where his son's body was thrown
and lost with his "niggers."

The ditch is nearer.
There are no statues for the last war here;
on Boylston Street, a commercial photograph 55
shows Hiroshima boiling

over a Mosler Safe, the "Rock of Ages"
that survived the blast. Space is nearer.
When I crouch to my television set,
the drained faces of Negro school-children rise like balloons. 60

Colonel Shaw
is riding on his bubble,
he waits
for the blessèd break.

The Aquarium is gone. Everywhere, 65
giant finned cars nose forward like fish;
a savage servility
slides by on grease.

COMMENTARY

In 1863, the third year of the Civil War, Governor Andrew of Massachusetts commissioned a new regiment, all of whose rank and file were Negroes although its officers were white men. The formation of the first Negro fighting unit had been undertaken only after considerable hesitation. It was felt by many that the war should not be exclusively a white man's war, that Negro citizens of the North should be allowed to take part in the liberation of their race. In addition to this principled consideration, there was the practical one that the Northern forces were in need of more fighting men. But the antislavery sentiment of the North was by no means unqualified and the considerable feeling against the war and against Negroes had to be taken into account. Such Negroes as might wish to bear arms in the fight against slavery had no military tradition, no one knew how they would perform as soldiers, and it would be a severe blow to the antislavery cause were they not to acquit themselves well.

The event proved that the doubts were quite groundless. Only a few months after it had been formed, the 54th Massachusetts took part in the assault on Fort Wagner, a Confederate stronghold on the South Carolina coast within sight and cannon shot of Fort Sumter; it is said to have been one of the strongest earthworks ever built. The 54th arrived on the field weary and hungry. It had previously given a good account of itself in minor engagements and now the field commander of the Union forces offered the regiment the honor of leading the attack, which its Colonel accepted. It charged the terrible guns and penetrated the outer defences of the fort. Before it was withdrawn an hour later, nearly half its men were killed within the fort or before its walls. The question of Negro soldierliness had been answered forever. "Wagner still defies us," a Union publicist said, "but prejudice is down." Before the end of the war 180,000 Negroes were under arms; President Lincoln said that they tipped the balance in favor of Union victory.

At least one Confederate officer gave the 54th its due measure of praise.

"The Negroes fought gallantly," Lieutenant Iredell Jones wrote after the engagement, "and were headed by as brave a Colonel as ever lived." The Colonel was killed at the beginning of the attack. When he fell from the parapet into the fort, eleven of his men leaped after him and were cut down by the defenders. Although the Confederate burial-parties followed custom and interred the other dead Union officers in separate graves, the Colonel of the 54th was buried in a trench with his men; when, at a later time, an effort was made to recover his body from the common grave, his father forbade it—his community in death with his Negro men, intended as an indignity, could be nothing but an appropriate honor for Colonel Shaw.

Robert Gould Shaw was twenty-five years old when he died. The only son of a wealthy and distinguished Boston family, he had, as the phrase goes, everything to live for; he was later to be remembered as "the blue-eyed child of fortune upon whose youth every divinity had smiled." In 1863 he was serving as captain in the 2nd Massachusetts Regiment, having risen to the rank from private; he had seen action at Cedar Mountain and Antietam. When the 54th Massachusetts was being formed, the Governor offered him its command because of his military record, his personal character, and his accord with the strong and well-known anti-slavery commitment of his parents. Shaw hesitated to undertake the arduous responsibility of the post, in part because he doubted his abilities, in part because he loved the regiment with which he was serving. Indeed, his first decision was to refuse the Governor's invitation, but second thoughts led him to believe that it was his duty to accept; it was he whom Emerson had in mind in writing the once-familiar lines:

> When Duty whispers low, *Thou must,*
> The youth replies, *I can.*

An intelligent and enthusiastic soldier, he won the devotion of his men and trained them thoroughly, to what effect their conduct at Fort Wagner makes plain.

The death of the young Colonel was deeply felt in Boston, and a year after the end of the war a committee was formed to erect a memorial to him. "The monument," it was said, "is intended not only to mark the public gratitude to the fallen hero, who at a critical moment assumed a perilous responsibility, but also to commemorate that great event, wherein he was a leader, by which the title of colored men as citizen-soldiers was fixed beyond recall." It was not, however, until 1897 that the monument was erected on Boston Common and dedicated at exercises held on Memorial Day in the Boston Music Hall. The work of Augustus St. Gaudens, the most notable American sculptor of the period, it is a large bronze stele which depicts in high relief the 54th Massachusetts marching in column, its flags furled, a boy drummer at its head; the young Colonel on a superb charger, his sabre unsheathed, rides beside his men; a symbolic female figure in flight over the column beckons it forward with one arm and holds in the other the palms of glory and the poppies of death. The faces of the men are set in calm, stern determination; their stride is long and vigorous; Shaw on his reined-in, slow-stepping great horse is erect and inflexible; his movelessness at the center of the composition, its fixed and still point, emphasizes the forward-thrusting energy of the marching column. The virtuosity with which a wealth of naturalistic detail is executed does not diminish but rather enhances the heroic aspect of the work.

The demeanor of Robert Lowell's poem about the memorial of his kinsman is significantly unlike that of the monument itself; the salient characteristic of the poem is its air of acknowledged fatigue. The units of utterance are fragmented and small, their movement is never of a forward or an upward kind; the diction is dry and sparse. At only one moment does the voice of the poem move with something like happy energy, at the lines:

> He is out of bounds now. He rejoices in man's lovely,
> peculiar power to choose life and die—

The recollection of Shaw's dying for the liberty that alone makes mere existence into what may rightly be called "life" arouses the tone of the poem from its sad discouragement to a moment of affirmation. A moment only; the dry minimal tone returns, to continue to the end, and we must read the poem as a lament for the death of the monument itself—this memorial has lost its power of awakening memory and "sticks like a fishbone / in the city's throat."

The poem tells us that William James was present at the dedication exercises, but it does not tell us that the famous philosopher was one of the speakers of the occasion. James's sense that he "could almost hear the bronze Negroes breathe" was expressed in the course of the speech he made—in praising St. Gaudens' work he said, "There on foot go the dark outcasts, so true to nature that one can almost hear them breathing as they march." Another passage from the speech finds its way into the poem, which, when it speaks of "a thousand small town New England greens" on which stand "the stone statues of the abstract Union Soldier," echoes a sentence of James's about "the abstract soldier's-monuments . . . reared on every village green." These small particular references that the poem makes to the speech do not comprise the whole of the relation between what Lowell is saying and what James said. So artful a poet as Lowell would not be likely to have read the speech as part of his preparation for writing the poem without being aware of the difference, and the significance of the difference, between the nature of James's utterance and of his own. Of the five speeches that were made on that Memorial Day of 1897, one was called a "report" and three were called "addresses," but James had been designated the "Orator" of the exercises and his speech was listed as an "oration." He had been asked, that is, to speak of Colonel Shaw in a certain way, with elevation and eloquence, to the end of affecting and "inspiring" the audience. He met the demand handsomely, and to the fluency and freedom of James's oration, which are consonant with the qualities of St. Gaudens' relief, the minimal fragmented style of Lowell's poem stands in a contrast that was surely intended.

If the orator of 1897 could speak in a freer and more open voice than the poet of 1963, it was because he spoke from more confidence in the possibility of social virtue than the poet can feel. In his eulogy of Shaw, James first praised his military courage, but went on to call it a courage that was "common and gregarious" and to set above it "another courage," which was Shaw's best glory. "That lonely kind of courage (civic courage as we call it in times of peace) is the kind of valor to which the monuments of nations should most of all be reared, for the survival of the fittest has not bred it into the bone of human beings as it has bred military valor; and of five hundred of us who could storm a battery side by side with others, perhaps not one would be found ready to risk his worldly fortunes all alone in resisting an enthroned abuse." And as James drew to his conclusion, he said, "The republic to which Robert Shaw and a quarter of a million like him were faithful unto death is no republic that can live at ease hereafter on the interest of what they have won. Democracy is still upon trial. The civic genius of our people is its only bulwark, and neither laws nor monuments, neither battleships nor public libraries, nor great newspapers nor booming stocks; neither mechanical invention nor political adroitness, nor churches nor universities . . . can save us from degeneration if the inner mystery is lost."

The orator was not wholly without apprehension about the outcome of the trial of democracy, but he could be of good cheer, as the poet cannot be. In Lowell's view, the "mystery" is already lost. His commemoration of a memorial of the struggle to free some men from the servile condition imposed upon them ends with the perception of the "savage servility" which has become the general condition, freely chosen. Of this the symbol is the "giant finned cars"; the "underworld garage" that is being constructed for them makes the circumstance that beleaguers and shakes the monument. Memory, or faith, has so far failed that "there are no statues for the last war here," only the inglorious memorial of the "commercial photograph" of a safe that survived the atomic bombing of Hiroshima. "The drained faces of Negro school-children" belie the promise that might once have been seen in the firm gaze of Colonel Shaw's "bell-cheeked Negro infantry."

The bitter sadness over the decline of public life from a better state in a former time—it is one of poetry's ancient sadnesses—begins with the evocation of the poet's own lost past. And the Aquarium of his childhood, now dismantled and forlorn, is the source, as it were, of an extended series of associations, having chiefly to do with fish, which makes a thematic line easy to trace but hard to explain. The Aquarium's deteriorated "bronze weathervane cod" is of course immediately appropriate to the purport of the poem, for the cod is the official emblem of the Commonwealth of Massachusetts. The "cowed, compliant fish" introduce the idea of servility and point toward the "savage servility" which is associated with the "giant finned cars" that "nose forward like fish," almost explicitly sharks. But a connection between the passive and the active servility is not readily apparent. Then, although one can understand that a despondent man might sigh "for the dark downward and vegetating kingdom / of the fish and reptile" as representing the comfortable passivity of childhood, other dark and downward things in the poem cannot well be the objects of nostalgia; these include the "underworld garage" and the burial "ditch" which is said to be "nearer." And if it is reptiles that are sighed for, they are at hand in the steam-shovels, which are likened to dinosaurs. What relation the "fishbone / in the city's throat" has to the other fish-references is not plain. In an effort to understand the "bubble" upon which Colonel Shaw is said to ride, some readers will recall Jaques's speech about the seven ages of man in *As You Like It,* in which the soldier is said to seek "the bubble reputation / Even in the cannon's mouth"; this reading has the advantage of seeming to explain why the Colonel "waits / for the blessèd break"—because it would release him from his public symbolic existence to the privacy for which "he seems to . . . suffocate."[1] But the bubbles of the fish that the boy's "hand tingled / to burst" come in to make this interpretation difficult, as does the simile of the "balloons" which is used to describe the faces of the Negro school children on the television screen. In short, although a rather tight system of associations is manifest in the poem, its syntax is difficult.

The epigraph of the poem is derived from an inscription on the face of the monument, "*Reliquit Omnia Servare Rem Publicam.*" The Latin sentence, which may be translated "He left everything behind to serve the nation," is the motto of the Society of the Cincinnati, whose members are descendants of American officers of the Revolutionary War; Robert Shaw was himself a member.[2] By changing the canonical form of the sentence to make it say, "*They* left everything behind to serve the nation," Lowell has given his epigraph a reference beyond Shaw himself; it now includes the rank and file of Shaw's regiment and all the Union dead. It is possible to read the variant as an implied criticism of the choice of the inscription.

[1] In a letter to his brother Henry, William James, who had known the colonel in their youth, wrote of "poor . . . Robert Shaw," who had been "erected into a great symbol of deeper things than he ever realized himself. . . ."

[2] Cincinnatus was the legendary Roman hero, who, at a time of military crisis, was chosen to be dictator of Rome; the legend is that the emissaries of the Senate found him plowing in his fields, that he left the plow standing and returned to it sixteen days later, having defeated the enemy and resigned the dictatorship. Because membership was hereditary and confined to the descendants of officers, the Society at its inception was denounced as an aristocratic organization, a charge that has since been repeated.

PART 2 POETRY FOR FURTHER READING

ANONYMOUS

A LYKE-WAKE[1] DIRGE

This ae nighte, this ae nighte,
    —Every nighte and alle,
Fire and fleet[2] and candle-lighte,
    And Christe receive thy saule.

When thou from hence away art past, 5
    —Every nighte and alle,
To Whinny-muir[3] thou com'st at last;
    And Christe receive thy saule.

If ever thou gavest hosen and shoon,[4]
    —Every nighte and alle, 10
Sit thee down and put them on;
    And Christe receive thy saule.

If hosen and shoon thou ne'er gav'st nane[5]
    —Every nighte and alle,
The whinnes sall prick thee to the bare bane; 15
    And Christe receive thy saule.

From Whinny-muir when thou may'st pass,
    —Every nighte and alle,
To Brig[6] o' Dread thou com'st at last;
    And Christe receive thy saule. 20

From Brig o' Dread when thou may'st pass,
    —Every nighte and alle,
To Purgatory fire thou com'st at last;
    And Christe receive thy saule.

[1] A watch kept at night over a dead body; a wake. [2] Place where water flows. [3] A moor where whins, or prickly shrubs, grow. [4] Hose and shoes. [5] None. [6] Bridge.

If ever thou gavest meat or drink, 25
—Every nighte and alle,
The fire shall never make thee shrink;
And Christe receive thy saule.

If meat or drink thou ne'er gav'st nane,
—Every nighte and alle, 30
The fire will burn thee to the bare bane;
And Christe receive thy saule.

This ae nighte, this ae nighte,
—Every nighte and alle,
Fire and fleet and candle-lighte, 35
And Christe receive thy saule.

THE CHERRY-TREE CAROL

Joseph was an old man,
and an old man was he,
When he wedded Mary,
in the land of Galilee.

Joseph and Mary walked 5
through an orchard good,
Where was cherries and berries,
so red as any blood.

Joseph and Mary walked
through an orchard green, 10
Where was berries and cherries,
as thick as might be seen.

O then bespoke Mary,
so meek and so mild:
"Pluck me one cherry, Joseph, 15
for I am with child."

O then bespoke Joseph:
with words most unkind:
"Let him pluck thee a cherry
that brought thee with child." 20

O then bespoke the babe,
    within his mother's womb:
"Bow down then the tallest tree,
    for my mother to have some."

Then bowed down the highest tree 25
    unto his mother's hand;
Then she cried, "See, Joseph,
    I have cherries at command."

O then bespoke Joseph:
    "I have done Mary wrong; 30
But cheer up, my dearest,
    and be not cast down."

Then Mary plucked a cherry,
    as red as the blood,
Then Mary went home 35
    with her heavy load.

Then Mary took her babe,
    and sat him on her knee,
Saying, "My dear son, tell me
    what this world will be." 40

"O I shall be as dead, mother,
    as the stones in the wall;
O the stones in the streets, mother,
    shall mourn for me all.

"Upon Easter-day, mother, 45
    my uprising shall be;
O the sun and the moon, mother,
    shall both rise with me."

THE THREE RAVENS

1. There were three ravens sat on a tree,
        Downe a downe, hay downe, hay downe
    There were three ravens sat on a tree,
        With a downe

There were three ravens sat on a tree, 5
They were as blacke as they might be.
With a downe derrie, derrie, derrie, downe, downe.

2. The one of them said to his mate,
"Where shall we our breakfast take?"

3. "Downe in yonder greene field, 10
There lies a knight slain under his shield.

4. "His hounds they lie downe at his feete,
So well they can their master keepe.

5. "His haukes they flie so eagerly,
There's no fowle dare him come nie." 15

6. Downe there comes a fallow doe,
As great with yong as she might goe.

7. She lift up his bloudy hed,
And kist his wounds that were so red.

8. She got him up upon her backe, 20
And carried him to earthen lake.[1]

9. She buried him before the prime,[2]
She was dead herselfe ere even-song time.

10. God send every gentleman,
Such haukes, such hounds, and such a leman.[3] 25

SIR PATRICK SPENS

The king sits in Dumferling toune,
Drinking the blude-reid wine:

[1] Pit in the earth. [2] *Prime* is the old ecclesiastical name for the first hour of the day; *even-song* is the service of vespers, held in the evening. [3] Lover.

"O whar will I get a guid sailor,
To sail this schip of mine?"

Up and spak an eldern knicht, 5
Sat at the kings richt kne:
"Sir Patrick Spens is the best sailor
That sails upon the se."

The king has written a braid[1] letter,
And signd it wi his hand, 10
And sent it to Sir Patrick Spens,
Was walking on the sand.

The first line that Sir Patrick red,
A loud lauch lauched he;
The next line that Sir Patrick red, 15
The teir blinded his ee.

"O wha is this has don this deid,
This ill deid don to me,
To send me out this time o' the yeir,
To sail upon the se! 20

'Mak hast, mak haste, my mirry men all,
Our guid schip sails the morne."
"O say na sae,[2] my master deir,
For I feir a deadlie storme.

"Late late yestreen[3] I saw the new moone, 25
Wi the auld moone in hir arme,
And I feir, I feir, my deir master,
That we will cum to harme."

O our Scots nobles wer richt laith[4]
To weet[5] their cork-heild schoone,[6] 30
Bot lang owre[7] a' the play wer playd,
Thair hats they swam aboone.[8]

[1] Broad; that is, emphatic, explicit. [2] Say not so. [3] Yesterday evening. [4] Right loath. [5] Wet. [6] Cork was not uncommonly used for the heels (and soles) of gentlemen's shoes in the sixteenth and seventeenth centuries. [7] Over; here, after. [8] Above; that is, on the water.

O lang, lang may their ladies sit,
    Wi thair fans into their hand,
Or eir they se Sir Patrick Spens   35
    Cum sailing to the land.

O lang, lang may the ladies stand,
    Wi thair gold kems in their hair,
Waiting for thair ain deir lords,
    For they'll se thame na mair.   40

Haf owre, half owre to Aberdour,
    It's fiftie fadom deip,
And thair lies guid Sir Patrick Spens,
    Wi the Scots lords at his feit.

MARY HAMILTON

Word's gane to the kitchen,
    And word's gane to the ha,[1]
That Marie Hamilton gangs[2] wi bairn[3]
    To the hichest[4] Stewart[5] of a'.

He's courted her in the kitchen,   5
    He's courted her in the ha,
He's courted her in the laigh[6] cellar,
    And that was warst of a'.

She's tyed it in her apron
    And she's thrown it in the sea   10
Says, "Sink ye, swim ye, bonny wee babe!
    You'l neer get mair o me."

Down then cam the auld queen,
    Goud[7] tassels tying her hair:
"O Marie, where's the bonny wee babe   15
    That I heard greet sae sair?"[8]

"There was never a babe intill[9] my room,
    As little designs to be;

[1] Hall. [2] Goes. [3] Child. [4] Highest. [5] Henry Stewart (1545–1567), second husband of Mary Queen of Scots. [6] Low. [7] Gold. [8] Cry so sore. [9] In.

It was but a touch o my sair side,
Come oer my fair bodie." 20

"O Marie, put on your robes o black,
Or else your robes o brown,
For ye maun gang wi me the night,
To see fair Edinbro town."

I winna put on my robes o black, 25
Nor yet my robes o brown;
But I'll put on my robes o white,
To shine through Edinbro town."

When she gaed up the Cannogate,[10]
She laughd loud laughters three; 30
But whan she cam down the Cannogate
The tear blinded her ee.

When she gaed up the Parliament stair,
The heel cam aff her shee;
And lang or she cam down again 35
She was condemned to dee.

When she cam down the Cannogate,
The Cannogate sae free,
Many a ladie lookd oer her window,
Weeping for this ladie. 40

"Ye need nae weep for me," she says,
"Ye need nae weep for me;
For had I not slain mine own sweet babe,
This death I wadna dee.

"Bring me a bottle of wine," she says, 45
"The best that eer ye hae,
That I may drink to my well-wishers,
And they may drink to me.

"Here's a health to the jolly sailors,
That sail upon the main; 50

[10] Cannongate, a section of Edinburgh.

Let them never let on to my father and mother
But what I'm coming hame.

"Here's a health to the jolly sailors,
That sail upon the sea;
Let them never let on to my father
and mother
That I cam here to dee. 55

"Oh little did my mother think,
The day she cradled me,
What lands I was to travel through,
What death I was to dee. 60

"Oh little did my father think,
The day he held up me,
What lands I was to travel through,
What death I was to dee.

"Last night I washd the queen's feet, 65
And gently laid her down;
And a' the thanks I've gotten the nicht[11]
To be hangd in Edinbro town!

"Last nicht there was four Maries,
The nicht there'l be but three; 70
There was Marie Seton, and Marie Beton,
And Marie Carmichael, and me."

WESTRON WINDE, WHEN WILL THOU BLOW

Westron winde, when will thou blow,
The smalle raine downe can raine?
Christ, if my love were in my armes,
And I in my bed againe.

[11] This night.

JOHN SKELTON

1460?–1529

TO MISTRESS ISABEL PENNELL

By Saint Mary, my lady,
Your mammy and your daddy
Brought forth a goodly baby!

My maiden Isabel,
Reflaring rosabel,[1] 5
The fragrant camomel;
The ruddy rosary,[2]
The sovereign rosemary,
The pretty strawberry;
The columbine, the nept,[3] 10
The jelofer[4] well set,
The proper violet:
Ennewèd[5] your colour
Is like the daisy flower
After the April shower; 15
Star of the morrow gray,
The blossom on the spray,
The freshest flower of May;
Maidenly demure,
Of womanhood the lure;[6] 20
Wherefore I make you sure
It were an heavenly health,
It were an endless wealth,
A life for God himself,
To hear this nightingale 25
Among the birdès smale
Warbeling in the vale,
Dug, dug,
Jug, jug,
Good year and good luck, 30
With chuck, chuck, chuck, chuck!

[1] Smelling like a beautiful rose. [2] Rose garden, rosarium. [3] Catnip. [4] Gillyflower. [5] Made new, restored. [6] That is, the most attractive (alluring) of women.

TO MISTRESS MARGARET HUSSEY

Merry Margaret,
As midsummer flower,
Gentle as falcon
Or hawk of the tower:
With solace and gladness, 5
Much mirth and no madness,
All good and no badness;
So joyously,
So maidenly,
So womanly 10
Her demeaning
In every thing,
Far, far passing
That I can indite,
Or suffice to write 15
Of Merry Margaret
As midsummer flower,
Gentle as falcon
Or hawk of the tower.
As patient and still 20
And as full of good will
As fair Isaphill,[1]
Coriander,
Sweet pomander,
Good Cassander,[2] 25
Steadfast of thought,
Well made, well wrought,
Far may be sought
Ere that ye can find
So courteous, so kind 30
As Merry Margaret,
This midsummer flower,
Gentle as falcon
Or hawk of the tower.

[1] Hypsipyle, in Greek legend, a queen of Lemnos who, when the women of the island killed their husbands for infidelity, saved her father. Later, when the Argonauts arrived on their way to find the Golden Fleece, she and her women were so hospitable that they repopulated the island. [2] Cassandra, who, in Greek mythology, was gifted with the power of prophecy. It was her fate that, although her predictions were always correct, no one believed her.

SIR THOMAS WYATT

1503–1542

MY GALLEY CHARGÈD WITH FORGETFULNESS

My galley chargèd with forgetfulness
Thorough sharp seas in winter nights doth pass
'Tween rock and rock; and eke mine enemy, alas,
That is my lord, steereth with cruelness;
And every oar a thought in readiness, 5
As though that death were light in such a case.
An endless wind doth tear the sail apace
Of forcèd sighs and trusty fearfulness.
A rain of tears, a cloud of dark disdain,
Hath done the wearied cords[1] great hinderance, 10
Wreathèd with error and eke with ignorance.
The stars be hid that led me to this pain;
Drownèd is reason that should me consort,[2]
And I remain despairing of the port.

FORGET NOT YET

Forget not yet the tried[1] intent
Of such a truth as I have meant,
My great travail so gladly spent
Forget not yet.

Forget not yet when first began 5
The weary life ye know since whan,
The suit,[2] the service none tell can,
Forget not yet.

Forget not yet the great assays,
The cruel wrong, the scornful ways, 10
The painful patience in denays,[3]
Forget not yet.

[1] Ropes. [2] Accompany.

[1] Proved. [2] Pursuit or courting. [3] Denials.

Forget not yet, forget not this,
How long ago hath been and is
The mind that never meant amiss, 15
Forget not yet.

Forget not then thine own approved,
The which so long hath thee loved,
Whose steadfast faith yet never moved,
Forget not this. 20

EDMUND SPENSER

1552?–1599

EPITHALAMION[1]

Ye learned sisters,[2] which have oftentimes
Been to me aiding, others to adorn,
Whom ye thought worthy of your graceful rhymes,
That even the greatest did not greatly scorn
To hear their names sung in your simple lays,[3] 5
But joyèd in their praise;
And when ye list[4] your own mishaps to mourn,
Which death, or love, or fortune's wreck did raise,
Your string could soon to sadder tenor turn,
And teach the woods and waters to lament 10
Your doleful dreariment:
Now lay those sorrowful complaints aside;
And, having all your heads with girlands crown'd,
Help me mine own love's praises to resound;
Ne let the same of any be envide:[5] 15
So Orpheus did for his own bride![6]
So I unto myself alone will sing;
The woods shall to me answer, and my echo ring.

[1] A nuptial song or poem in praise of the bride and bridegroom. [2] The Muses, nine sister goddesses charged, in Greek mythology, with care of the arts and sciences. [3] Poems. [4] Want. [5] That is, let no one be begrudged the ability to sing his love's praises. [6] Orpheus, in Greek mythology the husband of Eurydice, was famed as a singer.

Early, before the world's light-giving lamp
His golden beam upon the hills doth spread, 20
Having dispers'd the night's uncheerful damp,
Do ye awake; and with fresh lustihead
Go to the bower of my belovèd love,
My truest turtle-dove,
Bid her awake; for Hymen[7] is awake, 25
And long since ready forth his mask[8] to move,
With his bright tead[9] that flames with many a flake,
And many a bachelor[10] to wait on him,
In their fresh garments trim.
Bid her awake therefore, and soon her dight,[11] 30
For lo! the wishèd day is come at last,
That shall, for all the pains and sorrows past,
Pay to her usury[12] of long delight:
And whilst she doth her dight,
Do ye to her of joy and solace sing, 35
That all the woods may answer, and your echo ring.

Bring with you all the nymphs that you can hear
Both of the rivers and the forests green,
And of the sea that neighbours to her near:
All with gay girlands goodly well beseen.[13] 40
And let them also with them bring in hand
Another gay girland,
For my fair love, of lilies and of roses,
Bound true-love wise,[14] with a blue silk riband.
And let them make great store of bridal posies, 45
And let them eke bring store of other flowers,
To deck the bridal bowers
And let the ground whereas her foot shall tread,
For fear the stones her tender foot should wrong,
Be strewed with fragrant flowers all along, 50
And diap'red[15] like the discoloured mead.[16]
Which done, do at her chamber door await,
For she will waken straight;
The whiles do ye this song unto her sing,
The woods shall to you answer, and your echo ring. 55

Ye nymphs of Mulla,[17] which with careful heed
The silver scaly trouts do tend full well,
And greedy pikes which use[18] therein to feed

[7] A fictional figure associated with weddings who came to be though of as the god of marriage. [8] Masque. [9] Torch. [10] A young knight. [11] Get dressed. [12] Interest. [13] Very becoming (to the nymphs). [14] Like a truelove knot. [15] Decoratively covered. [16] Varicolored meadow. [17] A river. [18] Are accustomed.

(Those trouts and pikes all others do excel);
And ye likewise, which keep the rushy lake, 60
Where none do fishes take:
Bind up the locks the which hang scatter'd light,
And in his waters,[19] which your mirror make,
Behold your faces as the crystal bright,
That when you come whereas my love doth lie, 65
No blemish she may spy.
And eke, ye lightfoot maids, which keep the deer,
That on the hoary mountain used to tower;
And the wild wolves, which seek them to devour,
With your steel darts do chase from coming near; 70
Be also present here,
To help to deck her, and to help to sing,
That all the woods may answer, and your echo ring.

Wake now, my love, awake! for it is time;
The rosy Morn long since left Tithone's bed,[20] 75
All ready to her silver coach to climb;
And Phoebus[21] gins to shew his glorious head.
Hark! how the cheerful birds do chant their lays
And carol of Love's praise.
The merry lark her matins sings aloft; 80
The thrush replies; the mavis[22] descant plays;
The ouzel[23] shrills; the ruddock[24] warbles soft;
So goodly all[25] agree, with sweet consent,
To this day's merriment.
Ah! my dear love, why do ye sleep thus long? 85
When meeter[26] were that ye should now awake,
T' await the coming of your joyous make,[27]
And hearken to the birds' love-learnèd song,
The dewy leaves among!
For they of joy and pleasance[28] to you sing, 90
That all the woods them answer, and their echo ring.

My love is now awake out of her dreams,
And her fair eyes, like stars that dimmèd were
With darksome cloud, now shew their goodly beams
More bright than Hesperus[29] his head doth rear. 95
Come now, ye damsels, daughters of delight,
Help quickly her to dight:

[19] The water of the "rushy lake." [20] Eos, or Aurora, the dawn goddess ("Rosy Morn") was said to have a lover, Tithonus, whose bed she left every morning. She drove across the sky in a chariot and pair. [21] Phoebus Apollo, who, although not the sun god, was often associated with the sun. [22] Another thrush. [23] Blackbird. [24] Redbreast. [25] All these good creatures. [26] More appropriate. [27] Mate. [28] Pleasantness. [29] The evening star.

But first come, ye fair hours,[30] which were begot
In Jove's sweet paradise of Day and Night;
Which do the seasons of the year allot, 100
And all, that ever in this world is fair,
Do make and still repair:
And ye three handmaids of the Cyprian Queen,[31]
The which do still adorn her beauty's pride,
Help to adorn my beautifullest bride: 105
And, as ye her array, still throw between
Some graces to be seen;[32]
And, as ye use to Venus, to her sing,
The whiles the woods shall answer, and your echo ring.

Now is my love all ready forth to come: 110
Let all the virgins therefore well await:
And ye fresh[33] boys, that tend upon[34] her groom,
Prepare yourselves, for he is coming straight.
Set all your things in seemly good array,
Fit for so joyful day: 115
The joyfull'st day that ever sun did see.
Fair sun! shew forth thy favourable ray,
And let thy lifeful heat not fervent be,
For fear of burning her sunshiny face,
Her beauty to disgrace. 120
O fairest Phœbus! father of the Muse!
If ever I did honour thee aright,
Or sing the thing that mote thy mind delight,
Do not thy servant's simple boon refuse;
But let this day, let this one day, be mine; 125
Let all the rest be thine.
Then I thy sovereign praises loud will sing,
That all the woods shall answer, and their echo ring.

Hark: how the minstrels gin[35] to shrill aloud
Their merry music that resounds from far, 130
The pipe, the tabor, and the trembling croud,[36]
That well agree withouten breach or jar.[37]
But, most of all, the damsels do delight
When they their timbrels smite,
And thereunto do dance and carol sweet, 135
That all the senses they do ravish quite
The whiles the boys run up and down the street,

[30] The Hours (Horai), Greek goddesses of the seasons. [31] Aphrodite. [32] That is, as you dress her, be careful not to cover up all her beauty. [33] Untainted. [34] Serve, attend. [35] Begin. [36] An ancient Celtic musical instrument of the viol class. [37] That is, there is no break or disharmony in the music.

Crying aloud with strong confusèd noise,
As if it were one voice,
Hymen, iö Hymen, Hymen, they do shout; 140
That even to the heavens their shouting shrill
Doth reach, and all the firmament doth fill;
To which the people standing all about,
As in approvance,[38] do thereto applaud,
And loud advance her laud;[39] 145
And evermore they Hymen, Hymen sing,
That all the woods them answer, and their echo ring.

Lo! where she comes along with portly pace,
Like Phœbe,[40] from her chamber of the east,
Arising forth to run her mighty race, 150
Clad all in white, that 'seems[41] a virgin best.
So well it her beseems, that ye would ween[42]
Some angel she had been.
Her long loose yellow locks like golden wire,[43]
Sprinkled with pearl, and purling flowers atween, 155
Do like a golden mantle her attire;
And, being crownèd with a girland green,
Seem like some maiden queen.[44]
Her modest eyes, abashèd to behold
So many gazers as on her do stare, 160
Upon the lowly ground affixèd are;
Ne dare lift up her countenance too bold,
But blush to hear her praises sung so loud,
So far from being proud.
Nathless do ye still loud her praises sing, 165
That all the woods may answer, and your echo ring.

Tell me, ye merchants' daughters, did ye see
So fair a creature in your town before;
So sweet, so lovely, and so mild as she,
Adorned with beauty's grace and virtue's store? 170
Her goodly eyes like sapphires shining bright,
Her forehead ivory white,
Her cheeks like apples which the sun hath rudded,[45]
Her lips like cherries charming men to bite,
Her breast like to a bowl of cream uncrudded,[46] 175

[38] Approval. [39] Sing her praises. [40] A Titaness sometimes thought of as goddess of the moon. [41] Becomes (*beseemes,* in the following line, is synonymous). [42] Believe. [43] Strings of a musical instrument. [44] That is, her golden locks, because they are crowned with a green garland, make her seem like a maiden queen. [45] Made ruddy. [46] Uncurdled.

Her paps like lilies budded,
Her snowy neck like to a marble tower;
And all her body like a palace fair,
Ascending up, with many a stately stair,
To honour's seat and chastity's sweet bower. 180
Why stand we still, ye virgins, in amaze,[47]
Upon her so to gaze,
Whiles ye forget your former lay to sing,
To which the woods did answer, and your echo ring?

But if ye saw that which no eyes can see, 185
The inward beauty of her lively sprite,[48]
Garnisht with heavenly gifts of high degree,
Much more then would ye wonder at that sight,
And stand astonisht like to those which read[49]
Medusa's mazeful head.[50] 190
There dwells sweet love, and constant chastity,
Unspotted faith, and comely womanhood,
Regard of honour, and mild modesty;
There virtue reigns as queen in royal throne,
And giveth laws alone, 195
The which the base affections[51] do obey,
And yield their services unto her will;
Ne thought of thing uncomely ever may
Thereto approach to tempt her mind to ill.
Had ye once seen these her celestial treasures. 200
And unrevealèd pleasures,[52]
Then would ye wonder, and her praises sing,
That all the woods should answer, and your echo ring.

Open the temple gates unto my love,
Open them wide that she may enter in, 205
And all the posts adorn as doth behove,[53]
And all the pillars deck with girlands trim,
For to receive this saint[54] with honour due,
That cometh in to you.
With trembling steps, and humble reverence, 210
She cometh in, before th' Almighty's view:
Of her ye virgins learn obedience,
Whenso ye come into those holy places,
To humble your proud faces:
Bring her up to th' high altar, that she may 215

[47] Amazement. [48] Soul, spirit. [49] Gazed upon. [50] Medusa, a terrible monster in Greek mythology, had an ugly face, snakes instead of hair, and eyes that could transform people into stone. [51] Passions, instincts. [52] Hidden (interior) beauties. [53] As is fitting. [54] Note that Spenser's imagery, which has been classical pagan, here becomes Christian.

The sacred ceremonies there partake,
The which do endless matrimony make;
And let the roaring organs loudly play
The praises of the Lord in lively notes;
The whiles, with hollow throats, 220
The choristers the joyous anthem sing,
That all the woods should answer, and your echo ring.

Behold, whiles she before the altar stands,
Hearing the holy priest that to her speaks,
And blesseth her with his two happy hands, 225
How the red roses flush up in her cheeks,
And the pure snow, with goodly vermeil[55] stain
Like crimson dyed in grain:[56]
That even th' angels, which continually
About the sacred altar do remain, 230
Forget their service and about her fly,
Oft peeping in her face, that seems more fair
The more they on it stare.
But her sad eyes, still fastened on the ground,
Are governèd with goodly modesty, 235
That suffers not one look to glance awry,
Which may let in a little thought unsound.
Why blush ye, love, to give to me your hand,
The pledge of all our band![57]
Sing, ye sweet angels, Alleluia sing, 240
That all the woods may answer, and your echo ring.

Now all is done: bring home the bride again;
Bring home the triumph of our victory:
Bring home with you the glory of her gain
With joyance[58] bring her and with jollity. 245
Never had man more joyful day than this,
Whom heaven would heap with bliss.
Make feast therefore now all this livelong day;
This day for ever to me holy is.
Pour out the wine without restraint or stay,[59] 250
Pour not by cups, but by the bellyful,
Pour out to all that wull,[60]
And sprinkle all the posts and walls with wine,
That they may sweat, and drunken be withal.
Crown ye God Bacchus with a coronal, 255
And Hymen also crown with wreaths of vine;

[55] Vermillion. [56] Crimson cloth dyed while the material is still raw. [57] Bond. [58] Joy. [59] Check, pause. [60] Will, want.

And let the Graces[61] dance unto[62] the rest,
For they can do it best:
The whiles the maidens do their carol sing,
To which the woods shall answer, and their echo ring. 260

Ring ye the bells, ye young men of the town,
And leave your wonted[63] labours for this day:
This day is holy; do ye write it down,
That ye for ever it remember may.
This day the sun is in his chiefest height, 265
With Barnaby the bright,[64]
From whence declining daily by degrees,
He somewhat loseth of his heat and light,
When once the Crab[65] behind his back he sees.
But for this time it ill ordainèd was,[66] 270
To choose the longest day in all the year,
And shortest night, when longest fitter were:
Yet never day so long, but late would pass.[67]
Ring ye the bells, to make it wear away,
And bonfires make all day; 275
And dance about them, and about them sing
That all the woods may answer, and your echo ring.

Ah! when will this long weary day have end,
And lend me leave to come unto my love?
How slowly do the hours their numbers spend! 280
How slowly does sad Time his feathers move![68]
Haste thee, O fairest planet,[69] to thy home,
Within the western foam:
Thy tired steeds long since have need of rest.[70]
Long though it be, at last I see it gloom,[71] 285
And the bright evening-star with golden crest
Appear out of the east.
Fair child of beauty![72] glorious lamp of love!
That all the host of heaven in ranks dost lead,
And guidest lovers through the night's sad dread, 290
How cheerfully thou lookest from above,
And seem'st to laugh atween thy twinkling light,
As joying in the sight

[61] In Roman mythology, goddesses who embodied beauty and charm. [62] For. [63] Usual. [64] It is St. Barnabas' Day (Barnaby is a short form of Barnabas), June 11, once reckoned the longest day. [65] The constellation, Cancer. [66] Would have been. [67] Sooner or later it would pass. [68] Time is pictured as a bird or fowl. The image seems to be original with Spenser. [69] The sun. [70] In classical mythology, the sun was a chariot drawn across the skies by horses under the command of a sun god. [71] Darken, become dusk. [72] Hesperus, the evening star, pictured in art as a boy carrying a torch.

Of these glad many, which for joy do sing,
That all the woods them answer, and their echo ring! 295

Now cease, ye damsels, your delights forepast;[73]
Enough it is that all the day was yours:
Now day is done, and night is nighing[74] fast,
Now bring the bride into the bridal bowers.
The night is come, now soon her disarray, 300
And in her bed her lay;
Lay her in lilies and in violets,
And silken curtains over her display,[75]
And odour'd sheets, and arras coverlets,[76]
Behold how goodly[77] my fair love does lie, 305
In proud humility!
Like unto Maia,[78] whenas Jove her took
In Tempe,[79] lying on the flow'ry grass,
'Twixt sleep and wake, after she weary was,
With bathing in the Acidalian brook.[80] 310
Now it is night, ye damsels may be gone,
And leave my love alone,
And leave likewise your former lay to sing:[81]
The woods no more shall answer, nor your echo ring.

Now welcome, night! thou night so long expected, 315
That long day's labour dost at last defray,
And all my cares, which cruel Love collected,
Hast summ'd in one, and cancellèd for aye:
Spread thy broad wing over my love and me,
That no man us may see; 320
And in thy sable[82] mantle us enwrap,
From fear of peril and foul horror free.
Let no false treason seek us to entrap,
Nor any dread disquiet once annoy
The safety of our joy; 325
But let the night be calm, and quietsome,
Without tempestuous storms or sad affray:
Like as when Jove with fair Alcmena lay,
When he begot the great Tirynthian groom:[83]
Or like as when he with thyself did lie 330
And begot Majesty.[84]

[73] Delights of the past. [74] Drawing near. [75] Spread out, unfurl. [76] Coverlets embroidered in the manner of Arras tapestry. [77] Beautifully. [78] Mother of Hermes by Zeus (Jove). [79] A narrow valley in northern Thessaly. [80] The Acidalian brook was associated with Venus, the goddess of love. [81] That is, you may stop singing your lay now. [82] Black. [83] Heracles. [84] The poet here pays his bride the compliment of attributing to Jove and her the engendering of the god or goddess, Majesty; that is, she is the creator of majesty.

And let the maids and young men cease to sing,
Ne let the woods them answer, nor their echo ring.

Let no lamenting cries, nor doleful tears,
Be heard all night within, nor yet without: 335
Ne let false whispers, breeding hidden fears,
Break gentle sleep with misconceivèd doubt.
Let no deluding dreams, nor dreadful sights,
Make sudden sad affrights;
Ne let house-fires, nor lightning's helpless[85] harms, 340
Ne let the Pouke,[86] nor other evil sprites,
Ne let mischievous witches with their charms,
Ne let hobgoblins, names whose sense we see not,
Fray[87] us with things that be not:
Let not the shriek-owl nor the stork be heard, 345
Nor the night-raven, that still deadly yells;
Nor damnèd ghosts, called up with mighty spells,
Nor grisly vultures, make us once afeard:
Ne let th' unpleasant quire of frogs still croaking
Make us to wish their choking. 350
Let none of these their dreary accents sing;
Ne let the woods them answer, nor their echo ring.

But let still silence true night-watches keep,
That sacred peace may in assurance reign,
And timely sleep, when it is time to sleep, 355
May pour his limbs forth on your pleasant plain;[88]
The whiles an hundred little wingèd loves,
Like divers-feathered[89] doves,
Shall fly and flutter round your bed,
And in the secret dark, that[90] none reproves, 360
Their pretty stealths shall work, and snares shall
spread
To filch away sweet snatches of delight,
Concealed through covert night.
Ye sons of Venus[91] play your sports at will!
For greedy pleasure, careless of your toys, 365
Thinks more upon her paradise of joys,
Than what ye do, albeit good or ill.
All night therefore attend your merry play,
For it will soon be day:
Now none doth hinder you, that say or sing;[92] 370
Ne will the woods now answer, nor your echo ring.

[85] Unpreventable. [86] A fancied mischievous goblin or sprite. [87] Frighten. [88] The plain of your pleasant body. [89] Diversely feathered. [90] When. [91] "Little wingèd loves" or Cupids. [92] By talking or singing.

Who is the same, which[93] at my window peeps?
Or whose is that fair face that shines so bright?
Is it not Cynthia,[94] she that never sleeps,
But walks about high heaven all the night? 375
O! fairest goddess, do thou not envý
My love with me to spy:
For thou likewise didst love, though now unthought,
And for a fleece of wool, which privily
The Latmian shepherd once unto thee brought, 380
His pleasures with thee wrought.
Therefore to us be favourable now;
And sith[95] of women's labours thou hast charge,
And generation goodly dost enlarge,
Incline thy will t' effect our wishful vow, 385
And the chaste womb inform with timely seed,
That may our comfort breed:
Till which we cease our hopeful hap[96] to sing;
Ne let the woods us answer, nor our echo ring.

And thou, great Juno![97] which with awful might 390
The laws of wedlock still dost patronize;
And the religion of the faith first plight[98]
With sacred rites hast taught to solemnize;
And eke for comfort often callèd art
Of women in their smart;[99] 395
Eternally bind thou this lovely band,
And all thy blessings unto us impart.
And thou, glad Genius![100] in whose gentle hand
The bridal bower[101] and genial bed remain,
Without blemish or stain: 400
And the sweet pleasures of their love's delight
With secret aid dost succour and supply,
Till they bring forth the fruitful progeny;
Send us the timely fruit of this same night.
And thou fair Hebe![102] and thou, Hymen free! 405
Grant that it may so be.
Till which we cease your further praise to sing;
Ne any woods shall answer, nor your echo ring.

And ye high heavens, the temple of the gods,
In which a thousand torches flaming bright 410

[93] Who is it that. [94] The moon. Cynthia met Endymion, a remarkably beautiful young man, at the cave of Latmos; however, it was the god Pan who won her with a "fleece of wool." [95] Since. [96] Prosperity, good luck. [97] In Roman mythology, the consort of Jupiter and the protectress of marriage and of women. [98] Pledged. [99] Great pain; here, labor. [100] The god that governed the generation of all living beings and also watched over them, warding off evil. [101] Bedroom. [102] Greek goddess of youth and spring.

Do burn, that to us wretched earthly clods
In dreadful darkness lend desirèd light;
And all ye powers which in the same remain,
More than we men can feign,
Pour out your blessing on us plenteously, 415
And happy influence upon us rain,
That we may raise a large posterity,
Which from the earth, which they may long possess
With lasting happiness,
Up to your haughty palaces may mount; 420
And, for the guerdon of their glorious merit,
May heavenly tabernacles there inherit,
Of blessèd saints for to increase the count.
So let us rest, sweet love, in hope of this,
And cease till then our timely joys to sing; 425
The woods no more us answer, nor our echo ring!

Song! made in lieu of many ornaments,
With which my love should duly have been deckt,
Which cutting off through hasty accidents,
Ye would not stay your due time to expect,[103] 430
But promis'd both[104] *to recompense;*
Be unto her a goody ornament,
And for short time an endless monument.

CHRISTOPHER MARLOWE

1564–1593

THE PASSIONATE SHEPHERD TO HIS LOVE

Come live with me, and be my love,
And we will all the pleasures prove[1]
That valleys, groves, hills and fields,
Woods, or steepy mountain yields.

[103] That is, you would not wait as long as you should have. [104] That is, both the lack of ornaments and the accidents that precluded them.

[1] Experience.

And we will sit upon the rocks, 5
Seeing the shepherds feed their flocks,
By shallow rivers, to whose falls
Melodious birds sing madrigals.

And I will make thee beds of roses,
And a thousand fragrant posies, 10
A cap of flowers, and a kirtle,[2]
Embroider'd all with leaves of myrtle;

A gown made of the finest wool,
Which from our pretty lambs we pull,
Fair-linèd slippers for the cold, 15
With buckles of the purest gold;

A belt of straw, and ivy-buds,
With coral clasps and amber studs;
And if these pleasures may thee move,
Come live with me, and be my love. 20

The shepherd-swains shall dance and sing
For they delight each May morning;
If these delights thy mind may move,
Then live with me and be my love.

SIR WALTER RALEGH

1552?–1618

THE NYMPH'S REPLY

If all the world and love were young,
And truth in every shepherd's tongue,
These pretty pleasures might me move,
To live with thee, and be thy love.

[2] A long gown.

Time drives the flocks from field to fold, 5
When rivers rage, and rocks grow cold,
And Philomel[1] becometh dumb,
The rest complains of cares to come.

The flowers do fade, and wanton fields
To wayward winter reckoning yields, 10
A honey tongue, a heart of gall,
Is fancy's spring, but sorrow's fall.

Thy gowns, thy shoes, thy beds of roses,
Thy cap, thy kirtle, and thy posies,
Soon break, soon wither, soon forgotten: 15
In folly ripe, in reason rotten.

Thy belt of straw and ivy buds,
Thy coral clasps and amber studs,
All these in me no means can move,
To come to thee, and be thy love. 20

But could youth last, and love still breed,
Had joys no date, nor age no need,
Then these delights my mind might move,
To live with thee, and be thy love.

AS YOU CAME FROM THE HOLY LAND

As you came from the holy land
Of Walsinghame[1]
Met you not with my true love
By the way as you came?

How shall I know your true love 5
That have met many one
As I went to the holy land
That have come, that have gone?

She is neither white nor brown
But as the heavens fair; 10

[1] The nightingale.

[1] Probably the present Little Walsingham, a village in Norfolk, and site of Walsingham Abbey, one of the great shrines of medieval England.

There is none hath a form so divine
In the earth or the air.

Such an one did I meet, good Sir,
Such an Angelic face,
Who like a queen, like a nymph, did appear, 15
By her gait, by her grace.

She hath left me here all alone,
All alone as unknown,
Who sometimes did me lead with her self,
And me lov'd as her own. 20

What's the cause that she leaves you alone
And a new way doth take,
Who lovèd you once as her own
And her joy did you make?

I have lov'd her all my youth, 25
But now old, as you see,
Loves likes not the falling fruit
From the witherèd tree.

Know that love is a careless child
And forgets promise past: 30
He is blind, he is deaf when he list[2]
And in faith never fast.

His desire is a dureless[3] content
And a trustless joy;
He is won with a world of despair 35
And is lost with a toy.

Of women kind such indeed is the love
Or the word Love abus'd
Under which many childish desires
And conceits[4] are excus'd. 40

[2] Wants to be. [3] Transient. [4] Notions.

But true Love is a durable fire
    In the mind ever burning:
Never sick, never old, never dead,
    From itself never turning.

WILLIAM SHAKESPEARE

1564–1616

FULL FATHOM FIVE

Full fathom five thy father lies;
    Of his bones are coral made;
Those are pearls that were his eyes:
    Nothing of him that doth fade,
But doth suffer a sea-change 5
Into something rich and strange.
Sea-nymphs hourly ring his knell:
                                    Ding-dong
Hark! now I hear them—ding-dong bell.

TELL ME WHERE IS FANCY BRED

Tell me where is fancy bred,
Or in the heart or in the head?
How begot, how nourishèd?
    Reply, reply.

It is engender'd in the eyes, 5
With gazing fed; and fancy dies
In the cradle where it lies.
    Let us all ring fancy's knell:
    I'll begin it,—Ding, dong, bell.

O MISTRESS MINE

O mistress mine! where are you roaming?
O! stay and hear; you true love's coming,
That can sing both high and low.
Trip no further, pretty sweeting;
Journeys end in lovers meeting, 5
Every wise man's son doth know.

What is love? 'tis not hereafter;
Present mirth hath present laughter;
What's to come is still unsure:
In delay there lies no plenty; 10
Then come kiss me, sweet-and-twenty,
Youth's a stuff will not endure.

WHEN THAT I WAS AND A LITTLE TINY BOY

When that I was and a little tiny boy,
With hey, ho, the wind and the rain;
A foolish thing was but a toy,
For the rain it raineth every day.

But when I came to man's estate, 5
With hey, ho, the wind and the rain;
'Gainst knaves and thieves men shut their gates,
For the rain it raineth every day.

But when I came, alas! to wive,
With hey, ho, the wind and the rain; 10
By swaggering could I never thrive,
For the rain it raineth every day.

But when I came unto my beds,
With hey, ho, the wind and the rain;
With toss-pots still had drunken heads, 15
For the rain it raineth every day.

A great while ago the world begun,
With hey, ho, the wind and the rain;

But that's all one, our play is done,
And we'll strive to please you every day. 20

FEAR NO MORE

Fear no more the heat o' the sun,
Nor the furious winter's rages;
Thou thy worldly task hast done,
Home art gone, and ta'en thy wages:
Golden lads and girls all must, 5
As chimney-sweepers, come to dust.

Fear no more the frown o' the great;
Thou art past thy tyrant's stroke;
Care no more to clothe and eat;
To thee the reed is as the oak: 10
The sceptre, learning, physic,[1] must
All follow this, and come to dust.

Fear no more the lightning-flash,
Nor the all-dreaded thunder-stone;[2]
Fear not slander, censure rash; 15
Thou hast finish'd joy and moan:
All lovers young, all lovers must
Consign to[3] thee, and come to dust.

No exorciser harm thee!
Nor no witchcraft charm thee! 20
Ghost unlaid[4] forbear[5] thee!
Nothing ill come near thee!
Quiet consummation have;
And renownèd be thy grave!

SONNET 18

Shall I compare thee to a summer's day?
Thou art more lovely and more temperate:
Rough winds do shake the darling buds of May,
And summer's lease hath all too short a date:

[1] Kings, scholars, physicians. [2] Thunderbolt. [3] Come to terms with. [4] A ghost that cannot lie quiet in the grave. [5] Leave alone, shun.

Sometime too hot the eye of heaven shines, 5
And often is his gold complexion dimm'd;
And every fair from fair sometime declines,
By chance, or nature's changing course untrimm'd;
But thy eternal summer shall not fade,
Nor lose possession of that fair thou ow'st;[1] 10
Nor shall Death brag thou wander'st in his shade,
When in eternal lines to time thou grow'st.
So long as men can breathe or eyes can see,
So long lives this, and this gives life to thee.

SONNET 29

When in disgrace with fortune and men's eyes,
I all alone beweep my outcast state,
And trouble deaf heaven with my bootless cries,
And look upon myself and curse my fate,
Wishing me like to one more rich in hope, 5
Featur'd like him, like him with friends possess'd,
Desiring this man's art, and that man's scope,
With what I most enjoy contented least,
Yet in these thoughts myself almost despising,
Haply I think on thee, and then my state, 10
Like to the lark at break of day arising,
From sullen earth sings hymns at heaven's gate,
For thy sweet love rememb'red such wealth brings,
That when I scorn to change my state with kings.

SONNET 30

When to the sessions of sweet silent thought,
I summon up remembrance of things past,
I sigh the lack of many a thing I sought,
And with old woes new[1] wail my dear time's waste:
Then can I drown an eye, unus'd to flow, 5
For precious friends hid in death's dateless night,
And weep afresh love's long-since cancel'd woe,
And moan th' expense[2] of many a vanish'd sight.
Then can I grieve at grievances foregone,
And heavily from woe to woe tell o'er 10

[1] Ownest.

[1] Newly. [2] Loss.

The sad account of fore-bemoanèd moan,
Which I new pay as if not paid before.
But if the while I think on thee, dear friend,
All losses are restor'd, and sorrows end.

SONNET 33

Full many a glorious morning have I seen
Flatter the mountain-tops with sovereign[1] eye,
Kissing with golden face the meadows green;
Gilding pale streams with heavenly alchemy:
Anon permit the basest clouds to ride, 5
With ugly rack[2] on his celestial face,
And from the forlorn world his visage hide,
Stealing unseen to west with this disgrace:
Even so my sun one early morn did shine,
With all-triumphant splendor on my brow, 10
But out, alack, he was but one hour mine;
The region cloud[3] hath mask'd him from me now.
Yet him for this, my love no whit disdaineth;
Suns of the world may stain,[4] when heaven's sun staineth.

SONNET 55

Not marble, nor the gilded monuments
Of princes, shall outlive this powerful rhyme,
But you shall shine more bright in these contents
Than unswept stone,[1] besmear'd with sluttish time.
When wasteful war shall statues overturn, 5
And broils[2] root out the work of masonry,
Nor[3] Mars his sword,[4] nor war's quick fire shall burn
The living record of your memory.
'Gainst death and all-oblivious enmity
Shall you pace forth; your praise shall still find room, 10
Even in the eyes of all posterity
That wear this world out[5] to the ending doom.

[1] Efficacious, healing. [2] A group of storm clouds. [3] Cloud of the upper air. [4] Be darkened.

[1] Stone unswept by the wind and thus not eroded. [2] Tumults. This line essentially repeats the preceding one. [3] Neither. [4] The sword of Mars, the Roman god of war. [5] Stay with.

So till the judgment that yourself arise,
You live in this, and dwell in lovers' eyes.

SONNET 73

That time of year thou mayst in me behold,
When yellow leaves, or none, or few, do hang
Upon those boughs which shake against the cold,
Bare ruin'd choirs,[1] where late the sweet birds sang.
In me thou see'st the twilight of such day, 5
As after sunset fadeth in the west,
Which by and by black night doth take away,
Death's second self, that seals up all in rest.
In me thou see'st the glowing of such fire,
That on the ashes of his[2] youth doth lie, 10
As the death-bed whereon it must expire,
Consum'd with that which it was nourish'd by.
This thou perceiv'st, which makes thy love more strong,
To love that well, which thou must leave ere long.

SONNET 107

Not mine own fears, nor the prophetic soul
Of the wide world, dreaming on things to come,
Can yet the lease of my true love control,
Suppos'd as forfeit to a confin'd doom.[1]
The mortal moon hath her eclipse endur'd, 5
And the sad augurs mock their own presage;[2]
Incertainties now crown themselves assur'd,
And peace proclaims olives[3] of endless age.
Now with the drops[4] of this most balmy time,
My love looks fresh, and Death to me subscribes,[5] 10
Since, spite of him, I'll live in this poor rhyme,
While he insults[6] o'er dull and speechless tribes.
And thou in this shalt find thy monument,
When tyrants' crests and tombs of brass are spent.[7]

[1] Choir lofts. [2] Its (that is, the fire's).

[1] Judgment. [2] Prophesy. [3] The olive, or olive branch, symbolizes peace. [4] Dewdrops. [5] Yields. [6] Exalts insolently. [7] Gone.

SONNET 129

Th' expense of spirit in a waste of shame
Is lust in action; and till action, lust
Is perjur'd,[1] murd'rous, bloody, full of blame,
Savage, extreme, rude, cruel, not to trust,[2]
Enjoy'd no sooner but[3] despisèd straight, 5
Past reason hunted, and no sooner had
Past reason hated as a swallowed bait,
On purpose laid to make the taker mad:
Mad in pursuit, and in possession so,
Had,[4] having, and in quest to have, extreme, 10
A bliss in proof,—and prov'd, a very woe;
Before, a joy propos'd; behind, a dream.
All this the world well knows; yet none knows well,
To shun the heaven that leads men to this hell.

THOMAS NASHE

1567–1601

SPRING

Spring, the sweet spring, is the year's pleasant king;
Then blooms each thing, then maids dance in a ring,
Cold doth not sting, the pretty birds do sing:
Cuckoo, jug-jug, pu-we, to-witta-woo!

The palm and may[1] make country houses gay, 5
Lambs frisk and play, the shepherds pipe all day,
And we hear aye[2] birds tune this merry lay:
Cuckoo, jug-jug, pu-we, to-witta-woo!

The fields breathe sweet, the daisies kiss our feet,
Young lovers meet, old wives a-sunning sit, 10

[1] Made false to itself. [2] Not to be trusted. [3] Than. [4] In the process of being experienced.

[1] A branch of the hawthorn or similar plant used for May Day decorations. [2] Continually.

In every street these tunes our ears do greet:
Cuckoo, jug-jug, pu-we, to-witta-woo!
Spring, the sweet spring!

IN TIME OF PESTILENCE 1593

Adieu, farewell earth's bliss,
This world uncertain is;
Fond[1] are life's lustful joys,
Death proves them all but toys,
None from his darts can fly. 5
I am sick, I must die.
Lord, have mercy on us!

Rich men, trust not in wealth,
Gold cannot buy you health;
Physic himself[2] must fade, 10
All things to end are made.
The plague full swift goes by;
I am sick, I must die.
Lord, have mercy on us!

Beauty is but a flower 15
Which wrinkles will devour;
Brightness falls from the air,
Queens have died young and fair,
Dust hath closed Helen's[3] eye.
I am sick, I must die. 20
Lord, have mercy on us!

Strength stoops unto[4] the grave,
Worms feed on Hector[5] brave,
Swords may not fight with fate,
Earth still holds ope her gate. 25
Come! come! the bells do cry.
I am sick, I must die.
Lord, have mercy on us!

Wit with his wantonness
Tasteth death's bitterness; 30

[1] Foolish or vain. [2] The science of medicine itself. [3] The beautiful Helen of Troy (see Homer's *Iliad*). [4] Yields to. [5] The bravest of the Trojan heroes in the *Iliad*.

Hell's executioner
Hath no ears for to hear
What vain art can reply.
I am sick, I must die.
    Lord, have mercy on us! 35

Haste, therefore, each degree,[6]
To welcome destiny.
Heaven is our heritage,
Earth but a player's stage;
Mount we unto the sky. 40
I am sick, I must die.
    Lord, have mercy on us!

SIR JOHN DAVIES
1569–1626

AFFLICTION

If aught can teach us aught, Affliction's looks,
    Making us look into ourselves so near,
Teach us to know ourselves beyond all books,
    Or all the learnèd schools that ever were.

This mistress lately pluck'd me by the ear, 5
    And many a golden lesson hath me taught;
Hath made my senses quick, and reason clear,
    Reform'd my will, and rectified my thought.

So do the winds and thunders cleanse the air;
    So working seas settle and purge the wine; 10
So lopp'd and prunèd trees do flourish fair;
    So doth the fire the drossy gold refine.

[6] Class of people.

Neither Minerva[1] nor the learnèd Muse,[2]
Nor rules of art, nor precepts of the wise,
Could in my brain those beams of skill infuse, 15
As but the glance of this dame's angry eyes.

She within lists[3] my ranging mind hath brought,
That now beyond myself I list not[4] go:
Myself am centre of my circling thought,
Only myself I study, learn, and know. 20

I know my body's of so frail a kind
As force without, fevers within, can kill;
I know the heavenly nature of my mind,
But 'tis corrupted both in wit and will.

I know my soul hath power to know all things, 25
Yet is she blind and ignorant in all;
I know I am one of nature's little kings,
Yet to the least and vilest things am thrall.

I know my life's a pain and but a span,
I know my sense is mock'd with every thing: 30
And, to conclude, I know myself a man,
Which is a proud, and yet a wretched thing.

BEN JONSON

1572–1637

ON MY FIRST SON

Farewell, thou child of my right hand, and joy;
My sin was too much hope of thee, lov'd boy.
Seven years thou wert lent to me, and I thee pay,[1]

[1] The Roman goddess of wisdom. [2] Any of nine Greek goddesses of song, poetry, arts, and sciences. [3] Boundaries. [4] Do not desire to.

[1] I pay (for thee) with thee.

Exacted by thy fate, on the just day.
O, could I lose all father, now! For why 5
Will man lament the state he should envy?
To have so soon 'scap'd world's and flesh's rage,
And, if no other misery, yet age!
Rest in soft peace, and, ask'd, say, Here doth lie
Ben Jonson his[2] best piece of poetry. 10
For whose sake, henceforth, all his vows be such,
As what he loves may never like too much.

EPITAPH ON ELIZABETH, L.H.

Would'st thou hear what man can say
In a little? Reader, stay.
Underneath this stone doth lie
As much beauty as could die:
Which in life did harbour give 5
To more virtue than doth live.
If, at all, she had a fault,
Leave it buried in this vault.
One name was Elizabeth,
Th' other, let it sleep with death: 10
Fitter, where it died, to tell,
Than that it liv'd at all. Farewell.

TO PENSHURST[1]

Thou art not, Penshurst, built to envious show,
Of touch[2] or marble; nor canst boast a row
Of polish'd pillars, or a roof of gold:
Thou hast no lantern,[3] whereof tales are told;
Or stair, or courts; but stand'st an ancient pile,[4] 5
And these grudg'd at, are reverenc'd the while.
Thou joy'st in better marks,[5] of soil, of air,
Of wood, of water: therein thou art fair.
Thou hast thy walks for health, as well as sport:
Thy Mount, to which thy Dryads[6] do resort, 10
Where Pan and Bacchus[7] their high feasts have made,

[2] Ben Jonson's.

[1] The seat of the Sidneys, the family of the poet, Sir Philip Sidney (1554–1586). [2] Touchstone, a costly marble. [3] A small tower on top of a dome with glazed openings to admit light. [4] A group of buildings. [5] Characteristics. [6] Wood nymphs. [7] Pan was the Greek god of pastures and fields, and Bacchus the god of wine.

Beneath the broad beech and the chestnut shade;
That taller tree, which of a nut was set,[8]
At his great birth, where all the Muses met.[9]
There, in the writhèd bark, are cut the names 15
Of many a Sylvan, taken with his flames.[10]
And thence the ruddy satyrs oft provoke
The lighter Fauns to reach thy Lady's oak.[11]
Thy copse, too, nam'd of Gamage,[12] thou hast there,
That never fails to serve thee season'd[13] deer, 20
When thou wouldst feast, or exercise thy friends.
The lower land, that to the river bends,
Thy sheep, thy bullocks, kine, and calves do feed;
The middle grounds thy mares and horses breed.
Each bank doth yield thee conies;[14] and the tops 25
Fertile of wood, Ashore and Sidney's copse,
To crown thy open table, doth provide
The purpled pheasant, with the speckled side;
The painted partridge lies in every field,
And, for thy mess,[15] is willing to be kill'd. 30
And if the high-swoln Medway[16] fail thy dish,
Thou hast the ponds that pay thee tribute fish,
Fat agèd carps that run into thy net.
And pikes, now weary their own kind to eat,
As loth, the second draught,[17] or cast to stay,[18] 35
Officiously,[19] at first, themselves betray.
Bright eels that emulate them, leap on land,
Before the fisher, or into his hand.
Then hath thy orchard fruit, thy garden flowers,
Fresh as the air, and new as are the hours. 40
The early cherry, with the later plum,
Fig, grape, and quince, each in his time doth come;
The blushing apricot, and woolly peach
Hang on thy walls, that every child may reach.
And though thy walls be of the country stone, 45
They're rear'd with no man's ruin, no man's groan;
There's none that dwell about them wish them down;
But all come in, the farmer, and the clown,
And no one empty-handed, to salute
Thy lord, and lady, though they have no suit.[20] 50
Some bring a capon, some a rural cake,
Some nuts, some apples; some that think they make
The better cheeses, bring 'em; or else send

[8] Planted. [9] The allusion is to the birth of Sir Philip Sidney. [10] The passions inspired by Sidney's verses. [11] There is a tradition that Sir Robert Sidney's wife, Lady Leicester, went into labor at Penshurst under an oak, which was subsequently called "my lady's oak." [12] In this copse, Barbara Gamage, the first wife of Sir Robert Sidney, liked to feed the deer from her own hands. [13] Matured. [14] Rabbits. [15] Company of persons eating together. [16] A river bordering Penshurst Park. [17] The act of drawing a net for fish. [18] Wait for. [19] Obligingly. [20] Petition, request for favors.

By their ripe daughters, whom they would commend
This way to husbands, and whose baskets bear 55
An emblem of themselves in plum or pear.
But what can this, more than express their love,
Add to thy free provisions, far above
The need of such? whose liberal board doth flow
With all that hospitality doth know! 60
Where comes no guest but is allow'd to eat,
Without his fear, and of thy lord's own meat:
Where the same beer, and bread, and self-same wine,
That is his lordship's, shall be also mine.
And I not fain[21] to sit, as some, this day 65
At great men's tables, and yet dine away.
Here no man tells[22] my cups; nor, standing by,
A waiter doth my gluttony envý:
But gives me what I call, and lets me eat,
He knows, below, he shall find plenty of meat, 70
Thy tables hoard not up for the next day,
Nor, when I take my lodging, need I pray
For fire, or lights, or livery: all is there,
As if thou, then, wert mine, or I reign'd here:
There's nothing I can wish, for which I stay. 75
That found King James, when hunting late, this way,
With his brave son, the prince; they saw thy fires
Shine bright on every hearth, as[23] the desires
Of thy Penates[24] had been set on flame,
To entertain them; or the country came, 80
With all their zeal, to warm their welcome here.
What, great, I will not say, but, sudden cheer
Didst thou then make[25] 'em! and what praise was heap'd
On thy good lady, then! who therein reap'd
The just reward of all her housewifery; 85
To have her linen, plate, and all things nigh,
When she was far, and not a room but dress'd
As if it had expected such a guest!
These, Penshurst, are thy praise, and yet not all.
Thy lady's noble, fruitful, chaste withal. 90
His children thy great lord may call his own:
A fortune, in this age, but rarely known.
They are, and have been taught religion; thence
Their gentler spirits have suck'd innocence.
Each morn and even they are taught to pray, 95
With the whole household, and may, every day,
Read, in their virtuous parents' noble parts,[26]
The mysteries of manners, arms, and arts.

[21] Be obliged. [22] Counts. [23] As if. [24] Roman household gods. [25] Provide a feast for. [26] Abilities.

Now, Penshurst, they that will proportion[27] thee
With other edifices, when they see 100
Those proud, ambitious heaps, and nothing else,
May say, their lords have built, but thy lord dwells.

SONG, TO CELIA

Drink to me only with thine eyes,
And I will pledge with mine;
Or leave a kiss but in the cup,
And I'll not look for wine.
The thirst that from the soul doth rise 5
Doth ask a drink divine:
But might I of Jove's nectar sup,
I would not change for thine.

I sent thee late a rosy wreath,
Not so much honoring thee, 10
As giving it a hope that there
It could not withered be.
But thou thereon didst only breathe,
And sent'st it back to me:
Since when it grows, and smells, I swear, 15
Not of itself, but thee.

THE TRIUMPH OF CHARIS

See the chariot at hand here of Love,
Wherein my Lady rideth!
Each that draws is a swan or a dove,
And well the car Love guideth.
As she goes, all hearts do duty 5
Unto her beauty;
And enamor'd, do wish, so they might
But enjoy such a sight,
That they still were to run by her side,
Through swords, through seas, whither she would ride. 10

Do but look on her eyes, they do light
All that Love's world compriseth!

[27] Compare.

Do but look on her hair, it is bright
As Love's star when it riseth!
Do but mark, her forehead's smoother 15
Than words that soothe her!
And from her arched brows, such a grace
Sheds itself through the face
As alone there triumphs to the life
All the gain, all the good, of the elements' strife. 20

Have you seen but a bright lily grow,
Before rude hands have touch'd it?
Have you mark'd but the fall o' the snow
Before the soil hath smutch'd it?
Have you felt the wool o' the beaver? 25
Or swan's down ever?
Or have smelt o' the bud o' the briar?
Or the nard[1] i' the fire?
Or have tasted the bag o' the bee?[2]
O so white! O so soft! O so sweet is she! 30

HYMN TO DIANA[1]

Queen and huntress, chaste and fair,
Now the sun is laid to sleep,
Seated in thy silver chair,
State in wonted manner keep:
Hesperus[2] entreats thy light, 5
Goddess, excellently bright.

Earth, let not thy envious shade
Dare itself to interpose;
Cynthia's shining orb was made
Heaven to clear[3] when day did close: 10
Bless us then with wishèd sight,
Goddess, excellently bright.

Lay thy bow of pearl apart
And thy crystal-shining quiver;
Give unto the flying hart 15

[1] An aromatic balsam. [2] Honeycomb.

[1] The goddess Diana or Cynthia was associated with the moon and with hunting. [2] The evening star. [3] To make clear, illuminate.

Space to breathe, how short soever:
Thou that mak'st a day of night,
Goddess, excellently bright!

TO THE MEMORY OF MY BELOVED, THE AUTHOR, MR. WILLIAM SHAKESPEARE

To draw no envy,[1] Shakespeare, on thy name,
Am I thus ample[2] to thy book and fame:
While I confess thy writings to be such
As neither Man nor Muse can praise too much.
'Tis true, and all men's suffrage.[3] But these ways 5
Were not the paths I meant unto thy praise:
For silliest ignorance on these may light,
Which, when it sounds at best, but echoes right:
Or blind affection, which doth ne'er advance
The truth, but gropes, and urgeth all by chance; 10
Or crafty malice might pretend this praise,
And think to ruin, where it seem'd to praise.
These are as[4] some infamous bawd, or whore,
Should praise a matron.[5] What could hurt her more?
But thou art proof against them, and indeed 15
Above th' ill fortune of them, or the need.
I, therefore, will begin. Soul of the Age!
The applause, delight, the wonder of our stage!
My Shakespeare, rise. I will not lodge thee by
Chaucer or Spenser,[6] or bid Beaumont[7] lie 20
A little further to make thee a room:
Thou art a monument without a tomb,
And art alive still, while thy book doth live,
And we have wits to read, and praise to give.
That I not mix thee so, my brain excuses; 25
I mean with great, but disproportion'd Muses:[8]
For, if I thought my judgment were of years,
I should commit[9] thee surely with thy peers,
And tell how far thou didst our Lyly[10] outshine,

[1] Ill will. [2] Generous. [3] Opinion. [4] As if. [5] A dignified married woman. [6] Edmund Spenser (1552?–1599) was a great lyric and narrative poet (see his "Epithalamion"). [7] Francis Beaumont (1584–1616) was a poet and a collaborator with John Fletcher in dramatic works. Chaucer, Spenser, and Beaumont have neighboring graves in Westminster Abbey. [8] Here, poets; they are "disproportioned" in that they have less merit than Shakespeare. [9] Match, compare. [10] John Lyly (1554–1606) wrote drama and other works in prose.

Or sporting Kyd,[11] or Marlowe's[12] mighty line. 30
And though thou hadst small Latin, and less Greek,
From thence[13] to honour thee, I would not seek
For names, but call forth thund'ring Aeschylus,
Euripides and Sophocles[14] to us,
Pacuvius, Accius, him of Cordova dead,[15] 35
To life again, to hear thy buskin tread
And shake a stage; or, when thy socks were on,[16]
Leave thee alone for the comparison
Of all that insolent Greece or haughty Rome
Sent forth, or since did from their ashes come. 40
Triumph, my Britain, thou hast one to show,
To whom all scenes[17] of Europe homage owe.
He was not of an age, but for all time!
And all the Muses[18] still were in their prime
When like Apollo[19] he came forth to warm 45
Our ears, or like a Mercury[20] to charm.
Nature herself was proud of his designs,
And joy'd to wear the dressing of his lines;
Which were so richly spun, and woven so fit,
As, since,[21] she will vouchsafe[22] no other wit.[23] 50
The merry Greek, tart Aristophanes,[24]
Neat Terence, witty Plautus,[25] now not please;
But antiquated and deserted lie,
As they were not of Nature's[26] family.
Yet must I not give nature all: thy art, 55
My gentle Shakespeare, must enjoy a part.
For though the poet's matter nature be,
His art doth give the fashion. And that he
Who casts to write a living line must sweat,
(Such as thine are) and strike the second heat 60
Upon the Muses' anvil; turn the same[27]

[11] Thomas Kyd (1557?–1595?) was one of the best known tragic poets of his time. Very little is known of Kyd's life, but the fact that he died in debt perhaps explains the phrase "sporting Kyd." [12] Christopher Marlowe (1564–1593) was a poet and dramatist whose works are generally placed second only to Shakespeare's for the Elizabethan period. His best known play is *The Tragical History of Dr. Faustus.* [13] From the age of Latin and Greek literature. [14] Aeschylus, Euripedes, and Sophocles were the greatest of the Greek writers of tragedy. [15] Pacuvius, Accius, and Seneca ("him of Cordoba dead") were the best writers of Roman tragedy. [16] In Athenian drama, actors in tragedy wore a high, thick-soled boot (buskin) and those in comedy wore a low shoe (sock). Shakespeare's "buskin" is, thus, his tragic drama and his "sock," his comic drama. [17] Theatrical stages. [18] The Muses, in Greek mythology, were goddesses of the arts and learning. [19] Apollo was the Greek god of the sun. [20] Mercury is the Latin name of Hermes, who is best known as messenger of the gods. [21] That since then. [22] Acknowledge. [23] Genius. [24] Aristophanes was the foremost of Greek writers of comedy. [25] Terence and Plautus wrote the best comedies in Latin. [26] Nature, here, is a creative and regulative physical power conceived of as operating in the physical world and as the immediate cause of all its phenomena; it is contrasted with Art. [27] That is, the line of verse.

(And himself with it) that he thinks to frame;
Or for[28] the laurel he may gain a scorn,
For a good poet's made as well as born.
And such wert thou. Look how the father's face 65
Lives in his issue, even so the race
Of Shakespeare's mind and manners brightly shines
In his well-turnèd and true-filèd lines:
In each of which he seems to shake a lance
As[29] brandish'd at the eyes of ignorance. 70
Sweet swan of Avon![30] what a sight it were
To see thee in our waters yet[31] appear,
And make those flights upon the banks of Thames[32]
That so did take Eliza and our James![33]
But stay, I see thee in the Hemisphere 75
Advanc'd, and make[34] a constellation there.
Shine forth, thou star of Poets, and with rage,
Or influence,[35] chide, or cheer the drooping stage,
Which, since thy flight from hence, hath mourn'd like night,
And despairs[36] day, but for thy volume's light.[37] 80

JOHN DONNE

1572–1631

SONG

Go, and catch a falling star,
Get with child a mandrake root,[1]
Tell me where all past years are,
Or who cleft the Devil's foot,
Teach me to hear mermaids' singing, 5
Or to keep off envy's stinging,
And find
What wind
Serves to advance an honest mind.

[28] Instead of. [29] As if it were. [30] Shakespeare was born at Stratford, on the river Avon. [31] Again. [32] The Thames flows through London. [33] Elizabeth and James were, successively, rulers of England during Shakespeare's career. [34] Make out, discern. [35] Astral influence (Shakespeare is seen as the "Star of Poets"). [36] Despairs of, has no hope for. [37] The light that comes from thy plays (collectively).

[1] The forked root of the mandrake (mandragora) was thought to suggest the shape of the human body.

If thou be'st born to[2] strange sights, 10
Things invisible to see,
Ride ten thousand days and nights,
Till age snow white hairs on thee,
Thou, when thou return'st, wilt tell me
All strange wonders that befell thee, 15
And swear
No where
Lives a woman true, and fair.

If thou find'st one, let me know,
Such a pilgrimage were[3] sweet; 20
Yet do not, I would not go,
Though at next door we[4] might meet,
Though she were true, when you met her,
And last till you write your letter,
Yet she 25
Will be
False, ere I come, to two, or three.

THE INDIFFERENT

I can love both fair and brown,
Her whom abundance melts, and her whom want betrays,
Her who loves loneness best, and her who masks and plays,
Her whom the country form'd, and whom the town,
Her who believes, and her who tries,[1] 5
Her who still weeps with spongy eyes,
And her who is dry cork and never cries;
I can love her, and her, and you and you;
I can love any, so she be not true.

Will no other vice content you? 10
Will it not serve your turn to do as did your mothers?
Or have you all old vices spent,[2] and now would find out[3] others?
Or doth a fear that men are true torment you?
O, we are not, be not you so;
Let me, and do you, twenty know. 15

[2] Born for (seeing), prone to (see). [3] Would be. [4] The speaker and the "woman true and fair."

[1] Tests, examines. [2] Exhausted. [3] Discover.

If our two loves be one, or thou and I 20
Love so alike that none do slacken,[4] none can die.

THE UNDERTAKING

I have done one braver thing
Than all the Worthies did,
And yet a braver thence doth spring,
Which is, to keep that hid.

It were but madness now t'impart 5
The skill of specular[1] stone,
When he which can have learn'd the art
To cut it, can find none.

So, if I now should utter this,
Others (because no more 10
Such stuff to work upon there is)
Would love but as before.

But he who loveliness within
Hath found, all outward loathes,
For he who colour loves, and skin, 15
Loves but their[2] oldest clothes.

If, as I have, you also do
Virtue attir'd in woman see,
And dare love that, and say so too,
And forget the he and she; 20

And if this love, though placèd so,
From profane men you hide,
Which will no faith on this bestow,
Or, if they do, deride:

Then you have done a braver thing 25
Than all the Worthies did;

[4] Neither slackens.

[1] Mirror-like. "Specular stone" is probably an allusion to the astrologer's crystal.
[2] Women's.

And a braver thence will spring,
    Which is, to keep that hid.

HOLY SONNET VII

At the round earth's imagined corners,[1] blow
Your trumpets, angels, and arise, arise
From death, you numberless infinities
Of souls, and to your scattered bodies go;
All whom the flood did, and fire shall o'erthrow; 5
All whom war, dearth, age, agues, tyrannies,
Despair, law, chance, hath slain, and you whose eyes
Shall behold God, and never taste death's woe.
But let them sleep, Lord, and me mourn a space,
For, if above all these, my sins abound, 10
'Tis late to ask abundance of Thy grace,
When we are there; here on this lowly ground,[2]
Teach me how to repent; for that's as good
As if Thou hadst sealed my pardon, with Thy blood.

THE FUNERAL

Whoever comes to shroud me, do not harm
    Nor question much
That subtle wreath[1] of hair which crowns my arm;
The mystery, the sign you must not touch,
    For 'tis my outward soul, 5
Viceroy to that which, unto heaven being gone,
    Will leave this[2] to control,
And keep these limbs, her provinces, from dissolution.

For if the sinewy thread[3] my brain lets fall
    Through every part 10
Can tie those parts, and make me one of all,
Those hairs, which upward grew, and strength and art
    Have from a better brain,
Can better do it: except[4] she meant that I

[1] The "four corners" of the earth. [2] The earth.

[1] Circlet. [2] This soul (the circlet of hair). [3] Spinal cord. [4] Unless.

By this should know my pain, 15
As prisoners then[5] are manacled, when they're condemn'd to die.

Whate'er she meant by it, bury it with me,
For since I am
Love's martyr, it might breed idolatry,
If into other hands these reliques came; 20
As 'twas humility
To afford[6] to it all that a soul can do,
So 'tis some bravery[7]
That since you would save none of me, I bury some of you.

THE AUTUMNAL

No Spring, nor Summer beauty hath such grace,
As I have seen in one Autumnal face.
Young Beauties force our love, and that's a rape,
This doth but counsel, yet you cannot 'scape.
If 'twere a shame to love, here 'twere no shame, 5
Affection here takes Reverence's name.
Were her first years the Golden Age; that's true,
But now she's gold oft-tried and ever new.
That was her torrid and inflaming time,
This is her tolerable tropic clime. 10
Fair eyes, who asks more heat than comes from hence,
He in a fever wishes pestilence.
Call not these wrinkles, graves; if graves they were,
They were Love's graves; for else he is no where.
Yet lies not Love dead here, but here doth sit 15
Vow'd to this trench, like an anachorite.[1]
And here, till hers, which must be his death, come,
He doth not dig a grave, but build a tomb.
Here dwells he, though he sojourn ev'rywhere
In Progress, yet his standing house is here. 20
Here, where still evening is; not noon, nor night;
Where no voluptuousness, yet all delight.
In all her words, unto all hearers fit.
You may at Revels, you at Council sit.[2]
This is love's timber, youth his underwood; 25
There he, as wine in June, enrages blood,
Which then comes seasonabliest,[3] when our taste

[5] For that reason. [6] Give. [7] Boldness.

[1] Anchorite, hermit. [2] Revels are gay, mirthful gatherings, and councils are serious, judicial ones. The sense of the line is that her conversation is both witty and wise. [3] Most opportunely.

And appetite to other things is past.
Xerxes'[4] strange Lydian[5] love, the Platane tree,
Was lov'd for age, none being so large as she, 30
Or else because, being young, nature did bless
Her youth with age's glory, barrenness.
If we love things long sought, Age is a thing
Which we are fifty years in compassing;[6]
If transitory things, which soon decay, 35
Age must be loveliest at the latest day.
But name not Winter-faces, whose skin's slack,
Lank as an unthrift's purse,[7] but a soul's sack;[8]
Whose eyes seek light within, for all here's[9] shade;
Whose mouths are holes, rather worn out than made; 40
Whose every tooth to a several[10] place is gone
To vex their souls at Resurrection;
Name not these living Death's-heads unto me,
For these not ancient, but antique be.
I hate extremes; yet I had rather stay 45
With tombs than cradles to wear out[11] a day.
Since such love's natural lation[12] is, may still
My love descend, and journey down the hill,
Not panting after growing beauties, so
I shall ebb out with them who homeward go.[13] 50

JOHN WEBSTER

1580?–1625?

ALL THE FLOWERS OF THE SPRING

All the flowers of the spring
Meet to perfume our burying;
These have but their growing prime,
And man does flourish but his time.

[4] Xerxes, a king of Persia, in Lydia once found a plane (platane) tree so beautiful that he decorated it with gold and left it in the charge of a member of his elite bodyguard. [5] Lydia was an ancient country on the Aegean Sea. [6] Attaining. [7] An "unthrift" is an unthrifty person. [8] That is, although such skin is like a purse for an unthrift, it is like a sack (a formidable restraint) to a soul. [9] "Here" is outside the person with a "Winter-face." [10] Different. [11] Pass. [12] An astronomical term meaning "motion from one place to another." [13] Go towards death.

Survey our progress from our birth: 5
We are set, we grow, we turn to earth.
Courts adieu, and all delights,
All bewitching appetites.
Sweetest breath and clearest eye,
Like perfumes, go out and die; 10
And consequently this is done
As shadows wait upon the sun.
Vain the ambition of kings
Who seek by trophies and dead things
To leave a living name behind, 15
And weave but nets to catch the wind.

A DIRGE

Call for the robin-redbreast and the wren,
Since o'er shady groves they hover,
And with leaves and flowers do cover
The friendless bodies of unburied men.
Call unto his funeral dole[1] 5
The ant, the field-mouse, and the mole,
To rear him hillocks that shall keep him warm,
And, when gay tombs are robbed, sustain no harm;
But keep the wolf far thence, that's foe to men,
For with his nails he'll dig them up again. 10

ROBERT HERRICK

1591–1674

DELIGHT IN DISORDER

A sweet disorder in the dress
Kindles in clothes a wantonness:[1]
A lawn[2] about the shoulders thrown

[1] Lamentation.

[1] Capriciousness. [2] A scarf of fine linen.

Into a fine distraction,[3]
An erring lace, which here and there   5
Enthralls the crimson stomacher,[4]
A cuff neglectful, and thereby
Ribbands to flow confusedly,
A winning wave, deserving note,
In the tempestuous petticoat,   10
A careless shoe-string, in whose tie
I see a wild civility,
Do more bewitch me, than when art
Is too precise in every part.

TO THE VIRGINS, TO MAKE MUCH OF TIME

Gather ye rose-buds while ye may,
Old Time is still a-flying:
And this same flower that smiles today,
Tomorrow will be dying.

The glorious lamp of heaven, the Sun,   5
The higher he's a-getting,
The sooner will his race be run,
And nearer he's to setting.

That age is best, which is the first,
When youth and blood are warmer,   10
But being spent, the worse, and worst
Times, still succeed the former.

Then be not coy, but use your time;
And while ye may, go marry:
For having lost but once your prime,   15
You may for ever tarry.

UPON JULIA'S CLOTHES

Whenas[1] in silks my Julia goes,
Then, then (methinks) how sweetly flows
That liquefaction of her clothes.

[3] Confusion. [4] Part of a dress that is near the stomach.

[1] When.

Next, when I cast mine eyes and see
That brave[2] vibration each way free, 5
O how that glittering taketh me!

TO PHYLLIS,[1] TO LOVE AND LIVE WITH HIM

Live, live with me, and thou shalt see
The pleasures I'll prepare for thee:
What sweets the country can afford
Shall bless thy bed, and bless thy board.[2]
The soft sweet moss shall be thy bed, 5
With crawling woodbine overspread:
By which the silver-shedding streams
Shall gently melt thee into dreams.
Thy clothing, next, shall be a gown
Made of the fleece's purest down. 10
The tongues of kids shall be thy meat;
Their milk thy drink; and thou shalt eat
The paste of filberts for thy bread
With cream of cowslips butterèd.
Thy feasting-tables shall be hills 15
With Daisies spread, and Daffodils,
Where thou shalt sit, and Red-breast by,
For meat, shall give thee melody.
I'll give thee chains and carcanets[3]
Of Primroses and Violets. 20
A bag and bottle thou shalt have;
That[4] richly wrought, and this[5] as brave,[6]
So that as either shall express
The wearer's no mean shepherdess.
At shearing-times, and yearly wakes,[7] 25
When Themilis his pastime makes,
There thou shalt be, and be the wit,
Nay more, the feast, and grace of it.
On holy-days, when virgins meet
To dance the hays[8] with nimble feet, 30
Thou shalt come forth, and then appear
The Queen of Roses for that year,
And having danc'd, 'bove all the best,
Carry the garland from the rest.

[2] Handsome, splendid.

[1] A generic name for a rustic maiden. [2] Table used for meals; hence, meals. [3] Necklaces. [4] The bag. [5] The bottle. [6] Handsome. [7] Local festivals of English parishes. [8] A country dance.

In wicker baskets maids shall bring 35
To thee, my dearest shepherdling,
The blushing apple, bashful pear,
And shame-fac'd plum, all simp'ring there.
Walk in the groves, and thou shalt find
The name of Phyllis in the rind 40
Of every straight, and smooth-skin tree,
Where kissing that, I'll twice kiss thee.
To thee a sheep-hook I will send,
Beprank'd[9] with ribbands, to this end,
This, this alluring hook might be 45
Less for to catch a sheep, than me.
Thou shalt have possets,[10] wassails fine,
Not made of ale, but spicèd wine,
To make thy maids and self free[11] mirth,
All sitting near the glitt'ring hearth. 50
Thou shalt have ribbands, roses, rings,
Gloves, garters, stockings, shoes, and strings
Of winning colours, that shall move
Others to lust, but me to love.
These, nay, and more, thine own shall be, 55
If thou wilt love, and live with me.

CEREMONIES FOR CANDLEMAS EVE

Down with the rosemary and bays,[1]
Down with the mistletoe;
Instead of holly, now upraise
The greener box,[2] for show.

The holly hitherto did sway;[3] 5
Let box now domineer,
Until the dancing Easter Day
Or Easter's Eve appear.

Then youthful box which now hath grace
Your houses to renew, 10
Grown old, surrender must his place
Unto the crispèd yew.[4]

[9] Bedecked, adorned. [10] Drinks made of hot milk and some kind of liquor. [11] Frank and open.

[1] Boughs of bay or laurel. [2] Boxwood. [3] Predominate. [4] The yew is often associated with mourning.

When yew is out, then birch comes in,
    And many flowers beside,
Both of a fresh and fragrant kin   15
    To honour Whitsuntide.[5]

Green rushes then, and sweetest bents,[6]
    With cooler oaken boughs,
Come in for comely ornaments,
    To re-adorn the house.   20
Thus times do shift; each thing his turn does hold;
New things succeed, as former things grow old.

GEORGE HERBERT

1593–1633

THE QUIP

The merry World did on a day
With his train-bands[1] and mates agree
To meet together, where I lay,
And all in sport to jeer at me.

First, Beauty crept into a rose,   5
Which when I pluck'd not, Sir, said she,
Tell me, I pray, whose hands are those?[2]
But thou shalt answer, Lord, for me.

Then Money came, and chinking still,
What tune is this, poor man? said he: 10
I heard in music you had skill.
But thou shalt answer, Lord, for me.

[5] Whitsunday and the days immediately following. Whitsunday, the seventh Sunday after Easter, in the Christian Church is the festival of the descent of the Holy Spirit upon the Apostles. [6] Grasslike reeds.

[1] Citizen soldiers, here suggesting comrades. [2] "What kind of hands would not pluck the rose?"

Then came brave[3] Glory puffing by
In silks that whistled, who but he?
He scarce allow'd me half an eye. 15
But thou shalt answer, Lord, for me.

Then came quick Wit and Conversation,
And he would needs a comfort be,
And, to be short, make an oration.
But thou shalt answer, Lord, for me. 20

Yet when the hour of thy design
To answer these fine things shall come,
Speak not at large; say, I am thine;
And then they have their answer home.

THE COLLAR

I struck the board;[1] and cried, "No more.
I will abroad.
What? shall I ever sigh and pine?
My lines[2] and life are free; free as the road,
Loose as the wind, as large as store.[3] 5
Shall I be still in suit?[4]
Have I no harvest but a thorn
To let me blood,[5] and not restore
What I have lost with cordial[6] fruit?
Sure there was wine 10
Before my sighs did dry it: there was corn
Before my tears did drown it.
Is the year only lost to me?
Have I no bays[7] to crown it?
No flowers, no garlands gay? all blasted? 15
All wasted?
Not so, my heart: but there is fruit,
And thou hast hands.
Recover all thy sigh-blown age
On double pleasures; leave thy cold dispute 20

[3] Handsomely dressed.

[1] Table. [2] Appointed lot in life. [3] As large as abundance. [4] In attendance, in suit of (favor, reward). [5] To bleed myself, with reference to the practice of bleeding to cure ills. [6] Invigorating. [7] Honorary garland of bay, or laurel.

Of what is fit and not. Forsake thy cage,
Thy rope of sands,
Which petty thoughts have made, and made to thee
Good cable, to enforce and draw,
And be thy law, 25
While thou didst wink and wouldst not see.
Away; take heed:
I will abroad.
Call in thy death's-head there;[8] tie up thy fears.
He that forbears 30
To suit[9] and serve his need,
Deserves his load."
But as I rav'd and grew more fierce and wild
At every word,
Methought I heard one calling, *Child!* 35
And I replied, *My Lord.*

THE PULLEY

When God at first made man,
Having a glass of blessings standing by,
Let us, said he, pour on him all we can:
Let the world's riches, which dispersèd lie,
Contract into a span.[1] 5

So strength first made a way;
Then beauty flow'd, then wisdom, honour, pleasure.
When almost all was out, God made a stay,[2]
Perceiving that alone of all his treasure
Rest in the bottom lay. 10

For if I should, said he,
Bestow this jewel also on my creature,
He would adore my gifts instead of me,
And rest in[3] nature, not the God of nature:
So both[4] should losers be. 15

Yet let him keep the rest,
But keep them with repining restlessness:

[8] "Put aside thoughts of death." [9] To seek after, woo.

[1] A definitely limited space. [2] A halt. [3] Be content with. [4] Both God and man.

Let him be rich and weary, that at least,
If goodness lead him not, yet weariness
May toss him to my breast. 20

THOMAS CAREW

1595–1645?

SONG

Ask me no more where Jove bestows,
When June is past, the fading rose;
For in your beauty's orient deep[1]
These flowers, as in their causes,[2] sleep.

Ask me no more whither doth stray 5
The golden atoms[3] of the day;
For, in pure love, heaven did prepare
Those powders to enrich your hair.

Ask me no more whither doth haste
The nightingale when May is past; 10
For in your sweet dividing[4] throat
She winters, and keeps warm her note.

Ask me no more where those stars light
That downwards fall in dead of night;
For in your eyes they sit, and there 15
Fixèd become as in their sphere.[5]

Ask me no more if east or west
The Phoenix builds her spicy nest;[6]

[1] Lustrous depths; the adjective "orient" was once applied to exceptionally beautiful pearls and precious stones, because they came from the East. [2] In their seeds, or origins. [3] Sunbeams. [4] Able to articulate sweetly, harmoniously (a technical term in music). [5] According to Ptolemaic astronomy, from which seventeenth century poetry adopted images, the stars were attached to translucent spheres that were arranged around the earth. [6] The Phoenix, a mythical bird, was supposed to build for itself a pyre of spices every five hundred years, to die in the pyre's flames, and to be reborn from the ashes.

For unto you at last she flies,
And in your fragrant bosom dies. 20

JAMES SHIRLEY

1596–1666

DIRGE

The glories of our blood and state
Are shadows, not substantial things;
There is no armour against fate;
Death lays his icy hand on kings:
Scepter and crown 5
Must tumble down,
And in the dust be equal made
With the poor crooked scythe and spade.

Some men with swords may reap the field,
And plant fresh laurels[1] where they kill, 10
But their strong nerves at last must yield;
They tame but one another still;
Early or late
They stoop to fate,
And must give up their murmuring breath 15
When they, pale captives, creep to death.

The garlands wither on your brow;
Then boast no more your mighty deeds;
Upon Death's purple[2] altar now
See where the victor-victim bleeds; 20
Your heads must come
To the cold tomb:
Only the actions of the just
Smell sweet, and blossom in their dust.

[1] Win new emblems of victory (see line 17). [2] The color of royalty and also of blood.

EDMUND WALLER

1606–1687

GO, LOVELY ROSE

Go, lovely Rose—
Tell her that wastes her time and me
That now she knows,
When I resemble[1] her to thee,
How sweet and fair she seems to be. 5

Tell her that's young,
And shuns to have her graces spied,
That hadst thou sprung
In deserts, where no men abide,
Thou must have uncommended died. 10

Small is the worth
Of beauty from the light retired:
Bid her come forth,
Suffer herself to be desired,
And not blush so to be admired. 15

Then die—that she
The common fate of all things rare
May read in thee:
How small a part of time they share
That are so wondrous sweet and fair. 20

[1] Compare.

JOHN MILTON

1608–1674

ON THE MORNING OF CHRIST'S NATIVITY

I

This is the month, and this the happy morn,
Wherein the Son of Heav'ns eternal King,
Of wedded Maid, and Virgin Mother born,
Our great redemption from above did bring;
For so the holy sages[1] once did sing, 5
That he our deadly forfeit should release,[2]
And with his Father work[3] us a perpetual peace.

II

That glorious form, that light unsufferable,
And that far-beaming blaze of majesty,
Wherewith he wont[4] at Heav'n's high council-table 10
To sit the midst of Trinal Unity,
He laid aside; and here with us to be,
Forsook the courts of everlasting day,
And chose with us a darksome house of mortal clay.

III

Say, Heav'nly Muse,[5] shall not thy sacred vein 15
Afford a present to the infant God?
Hast thou no verse, no hymn, or solemn strain,
To welcome him to this his new abode,
Now while the Heav'n, by the sun's team untrod,[6]
Hath took no print of the approaching light, 20
And all the spangled host keep watch in squadrons bright?

[1] Old Testament prophets. [2] That he should release us from the penalty of death incurred because we, through Adam, forfeited eternal life. [3] Make. [4] Was wont or accustomed. [5] The practice (or convention) of appealing to the Muses or to a god or goddess for inspiration and of drawing metaphors from Greek or Roman mythology was so intimately associated with poetry that Milton and others used it, often very loosely, to treat even Christian themes. [6] Helios, the Greek sun god, every morning pulled the sun across the sky in his chariot.

IV

See how from far upon the eastern road
The star-led wizards[7] haste with odors sweet:
O run, prevent[8] them with thy humble ode,
And lay it lowly at his blessed feet; 25
Have thou the honor first thy Lord to greet,
And join thy voice unto the angel choir,
From out his secret altar touch'd with hallow'd fire.[9]

THE HYMN

I

It was the winter wild,
While the Heav'n-born child, 30
All meanly wrapp'd, in the rude manger lies;
Nature in awe to him
Had doff'd her gaudy trim,
With her great Master so to sympathize:
It was no season then for her 35
To wanton with the sun, her lusty paramour.

II

Only with speeches fair
She woos the gentle air
To hide her guilty front with innocent snow,[10]
And on her naked shame, 40
Pollute with sinful blame,
The saintly veil of maiden white to throw,
Confounded, that her Maker's eyes
Should look so near upon her foul deformities.

III

But he her fears to cease, 45
Sent down the meek-ey'd Peace;
She, crown'd with olive green, came softly sliding
Down through the turning sphere,[11]
His ready harbinger,
With turtle[12] wing the amorous clouds dividing, 50

[7] The Wise Men. [8] Anticipate, precede. [9] In Isaiah 6:6–7, a burning coal from the Lord's altar had the power of purifying the mouth, or speech. [10] Original sin is here attributed to nature as well as to man. [11] The translucent sphere that, according to ancient astronomy, contained the stars and, like all spheres, revolved about the earth. It was another convention of poetry to see the universe in terms of ancient astronomy, which was outmoded in 1543 by the Copernican system. [12] Turtledove; the turtledove is an emblem of meekness and conjugal affection.

And waving wide her myrtle[13] wand,
She strikes a universal peace through sea and land.

IV

No war or battle's sound
Was heard the world around:
The idle spear and shield were high uphung; 55
The hooked chariot[14] stood
Unstain'd with hostile blood;
The trumpet spake not to the armèd throng,
And kings sat still with awful[15] eye,
As if they surely knew their sovran Lord was by. 60

V

But peaceful was the night
Wherein the Prince of Light
His reign of peace upon the earth began:
The winds with wonder whist,[16]
Smoothly the waters kiss'd, 65
Whispering new joys to the mild ocëan,
Who now hath quite forgot to rave,
While birds of calm sit brooding on the charmèd wave.

VI

The stars with deep amaze[17]
Stand fix'd in steadfast gaze, 70
Bending one way their precious influence,[18]
And will not take their flight
For all the morning light,
Or Lucifer[19] that often warn'd them thence;
But in their glimmering orbs did glow, 75
Until their Lord himself bespake, and bid them go.

VII

And though the shady gloom
Had given day her room,[20]
The sun himself withheld his wonted speed,
And hid his head for shame, 80
As his inferior flame
The new-enlight'n'd world no more should need;

[13] An emblem of love. [14] A war chariot from which sharp hooks or blades project. [15] Full of awe, or reverence. [16] Hushed. [17] Amazement, awe. [18] According to astrology, the stars influence the lives of human beings. [19] The morning star, usually, but sometimes the sun. *Lucifer* means "light-bearer." [20] That is, night ("the shady gloom") made room, by passing, for day.

He saw a greater sun appear
Than his bright throne, or burning axletree[21] could bear.

VIII

The shepherds on the lawn,[22] 85
Or ere[23] the point of dawn,
Sat simply chatting in a rustic row;
Full little thought they then
That the mighty Pan[24]
Was kindly come to live with them below; 90
Perhaps their loves, or else their sheep,
Was all that did their silly[25] thoughts so busy keep.

IX

When such music sweet
Their hearts and ears did greet,
As never was by mortal finger struck, 95
Divinely warblèd voice
Answering the stringèd noise,[26]
As all their souls in blissful rapture took:[27]
The air, such pleasure loth to lose,
With thousand echoes still prolongs each heav'nly close.[28] 100

X

Nature that heard such sound
Beneath the hollow round
Of Cynthia's seat,[29] the airy region thrilling,
Now was almost won
To think her part was done, 105
And that her reign had here its last fulfilling;
She knew such harmony alone
Could hold all Heav'n and Earth in happier union.

XI

At last surrounds their sight[30]
A globe of circular light, 110
That with long beams the shame-fac'd Night array'd;
The helmèd Cherubim
And sworded Seraphim
Are seen in glitttering ranks with wings display'd,

[21] Allusions to the sun god and his chariot. [22] Pasture. [23] Even before. [24] Christ is here identified with the Greek god of nature. Shepherds might be supposed to see God in nature especially. [25] Simple, unsophisticated. [26] Melodious sound. [27] Captivated, charmed. [28] Cadence. [29] The sphere of the moon (Cynthia), which was just outside that of the earth (Nature). [30] Sight of them.

Harping in loud and solemn choir, 115
With unexpressive[31] notes to Heav'n's new-born Heir.

XII

Such music (as 'tis said)
Before was never made,
But[32] when of old the sons of morning[33] sung,
While the Creator great 120
His constellations set,
And the well-balanc'd world on hinges hung,
And cast the dark foundations deep,
And bid the welt'ring waves their oozy channel keep.

XIII

Ring out, ye crystal spheres, 125
Once bless our human ears
(If ye have power to touch our senses so),
And let your silver chime[34]
Move in melodious time;
And let the bass of Heaven's deep organ blow, 130
And with your ninefold[35] harmony
Make up full consort to th' angelic symphony.

XIV

For if such holy song
Enwrap our fancy long,
Time will run back, and fetch the age of gold,[36] 135
And speckl'd[37] Vanity
Will sicken soon and die,
And leprous sin will melt from earthly mold,
And Hell itself will pass away,
And leave her dolorous mansions to the peering day. 140

XV

Yea, Truth and Justice then
Will down return to men,
Orb'd in a rainbow; and, like[38] glories wearing,
Mercy will sit between,

[31] Inexpressible. [32] Except. [33] The Lord asked Job, "Where were you when I laid the foundation of the earth? . . . On what were its bases sunk, or who laid its corner-stone, when the morning stars sang together, and all the sons of God shouted for joy?" (Job 38:4–7). [34] Music. [35] The universe contained nine spheres (see line 125). [36] The golden age of man (rather than of Greece), before the Fall. [37] Blemished. [38] (The) similar.

Thron'd in celestial sheen, 145
With radiant feet the tissued[39] clouds down steering,
And Heav'n, as at some festival,
Will open wide the gates of her high palace hall.

XVI

But wisest Fate says no,
This must not yet be so, 150
The Babe lies yet in smiling infancy,
That on the bitter cross
Must redeem our loss:
So both himself and us to glorify;
Yet first to those ychain'd[40] in sleep, 155
The wakeful trump of doom[41] must thunder through the deep,

XVII

With such a horrid clang
As on Mount Sinai rang
While the red fire and smould'ring clouds outbrake:[42]
The aged Earth aghast 160
With terror of that blast,
Shall from the surface to the center shake,
When at the world's last session
The dreadful Judge in middle air shall spread his throne.

XVIII

And then at last our bliss 165
Full and perfect is,
But now begins; for from this happy day
Th' old Dragon[43] under ground,
In straiter limits bound,
Not half so far casts his usurpèd sway, 170
And, wroth to see his kingdom fail,
Swinges[44] the scaly horror of his folded tail.

XIX

The oracles are dumb,[45]
No voice or hideous hum
Runs through the archèd roof in words deceiving. 175

[39] Richly woven (with silver). [40] The prefix *y* survives from an Old English form of the word. [41] Doomsday trumpet. [42] "On the morning of the third day there were thunders and lightnings, and a thick cloud upon the mountain, and a very loud trumpet blast, so that all the people who were in the camp trembled" (Exodus 19:16). [43] Satan is called "the great dragon" in Revelation 12:9. [44] Lashes. [45] There is a legend that when Christ was born, pagan oracles could no longer prophesy.

Apollo from his shrine
Can no more divine,
With hollow shriek the steep of Delphos[46] leaving.
No nightly trance, or breathèd spell,
Inspires the pale-ey'd priest from the prophetic cell. 180

XX

The lonely mountains o'er,
And the resounding shore,
A voice of weeping heard, and loud lament;
From haunted spring and dale,
Edg'd with poplar pale, 185
The parting Genius[47] is with sighing sent;
With flow'r-inwov'n tresses torn
The nymphs in twilight shade of tangled thickets mourn.

XXI

In consecrated earth,
And on the holy hearth, 190
The Lars[48] and Lemures[49] moan with midnight plaint;
In urns and altars round,
A drear and dying sound
Affrights the Flamens[50] at their service quaint;[51]
And the chill marble seems to sweat,[52] 195
While each peculiar power forgoes his wonted seat.

XXII

Peor and Baalim[53]
Forsake their temples dim,
With that twice-batter'd god[54] of Palestine;
And moonèd Ashtaroth,[55] 200
Heav'n's queen and mother both,
Now sits not girt with tapers' holy shine;
The Libyc Hammon shrinks his horn,
In vain the Tyrian maids their wounded Thammuz mourn.

[46] Delphi. Apollo, god of light and healing, was thought to speak to mortals at Delphi in cryptic messages uttered by his medium and interpreted by priests. [47] The spirit that belongs to and guards a particular place. Milton is citing another illustration of the death of paganism. [48] Lares (singular: *Lar*), Roman household gods. [49] (Singular: *Lemur*), Roman spirits of the dead. [50] A flamen is a priest devoted to serving a particular god. [51] Strange, curious. [52] The statue of the god seems to sweat in apprehension of the god's fate. [53] These names and others in this and the following stanza belong to various Eastern deities of the ancient world. [54] Dagon, whose image twice fell down before the ark of the Lord (see I Samuel 5:1–5). [55] This goddess was sometimes associated with the moon.

XXIII

And sullen Moloch, fled, 205
Hath left in shadows dread
His burning idol all of blackest hue;
In vain with cymbals' ring
They call the grisly king,
In dismal dance about the furnace blue; 210
The brutish gods[56] of Nile as fast,
Isis and Orus, and the dog Anubis haste.

XXIV

Nor is Osiris seen
In Memphian[57] grove or green,
Trampling the unshow'r'd grass[58] with lowings loud: 215
Nor can he be at rest
Within his sacred chest,[59]
Nought but profoundest Hell can be his shroud,
In vain with timbrel'd anthems dark
The sable-stolèd[60] sorcerers bear his worship'd ark. 220

XXV

He feels from Judah's land
The dreaded Infant's hand,
The rays of Bethlehem blind his dusky eyn;[61]
Nor all the gods beside
Longer dare abide, 225
Nor Typhon[62] huge ending in snaky twine:
Our Babe, to show his Godhead true,
Can in his swaddling bands control the damnèd crew.

XXVI

So when the sun in bed,
Curtain'd with cloudy red, 230
Pillows his chin upon an orient[63] wave,
The flocking shadows pale
Troop to th' infernal jail;
Each fetter'd ghost slips to his several[64] grave,

[56] The gods referred to were represented as animals or as human beings with animal parts. [57] Memphis was the capital of ancient Egypt, where Osiris, who was represented as a bull, was the chief god. [58] It seldom rains in Egypt. [59] Images of Osiris were carried in small chests or arks. [60] Black-stoled. [61] Eyes (archaic). [62] A Greek monster that was half man, half snake. [63] Luxurious (because pearls and other gems and rich fabrics were associated with the Orient). [64] Particular, own.

And the yellow-skirted Fays 235
Fly after the night-steeds, leaving their moon-lov'd maze.[65]

XXVII

But see, the Virgin blest
Hath laid her Babe to rest.
Time is our tedious song should here have ending;
Heav'n's youngest-teemèd star[66] 240
Hath fix'd her polish'd car,
Her sleeping Lord with handmaid lamp attending;
And all about the courtly stable
Bright-harness'd[67] angels sit in order serviceable.[68]

ON SHAKESPEARE

What[1] needs my Shakespeare for his honor'd bones
The labor of an age in pilèd stones,
Or that his hallow'd relics should be hid
Under a star-ypointing[2] pyramid?
Dear son of memory, great heir of fame, 5
What need'st thou such weak witness of thy name?
Thou in our wonder and astonishment
Hast built thyself a livelong[3] monument.
For whilst to th' shame of slow-endeavoring art
Thy easy numbers[4] flow, and that each heart 10
Hath from the leaves of thy unvalu'd[5] book
Those Delphic[6] lines with deep impression took,
Then thou, our fancy of itself bereaving,
Dost make us marble with too much conceiving,[7]
And so sepúlcher'd in such pomp dost lie, 15
That kings for such a tomb would wish to die.

[65] Labyrinth of paths and trees, or forest. [66] Latest born star (the star of Bethlehem). [67] Brightly armored. [68] In an order suggesting their willingness to serve.

[1] Why. [2] The prefix *y* survives from an Old English form of the word. [3] Long-lasting. [4] Verses, measures. [5] Priceless, invaluable. [6] Oracular or inspired, as the priestess was who spoke for Apollo at Delphi. [7] Imagining.

L'ALLEGRO[1]

Hence, loathèd Melancholy,
 Of Cerberus[2] and blackest Midnight born,[3]
In Stygian cave[4] forlorn,
 'Mongst horrid shapes and shrieks, and sights unholy;
Find out some uncouth[5] cell, 5
 Where brooding darkness spreads his jealous wings,
And the night-raven sings;
 There, under ebon shades, and low-brow'd rocks,
As ragged as thy locks,
 In dark Cimmerian[6] desert ever dwell. 10
But come, thou goddess fair and free,
In Heav'n yclept[7] Euphrosyne,[8]
And by men, heart-easing Mirth,
Whom lovely Venus,[9] at a birth,
With two sister Graces more 15
To ivy-crownèd Bacchus[10] bore;
Or whether (as some sager sing)
The frolic wind that breathes the spring,
Zephyr[11] with Aurora[12] playing,
As he met her once a-Maying, 20
There on beds of violets blue,
And fresh-blown roses wash'd in dew,
Fill'd her with thee, a daughter fair,
So buxom,[13] blithe, and debonair.[14]
Haste thee, nymph, and bring with thee 25
Jest and youthful Jollity,
Quips and Cranks,[15] and wanton[16] Wiles,
Nods, and Becks,[17] and wreathèd Smiles,
Such as hang on Hebe's[18] cheek,
And love to live in dimple sleek; 30
Sport, that wrinkled Care derides,
And Laughter holding both his sides.
Come, and trip it as ye go
On the light fantastic toe,

[1] (Italian) The cheerful man. [2] In Greek mythology, a many-headed dog with a mane and a tail of snakes that guarded the gate of Hades, the underworld, where spirits of the dead (both good and evil) were believed to go. [3] This "myth" is of Milton's invention. [4] Hades was surrounded by the river Styx. [5] Unknown, unfamiliar. [6] The Cimmerians, according to Homer, were a people "on whom the sun never looks." He placed them in a land of never-ending darkness just this side of Hades. [7] Called, named (archaic). [8] One of the Graces; her name means "joy." [9] In Roman mythology, the goddess of love. [10] The Roman god of wine and joy. Zeus, or Jove, is usually considered the father of the Graces. [11] The west wind in classical mythology. [12] Roman goddess of the dawn. She is usually thought of as the mother of Zephyr. [13] Gracious, lively. [14] Courteous. [15] Twists or fanciful turns of speech; conceits. [16] Extravagant, impetuous. [17] Bows, curtsies. [18] Greek goddess of youth.

And in thy right hand lead with thee 35
The mountain nymph, sweet Liberty;
And if I give thee honor due,
Mirth, admit me of thy crew,
To live with her, and live with thee,
In unreprovèd[19] pleasures free: 40
To hear the lark begin his flight,
And, singing, startle the dull night,
From his watch-tow'r in the skies,
Till the dappled dawn doth rise;
Then to come in spite of sorrow, 45
And at my window bid good-morrow,
Through the sweet-briar, or the vine,
Or the twisted eglantine,[20]
While the cock, with lively din,
Scatters the rear of darkness thin, 50
And to the stack, or the barn door,
Stoutly struts his dames before;
Oft list'ning how the hounds and horn
Cheerly rouse the slumb'ring morn,
From the side of some hoar[21] hill, 55
Through the high wood echoing shrill;
Sometimes walking not unseen
By hedgerow elms, on hillocks green,
Right against[22] the eastern gate,
Where the great sun begins his state,[23] 60
Rob'd in flames, and amber light,
The clouds in thousand liveries dight;[24]
While the plowman near at hand,
Whistles o'er the furrow'd land,
And the milkmaid singeth blithe, 65
And the mower whets his scythe,
And every shepherd tells his tale[25]
Under the hawthorn in the dale.
Straight mine eye hath caught new pleasures
Whilst the landskip[26] round it measures: 70
Russet lawns and fallows[27] gray,
Where the nibbling flocks do stray;
Mountains on whose barren breast
The laboring clouds do often rest;
Meadows trim, with daisies pied,[28] 75
Shallow brooks, and rivers wide.
Towers, and battlements it sees
Bosom'd high in tufted trees,

[19] Innocent. [20] Probably woodbine or honeysuckle. (Eglantine is another name for sweetbrier.) [21] Gray, from absence of foliage. [22] Towards. [23] Stately procession. [24] Dressed. [25] Counts his sheep. [26] Landscape. [27] Plowed fields. [28] Parti-colored, speckled.

Where perhaps some beauty lies,
The cynosure of neighboring eyes. 80
Hard by, a cottage chimney smokes,
From betwixt two agèd oaks,
Where Corydon[29] and Thyrsis, met,
Are at their savory dinner set
Of herbs, and other country messes,[30] 85
Which the neat-handed Phillis dresses;
And then in haste her bow'r[31] she leaves,
With Thestylis to bind the sheaves;
Or, if the earlier season lead,
To the tannèd haycock in the mead. 90
Sometimes with secure[32] delight
The upland hamlets will invite,
When the merry bells ring round,
And the jocund rebecks[33] sound
To many a youth, and many a maid 95
Dancing in the checker'd shade;
And young and old come forth to play
On a sunshine holiday,
Till the livelong daylight fail;
Then to the spicy, nut-brown ale, 100
With stories told of many a feat,
How faery Mab[34] the junkets[35] eat;
She was pinch'd and pull'd, she said;
And he, by friar's lanthorn[36] led,
Tells how the drudging Goblin[37] sweat 105
To earn his cream-bowl duly set,
When in one night, ere glimpse of morn,
His shadowy flail hath thresh'd the corn
That ten day-laborers could not end;
Then lies him down the lubber[38] fiend, 110
And, stretch'd out all the chimney's length,
Basks at the fire his hairy strength;
And, crop-full,[39] out of doors he flings
Ere the first cock his matin rings.
Thus done the tales, to bed they creep, 115
By whispering winds soon lull'd asleep.
Tow'red cities please us then,
And the busy hum of men,
Where throngs of knights and barons bold,

[29] This and other names in the following lines are type names of shepherds and shepherdesses. [30] Dishes. [31] Cottage. [32] Confident. [33] Medieval fiddles. [34] Queen of the fairies. [35] Sweetened curds served with cream; *eat* (pronounced "ett") is the past tense. [36] Jack-o'-lantern, will-o'-the-wisp, *ignis fatuus*. [37] Hobgoblin, or Robin Goodfellow, an ugly sprite sometimes mischievous and sometimes (as here) helpful to the family. [38] Drudging. [39] With a full crop, or stomach.

In weeds[40] of peace, high triumphs[41] hold, 120
With store of ladies, whose bright eyes
Rain influence,[42] and judge the prize
Of wit, or arms, while both contend
To win her grace whom all commend.
There let Hymen[43] oft appear 125
In saffron robe, with taper clear,
And pomp, and feast, and revelry,
With masque,[44] and antique pageantry,
Such sights as youthful poets dream
On summer eves by haunted stream. 130
Then to the well-trod stage anon,
If Jonson's[45] learnèd sock[46] be on,
Or sweetest Shakespeare, Fancy's child,
Warble his native wood-notes wild.
And ever against eating cares, 135
Lap me in soft Lydian airs,[47]
Married to immortal verse,
Such as the meeting[48] soul may pierce
In notes, with many a winding bout[49]
Of linkèd sweetness long drawn out, 140
With wanton heed, and giddy cunning,[50]
The melting voice through mazes running,
Untwisting all the chains that tie
The hidden soul of harmony;
That Orpheus' self[51] may heave his head 145
From golden slumber on a bed
Of heap'd Elysian[52] flow'rs, and hear
Such strains as would have won the ear
Of Pluto, to have quite set free
His half-regain'd Eurydice. 150
These delights, if thou canst give,
Mirth, with thee, I mean to live.

[40] Garments. [41] Festivities. [42] That is, as the stars, according to astrology, influence men's lives. [43] The god of marriage. [44] Dramatic interlude performed by masked actors. [45] Ben Jonson (1572–1637), English dramatist who wrote comedies in the classical tradition. [46] In ancient Greece, the low shoe worn by comic actors, as opposed to the buskin, or raised shoe, worn for tragedy. [47] In ancient Greece, the Lydian "mode" of music was soft and delicate. [48] Responsive. [49] Turn, phrase. [50] Note the unusual adjective-noun combinations. Milton is suggesting a singer (or poet) abandoned to his art. [51] In Greek mythology, Orpheus was a musician whose wife Eurydice, was killed by a snake. Orpheus went to the underworld, Hades, to find her. He played the lyre so well that Pluto, ruler of Hades, permitted him to take Eurydice back, provided that he did not look at her during the journey to the upper world. When nearly there, however, he no longer heard her behind him and turned to look. Eurydice returned to Hades. [52] Delightful, from Elysium, the abode of the blessed in Greek mythology.

HOW SOON HATH TIME

How soon hath Time, the subtle thief of youth,
Stol'n on his wing my three and twentieth year!
My hasting days fly on with full career,[1]
But my late spring no bud or blossom shew'th.
Perhaps my semblance might deceive the truth, 5
That I to manhood am arriv'd so near,
And inward ripeness doth much less appear,
That[2] some more timely-happy spirits endu'th.[3]
Yet be it less or more, or soon or slow,
It shall be still in strictest measure ev'n 10
To that same lot, however mean or high,
Toward which Time leads me, and the will of Heav'n;
All is, if I have grace to use it so,
As ever in my great task-Master's eye.

WHEN I CONSIDER HOW MY LIGHT IS SPENT

When I consider how my light is spent
Ere half my days, in this dark world and wide,
And that one talent[1] which is death to hide,
Lodg'd with me useless, though my soul more bent
To serve therewith my Maker, and present 5
My true account, lest he returning chide,
"Doth God exact day labor, light denied?"
I fondly[2] ask. But Patience, to prevent
That murmur, soon replies, "God doth not need
Either man's work or his own gifts; who best 10
Bear his mild yoke,[3] they serve him best; his state
Is kingly: thousands at his bidding speed,
And post o'er land and ocean without rest:
They also serve who only stand and wait."

[1] Speed. [2] Refers to *manhood.* [3] Endows.

[1] See the "Parable of the Talents," Matthew 25:14–30. [2] Foolishly. [3] The yoke of servitude, bondage.

SIR JOHN SUCKLING

1609–1642

WHY SO PALE AND WAN?

Why so pale and wan, fond lover?
    Prithee, why so pale?
Will, when looking well can't move her,
    Looking ill prevail?
    Prithee, why so pale? 5

Why so dull and mute, young sinner?
    Prithee, why so mute?
Will, when speaking well can't win her,
    Saying nothing do't?
    Prithee, why so mute? 10

Quit, quit for shame, this will not move:
    This cannot take her.
If of herself she will not love,
    Nothing can make her:
    The devil take her! 15

A BALLAD UPON A WEDDING

I tell thee, Dick,[1] where I have been,
Where I the rarest things have seen,
    O, things without compare!
Such sights again cannot be found
In any place on English ground, 5
    Be it at wake[2] or fair.

At Charing Cross, hard by the way
Where we (thou know'st) do sell our hay[3]
    There is a house with stairs;

[1] The names used in this poem are type names for rustics. [2] Local annual festival of an English parish, an occasion of merrymaking. [3] London's Charing Cross and Haymarket are near one another.

And there did I see coming down 10
Such folk as are not in our town,
Vorty,[4] at least, in pairs.

Amongst the rest, one pest'lent fine[5]
(His beard no bigger, though, than thine)
Walk'd on before the rest; 15
Our landlord looks like nothing to him;
The King (God bless him!), 'twould undo him
Should he go still[6] so dress'd.

At Course-a-Park,[7] without all doubt,
He should have first been taken out 20
By all the maids i' th' town:
Though lusty Roger there had been,
Or little George upon the Green,[8]
Or Vincent of the Crown.[9]

But wot you what?[10] the youth was going 25
To make an end of all his wooing;
The parson for him staid:[11]
Yet by his leave (for all his haste)
He did not so much wish all past
(Perchance) as did the maid. 30

The maid—and thereby hangs a tale;
For such a maid no Whitson-ale[12]
Could ever yet produce:
No grape, that's kindly[13] ripe, could be
So round, so plump, so soft as she, 35
Nor half so full of juice.

Her finger was so small, the ring
Would not stay on, which they did bring;
It was too wide a peck:
And to say truth (for out it must) 40
It look'd like the great collar (just)
About our young colt's neck.

[4] Forty (the poem in part imitates rustic pronunciation). [5] Fine gentleman, with the countryman's scorn of city manners. [6] Always go about. [7] A country game in which a girl called the name of a young man, who then chased her. [8] A piece of grassy land, a small park (George lives near the green). [9] Probably an inn. [10] Do you know what? [11] Stayed; that is, waited. [12] A parish festival held on Whitsunday, the seventh Sunday after Easter. [13] Naturally, completely.

Her feet beneath her petticoat,
Like little mice, stole in and out,
As if they fear'd the light: 45
But O, she dances such a way!
No sun upon an Easter-day
Is half so fine a sight.

He would have kiss'd her once or twice;
But she would not, she was so nice,[14] 50
She would not do 't in sight:
And then she look'd as who should say,
'I will do what I list[15] to-day,
And you shall do 't at night.'

Her cheeks so rare a white was on, 55
No daisy makes comparison
(Who sees them is undone);
For streaks of red were mingled there,
Such as are on a Katherne pear[16]
(The side that's next the sun). 60

Her lips were red; and one was thin,
Compar'd to that was next her chin
(Some bee had stung it newly):
But, Dick, her eyes so guard her face,
I durst no more upon them gaze 65
Than on the sun in July.

Her mouth so small, when she does speak,
Thou 'dst swear her teeth her words did break,
That they might passage get;
But she so handled still the matter, 70
They came as good as ours, or better,
And are not spent a whit.[17]

If wishing should be any sin,
The parson himself had guilty been
(She look'd that day so purely[18]); 75
And, did the youth so oft the feat
At night, as some did in conceit,[19]
It would have spoil'd him surely.

[14] Shy, reluctant. [15] Want. [16] Catherine pear (a small variety). [17] That is, are not even a little deprived of force. [18] Pure. [19] Fancy, imagination.

Just in the nick the cook knock'd thrice,
And all the waiters in a trice[20] 80
His summons did obey:
Each serving-man, with dish in hand,
March'd boldly up, like our train'd band,
Presented, and away.

When all the meat was on the table, 85
What man of knife or teeth was able
To stay to be intreated?[21]
And this the very reason was—
Before the parson could say grace,
The company was seated. 90

The bus'ness of the kitchen's great,
For it is fit that man should eat;
Nor was it there deni'd—
Passion o' me, how I run on!
There's that that would be thought upon 95
(I trow[22]) besides the bride.

Now hats fly off, and youths carouse,
Healths first go round, and then the house:[23]
The bride's came thick and thick;
And, when 'twas nam'd another's health, 100
Perhaps he made it hers by stealth;
(And who could help it, Dick?)

O' th' sudden up they rise and dance;
Then sit again and sigh, and glance;
Then dance again and kiss: 105
Thus several ways the time did pass,
Whilst ev'ry woman wished her place,
And every man wished his.

By this time all were stol'n aside
To counsel and undress the bride; 110
But that he must not know:
But yet 'twas thought he guess'd her mind,
And did not mean to stay behind
Above an hour or so.

[20] In an instant, at once. [21] To wait to be entreated. [22] Trust, think.
[23] That is, healths, and then the house, are drunk to.

When in he came, Dick, there she lay 115
Like new-fall'n snow melting away
('Twas time, I trow, to part):
Kisses were now the only stay,
Which soon she gave, as who would say,
God b' w' ye, with all my heart. 120

But, just as Heav'ns would have, to cross it,
In came the bridemaids with the posset:[24]
The bridegroom eat[25] in spite;
For, had he left the women to 't,
It would have cost two hours to do 't, 125
Which were too much that night.

At length the candle's out; and now
All that they had not done they do:
What that is, who can tell?
But I believe it was no more 130
Than thou and I have done before
With Bridget and with Nell.

THE CONSTANT LOVER

Out upon it![1] I have lov'd
Three whole days together;
And am like to love three more,
If it prove fair weather.

Time shall moult away his wings, 5
Ere he shall discover
In the whole wide world again
Such a constant[2] lover.

But the spite on't is, no praise
Is due at all to me: 10
Love with me had made no stays,[3]
Had it any been but she.

[24] A drink of hot milk and ale, wine, or other liquor. [25] This is the past tense.

[1] Phrase implying abhorrence. [2] Faithful [3] Standstill.

Had it any been but she,
    And that very face,
There had been at least ere this   15
    A dozen dozen in her place.

RICHARD CRASHAW

1613?–1649

WISHES TO HIS (SUPPOSED) MISTRESS

Whoe'er she be,
That not impossible she
That shall command my heart and me;

Where'er she lie,
Lock'd up from mortal eye,   5
In shady leaves of destiny:

Till that ripe birth
Of studied fate stand forth,
And teach[1] her fair steps to our earth;

Till that divine   10
Idea take a shrine
Of crystal flesh, through which to shine;

Meet you her, my wishes,
Bespeak her to[2] my blisses,
And be ye call'd my absent kisses.   15

I wish her beauty,
That owes not all his[3] duty
To gaudy tire,[4] or glist'ring shoe-tie;

[1] Guide. [2] Speak to her about. [3] Its. [4] Attire.

Something more than
Taffeta or tissue can,[5]
Or rampant feather, or rich fan; 20

More than the spoil
Of shop, or silkworm's toil,
Or a bought blush, or a set smile;

A face that's best
By its own beauty dress'd, 25
And can alone commend[6] the rest;

A face made up
Out of no other shop
Than what nature's white hand sets ope; 30

A cheek where youth
And blood, with pen of truth
Write what the reader sweetly ru'th;[7]

A cheek where grows
More than a morning rose, 35
Which to no box his being owes;

Lips where all day
A lover's kiss may play,
Yet carry nothing[8] thence away;

Looks that oppress[9] 40
Their richest tires, but dress
And clothe their simplest nakedness.

Eyes that displace
The neighbour[10] diamond, and out-face
That sunshine by their own sweet grace; 45

Tresses that wear
Jewels but to declare
How much themselves more precious are;

[5] Can manage. [6] Recommend. [7] Rueth, regards with compassion. [8] None of the color or form. [9] Overpower by contrast. [10] Similar.

Whose native ray
Can tame the wanton day[11] 50
Of gems, that in their bright shades play—

Each ruby there,
Or pearl that dare appear,
Be its own blush, be its own tear;

A well-tam'd heart, 55
For whose more noble smart
Love may be long choosing a dart;

Eyes that bestow
Full quivers[12] on love's bow,
Yet pay less arrows than they owe; 60

Smiles that can warm
The blood, yet teach[13] a charm,
That chastity shall take no harm;

Blushes that bin[14]
The burnish of no sin, 65
Nor flames of aught too hot within;

Joys that confess
Virtue their mistress,
And have no other head to dress;

Fears, fond and flight,[15] 70
As the coy bride's, when night
First does the longing lover right;

Tears, quickly fled,
And vain, as those are shed
For a dying maidenhead; 75

Days that need borrow
No part of their good morrow
From a fore-spent night of sorrow;

[11] Light. [12] Containers for arrows. [13] Cast. [14] Be, are. [15] Foolish and fleeting.

Days that, in spite
Of darkness, by the light 80
Of a clear mind are day all night;

Nights, sweet as they,
Made short by lover's play,
Yet long by th' absence of the day;

Life that dares send 85
A challenge to his end,
And, when it comes, say, "Welcome, friend!"

Sidneian showers
Of sweet discourse,[16] whose powers
Can crown old winter's head with flowers; 90

Soft silken hours,
Open suns, shady bowers;
'Bove all, nothing within that lowers;

Whate'er delight
Can make day's forehead bright, 95
Or give down to the wings of night.

In her whole frame
Have nature all the name,[17]
Art and ornament the shame.

Her flattery, 100
Picture and poesy:
Her counsel her own virtue be.[18]

I wish her store
Of worth may leave her poor
Of wishes; and I wish—no more. 105

Now if time knows
That her[19] whose radiant brows
Weave them[20] a garland of my vows;

[16] A reference to the elegant conversations of Sir Philip Sidney's prose romance, *Arcadia* (1590), which was still widely read. [17] Credit. [18] That is, no matter how she is flattered in paintings and poems, let her accept only the judgment her own virtue gives. [19] Person. [20] Themselves.

Her whose just bays[21]
My future hopes can raise,[22] 110
A trophy to her present praise;

Her that dares be
What these lines wish to see:
I seek no further—it is she.

'Tis she, and here 115
Lo I unclothe and clear
My wishes' cloudy character.

May she enjoy it
Whose merit dare apply it,
But modesty dares still deny it. 120

Such worth as this is
Shall fix my flying wishes,
And determine them to[23] kisses.

Let her full glory,
My fancies, fly before ye; 125
Be ye my fictions—but her story.

RICHARD LOVELACE

1618–1658

TO AMARANTHA, THAT SHE WOULD DISHEVELE HER HAIR

Amarantha sweet and fair,
Ah, braid no more that shining hair!
As my curious hand or eye,
Hovering round thee, let it fly.

[21] Garlands of bay, or laurel, signifying excellence. [22] That is, I hope I can in the future create. [23] Resolve them into.

Let it fly as unconfin'd
As its calm ravisher, the wind,
Who hath left his darling, th' East,
To wanton o'er that spicy nest. 5

Ev'ry tress must be confest,[1]
But neatly tangled at the best; 10
Like a clue of golden thread,
Most excellently ravellèd.

Do not then wind up that light
In ribbands, and o'ercloud in night
Like the sun in's early ray, 15
But shake your head, and scatter day!

TO ALTHEA, FROM PRISON[1]

When Love with unconfinèd wings
Hovers within my gates,
And my divine Althea brings
To whisper at the grates;[2]
When I lie tangled in her hair 5
And fetter'd to her eye,
The gods that wanton in the air
Know no such liberty.

When flowing cups run swiftly round,
With no allaying Thames,[3] 10
Our careless heads with roses[4] bound,
Our hearts with loyal flames;
When thirsty grief in wine we steep,
When healths and draughts go free,
Fishes that tipple in the deep 15
Know no such liberty.

When, like committed[5] linnets, I
With shriller throat shall sing

[1] Admitted to, shown.

[1] Lovelace, a passionate supporter of the king (see stanzas 2 and 3), was imprisoned in 1642 by the Puritan Parliament when he presented them with a petition from the Loyalists of the Country of Kent. [2] Prison bars. [3] The Thames River; that is, water. [4] The rose is the emblem of England, hence, a symbol of loyalty. [5] Imprisoned, caged.

The sweetness, mercy, majesty,
    And glories of my King; 20
When I shall voice aloud how good
    He is, how great should be,
Enlargèd winds, that curl[6] the flood,
    Know no such liberty.

Stone walls do not a prison make, 25
    Nor iron bars a cage;
Minds innocent and quiet take
    That for an hermitage;
If I have freedom in my love,
    And in my soul am free, 30
Angels alone, that soar above,
    Enjoy such liberty.

TO LUCASTA, GOING TO THE WARS

Tell me not, Sweet, I am unkind,
That from the nunnery
Of thy chaste breast and quiet mind,
To war and arms I fly.

True, a new mistress now I chase, 5
The first foe in the field;
And with a stronger faith embrace
A sword, a horse, a shield.

Yet this inconstancy is such
As you too shall adore; 10
I could not love thee, Dear, so much,
Lov'd I not honour more.

THE GRASSHOPPER

To My Noble Friend, Mr. Charles Cotton

O thou that swing'st upon the waving hair
    Of some well-fillèd oaten beard,
Drunk ev'ry night with a delicious tear
    Dropp'd thee from heav'n, where now th'art reared;

[6] Push back.

The joys of earth and air are thine entire, 5
That with thy feet and wings dost hop and fly;
And when thy poppy works thou dost retire
To thy carv'd acorn-bed to lie.

Up with the day, the sun thou welcom'st then,
Sport'st in the gilt-plats[1] of his beams, 10
And all these merry days mak'st merry men,
Thyself, and melancholy streams.

But ah, the sickle! Golden ears are cropp'd;
Ceres and Bacchus[2] bid good night;
Sharp frosty fingers all your flow'rs have topp'd,[3] 15
And what scythes spar'd, winds shave off quite.

Poor verdant[4] fool! and now green ice! thy joys
Large and as lasting as thy perch of grass,
Bid us lay in 'gainst winter, rain, and poise[5]
Their floods with an o'erflowing glass. 20

Thou best of men and friends! we will create
A genuine summer in each other's breast;
And spite of this cold time and frozen fate
Thaw us a warm seat to[6] our rest.

Our sacred hearths shall burn eternally 25
As vestal flames; the North Wind, he
Shall strike his frost-stretch'd wings, dissolve, and fly
This Ætna[7] in epitome.

Dropping December shall come weeping in,
Bewail th' usurping of his reign; 30
But when in show'rs of old Greek[8] we begin,
Shall cry, he hath his crown again.

Night as clear Hesper[9] shall our tapers[10] whip
From the light casements where we play,

[1] Braids (see line 1). [2] The goddess of agriculture and the god of wine, respectively, in Roman mythology. [3] Picked. [4] Green, inexperienced. [5] Weight, worries. [6] For. [7] The Aetna (volcano) of "our sacred hearths." [8] Old Greek wine. [9] The evening star. [10] Candles.

And the dark hag[11] from her black mantle strip,   35
And stick there everlasting day.

Thus richer than untempted kings are we,
That asking nothing, nothing need:
Though lord of all what[12] seas embrace, yet he
That wants himself is poor indeed.   40

ANDREW MARVELL

1621–1678

THE GARDEN

How vainly men themselves amaze[1]
To win the palm, the oak, or bays;[2]
And their incessant labours see
Crown'd from some single herb or tree,
Whose short and narrow vergèd[3] shade   5
Does prudently their toils upbraid;
While all flow'rs and all trees do close[4]
To weave the garlands of repose.

Fair Quiet, have I found thee here,
And Innocence, thy sister dear!   10
Mistaken long, I sought you then
In busy companies of men.
Your sacred plants, if here below,
Only among the plants will grow.
Society is all but rude,   15
To[5] this delicious solitude.

No white nor red[6] was ever seen
So am'rous as this lovely green.

[11] That is, night. [12] That.

[1] Perplex [2] Crowns made of these types of leaves were symbols, respectively, of fame in war, civil life, poetry. [3] Bordered, limited. [4] Combine, join together. [5] In comparison to. [6] Of a woman's skin.

Fond lovers, cruel as their flame,[7]
Cut in these trees their mistress' name. 20
Little, alas, they know, or heed,
How far these beauties hers exceed!
Fair trees, wheres'e'er your barks I wound,
No name shall but your own be found.

When we have run our passion's heat, 25
Love hither makes his best retreat.
The gods, that mortal beauty chase,
Still in a tree did end their race:
Apollo hunted Daphne so,
Only that she might laurel grow; 30
And Pan did after Syrinx speed,
Not as a nymph, but for a reed.[8]

What wond'rous life is this I lead!
Ripe apples drop about my head;
The luscious clusters of the vine 35
Upon my mouth do crush their wine;
The nectarine, and curious peach,
Into my hands themselves do reach;
Stumbling on melons, as I pass,
Ensnar'd with flow'rs, I fall on grass. 40

Meanwhile the mind, from pleasure less,
Withdraws its happiness:
The mind, that ocean where each kind
Does straight[9] its own resemblance find;
Yet it creates, transcending these, 45
Far other worlds, and other seas;
Annihilating all that's made
To a green thought in a green shade.

Here at the fountain's sliding foot,
Or at some fruit-tree's mossy root, 50
Casting the body's vest aside,
My soul into the boughs does glide:
There, like a bird, it sits, and sings,
Then whets[10] and combs its silver wings,

[7] Passion. [8] Daphne and Syrinx, in Greek mythology, were nymphs who were pursued by Apollo (god of light and medicine) and Pan (god of forests and flocks), respectively. Both wanted to escape and both succeeded: Daphne was changed into a laurel and Syrinx into a reed. [9] Immediately. [10] Preens.

And, till prepar'd for longer flight, 55
Waves in its plumes the various light.

Such was that happy garden-state,
While man there walk'd without a mate:
After a place so pure, and sweet,
What other help could yet be meet! 60
But 'twas beyond a mortal's share
To wander solitary there:
Two paradises 'twere in one
To live in paradise alone.

How well the skilful gardner drew 65
Of flow'rs and herbs this dial new;[11]
Where, from above, the milder sun
Does through a fragrant zodiac run;
And, as it works, th' industrious bee
Computes its time as well as we. 70
How could such sweet and wholesome hours
Be reckon'd but with herbs and flow'rs!

THE MOWER AGAINST GARDENS

Luxurious[1] Man, to bring his vice in use,[2]
Did after him the world seduce:
And from the fields the flow'rs and plants allure,
Where Nature was most plain and pure.
He first enclos'd within the gardens square 5
A dead and standing pool of air:
And a more luscious earth for them did knead,
Which stupifi'd them while it fed.
The pink grew then as double as his mind;
The nutriment did change the kind. 10
With strange perfumes he did the roses taint.
And flow'rs themselves were taught to paint.
The tulip, white, did for complexion seek;
And learn'd to interline its cheek:
Its onion root[3] they then so high did hold, 15
That one was for a meadow sold.[4]

[11] The garden is planted in the form of a sundial.

[1] Lecherous. [2] That is, to make use of his vice. [3] The tulip bulb resembles an onion. [4] A reference to the tulip mania in Holland in the 1630's.

Another world was search'd, through Oceans new,
To find the Marvel of Peru.[5]
And yet these rarities might be allowed,
To Man, that sov'reign thing and proud, 20
Had he not dealt between the bark and tree,
Forbidden mixtures there to see.
No plant now knew the stock from which it came;
He grafts upon the wild the tame:
That the uncertain and adult'rate fruit 25
Might put the palate in dispute.
His green seraglio has its eunuchs too,
Lest any tyrant him outdo.
And in the cherry he does Nature vex,
To procreate without a sex.[6] 30
'Tis all enforc'd; the fountain and the grot;
While the sweet fields do lie forgot:
Where willing Nature does to all dispence
A wild and fragrant innocence:
And fauns and fairies do the meadows till, 35
More by their presence than their skill.
Their statues polish'd by some ancient hand,
May to adorn the gardens stand:
But howso'ere the figures do excel,
The gods[7] themselves with us do dwell. 40

THE MOWER'S SONG

My mind was once the true survey[1]
Of all these meadows fresh and gay;
And in the greenness of the grass
Did see its hopes as in a glass;
When *Juliana* came, and she 5
What I do to the grass, does to my thoughts and me.

But these, while I with sorrow pine,
Grew more luxuriant still and fine,
That not one blade of grass you spy'd,
But had a flower on either side; 10
When *Juliana* came, and she
What I do to the grass, does to my thoughts and me.

[5] A flower. [6] It has been conjectured that these lines refer to the growing of cherry trees by grafting. [7] Powers.

[1] Comprehensive view.

Unthankful meadows, could you so
A fellowship so true forego,
And in your gaudy May-games meet, 15
While I lay trodden under feet?
When *Juliana* came, and she
What I do to the grass, does to my thoughts and me.

But what you in compassion ought,
Shall now by my revenge be wrought: 20
And flow'rs, and grass, and I and all,
Will in one common ruin fall.
For *Juliana* comes, and she
What I do to the grass, does to my thoughts and me.

And thus, ye meadows, which have been 25
Companions of my thoughts more green,
Shall now the heraldry[2] become
With which I shall adorn my tomb;
For *Juliana* comes, and she
What I do to the grass, does to my thoughts and me. 30

BERMUDAS

Where the remote Bermudas ride
In th' ocean's bosom unespy'd,
From a small boat that row'd along,
The list'ning winds receiv'd this song[1]:
"What should we do but sing His praise, 5
That led us through the watery maze,
Unto an isle so long unknown,
And yet far kinder than our own?
Where He the huge sea-monsters wracks,
That lift the deep upon their backs. 10
He lands us on a grassy stage,
Safe from the storms, and prelate's rage.
He gave us this eternal spring,
Which here enamels everything;
And sends the fowls to us in care, 15
On daily visits through the air.
He hangs in shades the orange bright,
Like golden lamps in a green night;
And does in the pomegranates close

[2] Decorative insignia.

[1] Sung by the religious exiles from England who settled Bermuda in the early seventeenth century.

Jewels more rich than Ormus[2] shows.
He makes the figs our mouths to meet,
And throws the melons at our feet.
But apples[3] plants of such a price,
No tree could ever bear them twice.
With cedars, chosen by His hand,
From Lebanon, He stores the land,
And makes the hollow seas, that roar
Proclaim[4] the ambergris on shore.
He cast (of which we rather boast)
The Gospel's pearl upon our coast
And in these rocks for us did frame
A temple, where to sound His name.
Oh let our voice His praise exalt,
Till it arrive at Heaven's vault,
Which thence (perhaps) rebounding, may
Echo beyond the Mexique Bay."
Thus sung they, in the English boat,
An holy and a cheerful note;
And all the way, to guide their chime,
With falling oars they kept the time.

20

25

30

35

40

THE PICTURE OF LITTLE T.C. IN A PROSPECT[1] OF FLOWERS

See with what simplicity
This nymph begins her golden days!
In the green grass she loves to lie
And there with her fair aspect[2] tames
The wilder flow'rs and gives them names: 5
But only with the roses plays,
And them does tell
What colour best becomes them, and what smell.

Who can fortell for what high cause
This darling of the gods was born? 10
Yet this is she whose chaster laws
The wanton Love shall one day fear,
And, under her command severe,
See his bow broke and ensigns[3] torn.
Happy who can 15
Appease this virtuous enemy of man!

[2] Hormuz, an island of Iran that, in the twelfth and thirteenth centuries especially, was the market for the wares of India. [3] Pineapples. [4] Make known; that is, toss up.

[1] Scene, landscape. [2] Countenance, face. [3] Banners.

O then let me in time compound[4]
And parley with those conquering eyes,
Ere they have tried force to wound,
Ere, with their glancing wheels, they drive 20
In triumph over hearts that strive,
And them that yield but more despise.
Let me be laid
Where I may see the glories from some shade.

Meantime, whilst every verdant thing 25
Itself does at thy beauty charm,
Reform the errors of the spring;
Make that the tulips may have share
Of sweetness, seeing they are fair;
And roses of their thorns disarm: 30
But most procure
That violets may a longer age endure.

But O young beauty of the woods,
Whom Nature courts with fruit and flow'rs,
Gather the flow'rs, but spare the buds; 35
Lest Flora,[5] angry at thy crime,
To kill her infants in their prime,
Do quickly make th' example yours;
And, ere we see,
Nip in the blossom all our hopes and thee. 40

HENRY VAUGHAN

1622–1695

THE PURSUIT

Lord! what a busy, restless thing
Hast thou made man?
Each day, and hour he is on wing,
Rests not a span;

[4] Compromise, come to terms. [5] Roman goddess of flowers.

Then having lost[1] the sun, and light
By clouds surpriz'd
He keeps a commerce[2] in the night
With air disguis'd;
Hadst thou given to this active dust
A state untir'd, 10
The lost son had not left the huske
Nor home desir'd;[3]
That was thy secret, and it is
Thy mercy too,
For when all fails to bring to bliss, 15
Then, this[4] must do.
Ah! Lord! and what a purchase[5] will that be
To take us sick, that sound would not take thee?

THE RETREAT

Happy those early days! when I
Shin'd in my angel-infancy.
Before I understood this place
Appointed for my second race,
Or taught my soul to fancy aught 5
But a white, celestial thought,
When yet I had not walk'd above
A mile, or two, from my first love,
And looking back (at that short space),
Could see a glimpse of His bright face; 10
When on some gilded cloud, or flow'r,
My gazing soul would dwell an hour,
And in those weaker glories spy
Some shadows of eternity;
Before I taught my tongue to wound 15
My conscience with a sinful sound,
Or had the black art to dispense
A sev'ral sin[1] to ev'ry sense,
But felt through all this fleshly dress
Bright shoots of everlastingness. 20
O how I long to travel back
And tread again that ancient track!
That I might once more reach that plain
Where first I left my glorious train,

[1] Missed, wasted. [2] Carries on business, does his work. [3] A reference to the story of the prodigal son (see Luke 15:16–19). [4] Fatigue. [5] Acquisition, gain.

[1] Several sins.

From whence th' enlightened spirit sees 25
That shady city of palm trees;
But (ah!) my soul with too much stay
Is drunk, and staggers in the way.
Some men a forward motion love,
But I by backward steps would move, 30
And when this dust falls to the urn
In that state I came return.

CHILDHOOD

I cannot reach it; and my striving eye
Dazzles at it, as at eternity.
Were now that chronicle alive,
Those white designs which children drive,
And the thoughts of each harmless hour, 5
With their content, too, in my pow'r,
Quickly would I make my path even,
And by mere playing go to heaven.

Why should men love
A wolf more than a lamb or dove? 10
Or choose hell-fire and brimstone streams
Before bright stars and God's own beams?
Who kisseth thorns will hurt his face,
But flowers do both refresh and grace,
And sweetly living (fie on men!) 15
Are, when dead, medicinal then.
If seeing much should make staid eyes,
And long experience should make wise,
Since all that age doth teach is ill,
Why should I not love childhood still? 20
Why, if I see a rock or shelf,
Shall I from thence cast down myself,
Or by complying with the world,
From the same precipice be hurl'd?
Those observations are but foul 25
Which make me[1] wise to lose my soul.

And yet the practice worldlings call
Business, and weighty action all,
Checking[2] the poor child for his play,
But gravely cast themselves away. 30

[1] Say I am. [2] Reprimanding.

Dear, harmless age! the short, swift span
Where weeping virtue parts with man;
Where love without lust dwells, and bends
What way we please, without self-ends.[3]

An age of mysteries! which he 35
Must live twice that would God's face see;
Which angels guard, and with it play,
Angels! which foul men drive away.

How do I study now, and scan
Thee more than e'er I studied man, 40
And only see through a long night
Thy edges and thy bordering light!
O for thy center and mid-day!
For sure that is the Narrow Way![4]

THE WORLD

I saw eternity the other night
Like a great ring of pure and endless light,
All calm as it was bright,
And round beneath it, time in hours, days, years,
Driv'n by the spheres,[1] 5
Like a vast shadow mov'd, in which the world
And all her train were hurl'd;
The doting lover in his quaintest strain[2]
Did there complain;[3]
Near him, his lute, his fancy, and his flights, 10
Wit's sour delights,
With gloves and knots,[4] the silly snares of pleasure,
Yet his dear treasure
All scatter'd lay, while he his eyes did pour
Upon a flow'r. 15

The darksome statesman,[5] hung with weights and woe,
Like a thick midnight-fog, mov'd there so slow
He did nor stay nor go;

[3] Its own ends. [4] "Straight is the gate, and narrow is the way, which leadeth unto life" (Matthew 7:14).

[1] According to ancient astronomy, which Vaughan uses for figurative purposes, the heavens were a series of concentric, crystalline spheres arranged around the earth. [2] Most elaborate verse. [3] Plead his cause. [4] Love knots. [5] Unscrupulous politician.

Condemning thoughts, like sad eclipses, scowl
    Upon his soul, 20
And clouds of crying witnesses without
    Pursued him with one shout.
Yet digg'd the mole, and, lest his ways be found,
    Work'd under ground,
Where he did clutch his prey, but one[6] did see 25
    That policy:
Churches and altars fed him; perjuries
    Were gnats and flies;[7]
It rained about him blood and tears, but he
    Drank them as free.[8] 30

The fearful miser on a heap of rust
Sat pining all his life there, did scarce trust
    His own hands with the dust,
Yet would not place one piece[9] above, but lives
    In fear of thieves. 35
Thousands there were as frantic as himself,
    And hugg'd each one his pelf:
The downright epicure plac'd heav'n in sense[10]
    And scorn'd pretense
While others, slipp'd into a wide excess,[11] 40
    Said little less;
The weaker sort slight, trivial wares enslave,
    Who think them brave,[12]
And poor, despisèd Truth sat counting by[13]
    Their victory. 45

Yet some, who all this while did weep and sing,
And sing, and weep, soar'd up into the ring,[14]
    But most would use no wing.
"O fools!" said I, "thus to prefer dark night
    Before true light, 50
To live in grots, and caves, and hate the day
    Because it shows the way,
The way which from this dead and dark abode
    Leads up to God,
A way where you might tread the sun, and be 55
    More bright than he!"
But as I did their madness so discuss
    One whisper'd thus:

[6] The speaker. [7] Plentiful and of no importance. [8] As freely as they ran; that is, he thrived on others' misfortunes. [9] Invest one coin. See St. Matthew's admonition to invest in heavenly, rather than earthly, goods (Matthew 6:19–20). [10] Sensual pleasures. [11] Deviation from moderation. [12] Splendid, handsome. [13] Observing. [14] See line 2 above.

"This ring the Bridegroom did for none provide
But for His bride."[15] 60

JOHN DRYDEN

1631–1700

TO THE MEMORY OF MR. OLDHAM

Farewell, too little and too lately known,
Whom I began to think and call my own;
For sure our souls were near allied, and thine
Cast in the same poetic mold with mine.
One common note on either lyre did strike,[1] 5
And knaves and fools we both abhorr'd alike:
To the same goal did both our studies drive;
The last set out the soonest did arrive.[2]
Thus Nisus[3] fell upon the slippery place,
Whilst his young friend perform'd and won the race. 10
O early ripe! to thy abundant store
What could advancing age have added more?
It might (what nature never gives the young)
Have taught the numbers[4] of thy native tongue.
But satire needs not those, and wit will shine 15
Through the harsh cadence of a rugged line.
A noble error, and but seldom made,
When poets are by too much force betray'd.
Thy generous fruits, though gather'd ere their prime,
Still show'd a quickness;[5] and maturing time 20
But mellows what we write to the dull sweets[6] of rhyme.
Once more, hail, and farewell; farewell, thou young,

[15] In Revelation 21, the holy city of Jerusalem, the home of the twelve tribes of the children of Israel who are to be granted eternal life, is compared to a bride, and God to a bridegroom.

[1] Was struck. [2] Oldham was born twenty-two years after Dryden but died before him, at the age of thirty. [3] In Virgil's *Aeneid,* Nisus slipped on the spot where steers had been slain; knowing that he could not win the race, he threw himself in front of another runner, permitting his friend Euryalus to win the race. [4] Rhythm. [5] Acuteness of feeling or perception, but also sharpness of speech. [6] Sweetened wine or other liquor.

But ah too short, Marcellus[7] of our tongue;
Thy brows with ivy and with laurels bound;
But Fate and gloomy night encompass thee around. 25

HENRY WILMOT, EARL OF ROCHESTER

1612?–1658

UPON NOTHING

Nothing! thou elder brother ev'n to Shade,
That hadst a being e're the world was made,
And (well fixt) art alone, of ending not afraid.

E're time and place were, time and place were not,
When primitive Nothing something strait begot, 5
Then all proceeded from the great united—What?

Something, the gen'ral attribute of all,
Sever'd from thee, it's sole orginal,
Into thy boundless self must undistinguish'd fall.

Yet something did thy mighty pow'r command, 10
And from thy fruitful emptiness's hand,
Snatch'd men, beasts, birds, fire, water, air and land.

Matter, the wicked'st off-spring of thy race,
By Form assisted, flew from thy embrace,
And rebel Light obscur'd thy reverend dusky face. 15

With Form and Matter, Time and Place did join,
Body, thy foe, with these did leagues combine,[1]
To spoil thy peaceful realm, and ruine all thy line.[2]

[7] Son of Augustus' sister, Octavia, whose death is predicted in the *Aeneid*.

[1] Form. [2] Lineage.

But turn-coat Time assists the foe in vain,
And, brib'd by thee, destroys their short-liv'd reign, 20
And to thy hungry womb drives back thy slaves again.

Tho' mysteries are barr'd from laick eyes,
And the Divine alone, with warrant, pryes
Into thy bosom, where the truth in private lies,

Yet this of thee the wise may freely say, 25
Thou from the virtuous nothing tak'st away,
And to be part with thee the wicked wisely pray.

Great Negative, how vainly would the wise,
Enquire, define, distinguish, teach, devise?
Didst thou not stand to point[3] their dull philosophies. 30

Is, or *is not,* the two great ends of fate,
And, true or false, the subject of debate,
That perfect, or destroy, the vast designs of fate,

When they have rack'd the Politician's breast,
Within thy bosom most securely rest, 35
And, when reduc'd to thee, are least unsafe and best.

But, Nothing, why does Something still permit,
That sacred monarchs should at council sit,
With persons highly thought at best for nothing fit?

Whilst weighty Something modestly abstains, 40
From princes' coffers,[4] and from statesmen's brains,
And nothing there like stately Nothing reigns,

Nothing who dwell'st with fools in grave disguise,
For whom they rev'rend shapes, and forms devise,
Lawn sleeves, and furs, and gowns, when they like thee look wise. 45

French truth, Dutch prowess, Brittish policy,
Hibernian learning, Scotch civility,
Spaniards dispatch,[5] Danes wit, are mainly seen in thee.

[3] Sharpen, give a point to. [4] Treasuries. [5] Speed, expediency.

The great man's gratitude to his best friend,
Kings promises, whores vows, tow'rds thee they bend, 50
Flow swiftly into thee, and in thee ever end.

JONATHAN SWIFT

1667–1745

A DESCRIPTION OF A CITY SHOWER

In Imitation of Virgil's Georgics

Careful observers may foretell the hour
(By sure prognostics) when to dread a show'r:
While rain depends,[1] the pensive cat gives o'er
Her frolics, and pursues her tail no more.
Returning home at night, you'll find the sink[2] 5
Strike your offended sense with double stink.
If you be wise, then go not far to dine,
You'll spend in coach-hire more than save in wine.
A coming show'r your shooting corns presage,
Old aches throb, your hollow tooth will rage. 10
Saunt'ring in coffee-house is Dulman seen;
He damns the climate, and complains of spleen.

Meanwhile the South rising with dabbled[3] wings,
A sable cloud a-thwart the welkin[4] flings,
That swill'd more liquor than it could contain, 15
And like a drunkard gives it up again.
Brisk Susan whips her linen from the rope,
While the first drizzling show'r is borne aslope,[5]
Such is that sprinkling which some careless quean[6]
Flirts on you from her mop, but not so clean. 20
You fly, invoke the gods; then turning, stop
To rail; she singing, still whirls on her mop.
Not yet, the dust had shunn'd th' unequal strife,
But aided by the wind, fought still for life;

[1] Impends, is imminent. [2] Cesspool. [3] Bedabbled, bespattered. [4] Sky, firmament. [5] On the incline, crosswise. [6] Bold woman, jade, harlot.

And wafted with its foe[7] by violent gust, 25
'Twas doubtful which was rain, and which was dust.
Ah! where must needy poet seek for aid,
When dust and rain at once his coat invade;
His only coat! where dust confus'd with rain,
Roughen the nap, and leave a mingled stain. 30

Now in contiguous drops the flood comes down,
Threat'ning with deluge this *devoted* town.
To shops in crowds the daggled[8] females fly,
Pretend to cheapen[9] goods, but nothing buy.
The Templar[10] spruce, while ev'ry spout's a-broach,[11] 35
Stays till 'tis fair, yet seems to call a coach.
The tuck'd-up sempstress walks with hasty strides,
While streams run down her oil'd umbrella's sides.
Here various kinds by various fortunes led,
Commence acquaintance underneath a shed. 40
Triumphant Tories, and desponding Whigs,
Forget their feuds, and join to save their wigs.
Box'd in a chair[12] the beau impatient sits,
While spouts run clatt'ring o'er the roof by fits;
And ever and anon with frightful din 45
The leather sounds, he trembles from within.
So when Troy chair-men bore the wooden steed,[13]
Pregnant with Greeks impatient to be freed,
(Those bully Greeks, who, as the moderns do,
Instead of paying chair-men, run them thro'.) 50
Laocoon[14] struck the outside with his spear,
And each imprison'd hero quak'd for fear.

Now from all parts the swelling kennels[15] flow,
And bear their trophies with them as they go:
Filth of all hues and odours seem to tell 55
What street they sail'd from, by their sight and smell.
They, as each torrent drives, with rapid force
From Smithfield,[16] or St. Pulchre's shape their course,

[7] That is, rain, or water. [8] Wet, rained upon. [9] Price, bargain for. [10] A barrister or other person who occupies rooms in the Inner or Middle Temple in London. [11] Broached, pierced. [12] A sedan carried on poles. [13] The Trojan horse. The Greeks, having tried for ten years to capture Troy, built a huge wooden horse, hid their best soldiers inside, and had it presented to the Trojans as an offering to Athena which, if brought inside the city, would make Troy invulnerable. The Trojans dragged the horse inside. At night the hidden Greeks left the horse and opened the city's gates to their countrymen. Troy was quickly captured. [14] A Trojan priest who, in an attempt to dissuade Troy from accepting the Trojan horse, hurled his javelin into the hollow flank of the statue. There was a groan, but the Trojan's attention was diverted by a Greek who pretended to desert his countrymen. [15] Gutters. [16] This and the proper nouns that follow are the names of localities in London.

And in huge confluent[17] join at Snow-hill ridge,
Fall from the conduit prone to Holborn-bridge. 60
Sweepings from butchers' stalls, dung, guts, and blood,
Drown'd puppies, stinking sprats,[18] all drench'd in mud,
Dead cats and turnip-tops come tumbling down the flood.

STELLA'S BIRTHDAY[1]

March 13, 1726/7

This day, whate'er the Fates decree,
Shall still be kept with joy by me:
This day then, let us not be told,
That you are sick, and I grown old,
Nor think on our approaching ills, 5
And talk of spectacles and pills;
To-morrow will be time enough
To hear such mortifying stuff.
Yet, since from reason may be brought
A better and more pleasing thought, 10
Which can in spite of all decays,
Support a few remaining days:
From not the gravest of divines,[2]
Accept for once some serious lines.

Although we now can form no more 15
Long schemes of life, as heretofore;
Yet you, while time is running fast,
Can look with joy on what is past.

Were future happiness and pain,
A mere contrivance of the brain, 20
As atheists argue, to entice,
And fit their proselytes for vice;
(The only comfort they propose,
To have companions in their woes),
Grant this the case, yet sure 'tis hard, 25
That virtue, styled its own reward,
And by all sages understood
To be the chief of human good,

[17] A union of several streams. [18] Small sea-fish.

[1] Swift maintained a long friendship with Stella, who died of the illness spoken of here in January, 1728. [2] Swift, a clergyman, was Dean of St. Patrick's in Dublin.

Should acting, die, nor leave behind
Some lasting pleasure in the mind, 30
Which by remembrance will assuage,
Grief, sickness, poverty, and age;
And strongly shoot a radiant dart,
To shine through life's declining part.

Say, Stella, feel you no content, 35
Reflecting on a life well spent?
Your skilful hand employ'd to save
Despairing wretches from the grave;
And then supporting with your store,[3]
Those whom you dragg'd from death before: 40
So Providence on mortals waits,
Preserving what it first creates,
Your gen'rous boldness to defend
An innocent and absent friend;
That courage which can make you just 45
To merit humbled in the dust:
The detestation you express
For vice in all its glitt'ring dress;
That patience under tort'ring pain,
Where stubborn Stoics would complain. 50

Must these like empty shadows pass,
Or forms reflected from a glass?
Or mere chimaeras in the mind,
That fly, and leave no marks behind?
Does not the body thrive and grow 55
By food of twenty years ago?
And, had it not been still supplied,
It must a thousand times have died.
Then, who with reason can maintain,
That no effects of food remain? 60
And, is not virtue in mankind
The nutriment that feeds the mind?
Upheld by each good action past,
And still continued by the last?
Then, who with reason can pretend, 65
That all effects of virtue end?

Believe me Stella, when you show
That true contempt for things below,
Nor prize your life for other ends

[3] Abundance, here, of spiritual goods.

Than merely to oblige your friends; 70
Your former actions claim their part,
And join to fortify your heart.
For Virtue in her daily race,
Like Janus,[4] bears a double face;
Looks back with joy where she has gone, 75
And therefore goes with courage on.
She at your sickly couch will wait,
And guide you to a better state.

Oh then, whatever heav'n intends,
Take pity on your pitying friends; 80
Nor let your ills affect your mind,
To fancy they can be unkind.
Me, surely me, you ought to spare,
Who gladly would your suff'rings share;
Or give my scrap of life to you, 85
And think it far beneath your due;
You, to whose care so oft I owe,
That I'm alive to tell you so.

SAMUEL JOHNSON

1709–1784

ON THE DEATH OF DR. ROBERT LEVET

Condemn'd to hope's delusive mine,
As on we toil from day to day,
By sudden blasts, or slow decline,
Or social comforts drop away.

Well tried through many a varying year, 5
See Levet to the grave descend;
Officious,[1] innocent, sincere,
Of ev'ry friendless name the friend.

[4] In Roman mythology, the protector of doors and entrances. He was represented with two faces, one facing forward and the other backward.

[1] Kind, obliging.

Yet still he fills affection's eye,
    Obscurely wise, and coarsely kind; 10
Nor , letter'd arrogance, deny
    Thy praise to merit unrefin'd.

When fainting nature call'd for aid,
    And hov'ring death prepar'd the blow,
His vig'rous remedy display'd 15
    The power of art without the show.

In misery's darkest caverns known,
    His useful care was ever nigh.
Where hopeless anguish pour'd his groan,
    And lonely want retir'd to die. 20

No summons mock'd by chill delay,
    No petty gain disdain'd by pride,
The modest wants of ev'ry day
    The toil of ev'ry day supplied.

His virtues walk'd their narrow round, 25
    Nor made a pause, nor left a void;
And sure th' Eternal Master found
    The single talent well employ'd.

The busy day, the peaceful night,
    Unfelt, uncounted, glided by; 30
His frame was firm, his powers were bright,
    Tho' now his eightieth year was nigh.

Then with no throbbing fiery pain,
    No cold gradations of decay,
Death broke at once the vital chain, 35
    And freed his soul the nearest way.

THOMAS GRAY

1716–1771

ELEGY WRITTEN IN A COUNTRY CHURCHYARD

The curfew tolls the knell of parting day,
The lowing herd wind slowly o'er the lea,
The ploughman homeward plods his weary way,
And leaves the world to darkness and to me.

Now fades the glimmering landscape on the sight, 5
And all the air a solemn stillness holds,
Save where the beetle wheels his droning flight,
And drowsy tinklings lull the distant folds;

Save that from yonder ivy-mantled tow'r
The moping owl does to the moon complain 10
Of such, as wand'ring near her secret bow'r,
Molest her ancient solitary reign.

Beneath those rugged elms, that yew-tree's shade,
Where heaves the turf in many a mold'ring heap,
Each in his narrow cell forever laid, 15
The rude[1] forefathers of the hamlet sleep.

The breezy call of incense-breathing morn,
The swallow twitt'ring from the straw-built shed,
The cock's shrill clarion, or the echoing horn,
No more shall rouse them from their lowly bed. 20

For them no more the blazing hearth shall burn,
Or busy housewife ply her evening care;
No children run to lisp their sire's return,
Or climb his knees the envied kiss to share.

Oft did the harvest to their sickle yield; 25
Their furrow oft the stubborn glebe[2] has broke;

[1] Rustic. [2] Soil.

How jocund did they drive their team afield!
How bow'd the woods beneath their sturdy stroke!

Let not Ambition mock their useful toil,
Their homely joys, and destiny obscure; 30
Nor Grandeur hear with a disdainful smile
The short and simple annals of the poor.

The boast of heraldry,[3] the pomp of pow'r,
And all that beauty, all that wealth e'er gave,
Awaits alike th' inevitable hour: 35
The paths of glory lead but to the grave.

Nor you, ye proud, impute to these the fault,
If Mem'ry o'er their tomb no trophies raise,
Where through the long-drawn aisle and fretted vault
The pealing anthem swells the note of praise. 40

Can storied urn,[4] or animated[5] bust,
Back to its mansion call the fleeting breath?
Can Honour's voice provoke the silent dust,
Or Flatt'ry soothe the dull cold ear of Death?

Perhaps in this neglected spot is laid 45
Some heart once pregnant with celestial fire;
Hands that the rod of empire might have sway'd,
Or wak'd to ecstasy the living lyre.

But Knowledge to their eyes her ample page,
Rich with the spoils of time, did ne'er unroll; 50
Chill Penury repress'd their noble rage,
And froze the genial current of the soul.

Full many a gem of purest ray serene,
The dark unfathom'd caves of ocean bear;
Full many a flower is born to blush unseen, 55
And waste its sweetness on the desert air.

[3] Recorded genealogies and their heraldic symbols; hence, noble birth. [4] Funeral urn engraved with scenes from a story. [5] Lifelike.

Some village Hampden,[6] that with dauntless breast
    The little tyrant of his fields withstood;
Some mute inglorious Milton[7] here may rest,
    Some Cromwell,[8] guiltless of his country's blood. 60

Th' applause of list'ning senates to command,
    The threats of pain and ruin to despise,
To scatter plenty o'er a smiling land,
    And read their hist'ry in a nation's eyes,

Their lot forbade; nor circumscrib'd alone 65
    Their growing virtues, but their crimes confined;
Forbade to wade through slaughter to a throne,
    And shut the gates of mercy on mankind;

The struggling pangs of conscious truth to hide,
    To quench the blushes of ingenuous shame, 70
Or heap the shrine of Luxury and Pride
    With incense kindled at the Muse's flame.

Far from the madding[9] crowd's ignoble strife,
    Their sober wishes never learn'd to stray;
Along the cool sequester'd vale of life 75
    They kept the noiseless tenor of their way.

Yet ev'n these bones from insult to protect,
    Some frail memorial still erected nigh,
With uncouth rhymes and shapeless sculpture deck'd,
    Implores the passing tribute of a sigh. 80

Their name, their years, spelt by th' unletter'd Muse,
    The place of fame and elegy supply;
And many a holy text around she strews,
    That teach the rustic moralist to die.

For who, to dumb Forgetfulness a prey, 85
    This pleasing anxious being e'er resign'd,

[6] John Hampden (1594–1643), a Member of Parliament who resisted taxes levied by King Charles I because he thought them unjust. He was impeached but resisted arrest. [7] The poet John Milton (1608–1674). [8] Oliver Cromwell, a Puritan military leader during the English Civil War and Lord Protector of the Commonwealth (1653–1658). [9] Wild, restless.

Left the warm precincts of the cheerful day,
    Nor cast one longing ling'ring look behind?

On some fond breast the parting soul relies,
    Some pious drops the closing eye requires; 90
Ev'n from the tomb the voice of Nature cries,
    Ev'n in our ashes live their wonted[10] fires.

For thee, who mindful of th' unhonour'd dead
    Dost in these lines their artless tale relate;
If chance, by lonely contemplation led, 95
    Some kindred spirit shall inquire thy fate,

Haply some hoary-headed[11] swain may say,
    "Oft have we seen him at the peep of dawn
Brushing with hasty steps the dews away
    To meet the sun upon the upland lawn. 100

"There at the foot of yonder nodding beech
    That wreathes its old fantastic roots so high,
His listless length at noontide would he stretch,
    And pore upon the brook that babbles by.

"Hard by yon wood, now smiling as in scorn, 105
    Mutt'ring his wayward fancies he would rove;
Now drooping, woeful-wan, like one forlorn,
    Or craz'd with care, or cross'd in hopeless love.

"One morn I miss'd him on the custom'd hill,
    Along the heath, and near his fav'rite tree; 110
Another came; nor yet beside the rill,
    Nor up the lawn, nor at the wood was he;

"The next, with dirges due, in sad array,
    Slow through the church-way path we saw him borne.
Approach and read (for thou canst read) the lay, 115
    Grav'd on the stone beneath yon agèd thorn."

THE EPITAPH

Here rests his head upon the lap of earth,
    A youth to Fortune and to Fame unknown;

[10] Customary. [11] Gray- or white-haired.

Fair Science frown'd not on his humble birth,
And Melancholy mark'd him for her own. 120

Large was his bounty, and his soul sincere;
Heav'n did a recompense as largely send:
He gave to Mis'ry all he had, a tear;
He gain'd from Heav'n ('twas all he wish'd) a friend.

No farther seek his merits to disclose, 125
Or draw his frailties from their dread abode,
(There they alike in trembling hope repose)
The bosom of his Father and his God.

CHRISTOPHER SMART

1722–1771

OF JEOFFRY, HIS CAT

For I will consider my Cat Jeoffry.
For he is the servant of the Living God, duly and daily
serving him.
For at the first glance of the glory of God in the East he
worships in his way.
For is this done by wreathing[1] his body seven times round
with elegant quickness.
For then he leaps up to catch the musk,[2] which is the
blessing of God upon his prayer. 5
For he rolls upon prank to work it in.[3]
For having done duty and received blessing he begins to
consider himself.
For this he performs in ten degrees.
For first he looks upon his fore-paws to see if they are
clean.
For secondly he kicks up behind to clear away there. 10
For thirdly he works it upon stretch with the fore-paws
extended.

[1] Writhing. [2] Muskrat. [3] That is, as a prank, he rolls to digest the muskrat.

For fourthly he sharpens his paws by wood.
For fifthly he washes himself.
For sixthly he rolls upon wash.
For seventhly he fleas himself, that he may not be inter-
rupted upon the beat.[4] 15
For eighthly he rubs himself against a post.
For ninthly he looks up for his instructions.[5]
For tenthly he goes in quest of food.
For having consider'd God and himself he will consider
his neighbour.
For if he meets another cat he will kiss her in kindness. 20
For when he takes his prey he plays with it to give it
chance.
For one mouse in seven escapes by his dallying.
For when his day's work is done his business more
properly begins.
For [he] keeps the Lord's watch in the night against the
adversary.
For he counteracts the powers of darkness by his electrical
skin and glaring eyes. 25
For he counteracts the Devil, who is death, by brisking
about the life.
For in his morning orisons he loves the sun and the sun
loves him.
For he is of the tribe of Tiger.
For the Cherub Cat is a term[6] of the Angel Tiger.
For he has the subtlety and hissing of a serpent, which in
goodness he suppresses. 30
For he will not do destruction, if he is well-fed, neither
will he spit without provocation.
For he purrs in thankfulness, when God tells him he's a
good Cat.
For he is an instrument for the children to learn
benevolence upon.
For every house is incompleat without him and a blessing
is lacking in the spirit.
For the Lord commanded Moses concerning the cats at
the departure of the Children of Israel from Egypt. 35
For every family had one cat at least in the bag.
For the English Cats are the best in Europe.
For he is the cleanest in the use of his fore-paws of any
quadrupede.
For the dexterity of his defence is an instance of the love
of God to him exceedingly.
For he is the quickest to his mark of any creature. 40
For he is tenacious of his point.

[4] The territory he ranges over in pursuit of prey. [5] That is, he sniffs the air for a scent. [6] Period, step in the progression.

For he is a mixture of gravity and waggery.
For he knows that God is his Saviour.
For there is nothing sweeter than his peace when at rest.
For there is nothing brisker than his life when in motion. 45
For he is of the Lord's poor and so indeed is he called
by benevolence perpetually—Poor Jeoffry! poor
Jeoffry! the rat has bit thy throat.
For I bless the name of the Lord Jesus that Jeoffry is
better.
For the divine spirit comes about his body to sustain it in
compleat cat.
For his tongue is exceeding pure so that it has in purity
what it wants in musick.
For he is docile and can learn certain things. 50
For he can set up with gravity which is patience upon
approbation.
For he can fetch and carry, which is patience in employ-
ment.
For he can jump over a stick which is patience upon proof
positive.
For he can spraggle upon waggle at the word of
command.
For he can jump from an eminence into his master's
bosom. 55
For he can catch the cork and toss it again.
For he is hated by the hypocrite and miser.
For the former is affraid of detection.
For the latter refuses the charge.
For he camels his back to bear the first notion of
business. 60
For he is good to think on, if a man would express himself
neatly.
For he made a great figure in Egypt for his signal
services.
For he killed the Icneumon-rat[7] very pernicious by land.
For his ears are so acute that they sting again.
For from this proceeds the passing quickness of his
attention. 65
For by stroaking of him I have found out electricity.
For I perceived God's light about him both wax and fire.
For the Electrical fire is the spiritual substance, which
God sends from heaven to sustain the bodies both
of man and beast.
For God has blessed him in the variety of his movements.
For, tho' he cannot fly, he is an excellent clamberer. 70
For his motions upon the face of the earth are more than
any other quadrupede.

[7] Ichneumon, or mongoose.

For he can tread to all the measures upon the musick.
For he can swim for life.
For he can creep.

WILLIAM BLAKE

1757–1827

THE ECCHOING GREEN[1]

The Sun does arise,
And make happy the skies.
The merry bells ring
To welcome the Spring.
The skylark and thrush, 5
The birds of the bush,
Sing louder around
To the bells' cheerful sound;
While our sports shall be seen
On the Ecchoing Green. 10

Old John, with white hair,
Does laugh away care,
Sitting under the oak,
Among the old folk.
They laugh at our play, 15
And soon they all say:
Such, such were the joys,
When we all, girls and boys,
In our youth time were seen,
On the Ecchoing Green. 20

Till the little ones, weary,
No more can be merry;
The sun does descend,
And our sports have an end:
Round the laps of their mothers 25
Many sisters and brothers,

[1] The spelling of "Ecchoing" is Blake's.

Like birds in their nest,
Are ready for rest;
And sport no more seen,
On the darkening Green. 30

THE LAMB

Little Lamb, who made thee?
Dost thou know who made thee?
Gave thee life and bid thee feed,
By the stream and o'er the mead;
Gave thee clothing of delight, 5
Softest clothing wooly bright;
Gave thee such a tender voice,
Making all the vales rejoice?
Little Lamb, who made thee?
Dost thou know who made thee? 10

Little Lamb, I'll tell thee,
Little Lamb, I'll tell thee:
He is callèd by thy name,
For He calls Himself a Lamb:
He is meek, and He is mild; 15
He became a little child:
I a child, and thou a lamb,
We are callèd by His name.
Little Lamb, God bless thee.
Little Lamb, God bless thee. 20

THE CLOD AND THE PEBBLE

"Love seeketh not Itself to please,
Nor for itself hath any care,
But for another gives its ease,
And builds a Heaven in Hell's despair."

So sang a little Clod of Clay 5
Trodden with the cattle's feet,
But a Pebble of the brook
Warbled out these metres meet:

"Love seeketh only Self to please,
To bind another to its delight, 10
Joys in another's loss of ease,
And builds a Hell in Heaven's despite."[1]

A POISON TREE

I was angry with my friend:
I told my wrath, my wrath did end.
I was angry with my foe:
I told it not, my wrath did grow.

And I water'd it in fears, 5
Night and morning with my tears;
And I sunnèd it with smiles,
And with soft deceitful wiles.

And it grew both day and night,
Till it bore an apple bright. 10
And my foe beheld it shine,
And he knew that it was mine,

And into my garden stole
When the night had veil'd the pole;[1]
In the morning glad I see 15
My foe outstretch'd beneath the tree.

AH, SUN-FLOWER!

Ah, Sun-flower! weary of time,
Who countest the steps of the Sun:
Seeking after that sweet golden clime
Where the traveller's journey is done;

Where the Youth pined away with desire, 5
And the pale Virgin shrouded in snow,

[1] In spite of Heaven.

[1] Polestar or North Star.

Arise from their graves and aspire,[1]
Where my Sun-flower wishes to go.

LONDON

I wander through each charter'd[1] street,
Near where the charter'd Thames does flow,
And mark in every face I meet
Marks of weakness, marks of woe.

In every cry of every man, 5
In every infant's cry of fear,
In every voice, in every ban
The mind-forg'd manacles I hear.

How the chimney-sweeper's cry
Every black'ning church appalls, 10
And the hapless soldier's sigh
Runs in blood down palace walls.

But most through midnight streets I hear
How the youthful harlot's curse
Blasts the new-born infant's tear 15
And blights with plagues the marriage hearse.

STANZAS FROM *MILTON*

And did those feet in ancient time
Walk upon England's mountains green?
And was the holy Lamb of God
On England's pleasant pastures seen?

And did the Countenance Divine 5
Shine forth upon our clouded hills?
And was Jerusalem builded here,
Among these dark Satanic mills?

[1] Ascend.

[1] Privileged, licensed.

Bring me my bow of burning gold!
Bring me my arrows of desire! 10
Bring me my spear! O clouds, unfold!
Bring me my chariot of fire!

I will not cease from mental fight,
Nor shall my sword sleep in my hand:
Till we have built Jerusalem 15
In England's green and pleasant land.

ROBERT BURNS

1759–1796

MARY MORISON

O Mary, at thy window be!
It is the wish'd; the trysted hour.[1]
Those smiles and glances let me see,
That make the miser's treasure poor.
How blythely wad I bide the stoure,[2] 5
A weary slave frae sun to sun,
Could I the rich reward secure—
The lovely Mary Morison!

Yestreen,[3] when to the trembling string
The dance gaed[4] thro' the lighted ha', 10
To thee my fancy took its wing,
I sat, but neither heard or saw:
Tho' this was fair, and that was braw,[5]
And yon the toast of a' the town,
I sigh'd and said amang them a':— 15
"Ye are na Mary Morison!"

O Mary, canst thou wreck his peace
Wha[6] for thy sake wad gladly die?

[1] The hour appointed for a tryst. [2] Would I wait out the storm, or tumult. [3] Yesterday evening. [4] Went. [5] Brave; that is, splendid, showy. [6] Who.

Or canst thou break that heart of his
Whase only faut is loving thee? 20
If love for love thou wilt na gie,
At least be pity to me shown:
A thought ungentle canna be
The thought o' Mary Morison.

ADDRESS TO THE UNCO GUID[1]

or The Rigidly Righteous

My Son, these maxims make a rule,
An' lump them ay thegither:
The Rigid Righteous is a fool,
The Rigid Wise anither;
The cleanest corn that e'er was dight[2]
May hae some pyles o' caff[3] in;
So ne'er a fellow-creature slight
For random fits o' daffin.[4]
SOLOMON (Eccles. vii. 16)

O ye, wha are sae guid yoursel,
Sae pious and sae holy,
Ye've nought to do but mark and tell
Your neebours' fauts and folly,
Whase life is like a weel-gaun[5] mill, 5
Supplied wi' store o' water;
The heapet happer's[6] ebbing still,
An' still the clap[7] plays clatter!

Hear me, ye venerable core,
As counsel for poor mortals 10
That frequent pass douce[8] Wisdom's door
For glaikit[9] Folly's portals:
I for their thoughtless, careless sakes
Would here propone[10] defences—
Their donsie[11] tricks, their black mistakes, 15
Their failings and mischances.

Ye see your state wi' theirs compared,
And shudder at the niffer;[12]

[1] Uncommon good; that is, those who profess to be strict in matters of morals and religion. [2] Winnowed. [3] Chaff. [4] Fooling, frolicking. [5] Wheel-driven. [6] Heaped hopper. [7] Clapper (of the mill). [8] Sober. [9] Senseless, giddy. [10] Propound, propose. [11] Unfortunate. [12] Exchange.

But cast a moment's fair regard,
What makes the mighty differ?[13]
Discount what scant occasion[14] gave;
That purity ye pride in;
And (what's aft mair than a' the lave[15])
Your better art o' hidin.

Think, when your castigated pulse (25)
Gies now and then a wallop,
What ragings must his veins convulse,
That still eternal gallop!
Wi' wind and tide fair i' your tail,
Right on ye scud[16] your sea-way; (30)
But in the teeth o' baith to sail,
It makes an unco[17] lee-way.

See Social-life and Glee sit down
All joyous and unthinking,
Till, quite transmugrify'd,[18] they're grown (35)
Debauchery and Drinking:
O, would they stay to calculate
Th' eternal consequences,
Or—your more dreaded hell to state—
Damnation of expenses! (40)

Ye high, exalted, virtuous dames,
Tied up in godly laces,
Before ye gie poor Frailty names,
Suppose a change o' cases:
A dear-lov'd lad, convenience snug, (45)
A treach'rous inclination—
But, let me whisper i' your lug,[19]
Ye're aiblins[20] nae temptation.

Then gently scan your brother man,
Still gentler sister woman; (50)
Tho' they may gang a kennin[21] wrang,
To step aside is human:
One point must still be greatly dark,
The moving[22] *why* they do it;

[13] Difference. [14] Chance, coincidence. [15] What's often more than all the rest. [16] Sail swiftly, before the wind. [17] Strange, uncommon. [18] Transmogrified; that is, transformed, metamorphosed (humorous). [19] Ear. [20] Perhaps. [21] Just enough to be perceived; a little. [22] Reason.

And just as lamely can ye mark 55
How far perhaps they rue it.

Who made the heart, 't is He alone
Decidedly can try us:
He knows each chord, its various tone,
Each spring, its various bias: 60
Then at the balance[23] let's be mute,
We never can adjust it;
What's done we partly may compute,
But know not what's resisted.

AULD LANG SYNE[1]

Should auld acquaintance be forgot,
And never brought to mind?
Should auld acquaintance be forgot,
And auld lang syne!

CHORUS

For auld lang syne, my dear, 5
For auld lang syne,
We'll tak a cup o' kindness yet
For auld lang syne!

And surely ye'll be your pint-stowp,[2]
And surely I'll be mine, 10
And we'll tak a cup o' kindness yet
For auld lang syne!

We twa hae run about the braes,[3]
And pou'd[4] the gowans[5] fine,
But we've wander'd monie a weary fit[6] 15
Sin' auld lang syne.

We twa hae paidl'd in the burn[7]
Frae morning sun till dine,[8]

[23] Scale (of justice).

[1] Old long-since; that it, old times. [2] Pint-stoup; tankard holding a pint (of beer or ale). [3] Hillsides. [4] Pulled, picked. [5] Daisies. [6] Spell (period of time). [7] Stream, brook. [8] Dinner.

But seas between us braid hae roar'd
    Sin' auld lang syne. 20

And there's a hand, my trusty fiere,[9]
    And gie's a hand o' thine,
And we'll tak a right guid-willie waught[10]
    For auld lang syne!

ROBERT BRUCE'S MARCH TO BANNOCKBURN[1]

Scots, wha hae wi' Wallace[2] bled,
Scots, wham Bruce has aften led;
Welcome to your gory bed,
    Or to victorie!

Now's the day, and now's the hour; 5
See the front o' battle lour:[3]
See approach proud Edward's pow'r—
    Chains and slaverie!

Wha will be a traitor-knave?
Wha can fill a coward's grave? 10
Wha sae base as be a slave?
    Let him turn and flee!

Wha for Scotland's king and law
Freedom's sword will strongly draw,
Freeman stand, or freeman fa'; 15
    Let him follow me!

By oppression's woes and pains!
By our sons in servile chains!
We will drain our dearest veins,
    But they shall be free! 20

[9] Fellow, friend. [10] Good-will draught.

[1] In 1314, Robert Bruce routed the English under Edward II at Bannockburn. [2] Sir William Wallace (1272?–1305), a Scottish patriot who devoted his life to resisting the English. [3] Scowl; look dark and threatening.

Lay the proud usurpers low!
Tyrants fall in every foe!
Liberty's in every blow!—
Let us do or die!

A RED, RED ROSE

O, my luve is like a red, red rose,
That's newly sprung[1] in June.
O, my luve is like the melodie,
That's sweetly play'd in tune.

As fair art thou, my bonie[2] lass,
So deep in luve am I,
And I will luve thee still, my dear,
Till a' the seas gang dry.

Till a' the seas gang dry, my dear,
And the rocks melt wi' the sun! 10
And I will luve thee still, my dear,
While the sands o' life shall run.

And fare thee weel, my only luve,
And fare thee weel a while!
And I will come again, my luve, 15
Tho' it were ten thousand mile!

A MAN'S A MAN FOR A' THAT

Is there for honest poverty
That hings his head, an' a' that?
The coward slave, we pass him by,
We dare be poor for a' that!
For a' that, an' a' that, 5
Our toils obscure, an' a' that,
The rank is but the guinea's stamp;[1]
The man's the gowd[2] for a' that.

[1] Burst forth; bloomed. [2] Bonny.

[1] The guinea is the highest valued English coin. [2] Gold.

What though on hamely fare we dine,
    Wear hodd'n grey,[3] an' a' that? 10
Gie fools their silks, and knaves their wine,
    A man's a man for a' that.
For a' that, an' a' that,
    Their tinsel show, an' a' that,
The honest man, tho' e'er sae poor, 15
    Is king o' men for a' that.

Ye see yon birkie[4] ca'd a lord,
    Wha struts, an' stares, an' a' that;
Tho' hundreds worship at his word,
    He's but a coof[5] for a' that. 20
For a' that, an' a' that,
    His ribband, star, an' a' that.
The man o' independent mind,
    He looks an' laughs at a' that.

A prince can mak a belted knight, 25
    A marquis, duke, an' a' that;
But an honest man's aboon[6] his might,
    Guid faith, he mauna fa'[7] that!
For a' that, an' a' that,
    Their dignities, an' a' that, 30
The pith o' sense, an' pride o' worth,
    Are higher rank than a' that.

Then let us pray that come it may,
    As come it will, for a' that,
That sense and worth o'er a' the earth 35
    Shall bear the gree,[8] an' a' that!
For a' that an' a' that,
    It's comin yet, for a' that,
That man to man the world o'er,
    Shall brithers be for a' that. 40

[3] Hodden grey, a course woolen cloth worn by the peasantry. [4] Strutting fellow. [5] Dull fellow. [6] Above. [7] Cannot depreciate. [8] Victory, prize.

WILLIAM WORDSWORTH

1770–1850

EXPOSTULATION AND REPLY

"Why, William, on that old grey stone,
Thus for the length of half a day,
Why, William, sit you thus alone,
And dream your time away?

"Where are your books?—that light bequeathed 5
To Beings else forlorn and blind!
Up! up! and drink the spirit breathed
From dead men to their kind.

"You look round on your Mother Earth,
As if she for no purpose bore you; 10
As if you were her first-born birth,
And none had lived before you!"

One morning thus, by Esthwaite lake,
When life was sweet, I knew not why,
To me my good friend Matthew spake, 15
And thus I made reply:

"The eye—it cannot choose but see;
We cannot bid the ear be still;
Our bodies feel, where'er they be,
Against or with our will. 20

"Nor less I deem that there are Powers
Which of themselves our minds impress;
That we can feed this mind of ours
In a wise passiveness.

"Think you, 'mid all this mighty sum 25
Of things forever speaking,
That nothing of itself will come,
But we must still be seeking?

"—Then ask not wherefore, here, alone,
Conversing as I may, 30
I sit upon this old gray stone,
And dream my time away."

THE TABLES TURNED

An Evening Scene on the Same Subject

Up! up! my Friend, and quit your books;
Or surely you'll grow double:
Up! up! my Friend, and clear your looks;
Why all this toil and trouble?

The sun, above the mountain's head, 5
A freshening lustre mellow
Through all the long green fields has spread,
His first sweet evening yellow.

Books! 'tis a dull and endless strife:
Come, hear the woodland linnet, 10
How sweet his music! on my life,
There's more of wisdom in it.

And hark! how blithe the throstle sings!
He, too, is no mean preacher:
Come forth into the light of things, 15
Let Nature be your Teacher.

She has a world of ready wealth,
Our minds and hearts to bless—
Spontaneous wisdom breathed by health,
Truth breathed by cheerfulness. 20

One impulse from a vernal wood
May teach you more of man,
Of moral evil and of good,
Than all the sages can.

Sweet is the lore which Nature brings; 25
Our meddling intellect

Mis-shapes the beauteous forms of things:—
We murder to dissect.

Enough of Science and of Art;
Close up those barren leaves; 30
Come forth, and bring with you a heart
That watches and receives.

SHE DWELT AMONG THE UNTRODDEN WAYS

She dwelt among the untrodden ways
Beside the springs of Dove,
A Maid whom there were none to praise
And very few to love:

A violet by a mossy stone 5
Half hidden from the eye!
—Fair as a star, when only one
Is shining in the sky.

She lived unknown, and few could know
When Lucy ceased to be; 10
But she is in her grave, and, oh,
The difference to me!

THERE WAS A BOY

There was a Boy: ye knew him well, ye cliffs
And islands of Winander!—many a time
At evening, when the earliest stars began
To move along the edges of the hills,
Rising or setting, would he stand alone 5
Beneath the trees or by the glimmering lake,
And there, with fingers interwoven, both hands
Pressed closely palm to palm, and to his mouth
Uplifted, he, as through an instrument,
Blew mimic hootings to the silent owls, 10
That they might answer him; and they would shout
Across the watery vale, and shout again,
Responsive to his call, with quivering peals,

And long halloos and screams, and echoes loud,
Redoubled and redoubled, concourse wild 15
Of jocund din; and, when a lengthened pause
Of silence came and baffled his best skill,
Then sometimes, in that silence while he hung
Listening, a gentle shock of mild surprise
Has carried far into his heart the voice 20
Of mountain torrents; or the visible scene
Would enter unawares into his mind,
With all its solemn imagery, its rocks,
Its woods, and that uncertain heaven, received
Into the bosom of the steady lake. 25

This Boy was taken from his mates, and died
In childhood, ere he was full twelve years old.
Fair is the spot, most beautiful the vale
Where he was born; the grassy churchyard hangs
Upon a slope above the village school, 30
And through that churchyard when my way has led
On summer evenings, I believe that there
A long half hour together I have stood
Mute, looking at the grave in which he lies!

NUTTING

—It seems a day
(I speak of one from many singled out)
One of those heavenly days that cannot die;
When, in the eagerness of boyish hope,
I left our cottage-threshold, sallying forth 5
With a huge wallet o'er my shoulders slung,
A nutting-crook[1] in hand; and turned my steps
Tow'rd some far-distant wood, a Figure quaint,
Tricked out in proud disguise of cast-off weeds[2]
Which for that service had been husbanded, 10
By exhortation of my frugal Dame—
Motley accoutrement, of power to smile
At thorns, and brakes, and brambles,—and, in truth,
More ragged than need was! O'er pathless rocks,
Through beds of matted fern, and tangled thickets 15
Forcing my way, I came to one dear nook
Unvisited, where not a broken bough
Drooped with its withered leaves, ungracious sign

[1] A hooked implement for gathering nuts. [2] Clothes.

Of devastation; but the hazels rose
Tall and erect, with tempting clusters hung, 20
A virgin scene!—A little while I stood,
Breathing with such suppression of the heart
As joy delights in; and with wise restraint
Voluptuous, fearless of a rival, eyed
The banquet;—or beneath the trees I sate 25
Among the flowers, and with the flowers I played;
A temper known to those who, after long
And weary expectation, have been blest
With sudden happiness beyond all hope.
Perhaps it was a bower beneath whose leaves 30
The violets of five seasons re-appear
And fade, unseen by any human eye;
Where fairy water-breaks[3] do murmur on
For ever; and I saw the sparkling foam,
And—with my cheek on one of those green stones 35
That, fleeced with moss, under the shady trees,
Lay round me, scattered like a flock of sheep—
I heard the murmur and the murmuring sound.
In that sweet mood when pleasure loves to pay
Tribute to ease; and, of its joy secure, 40
The heart luxuriates with indifferent things,
Wasting its kindliness on stocks and stones,
And on the vacant air. Then up I rose,
And dragged to earth both branch and bough, with crash
And merciless ravage: and the shady nook 45
Of hazels, and the green and mossy bower,
Deformed and sullied, patiently gave up
Their quiet being: and unless I now
Confound my present feelings with the past,
Ere from the mutilated bower I turned 50
Exulting, rich beyond the wealth of kings,
I felt a sense of pain when I beheld
The silent trees, and saw the intruding sky.—
Then, dearest Maiden, move along these shades
In gentleness of heart; with gentle hand 55
Touch—for there is a spirit in the woods.

COMPOSED UPON WESTMINSTER BRIDGE

Earth has not anything to show more fair:
Dull would he be of soul who could pass by
A sight so touching in its majesty:

[3] Broken water.

This city now doth, like a garment, wear
The beauty of the morning; silent, bare, 5
Ships, towers, domes, theatres, and temples lie
Open unto the fields, and to the sky;
All bright and glittering in the smokeless air.
Never did sun more beautifully steep
In his first splendour, valley, rock, or hill; 10
Ne'er saw I, never felt, a calm so deep!
The river glideth at his own sweet will:
Dear God! the very houses seem asleep;
And all that mighty heart is lying still!

THE WORLD IS TOO MUCH WITH US

The world is too much with us; late and soon,
Getting and spending, we lay waste our powers:
Little we see in Nature that is ours;
We have given our hearts away, a sordid boon!
This Sea that bares her bosom to the moon; 5
The winds that will be howling at all hours,
And are up-gathered now like sleeping flowers;
For this, for everything, we are out of tune;
It moves us not.—Great God! I'd rather be
A Pagan suckled in a creed outworn; 10
So might I, standing on this pleasant lea,
Have glimpses that would make me less forlorn;
Have sight of Proteus[1] rising from the sea;
Or hear old Triton blow his wreathèd horn.

SURPRISED BY JOY

Surprised by joy—impatient as the Wind
I turned to share the transport—Oh! with whom
But Thee,[1] deep buried in the silent tomb,
That spot which no vicissitude can find?
Love, faithful love, recalled thee to my mind— 5
But how could I forget thee? Through what power,
Even for the least division of an hour,

[1] Proteus, like Triton (line 14), was a sea god. Both were sons of Poseidon (or Neptune), principal god of the sea. Proteus could change his shape at will; Triton controlled the waves by blowing on a conch shell.

[1] Wordsworth's daughter Catherine.

Have I been so beguiled as to be blind
To my most grievous loss!—That thought's return
Was the worst pang that sorrow ever bore, 10
Save one, one only, when I stood forlorn,
Knowing my heart's best treasure was no more;
That neither present time, nor years unborn
Could to my sight that heavenly face restore.

THE SOLITARY REAPER

Behold her, single in the field,
Yon solitary Highland Lass!
Reaping and singing by herself;
Stop here, or gently pass!
Alone she cuts and binds the grain, 5
And sings a melancholy strain;
O listen! for the Vale profound
Is overflowing with the sound.

No Nightingale did ever chaunt
More welcome notes to weary bands 10
Of travellers in some shady haunt,
Among Arabian sands:
A voice so thrilling ne'er was heard
In springtime from the Cuckoo-bird,
Breaking the silence of the seas 15
Among the farthest Hebrides.[1]

Will no one tell me what she sings?—
Perhaps the plaintive numbers flow
For old, unhappy, far-off things,
And battles long ago: 20
Or is it some more humble lay,
Familiar matter of to-day?
Some natural sorrow, loss, or pain,
That has been, and may be again?

Whate'er the theme, the Maiden sang 25
As if her song could have no ending;
I saw her singing at her work,
And o'er the sickle bending:—

[1] Islands off the west coast of Scotland.

I listened, motionless and still;
And, as I mounted up the hill, 30
The music in my heart I bore,
Long after it was heard no more.

STEPPING WESTWARD

"What, you are stepping westward?"—"Yea."
—'T would be a *wildish* destiny,
If we, who thus together roam
In a strange Land, and far from home,
Were in this place the guests of Chance: 5
Yet who would stop, or fear to advance,
Though home or shelter he had none,
With such a sky to lead him on?

The dewy ground was dark and cold;
Behind, all gloomy to behold; 10
And stepping westward seemed to be
A kind of *heavenly* destiny:
I liked the greeting;[1] 't was a sound
Of something without place or bound;
And seemed to give me spiritual right 15
To travel through that region bright.

The voice was soft, and she who spake
Was walking by her native lake:
The salutation had to me
The very sound of courtesy: 20
Its power was felt; and while my eye
Was fixed upon the glowing Sky,
The echo of the voice enwrought
A human sweetness with the thought
Of travelling through the world that lay 25
Before me in my endless way.

[1] The greeting is in the first line of the poem.

ODE: INTIMATIONS OF IMMORTALITY FROM RECOLLECTIONS OF EARLY CHILDHOOD

The Child is father of the Man;
And I could wish my days to be
Bound each to each by natural piety.[1]

I

There was a time when meadow, grove, and stream,
The earth, and every common sight,
To me did seem
Apparelled in celestial light,
The glory and the freshness of a dream. 5
It is not now as it hath been of yore;—
Turn wheresoe'er I may,
By night or day,
The things which I have seen I now can see no more.

II

The Rainbow comes and goes, 10
And lovely is the Rose;
The Moon doth with delight
Look round her when the heavens are bare;
Waters on a starry night
Are beautiful and fair; 15
The sunshine is a glorious birth;
But yet I know, where'er I go,
That there hath passed away a glory from the earth.

III

Now, while the birds thus sing a joyous song,
And while the young lambs bound 20
As to the tabor's sound,
To me alone there came a thought of grief:
A timely utterance gave that thought relief,
And I again am strong:
The cataracts blow their trumpets from the steep; 25

[1] As the epigraph to the Ode, Wordsworth uses the last three lines of a poem of his own:

My heart leaps up when I behold
A rainbow in the sky:
So was it when my life began;
So is it now I am a man;
So be it when I shall grow old,
Or let me die!
The child is father . . . [etc.]

No more shall grief of mine the season wrong;
I hear the Echoes through the mountains throng,
The Winds come to me from the fields of sleep,
And all the earth is gay;
Land and sea 30
Give themselves up to jollity,
And with the heart of May
Doth every Beast keep holiday;—
Thou Child of Joy,
Shout round me, let me hear thy shouts, thou happy Shepherd-boy! 35

IV

Ye blessèd Creatures, I have heard the call
Ye to each other make; I see
The heavens laugh with you in your jubilee;
My heart is at your festival,
My head hath its coronal, 40
The fulness of your bliss, I feel—I feel it all.
Oh, evil day! if I were sullen
While Earth herself is adorning,
This sweet May-morning,
And the Children are culling 45
On every side,
In a thousand valleys far and wide,
Fresh flowers; while the sun shines warm,
And the Babe leaps up on his Mother's arm:—
I hear, I hear, with joy I hear! 50
—But there's a Tree, of many, one,
A single Field which I have looked upon,
Both of them speak of something that is gone:
The Pansy at my feet
Doth the same tale repeat: 55
Whither is fled the visionary gleam?
Where is it now, the glory and the dream?

V

Our birth is but a sleep and a forgetting:
The Soul that rises with us, our life's Star,
Hath had elsewhere its setting, 60
And cometh from afar:
Not in entire forgetfulness,
And not in utter nakedness,
But trailing clouds of glory do we come
From God, who is our home: 65
Heaven lies about us in our infancy!
Shades of the prison-house begin to close
Upon the growing Boy,

But he beholds the light, and whence it flows
        He sees it in his joy; 70
The Youth, who daily farther from the east
        Must travel, still is Nature's Priest,
        And by the vision splendid
        Is on his way attended;
At length the Man perceives it die away, 75
And fade into the light of common day.

VI

Earth fills her lap with pleasures of her own;
Yearnings she hath in her own natural kind,
And, even with something of a Mother's mind,
        And no unworthy aim, 80
        The homely Nurse doth all she can
To make her Foster-child, her Inmate Man,
        Forget the glories he hath known,
And that imperial palace whence he came.

VII

Behold the Child among his new-born blisses, 85
A six years' Darling of a pigmy size!
See, where 'mid work of his own hand he lies,
Fretted by sallies of his mother's kisses,
With light upon him from his father's eyes!
See, at his feet, some little plan or chart, 90
Some fragment from his dream of human life,
Shaped by himself with newly-learnèd art;
        A wedding or a festival,
        A mourning or a funeral,
            And this hath now his heart, 95
        And unto this he frames his song:
            Then will he fit his tongue
To dialogues of business, love, or strife;
        But it will not be long
        Ere this be thrown aside, 100
        And with new joy and pride
The little Actor cons another part;
Filling from time to time his "humorous stage"
With all the Persons, down to palsied Age,
That Life brings with her in her equipage; 105
        As if his whole vocation
        Were endless imitation.

VIII

Thou, whose exterior semblance doth belie
        Thy Soul's immensity;

Thou best Philosopher, who yet dost keep 110
Thy heritage, thou Eye among the blind,
That, deaf and silent, read'st the eternal deep,
Haunted for ever by the eternal mind,—
Mighty Prophet! Seer blest!
On whom those truths do rest, 115
Which we are toiling all our lives to find,
In darkness lost, the darkness of the grave;
Thou, over whom thy Immortality
Broods like the Day, a Master o'er a Slave,
A Presence which is not to be put by; 120
Thou little Child, yet glorious in the might
Of heaven-born freedom on thy being's height,
Why with such earnest pains dost thou provoke
The years to bring the inevitable yoke,
Thus blindly with thy blessedness at strife? 125
Full soon thy Soul shall have her earthly freight,
And custom lie upon thee with a weight,
Heavy as frost, and deep almost as life!

IX

O joy! that in our embers
Is something that doth live, 130
That nature yet remembers
What was so fugitive!
The thought of our past years in me doth breed
Perpetual benediction: not indeed
For that which is most worthy to be blest; 135
Delight and liberty, the simple creed
Of Childhood, whether busy or at rest,
With new-fledged hope still fluttering in his breast:—
Not for these I raise
The song of thanks and praise; 140
But for those obstinate questionings
Of sense and outward things,
Fallings from us, vanishings;
Blank misgivings of a Creature
Moving about in worlds not realised, 145
High instincts, before which our mortal Nature
Did tremble like a guilty Thing surprised:
But for those first affections,
Those shadowy recollections,
Which, be they what they may, 150
Are yet the fountain-light of all our day,
Are yet a master-light of all our seeing;
Uphold us, cherish, and have power to make
Our noisy years seem moments in the being

Of the eternal Silence: truths that wake, 155
To perish never;
Which neither listlessness, nor mad endeavour,
Nor Man nor Boy,
Nor all that is at enmity with joy,
Can utterly abolish or destroy! 160
Hence in a season of calm weather
Though inland far we be,
Our souls have sight of that immortal sea
Which brought us hither;
Can in a moment travel thither,— 165
And see the Children sport upon the shore,
And hear the mighty waters rolling evermore.

X

Then, sing, ye Birds, sing, sing a joyous song!
And let the young Lambs bound
As to the tabor's sound! 170
We, in thought, will join your throng,
Ye that pipe and ye that play,
Ye that through your hearts to-day
Feel the gladness of the May!
What though the radiance which was once so bright 175
Be now for ever taken from my sight,
Though nothing can bring back the hour
Of splendour in the grass, of glory in the flower;
We will grieve not, rather find
Strength in what remains behind; 180
In the primal sympathy
Which having been must ever be;
In the soothing thoughts that spring
Out of human suffering;
In the faith that looks through death, 185
In years that bring the philosophic mind.

XI

And O, ye Fountains, Meadows, Hills, and Groves,
Forbode not any severing of our loves!
Yet in my heart of hearts I feel your might;
I only have relinquished one delight 190
To live beneath your more habitual sway.
I love the Brooks which down their channels fret,
Even more than when I tripped lightly as they;
The innocent brightness of a new-born Day
Is lovely yet; 195
The Clouds that gather round the setting sun
Do take a sober colouring from an eye

That hath kept watch o'er man's mortality;
Another race hath been, and other palms are won.
Thanks to the human heart by which we live, 200
Thanks to its tenderness, its joys, and fears,
To me the meanest flower that blows can give
Thoughts that do often lie too deep for tears.

SAMUEL TAYLOR COLERIDGE

1772–1834

FROST AT MIDNIGHT

The Frost performs its secret ministry,
Unhelped by any wind. The owlet's cry
Came loud—and hark, again! loud as before.
The inmates of my cottage, all at rest,
Have left me to that solitude, which suits 5
Abstruser musings: save that at my side
My cradled infant slumbers peacefully.

'Tis calm indeed! so calm, that it disturbs
And vexes meditation with its strange
And extreme silentness. Sea, hill, and wood, 10
This populous village! Sea, and hill, and wood,
With all the numberless goings-on of life,
Inaudible as dreams! the thin blue flame
Lies on my low-burnt fire, and quivers not;
Only that film, which fluttered on the grate, 15
Still flutters there, the sole unquiet thing.
Methinks, its motion in this hush of nature
Gives it dim sympathies with me who live,
Making it a companionable form,
Whose puny flaps and freaks the idling Spirit 20
By its own moods interprets, every where
Echo or mirror seeking of itself,
And makes a toy of Thought.
But O! how oft,
How oft, at school, with most believing mind,
Presageful, have I gazed upon the bars, 25

To watch that fluttering *stranger!* and as oft
With unclosed lids, already had I dreamt
Of my sweet birth-place, and the old church-tower,
Whose bells, the poor man's only music, rang
Form morn to evening, all the hot Fair-day, 30
So sweetly, that they stirred and haunted me
With a wild pleasure, falling on mine ear
Most like articulate sounds of things to come!
So gazed I, till the soothing things, I dreamt,
Lulled me to sleep, and sleep prolonged my dreams! 35
And so I brooded all the following morn,
Awed by the stern preceptor's face, mine eye
Fixed with mock study on my swimming book:
Save if the door half opened, and I snatched
A hasty glance, and still my heart leaped up, 40
For still I hoped to see the *stranger's* face,
Townsman, or aunt, or sister more beloved,
My play-mate when we both were clothed alike!

Dear Babe, that sleepest cradled by my side,
Whose gentle breathings, heard in this deep calm, 45
Fill up the interspersed vacancies
And momentary pauses of the thought!
My babe so beautiful! it thrills my heart
With tender gladness, thus to look at thee,
And think that thou shalt learn far other lore, 50
And in far other scenes! For I was reared
In the great city, pent 'mid cloisters dim,
And saw nought lovely but the sky and stars.
But *thou*, my babe! shalt wander like a breeze
By lakes and sandy shores, beneath the crags 55
Of ancient mountain, and beneath the clouds,
Which image in their bulk both lakes and shores
And mountain crags: so shalt thou see and hear
The lovely shapes and sounds intelligible
Of that eternal language, which thy God 60
Utters, who from eternity doth teach
Himself in all, and all things in himself.
Great universal Teacher! he shall mould
Thy spirit, and by giving make it ask.

Therefore all seasons shall be sweet to thee, 65
Whether the summer clothe the general earth
With greenness, or the redbreast sit and sing
Betwixt the tufts of snow on the bare branch
Of mossy apple-tree, while the night thatch

Smokes in the sun-thaw; whether the eave-drops[1] fall 70
Heard only in the trances[2] of the blast,
Or if the secret ministry of frost
Shall hang them up in silent icicles,
Quietly shining to the quiet Moon.

DEJECTION: AN ODE

Late, late yestreen I saw the new Moon,
With the old Moon in her arms;
And I fear, I fear, my Master dear!
We shall have a deadly storm.
Ballad of Sir Patrick Spence.[1]

I

Well! If the Bard was weather-wise, who made
The grand old ballad of Sir Patrick Spence,
This night, so tranquil now, will not go hence
Unroused by winds, that ply a busier trade
Than those which mould yon cloud in lazy flakes, 5
Or the dull sobbing draft, that moans and rakes
Upon the strings of this Æolian lute,[2]
Which better far were mute.
For lo! the New-moon winter-bright!
And overspread with phantom light, 10
(With swimming phantom light o'erspread
But rimmed and circled by a silver thread)
I see the old Moon in her lap, foretelling
The coming-on of rain and squally blast.
And oh! that even now the gust were swelling, 15
And the slant night-shower driving loud and fast!
Those sounds which oft have raised me, whilst they awed,
And sent my soul abroad,
Might now perhaps their wonted[3] impulse give,
Might startle this dull pain, and make it move and live! 20

II

A grief without a pang, void, dark, and drear,
A stifled, drowsy, unimpassioned grief,

[1] Drops of rainwater from the eaves. [2] Suspensions, pauses.

[1] See "Sir Patrick Spens," p. 158. [2] In Greek mythology, Aeolus was god of the winds. An Aeolian lute is a stringed instrument that is hung so that the wind can blow over it, producing sounds of a rather melancholy kind. [3] Customary, usual.

Which finds no natural outlet, no relief,
In word, or sigh, or tear—
O Lady! in this wan and heartless mood, 25
To other thoughts by yonder throstle[4] woo'd,
All this long eve, so balmy and serene,
Have I been gazing on the western sky,
And its peculiar tint of yellow green:
And still I gaze—and with how blank an eye! 30
And those thin clouds above, in flakes and bars,
That give away their motion to the stars;
Those stars, that glide behind them or between,
Now sparkling, now bedimmed, but always seen:
Yon crescent Moon, as fixed as if it grew 35
In its own cloudless, starless lake of blue;
I see them all so excellently fair,
I see, not feel, how beautiful they are!

III

My genial spirits fail;
And what can these avail 40
To lift the smothering weight from off my breast?
It were a vain endeavour,
Though I should gaze for ever
On that green light that lingers in the west:
I may not hope from outward forms to win 45
The passion and the life, whose fountains are within.

IV

O Lady! we receive but what we give,
And in our life alone does Nature live:
Ours is her wedding garment, ours her shroud!
And would we aught behold, of higher worth, 50
Than that inanimate cold world allowed
To the poor loveless ever-anxious crowd,
Ah! from the soul itself must issue forth
A light, a glory, a fair luminous cloud
Enveloping the Earth— 55
And from the soul itself must there be sent
A sweet and potent voice, of its own birth,
Of all sweet sounds the life and element!

V

O pure of heart! thou need'st not ask of me
What this strong music in the soul may be! 60

[4] Thrush.

What, and wherein it doth exist,
This light, this glory, this fair luminous mist,
This beautiful and beauty-making power.
Joy, virtuous Lady! Joy that ne'er was given,
Save to the pure, and in their purest hour, 65
Life, and Life's effluence, cloud at once and shower,
Joy, Lady! is the spirit and the power,
Which wedding Nature to us gives in dower
A new Earth and new Heaven,
Undreamt of by the sensual and the proud— 70
Joy is the sweet voice, Joy the luminous cloud—
We in ourselves rejoice!
And thence flows all that charms or ear or sight,
All melodies the echoes of that voice,
All colours a suffusion from that light. 75

VI

There was a time when, though my path was rough,
This joy within me dallied with distress,
And all misfortunes were but as the stuff
Whence Fancy made me dreams of happiness:
For hope grew round me, like the twining vine, 80
And fruits, and foliage, not my own, seemed mine.
But now afflictions bow me down to earth:
Nor care I that they rob me of my mirth;
But oh! each visitation
Suspends what nature gave me at my birth, 85
My shaping spirit of Imagination.
For not to think of what I needs must feel,
But to be still and patient, all I can;
And haply by abstruse research to steal
From my own nature all the natural man— 90
This was my sole resource, my only plan:
Till that which suits a part infects the whole,
And now is almost grown the habit of my soul.

VII

Hence, viper thoughts, that coil around my mind,
Reality's dark dream! 95
I turn from you, and listen to the wind,
Which long has raved unnoticed. What a scream
Of agony by torture lengthened out
That lute sent forth! Thou Wind, that rav'st without,
Bare crag, or mountain-tairn, or blasted tree, 100
Or pine-grove whither woodman never clomb,
Or lonely house, long held the witches' home,
Methinks were fitter instruments for thee,

Mad Lutanist! who in this month of showers,
Of dark-brown gardens, and of peeping flowers, 105
Mak'st Devils' yule, with worse than wintry song,
The blossoms, buds, and timorous leaves among.
Thou Actor, perfect in all tragic sounds!
Thou mighty Poet, e'en to frenzy bold!
What tell'st thou now about? 110
'Tis of the rushing of an host in rout,
With groans, of trampled men, with smarting wounds—
At once they groan with pain, and shudder with the cold!
But hush! there is a pause of deepest silence!
And all that noise, as of a rushing crowd, 115
With groans, and tremulous shudderings—all is over—
It tells another tale, with sounds less deep and loud!
A tale of less affright,
And tempered with delight,
As Otway's self[5] had framed the tender lay,— 120
'Tis of a little child
Upon a lonesome wild,
Not far from home, but she hath lost her way:
And now moans low in bitter grief and fear,
And now screams loud, and hopes to make her mother hear. 125

VIII

'Tis midnight, but small thoughts have I of sleep:
Full seldom may my friends such vigils keep!
Visit her, gentle Sleep! with wings of healing,
And may this storm be but a mountain-birth,
May all the stars hang bright above her dwelling, 130
Silent as though they watched the sleeping Earth!
With light heart may she rise,
Gay fancy, cheerful eyes,
Joy lift her spirit, joy attune her voice;
To her may all things live, from pole to pole, 135
Their life the eddying of her living soul!
O simple spirit, guided from above,
Dear Lady! friend devoutest of my choice,
Thus mayest thou ever, evermore rejoice.

[5] Thomas Otway (1642–1685) wrote tragedies in blank verse.

GEORGE GORDON, LORD BYRON

1788–1824

DARKNESS

I had a dream, which was not all a dream.
The bright sun was extinguish'd, and the stars
Did wander darkling in the eternal space,
Rayless, and pathless, and the icy earth
Swung blind and blackening in the moonless air; 5
Morn came and went—and came, and brought no day,
And men forgot their passions in the dread
Of this their desolation; and all hearts
Were chill'd into a selfish prayer for light:
And they did live by watchfires—and the thrones, 10
The palaces of crowned kings—the huts,
The habitations of all things which dwell,
Were burnt for beacons; cities were consumed,
And men were gather'd round their blazing homes
To look once more into each other's face; 15
Happy were those who dwelt within the eye
Of the volcanos, and their mountain-torch:
A fearful hope was all the world contain'd;
Forests were set on fire—but hour by hour
They fell and faded—and the crackling trunks 20
Extinguish'd with a crash—and all was black.
The brows of men by the despairing light
Wore an unearthly aspect, as by fits
The flashes fell upon them; some lay down
And hid their eyes and wept; and some did rest 25
Their chins upon their clenchèd hands, and smiled;
And others hurried to and fro, and fed
Their funeral piles with fuel, and look'd up
With mad disquietude on the dull sky,
The pall of a past world; and then again 30
With curses cast them down upon the dust,
And gnash'd their teeth and howl'd: the wild birds shriek'd,
And, terrified, did flutter on the ground,
And flap their useless wings; the wildest brutes
Came tame and tremulous; and vipers crawl'd 35
And twined themselves among the multitude,

Hissing, but stingless—they were slain for food;
And War, which for a moment was no more,
Did glut himself again:—a meal was bought
With blood, and each sate sullenly apart 40
Gorging himself in gloom: no love was left;
All earth was but one thought—and that was death,
Immediate and inglorious; and the pang
Of famine fed upon all entrails—men
Died, and their bones were tombless as their flesh; 45
The meagre by the meagre were devour'd,
Even dogs assail'd their masters, all save one,
And he was faithful to a corse,[1] and kept
The birds and beasts and famish'd men at bay,
Till hunger clung[2] them, or the dropping dead 50
Lured their lank jaws; himself sought out no food,
But with a piteous and perpetual moan,
And a quick desolate cry, licking the hand
Which answer'd not with a caress—he died.
The crowd was famish'd by degrees; but two 55
Of an enormous city did survive,
And they were enemies: they met beside
The dying embers of an altar-place
Where had been heap'd a mass of holy things
For an unholy usage; they raked up, 60
And shivering scraped with their cold skeleton hands
The feeble ashes, and their feeble breath
Blew for a little life, and made a flame
Which was a mockery; then they lifted up
Their eyes as it grew lighter, and beheld 65
Each other's aspects—saw, and shriek'd, and died—
Even of their mutual hideousness they died,
Unknowing who he was upon whose brow
Famine had written Fiend. The world was void,
The populous and the powerful was a lump, 70
Seasonless, herbless, treeless, manless, lifeless—
A lump of death—a chaos of hard clay.
The rivers, lakes, and ocean all stool still,
And nothing stirr'd within their silent depths;
Ships sailorless lay rotting on the sea, 75
And their masts fell down piecemeal: as they dropp'd
They slept on the abyss without a surge—
The waves were dead; the tides were in their grave,
The Moon, their mistress, had expired before;
The winds were wither'd in the stagnant air, 80
And the clouds perish'd; Darkness had no need
Of aid from them—She was the Universe.

[1] Corpse. [2] Shriveled, parched.

SHE WALKS IN BEAUTY

She walks in beauty, like the night
Of cloudless climes and starry skies;
And all that's best of dark and bright
Meet in her aspect and her eyes:
Thus mellow'd to that tender light 5
Which heaven to gaudy day denies.

One shade the more, one ray the less,
Had half impair'd the nameless grace
Which waves in every raven tress,
Or softly lightens o'er her face; 10
Where thoughts serenely sweet express
How pure, how dear their dwelling-place.

And on that cheek, and o'er that brow,
So soft, so calm, yet eloquent,
The smiles that win, the tints that glow, 15
But tell of days in goodness spent,
A mind at peace with all below,
A heart whose love is innocent!

WHEN WE TWO PARTED

When we two parted
In silence and tears,
Half broken-hearted
To sever for years,
Pale grew thy cheek and cold, 5
Colder thy kiss;
Truly that hour foretold
Sorrow to this.

The dew of the morning
Sunk chill on my brow— 10
It felt like the warning
Of what I feel now.
Thy vows are all broken,
And light is thy fame:
I hear thy name spoken, 15
And share in its shame.

They name thee before me,
A knell to mine ear;
A shudder comes o'er me—
Why wert thou so dear? 20
They know not I knew thee,
Who knew thee too well:—
Long, long shall I rue thee,
Too deeply to tell.

In secret we met— 25
In silence I grieve,
That thy heart could forget,
Thy spirit deceive.
If I should meet thee
After long years, 30
How should I greet thee?—
With silence and tears.

SO, WE'LL GO NO MORE A-ROVING

So, we'll go no more a-roving
So late into the night,
Though the heart be still as loving,
And the moon be still as bright.

For the sword outwears its sheath, 5
And the soul wears out the breast,
And the heart must pause to breathe,
And love itself have rest.

Though the night was made for loving,
And the day returns too soon, 10
Yet we'll go no more a-roving
By the light of the moon.

PERCY BYSSHE SHELLEY

1792–1822

HYMN TO INTELLECTUAL BEAUTY

The awful shadow of some unseen Power
    Floats tho' unseen among us; visiting
    This various world with as inconstant wing
As summer winds that creep from flower to flower;
Like moonbeams that behind some piny mountain shower, 5
        It visits with inconstant glance
        Each human heart and countenance;
Like hues and harmonies of evening,
        Like clouds in starlight widely spread,
        Like memory of music fled, 10
        Like aught that for its grace may be
Dear, and yet dearer for its mystery.

Spirit of BEAUTY, that dost consecrate
    With thine own hues all thou dost shine upon
    Of human thought or form, where art thou gone? 15
Why dost thou pass away and leave our state,
This dim vast vale of tears, vacant and desolate?
        Ask why the sunlight not forever
        Weaves rainbows o'er yon mountain river,
Why aught should fail and fade that once is shewn, 20
        Why fear and dream and death and birth
        Cast on the daylight of this earth
        Such gloom, why man has such a scope
For love and hate, despondency and hope?

No voice from some sublimer world hath ever 25
    To sage or poet these responses given:
    Therefore the names of Demon, Ghost, and Heaven,
Remain the records of their vain endeavour:
Frail spells, whose uttered charm might not avail to sever,
        From all we hear and all we see, 30
        Doubt, chance, and mutability.
Thy light alone, like mist o'er mountains driven,
        Or music by the night wind sent
        Through strings of some still instrument,

Or moonlight on a midnight stream, 35
Gives grace and truth to life's unquiet dream.

Love, Hope, and Self-esteem, like clouds, depart
And come, for some uncertain moments lent.
Man were immortal, and omnipotent,
Didst thou, unknown and awful as thou art, 40
Keep with thy glorious train firm state within his heart.
Thou messenger of sympathies,
That wax and wane in lovers' eyes;
Thou, that to human thought art nourishment,
Like darkness to a dying flame! 45
Depart not as thy shadow came:
Depart not, lest the grave should be,
Like life and fear, a dark reality.

While yet a boy I sought for ghosts, and sped
Through many a listening chamber, cave and ruin, 50
And starlight wood, with fearful steps pursuing
Hopes of high talk with the departed dead.
I called on poisonous names with which our youth is fed:
I was not heard: I saw them not:
When musing deeply on the lot 55
Of life, at that sweet time when winds are wooing
All vital things that wake to bring
News of birds and blossoming,
Sudden, thy shadow fell on me:
I shrieked, and clasped my hands in ecstacy! 60

I vowed that I would dedicate my powers
To thee and thine: have I not kept the vow?
With beating heart and streaming eyes, even now
I call the phantoms of a thousand hours
Each from his voiceless grave: they have in visioned bowers 65
Of studious zeal or love's delight
Outwatched with me the envious night:
They know that never joy illumed my brow,
Unlinked with hope that thou wouldst free
This world from its dark slavery, 70
That thou, O awful LOVELINESS,
Wouldst give whate'er these words cannot express.

The day becomes more solemn and serene
When noon is past: there is a harmony
In autumn, and a lustre in its sky, 75

Which through the summer is not heard or seen,
As if it could not be, as if it had not been!
Thus let thy power, which like the truth
Of nature on my passive youth
Descended, to my onward life supply 80
Its calm, to one who worships thee,
And every form containing thee,
Whom, SPIRIT fair, thy spells did bind
To fear himself, and love all human kind.

OZYMANDIAS[1]

I met a traveller from an antique land
Who said: Two vast and trunkless legs of stone
Stand in the desert. Near them, on the sand,
Half sunk, a shattered visage lies, whose frown,
And wrinkled lip, and sneer of cold command, 5
Tell that its sculptor well those passions read
Which yet survive, stamped on these lifeless things,
The hand that mocked them and the heart that fed;
And on the pedestal these words appear:
"My name is Ozymandias, king of kings: 10
Look on my works, ye Mighty, and despair!"
Nothing beside remains. Round the decay
Of that colossal wreck, boundless and bare
The lone and level sands stretch far away.

SONNET: ENGLAND IN 1819

An old, mad, blind, despised, and dying king,—
Princes, the dregs of their dull race, who flow
Through public scorn,—mud from a muddy spring;
Rulers who neither see, nor feel, nor know,
But leech-like to their fainting country cling, 5
Till they drop, blind in blood, without a blow;
A people starved and stabbed in the untilled field,—
An army, which liberticide[1] and prey
Makes a two-edged sword to all who wield,—
Golden and sanguine laws which tempt and slay,— 10
Religion Christless, Godless—a book sealed;

[1] Rameses II, Pharaoh of Egypt, whose statue stood at Thebes.

[1] Destruction of liberty.

A Senate, Time's worst statute unrepealed,—
Are graves, from which a glorious Phantom may
Burst, to illumine our tempestuous day.

TO NIGHT

Swiftly walk over the western Wave,
　　　Spirit of Night!
Out of the misty eastern cave
Where, all the long and lone daylight,
Thou wovest dreams of joy and fear, 5
Which make thee terrible and dear,—
　　　Swift be thy flight!

Wrap thy form in a mantle gray,
　　　Star-inwrought!
Blind with thine hair the eyes of Day, 10
Kiss her until she be wearied out,
Then wander o'er city, and sea, and land,
Touching all with thine opiate wand—
　　　Come, long-sought!

When I arose and saw the dawn, 15
　　　I sighed for thee;
When light rode high, and the dew was gone,
And noon lay heavy on flower and tree,
And the weary Day turned to his rest,
Lingering like an unloved guest, 20
　　　I sighed for thee.

Thy brother Death came, and cried,
　　　Wouldst thou me?
Thy sweet child Sleep, the filmy-eyed,
Murmured like a noon tide bee, 25
Shall I nestle near thy side?
Wouldst thou me?—And I replied,
　　　No, . . . not thee!

Death will come when thou art dead,
　　　Soon, too soon— 30
Sleep will come when thou art fled;
Of neither would I ask the boon
I asked of thee, belovèd Night—

Swift be thine approaching flight,
    Come soon, soon! 35

TO ———

Music, when soft voices die,
Vibrates in the memory—
Odours, when sweet violets sicken,
Live within the sense they quicken.

Rose leaves, when the rose is dead, 5
Are heaped for the belovèd's bed;
And so thy thoughts, when thou art gone,
Love itself shall slumber on.

CHORUS FROM *HELLAS*

The world's great age begins anew,
    The golden years return,
The earth doth like a snake renew
    Her winter weeds outworn:
Heaven smiles, and faiths and empires gleam, 5
Like wrecks of a dissolving dream.

A brighter Hellas[1] rears its mountains
    From waves serener far:
A new Peneus[2] rolls his fountains
    Against the morning-star. 10
Where fairer Tempes[3] bloom, there sleep
Young Cyclads[4] on a sunnier deep.

A loftier Argo[5] cleaves the main,
    Fraught with a later prize;

[1] Greece. [2] A river in Thessaly, a district in Greece. [3] *Tempe,* the name of a valley in ancient Greece, was used as a synonym for any valley noted for its cool shades, singing birds, and romantic scenery. [4] The Cyclades, Greek islands where a very early culture flourished. [5] Galley that carried Jason and the Argonauts in search of the Golden Fleece to return it to Greece, where it belonged. The ship was thought to be the first seagoing vessel.

Another Orpheus[6] sings again, 15
And loves, and weeps, and dies.
A new Ulysses[7] leaves once more
Calypso[8] for his native shore.

O, write no more the tale of Troy,
If earth Death's scroll must be! 20
Nor mix with Laian rage[9] the joy
Which dawns upon the free:
Although a subtler Sphinx renew
Riddles of death Thebes never knew.[10]

Another Athens shall arise, 25
And to remoter time
Bequeath, like sunset to the skies,
The splendour of its prime;
And leave, if nought so bright may live,
All earth can take or heaven can give. 30

Saturn[11] and Love their long repose
Shall burst, more bright and good
Than all who fell, than One[12] who rose,
Than many unsubdued:
Not gold, not blood, their altar dowers,[13] 35
But votive tears and symbol flowers.

O cease! must hate and death return?
Cease! must men kill and die?
Cease! drain not to its dregs the urn
Of bitter prophecy. 40
The world is weary of the past,
O might it die or rest at last!

[6] In Greek mythology, a fabulous musician whose marriage to Eurydice ended tragically. [7] Odysseus, hero of Homer's *Odyssey,* which tells of the Trojan War and Odysseus' wanderings after it. [8] In the *Odyssey,* a nymph who detained Odysseus on an island for seven years. [9] Laius, the father of Oedipus, was known for his fierce anger. [10] Oedipus saved Thebes from destruction by answering a riddle posed by the Sphinx, a hideous monster. [11] Roman god of agriculture. [12] Christ. [13] Endowments.

JOHN KEATS

1795–1821

ON FIRST LOOKING INTO CHAPMAN'S HOMER[1]

Much have I travell'd in the realms of gold,
And many goodly states and kingdoms seen;
Round many western islands have I been
Which bards in fealty to Apollo[2] hold.
Oft of one wide expanse had I been told 5
That deep-brow'd Homer ruled as his demesne;
Yet did I never breathe its pure serene
Till I heard Chapman speak out loud and bold:
Then felt I like some watcher of the skies
When a new planet swims into his ken; 10
Or like stout Cortez[3] when with eagle eyes
He star'd at the Pacific—and all his men
Look'd at each other with a wild surmise—
Silent, upon a peak in Darien.[4]

WHEN I HAVE FEARS

When I have fears that I may cease to be
Before my pen has glean'd my teeming brain,
Before high-pilèd books, in charact'ry,
Hold like rich garners the full-ripen'd grain;
When I behold, upon the night's starr'd face, 5
Huge cloudy symbols of a high romance,[1]
And think that I may never live to trace
Their shadows, with the magic hand of chance;
And when I feel, fair creature of an hour!
That I shall never look upon thee more, 10
Never have relish in the faery power
Of unreflecting love!—then on the shore

[1] George Chapman, an Elizabethan poet, translated both the *Iliad* (1611) and the *Odyssey* (1614) of Homer. [2] God of light and medicine and probably the most widely revered god of ancient Greece. [3] A mistake for Balboa. [4] Former name for Panama.

[1] Here, romantic story.

Of the wide world I stand alone, and think
Till love and fame to nothingness do sink.

BRIGHT STAR, WOULD I WERE STEADFAST AS THOU ART

Bright star! would I were steadfast as thou art—
Not in lone splendour hung aloft the night
And watching, with eternal lids apart,
Like nature's patient, sleepless Eremite,
The moving waters at their priestlike task 5
Of pure ablution round earth's human shores,
Or gazing on the new soft fallen mask
Of snow upon the mountains and the moors—
No—yet still steadfast, still unchangeable,
Pillow'd upon my fair love's ripening breast, 10
To feel for ever its soft fall and swell,
Awake for ever in a sweet unrest,
Still, still to hear her tender-taken breath,
And so live ever—or else swoon to death.

LA BELLE DAME SANS MERCI[1]

O what can ail thee, knight-at-arms,
Alone and palely loitering?
The sedge has wither'd from the lake,
And no birds sing.

O what can ail thee, knight at arms, 5
So haggard and so woe-begone?
The squirrel's granary is full,
And the harvest's done.

I see a lily on thy brow,
With anguish moist and fever dew, 10
And on thy cheeks a fading rose
Fast withereth too.

"I met a lady in the meads,
Full beautiful—a faery's child;

[1] The title can be translated as "The Fair Lady without Pity." Keats revised this poem, but his first version, which is printed here, is generally regarded as superior.

Her hair was long, her foot was light,
And her eyes were wild. 15

"I made a garland for her head,
And bracelets too, and fragrant zone;[2]
She look'd at me as she did love,
And made sweet moan. 20

"I set her on my pacing steed,
And nothing else saw all day long,
For side-long would she bend, and sing
A faery's song.

"She found me roots of relish sweet, 25
And honey wild, and manna dew,
And sure in language strange she said—
'I love thee true.'

"She took me to her elfin grot,[3]
And there she wept, and sigh'd full sore, 30
And there I shut her wild wild eyes
With kisses four.

"And there she lullèd me asleep,
And there I dream'd—Ah! woe betide!—
The latest dream I ever dream'd 35
On the cold hill side.

"I saw pale kings and princes too,
Pale warriors, death-pale were they all;
They cried—'La Belle Dame sans Merci
Hath thee in thrall!' 40

"I saw their starved lips in the gloam,
With horrid warning gapèd wide,
And I awoke, and found me here,
On the cold hill's side.

"And this is why I sojourn here, 45
Alone and palely loitering,

[2] An encircling band, belt, girdle. [3] Fairy cave.

Though the sedge is wither'd from the lake,
And no birds sing."

ODE ON A GRECIAN URN

Thou still unravish'd bride of quietness,
Thou foster-child of silence and slow time,
Sylvan historian, who canst thus express
A flowery tale more sweetly than our rhyme:
What leaf-fring'd legend haunts about thy shape 5
Of dieties or mortals, or of both,
In Tempe[1] or the dales of Arcady?[2]
What men or gods are these? What maidens loth?
What mad pursuit? What struggle to escape?
What pipes and timbrels? What wild ecstasy? 10

Heard melodies are sweet, but those unheard
Are sweeter; therefore, ye soft pipes, play on;
Not to the sensual ear, but, more endear'd,
Pipe to the spirit ditties of no tone:
Fair youth, beneath the trees, thou canst not leave 15
Thy song, nor ever can those trees be bare;
Bold lover, never, never canst thou kiss,
Though winning near the goal—yet, do not grieve;
She cannot fade, though thou hast not thy bliss,
Forever wilt thou love, and she be fair! 20

Ah, happy, happy boughs! that cannot shed
Your leaves, nor ever bid the Spring adieu;
And, happy melodist, unweariéd,
For ever piping songs for ever new;
More happy love! more happy, happy love! 25
For ever warm and still to be enjoy'd,
For ever panting, and for ever young;
All breathing human passion far above,
That leaves a heart high-sorrowful and cloy'd,
A burning forehead, and a parching tongue. 30

Who are these coming to the sacrifice?
To what green altar, O mysterious priest,

[1] The name of a valley in Thessaly, in ancient Greece, that came to be a synonym for any beautiful rural spot. [2] Arcadia, a region in ancient Greece that is taken as the ideal region of rural felicity.

Lead'st thou that heifer lowing at the skies,
And all her silken flanks with garlands drest?
What little town by river or sea shore, 35
Or mountain-built with peaceful citadel,
Is emptied of this folk, this pious morn?
And, little town, thy streets for evermore
Will silent be; and not a soul to tell
Why thou art desolate, can e'er return. 40

O Attic[3] shape! Fair attitude! with brede[4]
Of marble men and maidens overwrought,
With forest branches and the trodden weed;
Thou, silent form, dost tease us out of thought
As doth eternity: Cold Pastoral! 45
When old age shall this generation waste,
Thou shalt remain, in midst of other woe
Than ours, a friend to man, to whom thou say'st,
Beauty is truth, truth beauty,—that is all
Ye know on earth, and all ye need to know 50

TO AUTUMN

Season of mists and mellow fruitfulness,
Close bosom-friend of the maturing sun;
Conspiring with him how to load and bless
With fruit the vines that round the thatch-eaves run;
To bend with apples the moss'd cottage-trees, 5
And fill all fruit with ripeness to the core;
To swell the gourd, and plump the hazel shells
With a sweet kernel; to set budding more,
And still more, later flowers for the bees,
Until they think warm days will never cease, 10
For summer has o'er-brimm'd their clammy cells.

Who hath not seen thee oft amid thy store?
Sometimes whoever seeks abroad may find
Thee sitting careless on a granary floor,
Thy hair soft-lifted by the winnowing wind; 15
Or on a half-reap'd furrow sound asleep,
Drows'd with the fume of poppies, while thy hook
Spares the next swath and all its twinèd flowers:

[3] Of Attica, the ancient region of which Athens was the capital. *Attic* has come to suggest simplicity, purity, and refinement. [4] Embroidery, interweaving.

And sometimes like a gleaner thou dost keep
Steady thy laden head across a brook; 20
Or by a cider-press, with patient look,
Thou watchest the last oozings hours by hours.

Where are the songs of Spring? Ay, where are they?
Think not of them, thou hast thy music too,—
While barrèd clouds bloom the soft-dying day, 25
And touch the stubble-plains with rosy hue;
Then in a wailful choir the small gnats mourn
Among the river sallows,[1] borne aloft
Or sinking as the light wind lives or dies;
And full-grown lambs loud bleat from hilly bourn,[2] 30
Hedge-crickets sing; and now with treble soft
The red-breast whistles from a garden-croft;
And gathering swallows twitter in the skies.

ODE ON MELANCHOLY

No, no, go not to Lethe,[1] neither twist
Wolf's-bane,[2] tight-rooted, for its poisonous wine;
Nor suffer thy pale forehead to be kiss'd
By nightshade, ruby grape of Proserpine;[3]
Make not your rosary of yew-berries, 5
Nor let the beetle, nor the death-moth[4] be
Your mournful Psyche,[5] nor the downy owl[6]
A partner in your sorrow's mysteries;
For shade to shade will come too drowsily,
And drown the wakeful anguish of the soul. 10

But when the melancholy fit shall fall
Sudden from heaven like a weeping cloud,
That fosters the droop-headed flowers all,
And hides the green hill in an April shroud;

[1] Willows. [2] Domain, land.

[1] In Greek mythology, a river in Hades whose water, if drunk, causes forgetfulness; hence, forgetfulness, oblivion. [2] Wolf's-bane, nightshade, and Yew-berries are poisonous plants. [3] Queen of Hades. [4] Both the beetle and the death's-head moth have markings on the back of the thorax suggesting a human skull or death's-head. [5] In Greek, the soul, with was recognized as the seat of the passions. It was pictorially represented as a beautiful maiden with the wings of a butterfly, and sometimes as a butterfly. [6] The note of the owl is generally thought to be doleful.

Then glut thy sorrow on a morning rose, 15
Or on the rainbow of the salt sand-wave,
Or on the wealth of globèd peonies;
Or if thy mistress some rich anger shows,
Emprison her soft hand, and let her rave,
And feed deep, deep upon her peerless eyes. 20

She dwells with Beauty—Beauty that must die;
And Joy, whose hand is ever at his lips
Bidding adieu; and aching Pleasure nigh,
Turning to poison while the bee-mouth sips:
Ay, in the very temple of Delight 25
Veil'd Melancholy has her sovran shrine,
Though seen of none save him whose strenuous tongue
Can burst Joy's grape against his palate fine;
His soul shall taste the sadness of her might,
And be among her cloudy trophies hung. 30

RALPH WALDO EMERSON

1803–1882

HAMATREYA[1]

Bulkeley, Hunt, Willard, Hosmer, Meriam, Flint,
Possessed the land which rendered to their toil
Hay, corn, roots, hemp, flax, apples, wool and wood.
Each of these landlords walked amidst his farm,
Saying, " 'Tis mine, my children's and my name's. 5
How sweet the west wind sounds in my own trees!
How graceful climb those shadows on my hill!
I fancy these pure waters and the flags
Know me, as does my dog: we sympathize;
And, I affirm, my actions smack of the soil." 10

[1] This poem is a free rendering of a passage in the *Vishnu Purana*. The title seems to be a version of *Maitreya,* the name of the next future Buddha, to whom Emerson addresses, in his journal, some "stanzas that were chanted by Earth" on the "folly of princes" (in acquiring land).

Where are these men? Asleep beneath their grounds:
And strangers, fond[2] as they, their furrows plough.
Earth laughs in flowers, to see her boastful boys
Earth-proud, proud of the earth which is not theirs;
Who steer the plough, but cannot steer their feet 15
Clear of the grave.
They added ridge to valley, brook to pond,
And sighed for all that bounded their domain;
"This suits me for a pasture; that's my park;
We must have clay, lime, gravel, granite-ledge,[3] 20
And misty lowland, where to go for peat.
The land is well,—lies fairly to the south.
'Tis good, when you have crossed the sea and back,
To find the sitfast acres where you left them."
Ah! the hot owner sees not Death, who adds 25
Him to his land, a lump of mould the more.
Hear what the Earth says:—

EARTH-SONG

"Mine and yours;
Mine, not yours.
Earth endures; 30
Stars abide—
Shine down in the old sea;
Old are the shores;
But where are old men?
I who have seen much, 35
Such have I never seen.

"The lawyer's deed
Ran sure,
In tail,[4]
To them, and to their heirs 40
Who shall succeed,
Without fail,
Forevermore.

"Here is the land,
Shaggy with wood, 45
With its old valley,
Mound and flood.
But the heritors?—
Fled like the flood's foam.

[2] Foolish. [3] A deposit of granite to be mined. [4] In entail, or transmission as an inalienable inheritance.

The lawyer, and the laws,
And the kingdom,
Clean swept herefrom. 50

"They called me theirs,
Who so controlled me;
Yet every one 55
Wished to stay, and is gone,
How am I theirs,
If they cannot hold me,
But I hold them?"

When I heard the Earth-song, 60
I was no longer brave;
My avarice cooled
Like lust in the chill of the grave.

GIVE ALL TO LOVE

Give all to love;
Obey thy heart;
Friends, kindred, days,
Estate, good-fame,
Plans, credit and the Muse,— 5
Nothing refuse.

'Tis a brave master;
Let it have scope:
Follow it utterly,
Hope beyond hope: 10
High and more high
It dives into noon,
With wing unspent,
Untold intent;
But it is a god, 15
Knows its own path
And the outlets of the sky.

It was never for the mean;
It requireth courage stout.
Souls above doubt, 20
Valor unbending,

It will reward,—
They shall return
More than they were,
And ever ascending. 25

Leave all for love;
Yet, hear me, yet,
One word more thy heart behoved,
One pulse more of firm endeavor,—
Keep thee today, 30
Tomorrow, forever,
Free as an Arab
Of thy beloved.

Cling with life to the maid;
But when the surprise, 35
First vague shadow of surmise
Flits across her bosom young,
Of a joy apart from thee,
Free be she, fancy-free;
Nor thou detain her vesture's hem, 40
Nor the palest rose she flung
From her summer diadem.

Though thou loved her as thyself,
As a self of purer clay,
Though her parting dims the day, 45
Stealing grace from all alive;
Heartily know,
When half-gods go,
The gods arrive.

BRAHMA[1]

If the red slayer thinks he slays,
 Or if the slain think he is slain,
They know not well the subtle ways
 I keep, and pass, and turn again.

Far or forgot to me is near; 5
 Shadow and sunlight are the same;

[1] The creator god of Hinduism. This poem was inspired by several passages of the *Bhagavat-Gita*.

The vanished gods to me appear;
    And one to me are shame and fame.

They reckon ill who leave me out;
    When me they fly, I am the wings; 10
I am the doubter and the doubt,
    And I the hymn the Brahmin[2] sings.

The strong gods[3] pine for my abode,
    And pine in vain the sacred Seven;[4]
But thou, meek lover of the good! 15
    Find me, and turn thy back on heaven.

EDGAR ALLAN POE

1809–1849

THE VALLEY OF UNREST

Once it smiled a silent dell
Where the people did not dwell;
They had gone unto the wars,
Trusting to the mild-eyed stars,
Nightly, from their azure towers, 5
To keep watch above the flowers,
In the midst of which all day
The red sun-light lazily lay.
Now each visitor shall confess
The sad valley's restlessness. 10
Nothing there is motionless—
Nothing save the airs that brood
Over the magic solitude.
Ah, by no wind are stirred those trees
That palpitate like the chill seas 15

[2] Member of the priestly and meditative caste of Hinduism. [3] Indra, god of the sky and wielder of the thunderbolt; Agni, god of fire; and Yoma, god of death and judgment. These gods eventually will be absorbed into Brahma. [4] Maharshis or highest saints.

Around the misty Hebrides!
Ah, by no wind those clouds are driven
That rustle through the unquiet Heaven
Uneasily, from morn till even,
Over the violets there that lie 20
In myriad types of the human eye—
Over three lilies there that wave
And weep above a nameless grave!
They wave:—from out their fragment tops
Eternal dews come down in drops. 25
They weep:—from off their delicate stems
Perennial tears descend in gems.

TO HELEN

Helen, thy beauty is to me
Like those Nicèan[1] barks of yore,
That gently, o'er a perfumed sea,
The weary, way-worn wanderer bore
To his own native shore. 5

On desperate seas long wont to roam,
Thy hyacinth hair, thy classic face,
Thy Naiad[2] airs have brought me home
To the glory that was Greece
And the grandeur that was Rome. 10

Lo! in yon brilliant window-niche
How statue-like I see thee stand,
The agate lamp within thy hand!
Ah, Psyche,[3] from the regions which
Are Holy Land! 15

ALONE

From childhood's hour I have not been
As others were—I have not seen
As others saw—I could not bring
My passions from a common spring—

[1] Of Nicaea, an ancient city in Asia Minor. [2] A water nymph. [3] The reference is to the legend of Psyche, who, beloved of Cupid, lit a lamp to see him while asleep.

From the same source I have not taken
My sorrow—I could not awaken
Hy heart to joy at the same tone—
And all I loved—*I* loved alone—
Then—in my childhood, in the dawn
Of a most stormy life—was drawn
From every depth of good and ill
The mystery which binds me still—
From the torrent, or the fountain—
From the red cliff of the mountain—
From the sun that round me rolled
In its autumn tint of gold—
From the lightning in the sky
As it pass'd me flying by—
From the thunder and the storm—
And the cloud that took the form
When the rest of Heaven was blue
Of a demon in my view.—

ALFRED, LORD TENNYSON

1809–1892

ULYSSES

It little profits that an idle king,
By this still hearth, among these barren crags,
Match'd with an agèd wife, I mete and dole[1]
Unequal laws unto a savage race,
That hoard, and sleep, and feed, and know not me.
I cannot rest from travel; I will drink
Life to the lees; all times I have enjoy'd
Greatly, have suffer'd greatly, both with those
That loved me, and alone; on shore, and when
Through scudding drifts the rainy Hyades[2]
Vext the dim sea: I am become a name;
For always roaming with a hungry heart
Much have I seen and known;—cities of men

[1] The speaker is Ulysses (Odysseus). The time is after his return to his kingdom of Ithaca from the travels described in Homer's *Odyssey*. [2] A cluster of stars believed to cause rainy weather.

And manners, climates, councils, governments,
Myself not least, but honour'd of them all;— 15
And drunk delight of battle with my peers,
Far on the ringing plains of windy Troy.
I am a part of all that I have met;
Yet all experience is an arch wherethrough
Gleams that untravell'd world, whose margin fades 20
For ever and for ever when I move.
How dull it is to pause, to make an end,
To rust unburnish'd, not to shine in use!
As though to breathe were life! Life piled on life
Were all too little, and of one to me 25
Little remains; but every hour is saved
From that eternal silence, something more,
A bringer of new things; and vile it were
For some three suns to store and hoard myself,
And this grey spirit yearning in desire 30
To follow knowledge, like a sinking star,
Beyond the utmost bound of human thought.

This is my son, mine own Telemachus,
To whom I leave the sceptre and the isle—
Well-loved of me, discerning to fulfil 35
This labour, by slow prudence to make mild
A rugged people, and through soft degrees
Subdue them to the useful and the good.
Most blameless is he, centred in the sphere
Of common duties, decent not to fail 40
In offices of tenderness, and pay
Meet adoration to my household gods,
When I am gone. He works his work, I mine.

There lies the port; the vessel puffs her sail;
There gloom the dark, broad seas. My mariners, 45
Souls that have toil'd, and wrought, and thought with me—
That ever with a frolic welcome took
The thunder and the sunshine, and opposed
Free hearts, free foreheads—you and I are old;
Old age hath yet his honour and his toil; 50
Death closes all; but something ere the end,
Some work of noble note, may yet be done,
Not unbecoming men that strove with Gods.
The lights begin to twinkle from the rocks;
The long day wanes; the slow moon climbs; the deep 55
Moans round with many voices. Come, my friends,
'Tis not too late to seek a newer world.
Push off, and sitting well in order smite
The sounding furrows; for my purpose holds
To sail beyond the sunset, and the baths 60
Of all the western stars, until I die.
It may be that the gulfs will wash us down;

It may be we shall touch the Happy Isles,[3]
And see the great Achilles,[4] whom we knew.
Though much is taken, much abides; and though 65
We are not now that strength which in old days
Moved earth and heaven; that which we are, we are;—
One equal temper of heroic hearts,
Made weak by time and fate, but strong in will
To strive, to seek, to find, and not to yield. 70

THE LOTOS-EATERS[1]

"Courage!" he[2] said, and pointed toward the land,
"This mounting wave will roll us shoreward soon."
In the afternoon they came unto a land
In which it seemed always afternoon.
All round the coast the languid air did swoon, 5
Breathing like one that hath a weary dream.
Full-faced above the valley stood the moon;
And like a downward smoke, the slender stream
Along the cliff to fall and pause and fall did seem.

A land of streams; some, like a downward smoke, 10
Slow-dropping veils of thinnest lawn, did go;
And some through wavering lights and shadows broke,
Rolling a slumbrous sheet of foam below.
They saw the gleaming river seaward flow
From the inner land; far off, three mountain-tops, 15
Three silent pinnacles of aged snow,
Stood sunset-flush'd; and, dew'd with showery drops,
Up-clomb the shadowy pine above the woven copse.

The charmed sunset linger'd low adown
In the red West; through mountain clefts the dale 20
Was seen far inland, and the yellow down
Border'd with palm, and many a winding vale
And meadow, set with slender galingale;[3]
A land where all things always seemed the same!
And round about the keel with faces pale, 25

[3] Elysium, the Greek paradise for heroes. [4] Hero of the *Iliad,* as Ulysses is of the *Odyssey*. Both epics deal with the Trojan war.

[1] In Homer's *Odyssey,* the Lotophagi, or lotos-eaters, ate fruit that caused a state of dreamy forgetfulness and loss of all desire to return home. [2] Odysseus, or Ulysses. [3] A kind of sedge.

Dark faces pale against that rosy flame,
The mild-eyed melancholy Lotos-eaters came.

Branches they bore of that enchanted stem,
Laden with flower and fruit, whereof they gave
To each, but whoso did receive of them, 30
And taste, to him the gushing of the wave
Far far away did seem to mourn and rave
On alien shores; and if his fellow spake,
His voice was thin, as voices from the grave;
And deep-asleep he seem'd, yet all awake, 35
And music in his ears his beating heart did make.

They sat them down upon the yellow sand,
Between the sun and moon upon the shore;
And sweet it was to dream of Fatherland,
Of child, and wife, and slave; but evermore 40
Most weary seem'd the sea, weary the oar,
Weary the wandering fields of barren foam.
Then someone said, "We will return no more";
And all at once they sang, "Our island home
Is far beyond the wave; we will no longer roam." 45

CHORIC SONG

I

There is sweet music here that softer falls
Than petals from blown roses on the grass,
Or night-dews on still waters between walls
Of shadowy granite, in a gleaming pass;
Music that gentlier on the spirit lies, 50
Than tired eyelids upon tired eyes;
Music that brings sweet sleep down from the blissful skies.
Here are cool mosses deep,
And through the moss the ivies creep,
And in the stream the long-leaved flowers weep, 55
And from the craggy ledge the poppy hangs in sleep.

II

Why are we weigh'd upon with heaviness,
And utterly consumed with sharp distress,
While all things else have rest from weariness?
All things have rest: why should we toil alone, 60
We only toil, who are the first of things,

And make perpetual moan,
Still from one sorrow to another thrown:
Nor ever fold our wings,
And cease from wanderings, 65
Nor steep our brows in slumber's holy balm;
Nor hearken what the inner spirit sings,
"There is no joy but calm!"
Why should we only toil, the roof and crown of things?

III

Lo! in the middle of the wood, 70
The folded leaf is woo'd from out the bud
With winds upon the branch, and there
Grows green and broad, and takes no care,
Sun-steep'd at noon, and in the moon
Nightly dew-fed; and turning yellow 75
Falls, and floats adown the air.
Lo! sweeten'd with the summer light,
The full-juiced apple, waxing over-mellow,
Drops in a silent autumn night.
All its allotted length of days 80
The flower ripens in its place,
Ripens and fades, and falls, and hath no toil,
Fast-rooted in the fruitful soil.

IV

Hateful is the dark-blue sky,
Vaulted o'er the dark-blue sea. 85
Death is the end of life; ah, why
Should life all labour be?
Let us alone. Time driveth onward fast
And in a little while our lips are dumb.
Let us alone. What is it that will last? 90
All things are taken from us, and become
Portions and parcels of the dreadful Past.
Let us alone. What pleasure can we have
To war with evil? Is there any peace
In ever climbing up the climbing wave? 95
All things have rest, and ripen toward the grave
In silence—ripen, fall and cease:
Give us long rest or death, dark death, or dreamful ease.

V

How sweet it were, hearing the downward stream,
With half-shut eyes ever to seem 100

Falling asleep in a half-dream!
To dream and dream, like yonder amber light,
Which will not leave the myrrh-bush on the height;
To hear each other's whisper'd speech;
Eating the Lotos day by day, 105
To watch the crisping ripples on the beach,
And tender curving lines of creamy spray;
To lend our hearts and spirits wholly
To the influence of mild-minded melancholy;
To muse and brood and live again in memory, 110
With those old faces of our infancy
Heap'd over with a mound of grass,
Two handfuls of white dust, shut in an urn of brass!

VI

Dear is the memory of our wedded lives,
And dear the last embraces of our wives 115
And their warm tears; but all hath suffer'd change;
For surely now our household hearths are cold:
Our sons inherit us: our looks are strange:
And we should come like ghosts to trouble joy.
Or else the island princes over-bold 120
Have eat our substance, and the minstrel sings
Before them of the ten-years' war in Troy,
And our great deeds, as half-forgotten things.
Is there confusion in the little isle?
Let what is broken so remain. 125
The Gods are hard to reconcile:
'Tis hard to settle order once again.
There *is* confusion worse than death,
Trouble on trouble, pain on pain,
Long labour unto agèd breath, 130
Sore task to hearts worn out with many wars
And eyes grown dim with gazing on the pilot-stars.

VII

But, propt on beds of amaranth and moly,
How sweet (while warm airs lull us, blowing lowly)
With half-dropt eyelids still, 135
Beneath a heaven dark and holy,
To watch the long bright river drawing slowly
His waters from the purple hill—
To hear the dewy echoes calling
From cave to cave through the thick-twinèd vine— 140
To watch the emerald-colour'd water falling
Through many a wov'n acanthus-wreath divine!

Only to hear and see the far-off sparkling brine,
Only to hear were sweet, stretch'd out beneath the pine.

VIII

The Lotos blooms below the barren peak: 145
The Lotos blows by every winding creek:
All day the wind breathes low with mellower tone;
Through every hollow cave and alley lone
Round and round the spicy downs the yellow Lotos-dust is blown.
We have had enough of action, and of motion we, 150
Roll'd to starboard, roll'd to larboard, when the surge was seething free,
Where the wallowing monster spouted his foam-fountains in the sea.
Let us swear an oath, and keep it with an equal mind,
In the hollow Lotos-land to live and lie reclined
On the hills like Gods together, careless of mankind. 155
For they lie beside their nectar, and the bolts are hurl'd
Far below them in the valleys, and the clouds are lightly curl'd
Round their golden houses, girdled with the gleaming world:
Where they smile in secret, looking over wasted lands,
Blight and famine, plague and earthquake, roaring deeps and fiery
sands, 160
Clanging fights, and flaming towns, and sinking ships, and praying
hands.
But they smile, they find a music centred in a doleful song
Steaming up, a lamentation and an ancient tale of wrong,
Like a tale of little meaning though the words are strong;
Chanted from an ill-used race of men that cleave the soil, 165
Sow the seed, and reap the harvest with enduring toil,
Storing yearly little dues of wheat, and wine and oil;
Till they perish and they suffer—some, 'tis whisper'd—down in hell
Suffer endless anguish, others in Elysian valleys dwell,
Resting weary limbs at last on beds of asphodel. 170
Surely, surely, slumber is more sweet than toil, the shore
Than labour in the deep mid-ocean, wind and wave and oar;
Oh, rest ye, brother mariners, we will not wander more.

NOW SLEEPS THE CRIMSON PETAL

Now sleeps the crimson petal, now the white;
Nor waves the cypress in the palace walk;
Nor winks the gold fin in the porphyry font:
The fire-fly wakens: waken thou with me.

Now droops the milkwhite peacock like a ghost, 5
And like a ghost she glimmers on to me.

Now lies the Earth all Danaë[1] to the stars,
And all thy heart lies open unto me.

Now slides the silent meteor on, and leaves
A shining furrow, as thy thoughts in me. 10

Now folds the lily all her sweetness up,
And slips into the bosom of the lake:
So fold thyself, my dearest, thou, and slip
Into my bosom and be lost in me.

COME DOWN, O MAID

Come down, O maid, from yonder mountain height:
What pleasure lives in height (the shepherd sang)
In height and cold, the splendour of the hills?
But cease to move so near the Heavens, and cease
To glide a sunbeam by the blasted[1] Pine, 5
To sit a star upon the sparkling spire;
And come, for Love is of the valley, come,
For Love is of the valley, come thou down
And find him; by the happy threshold, he,
Or hand in hand with Plenty in the maize, 10
Or red with spirited purple of the vats,
Or foxlike in the vine; nor cares to walk
With Death and Morning on the silver horns,[2]
Nor wilt thou snare him in the white ravine,
Nor find him dropt upon the firths of ice, 15
That huddling slant in furrow-cloven falls
To roll the torrent out of dusky doors:
But follow; let the torrent dance thee down
To find him in the valley; let the wild
Lean-headed Eagles yelp alone, and leave 20
The monstrous ledges there to slope, and spill
Their thousand wreaths of dangling water-smoke,[3]
That like a broken purpose waste in air:
So waste not thou; but come; for all the vales
Await thee; azure pillars of the hearth 25
Arise to thee; the children call, and I
Thy shepherd pipe, and sweet is every sound,

[1] A princess who was visited by Zeus in the form of a golden shower. Tennyson's figure parallels the Earth and "thy heart" with Danaë, and the stars and "me" with Zeus.

[1] Blighted. [2] The icy horns of mountains. [3] Water vapor.

Sweeter thy voice, but every sound is sweet;
Myriads of rivulets hurrying through the lawn,
The moan of doves in immemorial elms, 30
And murmuring of innumerable bees.

MORTE D'ARTHUR

So all day long the noise of battle roll'd
Among the mountains by the winter sea,
Until King Arthur's table,[1] man by man,
Had fall'n in Lyonness about their lord,
King Arthur; then, because his wound was deep, 5
The bold Sir Bedivere uplifted him,
Sir Bedivere, the last of all his knights,
And bore him to a chapel nigh the field,
A broken chancel with a broken cross,
That stood on a dark strait of barren land. 10
On one side lay the ocean, and on one
Lay a great water, and the moon was full.
Then spake King Arthur to Sir Bedivere:
"The sequel of to-day unsolders all
The goodliest fellowship of famous knights 15
Whereof this world holds record. Such a sleep
They sleep—the men I loved. I think that we
Shall never more, at any future time,
Delight our souls with talk of knightly deeds,
Walking about the gardens and the halls 20
Of Camelot, as in the days that were.
I perish by this people which I made,—
Tho' Merlin[2] sware that I should come again
To rule once more—but let what will be be,
I am so deeply smitten through the helm 25
That without help I cannot last till morn.
Thou therefore take my brand[3] Excalibur,
Which was my pride; for thou rememberest how
In those old days, one summer noon, an arm
Rose up from out the bosom of the lake, 30
Clothed in white samite, mystic, wonderful,
Holding the sword—and how I row'd across
And took it, and have worn it, like a king;
And, wheresoever I am sung or told
In aftertime, this also shall be known. 35
But now delay not; take Excalibur,

[1] The famous "round table"; hence, the men that sat there. [2] Magician of Arthurian legend. [3] Sword.

And fling him far into the middle mere;[4]
Watch what thou seest, and lightly[5] bring me word."
To him replied the bold Sir Bedivere:
It is not meet, Sir King, to leave thee thus, 40
Aidless, alone, and smitten through the helm.
A little thing may harm a wounded man.
Yet I thy hest will all perform at full,
Watch what I see, and lightly bring thee word."
So saying, from the ruin'd shrine he stept 45
And in the moon athwart[6] the place of tombs,
Where lay the mighty bones of ancient men,
Old knights, and over them the sea-wind sang
Shrill, chill, with flakes of foam. He, stepping down
By zigzag paths and juts of pointed rock, 50
Came on the shining levels of the lake.
There drew he forth the brand Excalibur,
And o'er him drawing it, the winter moon,
Brightening the skirts of a long cloud, ran forth
And sparkled keen with frost against the hilt; 55
For all the haft twinkled with diamond sparks,
Myriads of topaz-lights and jacinth-work
Of subtlest jewellery. He gazed so long
That both his eyes were dazzled, as he stood,
This way and that dividing the swift mind, 60
In act to throw; but at the last it seem'd
Better to leave Excalibur conceal'd
There in the many-knotted water-flags,
That whistled stiff and dry about the marge.[7]
So strode he back slow to the wounded king. 65
Then spake King Arthur to Sir Bedivere:
"Hast thou perform'd my mission which I gave?
What is it thou hast seen, or what hast heard?"
And answer made the bold Sir Bedivere:
"I heard the ripple washing in the reeds, 70
And the wild water lapping on the crag."
To whom replied King Arthur, faint and pale:
"Thou hast betray'd thy nature and thy name,
Not rendering true answer, as beseem'd
Thy fealty, nor like a noble knight; 75
For surer sign had follow'd, either hand,
Or voice, or else a motion of the mere.
This is a shameful thing for men to lie.
Yet now, I charge thee, quickly go again
As thou art lief and dear, and do the thing 80
I bade thee, watch, and lightly bring me word."
Then went Sir Bedivere the second time

[4] The middle of the mere, or lake. [5] Quickly. [6] Across. [7] Margin (of the lake).

Across the ridge, and paced beside the mere,
Counting the dewy pebbles, fix'd in thought;
But when he saw the wonder of the hilt, 85
How curiously and strangely chased, he smote
His palms together, and he cried aloud:

"And if indeed I cast the brand away,
Surely a precious thing, one worthy note,
Should thus be lost forever from the earth, 90
Which might have pleased the eyes of many men.
What good should follow this, if this were done?
What harm, undone? deep harm to disobey,
Seeing obedience is the bond of rule.
Were it well to obey then, if a king demand 95
An act unprofitable, against himself?
The king is sick, and knows not what he does.
What record or what relic of my lord
Should be to aftertime, but empty breath
And rumors of a doubt? but were this kept, 100
Stored in some treasure-house of mighty kings,
Some one might show it at a joust of arms,
Saying, 'King Arthur's sword, Excalibur,
Wrought by the lonely maiden of the lake;[8]
Nine years she wrought it, sitting in the deeps 105
Upon the hidden bases of the hills.'
So might some old man speak in the aftertime
To all the people, winning reverence;
But now much honor and much fame were lost."

So spake he, clouded with his own conceit,[9] 110
And hid Excalibur the second time,
And so strode back slow to the wounded king.

Then spoke King Arthur, breathing heavily:
"What is it thou hast seen, or what hast heard?"

And answer made the bold Sir Bedivere: 115
"I heard the water lapping on the crag,
And the long ripple washing in the reeds."

To whom replied King Arthur, much in wrath:
"Ah, miserable and unkind, untrue,
Unknightly, traitor-hearted! Woe is me! 120
Authority forgets a dying king,
Laid widow'd of the power in his eye
That bow'd the will. I see thee what thou art,
For thou, the latest-left of all my knights,
In whom should meet the offices of all, 125
Thou wouldst betray me for the precious hilt;
Either from lust of gold, or like a girl
Valuing the giddy pleasure of the eyes.
Yet, for a man may fail in duty twice,

[8] The "lady of the lake," who, according to legend, gave Arthur his miraculous sword.
[9] Thought.

And the third time may prosper, get thee hence; 130
But, if thou spare to fling Excalibur,
I will arise and slay thee with my hands."

Then quickly rose Sir Bedivere, and ran,
And, leaping down the ridges lightly, plunged
Among the bulrush-beds, and clutch'd the sword, 135
And strongly wheel'd and threw it. The great brand
Made lightnings in the splendour of the moon,
And flashing round and round, and whirl'd in an arch,
Shot like a streamer of the northern morn,
Seen where the moving isles of winter shock 140
By night, with noises of the northern sea.
So flash'd and fell the brand Excalibur;
But ere he dipt the surface, rose an arm
Cloth'd in white samite, mystic, wonderful,
And caught him by the hilt, and brandish'd him 145
Three times, and drew him under in the mere.
And lightly went the other to the king.

Then spoke King Arthur, drawing thicker breath:
"Now see I by thine eyes that this is done.
Speak out; what is it thou hast heard, or seen?" 150

And answer made the bold Sir Bedivere:
"Sir King, I closed mine eyelids, lest the gems
Should blind my purpose, for I never saw,
Nor shall see, here or elsewhere, till I die,
Not tho' I live three lives of mortal men, 155
So great a miracle as yonder hilt.
Then with both hands I flung him, wheeling him;
But when I look'd again, behold an arm,
Clothed in white samite, mystic, wonderful,
That caught him by the hilt, and brandish'd him 160
Three times, and drew him under in the mere."

And answer made King Arthur, breathing hard:
"My end draws nigh; 't is time that I were gone.
Make broad thy shoulders to receive my weight,
And bear me to the margin; yet I fear 165
My wound hath taken cold, and I shall die."

So saying, from the pavement he half rose,
Slowly, with pain, reclining on his arm,
And looking wistfully with wide blue eyes
As in a picture. Him Sir Bedivere 170
Remorsefully regarded through his tears,
And would have spoken, but he found not words,
Then took with care, and kneeling on one knee,
O'er both his shoulders drew the languid hands,
And rising bore him through the place of tombs. 175

But, as he walk'd, King Arthur panted hard,
Like one that feels a nightmare on his bed
When all the house is mute. So sigh'd the king,

Muttering and murmuring at his ear, "Quick, quick!
I fear it is too late, and I shall die." 180
But the other swiftly strode from ridge to ridge,
Clothed with his breath, and looking, as he walk'd,
Larger than human on the frozen hills.
He heard the deep behind him, and a cry
Before. His own thought drove him like a goad. 185
Dry clash'd his harness[10] in the icy caves
And barren chasms, and all to left and right
The bare black cliff clang'd round him, as he based
His feet on juts of slippery crag that rang
Sharp-smitten with the dint of armed heels— 190
And on a sudden, lo! the level lake,
And the long glories of the winter moon.

Then saw they how there hove a dusky barge,
Dark as a funeral scarf from stem to stern,
Beneath them; and descending they were ware 195
That all the decks were dense with stately forms
Black-stoled, black-hooded, like a dream—by these
Three queens with crowns of gold—and from them rose
A cry that shiver'd to the tingling stars,
And, as it were one voice, an agony 200
Of lamentation, like a wind that shrills
All night in a waste land, where no one comes,
Or hath come, since the making of the world.

Then murmur'd Arthur, "Place me in the barge,"
And to the barge they came. There those three queens 205
Put forth their hands, and took the king, and wept.
But she that rose the tallest of them all
And fairest laid his head upon her lap,
And loosed the shatter'd casque,[11] and chafed his hands,
And call'd him by his name, complaining[12] loud, 210
And dropping bitter tears against his brow
Striped with dark blood; for all his face was white
And colourless, and like the wither'd moon
Smote by the fresh beam of the springing east;
And all his greaves and cuisses[13] dash'd with drops 215
Of onset; and the light and lustrous curls—
That made his forehead like a rising sun
High from the dais-throne—were parch'd with dust;
Or, clotted into points and hanging loose,
Mix'd with the knightly growth that fringed his lips. 220
So like a shatter'd column lay the king;
Not like that Arthur who, with lance in rest,
From spur to plume a star of tournament,[14]
Shot through the lists[15] at Camelot, and charged

[10] Armor. [11] Helmet. [12] Expressing grief. [13] Leg and thigh armor.
[14] The knightly sport of jousting or tilting with a blunted lance. [15] Arenas.

Before the eyes of ladies and of kings. 225
Then loudly cried the bold Sir Bedivere:
"Ah! my Lord Arthur, whither shall I go?
Where shall I hide my forehead and my eyes?
For now I see the true old times are dead,
When every morning brought a noble chance, 230
And every chance brought out a noble knight.
Such times have been not since the light that led
The holy Elders with the gift of myrrh.[16]
But now the whole ROUND TABLE is dissolved
Which was an image of the mighty world; 235
And I, the last, go forth companionless,
And the days darken round me, and the years,
Among new men, strange faces, other minds."
And slowly answer'd Arthur from the barge:
"The old order changeth, yielding place to new, 240
And God fulfils himself in many ways,
Lest one good custom should corrupt the world.
Comfort thyself: what comfort is in me?
I have lived my life, and that which I have done
May He within himself make pure! but thou, 245
If thou shouldst never see my face again,
Pray for my soul. More things are wrought by prayer
Than this world dreams of. Wherefore, let thy voice
Rise like a fountain for me night and day.
For what are men better than sheep or goats 250
That nourish a blind life within the brain,
If, knowing God, they lift not hands of prayer
Both for themselves and those who call them friend?
For so the whole round earth is every way
Bound by gold chains about the feet of God. 255
But now farewell. I am going a long way
With these thou seest—if indeed I go—
For all my mind is clouded with a doubt—
To the island-valley of Avilion;[17]
Where falls not hail, or rain, or any snow, 260
Nor ever wind blows loudly, but it lies
Deep-meadow'd, happy, fair with orchard lawns
And bowery hollows crown'd with summer sea,
Where I will heal me of my grievous wound."
So said he, and the barge with oar and sail 265
Moved from the brink, like some full-breasted swan
That, fluting a wild carol ere her death,
Ruffles her pure cold plume, and takes the flood
With swarthy webs. Long stood Sir Bedivere
Revolving many memories, till the hull 270

[16] The Wise Men. [17] Avalon, the island to which Arthur was taken to die, according to legend.

Look'd one black dot against the verge of dawn,
And on the mere the wailing died away.

THE REVENGE[1]

A Ballad of the Fleet

I

At Flores in the Azores Sir Richard Grenville lay,
And a pinnace, like a flutter'd bird, came flying from far away:
"Spanish ships of war at sea! we have sighted fifty-three!"
Then sware Lord Thomas Howard: " 'Fore God I am no coward;
But I cannot meet them here, for my ships are out of gear, 5
And the half my men are sick. I must fly, but follow quick.
We are six ships of the line; can we fight with fifty-three?"

II

Then spake Sir Richard Grenville: "I know you are no coward;
You fly them for a moment to fight with them again.
But I've ninety men and more that are lying sick ashore. 10
I should count myself the coward if I left them, my Lord Howard,
To these Inquisition dogs and the devildoms of Spain."

III

So Lord Howard past away with five ships of war that day,
Till he melted like a cloud in the silent summer heaven;
But Sir Richard bore in hand all his sick men from the land 15
Very carefully and slow,
Men of Bideford in Devon,
And we laid them on the ballast down below;
For we brought them all aboard,
And they blest him in their pain, that they were not left to Spain, 20
To the thumb-screw and the stake, for the glory of the Lord.

IV

He had only a hundred seamen to work the ship and to fight,
And he sailed away from Flores till the Spaniard came in sight,
With his huge sea-castles heaving upon the weather[2] bow.
"Shall we fight or shall we fly? 25
Good Sir Richard, tell us now,
For to fight is but to die!

[1] The battle described here took place in 1591. The *Revenge* was Sir Richard Grenville's ship. [2] Windward.

There'll be little of us left by the time this sun be set."
And Sir Richard said again: "We be all good English men.
Let us bang these dogs of Seville, the children of the devil, 30
For I never turn'd my back upon Don or devil yet."

V

Sir Richard spoke and he laugh'd, and we roar'd a hurrah, and so
The little Revenge ran on sheer into the heart of the foe,
With her hundred fighters on deck, and her ninety sick below;
For half of their fleet to the right and half to the left were seen, 35
And the little Revenge ran on through the long sea-lane between.

VI

Thousands of their soldiers look'd down from their decks and laugh'd,
Thousands of their seamen made mock at the mad little craft
Running on and on, till delay'd
By their mountain-like San Philip that, of fifteen hundred tons, 40
And up-shadowing high above us with her yawning tiers of guns,
Took the breath from our sails, and we stay'd.

VII

And while now the great San Philip hung above us like a cloud
Whence the thunderbolt will fall
Long and loud, 45
Four galleons drew away
From the Spanish fleet that day,
And two upon the larboard and two upon the starboard lay,
And the battle-thunder broke from them all.

VIII

But anon the great San Philip, she bethought herself and went, 50
Having that within her womb that had left her ill content;
And the rest they came aboard us, and they fought us hand to hand,
For a dozen times they came with their pikes and musqueteers,[3]
And a dozen times we shook 'em off as a dog that shakes his ears
When he leaps from the water to the land. 55

IX

And the sun went down, and the stars came out far over the summer sea,
But never a moment ceased the fight of the one and the fifty-three.
Ship after ship, the whole night long, their high-built galleons came,
Ship after ship, the whole night long, with her battle-thunder and flame;

[3] Musketeers.

Ship after ship, the whole night long, drew back with her dead and her
shame. 60
For some were sunk and many were shatter'd, and so could fight us no
more—
God of battles, was ever a battle like this in the world before?

X

For he said, "Fight on! fight on!"
Tho' his vessel was all but a wreck;
And it chanced that, when half of the short summer night was gone, 65
With a grisly wound to be drest he had left the deck,
But a bullet struck him that was dressing it suddenly dead,
And himself he was wounded again in the side and the head,
And he said, "Fight on! fight on!"

XI

And the night went down, and the sun smiled out far over the summer
sea, 70
And the Spanish fleet with broken sides lay round us all in a ring;
But they dared not touch us again, for they fear'd that we still could sting,
So they watch'd what the end would be.
And we had not fought them in vain,
But in perilous plight were we, 75
Seeing forty of our poor hundred were slain,
And half the rest of us maim'd for life
In the crash of the cannonades and the desperate strife;
And the sick men down in the hold were most of them stark and cold,
And the pikes were all broken or bent, and the powder was all of it
spent; 80
And the masts and the rigging were lying over the side;
But Sir Richard cried in his English pride:
"We have fought such a fight for a day and a night
As may never be fought again!
We have won great glory, my men! 85
And a day less or more
At sea or ashore,
We die—does it matter when?
Sink me the ship, Master Gunner—sink her, split her in twain!
Fall into the hands of God, not into the hands of Spain!" 90

XII

And the gunner said, "Ay, ay," but the seamen made reply:
"We have children, we have wives,
And the Lord hath spared our lives.
We will make the Spaniard promise, if we yield, to let us go;

We shall live to fight again and to strike another blow." 95
And the lion there lay dying, and they yielded to the foe.

XIII

And the stately Spanish men to their flagship bore him then,
Where they laid him by the mast, old Sir Richard caught at last,
And they praised him to his face with their courtly foreign grace;
But he rose upon their decks, and he cried: 100
"I have fought for Queen and Faith like a valiant man and true;
I have only done my duty as a man is bound to do.
With a joyful spirit I Sir Richard Grenville die!"
And he fell upon their decks, and he died.

XIV

And they stared at the dead that had been so valiant and true, 105
And had holden the power and glory of Spain so cheap
That he dared her with one little ship and his English few;
Was he devil or man? He was devil for aught they knew,
But they sank his body with honor down into the deep,
And they mann'd the Revenge with a swarthier alien crew, 110
And away she sail'd with her loss and long'd for her own;
When a wind from the lands they had ruin'd awoke from sleep,
And the water began to heave and the weather to moan,
And or ever that evening ended a great gale blew,
And a wave like the wave that is raised by an earthquake grew, 115
Till it smote on their hulls and their sails and their masts and their flags,
And the whole sea plunged and fell on the shot-shatter'd navy of Spain,
And the little Revenge herself went down by the island crags
To be lost evermore in the main.

EDWARD LEAR

1812–1888

THE JUMBLIES

I

They went to sea in a Sieve, they did;
In a Sieve they went to sea:
In spite of all their friends could say,

On a winter's morn, on a stormy day,
    In a Sieve they went to sea! 5
And when the Sieve turned round and round,
And every one cried, "You'll all be drowned!"
They called aloud, "Our Sieve ain't big,
But we don't care a button! we don't care a fig!
    In a Sieve we'll go to sea!" 10
        Far and few, far and few,
            Are the lands where the Jumblies live;
        Their heads are green, and their hands are blue;
            And they went to sea in a Sieve.

II

They sailed away in a Sieve, they did, 15
    In a Sieve they sailed so fast,
With only a beautiful pea-green veil
Tied with a riband, by way of a sail,
    To a small tobacco-pipe mast;
And every one said, who saw them go, 20
"O won't they be soon upset, you know!
For the sky is dark, and the voyage is long,
And happen what may, it's extremely wrong
    In a Sieve to sail so fast!"
        Far and few, far and few, 25
            Are the lands where the Jumblies live;
        Their heads are green, and their hands are blue,
            And they went to sea in a Sieve.

III

The water it soon came in, it did,
    The water it soon came in; 30
So to keep them dry, they wrapped their feet
In a pinky paper all folded neat,
    And they fastened it down with a pin.
And they passed the night in a crockery-jar,
And each of them said, "How wise we are! 35
Though the sky be dark, and the voyage be long,
Yet we never can think we were rash or wrong,
    While round in our Sieve we spin!"
        Far and few, far and few,
            Are the lands where the Jumblies live; 40
        Their heads are green, and their hands are blue,
            And they went to sea in a Sieve.

IV

And all night long they sailed away;
    And when the sun went down,

They whistled and warbled a moony song 45
To the echoing sound of a coppery gong,
    In the shade of the mountains brown.
"O Timballo! How happy we are,
When we live in a Sieve and a crockery-jar,
And all night long in the moonlight pale, 50
We sail away with a pea-green sail,
    In the shade of the mountains brown."
        Far and few, far and few,
            Are the lands where the Jumblies live;
        Their heads are green, and their hands are blue, 55
            And they went to sea in a Sieve.

V

They sailed to the Western Sea, they did,
    To a land all covered with trees,
And they bought an Owl, and a useful Cart,
And a pound of Rice, and a Cranberry Tart, 60
    And a hive of silvery Bees.
And they bought a Pig, and some green Jackdaws,
And a lovely Monkey with lollipop paws,
And forty bottles of Ring-Bo-Ree,
    And no end of Stilton cheese. 65
        Far and few, far and few,
            Are the lands where the Jumblies live;
        Their heads are green, and their hands are blue,
            And they went to sea in a Sieve.

VI

And in twenty years they all came back, 70
    In twenty years or more,
And every one said, "How tall they've grown!
For they've been to the Lakes, and the Torrible Zone,
    And the hills of the Chankly Bore."
And they drank their health, and gave them a feast 75
Of dumplings made of beautiful yeast;
And every one said, "If we only live,
We, too, will go to sea in a Sieve,
    To the hills of the Chankly Bore."
        Far and few, far and few, 80
            Are the lands where the Jumblies live;
        Their heads are green, and their hands are blue,
            And they went to sea in a Sieve.

ROBERT BROWNING

1812–1889

MY LAST DUCHESS

FERRARA

That's my last Duchess painted on the wall,
Looking as if she were alive. I call
That piece a wonder, now: Frà Pandolf's[1] hands
Worked busily a day, and there she stands.
Will't please you sit and look at her? I said 5
"Frà Pandolf" by design, for never read
Strangers like you that pictured countenance,
The depth and passion of its earnest glance,
But to myself they turned (since none puts by
The curtain I have drawn for you, but I) 10
And seemed as they would ask me, if they durst,
How such a glance came there; so, not the first
Are you to turn and ask thus. Sir, 'twas not
Her husband's presence only, called that spot
Of joy into the Duchess' cheek: perhaps 15
Frà Pandolf chanced to say, "Her mantle laps
Over my lady's wrist too much," or "Paint
Must never hope to reproduce the faint
Half-flush that dies along her throat": such stuff
Was courtesy, she thought, and cause enough 20
For calling up that spot of joy. She had
A heart—how shall I say?—too soon made glad,
Too easily impressed: she liked whate'er
She looked on, and her looks went everywhere.
Sir, 'twas all one! My favor at her breast, 25
The dropping of the daylight in the West,
The bough of cherries some officious fool
Broke in the orchard for her, the white mule
She rode with round the terrace—all and each
Would draw from her alike the approving speech, 30
Or blush, at least. She thanked men,—good! but thanked
Somehow—I know not how—as if she ranked
My gift of a nine-hundred-years-old name
With anybody's gift. Who'd stoop to blame
This sort of trifling? Even had you skill 35

[1] An imaginary painter.

In speech—(which I have not)—to make your will
Quite clear to such an one, and say, "Just this
Or that in you disgusts me; here you miss,
Or there exceed the mark"—and if she let
Herself be lessoned so, nor plainly set 40
Her wits to yours, forsooth, and made excuse,
—E'en then would be some stooping; and I choose
Never to stoop. Oh sir, she smiled, no doubt,
Whene'er I passed her; but who passed without
Much the same smile? This grew; I gave commands; 45
Then all smiles stopped together. There she stands
As if alive. Will't please you rise? We'll meet
The company below, then. I repeat,
The Count your master's known munificence
Is ample warrant that no just pretence 50
Of mine for dowry will be disallowed;
Though his fair daughter's self, as I avowed
At starting, is my object. Nay, we'll go
Together down, sir. Notice Neptune, though,
Taming a sea-horse, thought a rarity, 55
Which Claus of Innsbruck cast in bronze for me!

SOLILOQUY OF THE SPANISH CLOISTER

Gr-r-r—there go, my heart's abhorrence!
    Water your damned flower-pots, do!
If hate killed men, Brother Lawrence,
    God's blood, would not mine kill you!
What? your myrtle-bush wants trimming? 5
    Oh, that rose has prior claims—
Needs its leaden vase filled brimming?
    Hell dry you up with its flames!

At the meal we sit together:
    Salve tibi![1] I must hear 10
Wise talk of the kind of weather,
    Sort of season, time of year:
Not a plenteous cork-crop: scarcely
    Dare we hope oak-galls, I doubt:
What's the Latin name for 'parsley'? 15
    What's the Greek name for Swine's Snout?

Whew! We'll have our platter burnished,
    Laid with care on our own shelf!

[1] (Latin) Hail to thee.

With a fire-new spoon we're furnished,
And a goblet for ourself, 20
Rinsed like something sacrificial
Ere 'tis fit to touch our chaps—
Marked with L for our initial!
(He-he! There his lily snaps!)

Saint, forsooth! While brown Dolores 25
Squats outside the Convent bank
With Sanchicha, telling stories,
Steeping tresses in the tank,[2]
Blue-black, lustrous, thick like horsehairs,
—Can't I see his dead eye glow, 30
Bright as 'twere a Barbary corsair's?
(That is, if he'd let it show!)

When he finishes refection,
Knife and fork he never lays
Cross-wise, to my recollection, 35
As do I, in Jesu's praise.
I the Trinity illustrate,
Drinking watered orange-pulp—
In three sips the Arian[3] frustrate;
While he drains his at one gulp. 40

Oh, those melons? If he's able
We're to have a feast! so nice!
One goes to the Abbot's table,
All of use get each a slice.
How go on your flowers? None double? 45
Not one fruit-sort can you spy?
Strange!—And I, too, at such trouble,
Keep them close-nipped on the sly!

There's a great text in Galatians,[4]
Once you trip on it, entails 50
Twenty-nine distinct damnations,
One sure, if another fails:
If I trip him just a-dying,
Sure of heaven as sure can be,

[2] Of rain water. [3] The Arian heresy, which maintained that Father and Son were entirely separate beings and that Christ was a created being, inferior to the Father. [4] Probably Galatians 3:10: For as many as are of the works of the law are under the curse: for it is written, Cursed is every one that continueth not in all things which are written in the book of the law to do them.

Spin him round and send him flying 55
    Off to hell, a Manichee?[5]

Or, my scrofulous French novel
    On grey paper with blunt type!
Simply glance at it, you grovel
    Hand and foot in Belial's[6] gripe: 60
If I double down its pages
    At the woeful sixteenth print,
When he gathers his greengages,
    Ope a sieve[7] and slip it in't?[7]

Or, there's Satan—one might venture 65
    Pledge one's soul to him, yet leave
Such a flaw in the endenture
    As he'd miss till, past retrieve,
Blasted lay that rose-acacia
    We're so proud of! *Hy, Zy Hine . . .* 70
'St, there's Vespers! *Plena gratiâ*
    Ave, Virgo![8] Gr-r-r—you swine!

A WOMAN'S LAST WORD

I

Let's contend no more, Love,
    Strive nor weep:
All be as before, Love,
    —Only sleep!

II

What so wild as words are? 5
    I and thou
In debate, as birds are,
    Hawk on bough!

III

See the creature stalking
    While we speak! 10

[5] A believer in the Manichean heresy, which holds that the world is composed of two irreducible opposing principles, light (or good) and darkness (or evil). [6] Satan's. [7] Basket used chiefly for produce. [8] Full of grace, Hail, Virgin (usually, *Ave Maria gratia plena*).

Hush and hide the talking,
    Cheek on cheek!

IV

What so false as truth is,
    False to thee?
Where the serpent's tooth is   15
    Shun the tree—

V

Where the apple reddens
    Never pry—
Lest we lose our Edens,
    Eve and I.   20

VI

Be a god and hold me
    With a charm!
Be a man and fold me
    With thine arm!

VII

Teach me, only teach, Love.   25
    As I ought
I will speak thy speech, Love,
    Think thy thought—

VIII

Meet, if thou require it,
    Both demands,   30
Laying flesh and spirit
    In thy hands.

IX

That shall be to-morrow
    Not to-night:
I must bury sorrow   35
    Out of sight:

X

—Must a little weep, Love,
    (Foolish me!)

And so fall asleep, Love,
    Loved by thee. 40

"CHILDE ROLAND[1] TO THE DARK TOWER CAME"

(*See Edgar's song in* Lear)

I

My first thought was, he lied in every word,
    That hoary cripple, with malicious eye
    Askance to watch the working of his lie
On mine, and mouth scarce able to afford
Suppression of the glee, that pursed and scored 5
    Its edge, at one more victim gained thereby.

II

What else should he be set for, with his staff?
    What, save to waylay with his lies, ensnare
    All travellers who might find him posted there,
And ask the road? I guessed what skull-like laugh 10
Would break, what crutch 'gin write my epitaph
    For pastime in the dusty thoroughfare,

III

If at his counsel I should turn aside
    Into that ominous tract which, all agree,
    Hides the Dark Tower. Yet acquiescingly 15
I did turn as he pointed: neither pride
Nor hope rekindling at the end descried,
    So much as gladness that some end might be.

IV

For, what with my whole world-wide wandering,
    What with my search drawn out through years, my hope 20
    Dwindled into a ghost not fit to cope
With that obstreperous joy success would bring,
I hardly tried now to rebuke the spring
    My heart made, finding failure in its scope.

[1] Childe Roland, in legend, was a son of King Arthur whose sister was carried away by fairies to the castle of the king of Elfland. He rescues her. In Shakespeare's *King Lear,* Edgar, in feigned madness, sings "Child Rowland to the dark tower came" (see *Drama,* p. 88).

V

As when a sick man very near to death 25
Seems dead indeed, and feels begin and end
The tears and takes the farewell of each friend,
And hears one bid the other go, draw breath
Freelier outside, ("since all is o'er," he saith,
"And the blow fallen no grieving can amend;") 30

VI

While some discuss if near the other graves
Be room enough for this, and when a day
Suits best for carrying the corpse away,
With care about the banners, scarves and staves:
And still the man hears all, and only craves 35
He may not shame such tender love and stay.

VII

Thus, I had so long suffered in this quest,
Heard failure prophesied so oft, been writ
So many times among "The Band"—to wit,
The knights who to the Dark Tower's search addressed 40
Their steps—that just to fail as they, seemed best,
And all the doubt was now—should I be fit?

VIII

So, quiet as despair, I turned from him,
That hateful cripple, out of his highway
Into the path he pointed. All the day 45
Had been a dreary one at best, and dim[2]
Was settling to its close, yet shot one grim
Red leer to see the plain catch its estray.[3]

IX

For mark! no sooner was I fairly found
Pledged to the plain, after a pace or two, 50
Than, pausing to throw backward a last view
O'er the safe road, 'twas gone; grey plain all round:
Nothing but plain to the horizon's bound.
I might go on; nought else remained to do.

X

So, on I went. I think I never saw 55
Such starved ignoble nature; nothing throve:

[2] Twilight. [3] Stray (red glow).

For flowers—as well expect a cedar grove!
But cockle, spurge, according to their law
Might propagate their kind, with none to awe,
You'd think; a burr had been[4] a treasure-trove. 60

XI

No! penury, inertness and grimace,
In some strange sort, were the land's portion. "See
Or shut your eyes," said Nature peevishly,
"It nothing skills:[5] I cannot help my case:
'Tis the Last Judgment's fire must cure this place, 65
Calcine its clods and set my prisoners[6] free."

XII

If there pushed any ragged thistle-stalk
Above its mates, the head was chopped; the bents[7]
Were jealous else. What made those holes and rents
In the dock's harsh swarth leaves,[8] bruised as to balk 70
All hope of greenness? 'tis a brute must walk
Pashing[9] their life out, with a brute's intents.

XIII

As for the grass, it grew as scant as hair
In leprosy; thin dry blades pricked the mud
Which underneath looked kneaded up with blood. 75
One stiff blind horse, his every bone a-stare,
Stood stupefied, however he came there:[10]
Thrust out past service from the devil's stud![11]

XIV

Alive? he might be dead for aught I know,
With that red gaunt and colloped[12] neck a-strain, 80
And shut eyes underneath the rusty mane;
Seldom went such grotesqueness with such woe;
I never saw a brute I hated so;
He must be wicked to deserve such pain.

XV

I shut my eyes and turned them on my heart. 85
As a man calls for wine before he fights,

[4] Would have been (had it been there). [5] It doesn't matter, makes no difference. [6] My possessions, that is, plants that grow in the "clods" (soil). [7] Stalks of stiff coarse grass. [8] The dock is a coarse weedy plant. [9] Smashing. [10] That is, he looked as if he wondered however he came there. [11] Place for keeping a group of animals, especially horses. [12] Having fatty folds; wrinkled.

I asked one draught of earlier, happier sights,
Ere fitly I could hope to play my part.
Think first, fight afterwards—the soldier's art:
One taste of the old time sets all to rights. 90

XVI

Not it! I fancied Cuthbert's reddening face[13]
Beneath its garniture of curly gold,
Dear fellow, till I almost felt him fold
An arm in mine to fix me to the place,
That way he used. Alas, one night's disgrace! 95
Out went my heart's new fire and left it cold.

XVII

Giles then, the soul of honour—there he stands
Frank as ten years ago when knighted first.
What honest man should dare (he said) he durst.
Good—but the scene shifts—faugh! what hangman hands 100
Pin to his breast a parchment? His own bands
Read it. Poor traitor, spit upon and curst!

XVIII

Better this present than a past like that;
Back therefore to my darkening path again!
No sound, no sight as far as eye could strain. 105
Will the night send a howlet[14] or a bat?
I asked: when something on the dismal flat[15]
Came to arrest my thoughts and change their train.

XIX

A sudden little river crossed my path
As unexpected as a serpent comes. 110
No sluggish tide congenial to the glooms;
This, as it frothed by, might have been a bath
For the fiend's glowing hoof[16]—to see the wrath
Of its black eddy bespate[17] with flakes and spumes.

XX

So petty yet so spiteful! All along, 115
Low scrubby alders kneeled down over it;
Drenched willows flung them headlong in a fit

[13] Cuthbert and Giles are former companions of Roland. [14] Owlet. [15] Plain.
[16] The cloven hoof often attributed to Satan. [17] Bespattered.

Of mute despair, a suicidal throng:
The river which had done them all the wrong,
Whate'er that was, rolled by, deterred no whit. 120

XXI

Which, while I forded,—good saints, how I feared
To set my foot upon a dead man's cheek,
Each step, or feel the spear I thrust to seek
For hollows, tangled in his hair or beard!
—It may have been a water-rat I speared, 125
But, ugh! it sounded like a baby's shriek.

XXII

Glad was I when I reached the other bank.
Now for a better country. Vain presage!
Who were the strugglers, what war did they wage,
Whose savage trample thus could pad the dank 130
Soil to a plash?[18] Toads in a poisoned tank,
Or wild cats in a red-hot iron cage—

XXIII

The fight must so have seemed in that fell cirque.[19]
What penned them there, with all the plain to choose?
No foot-print leading to that horrid mews,[20] 135
None out of it. Mad brewage set to work
Their brains, no doubt, like galley-slaves the Turk
Pits for his pastime, Christians against Jews.

XXIV

And more than that—a furlong on—why, there!
What bad use was that engine for, that wheel, 140
Or brake, not wheel—that harrow fit to reel
Men's bodies out like silk? with all the air
Of Tophet's tool,[21] on earth left unaware,
Or brought to sharpen its rusty teeth of steel.

XXV

Then came a bit of stubbed ground, once a wood, 145
Next a marsh, it would seem, and now mere earth
Desperate and done with; (so a fool finds mirth,

[18] Puddle. [19] A theatre or arena (a "circle"). [20] Stable or collection of cages.
[21] Tophet was a place near Jerusalem where Jews were supposed to have made human sacrifices (Jeremiah 19:4). Later the place was used to burn rubbish and, partly because bonfires burned continually, became symbolic of the torments of hell.

Makes a thing and then mars it, till his mood
Changes and off he goes!) within a rood—[22]
Bog, clay and rubble, sand and stark black dearth. 150

XXVI

Now blotches rankling, coloured gay and grim,
Now patches where some leanness of the soil's
Broke into moss or substances like boils;
Then came some palsied oak, a cleft in him
Like a distorted mouth that splits its rim 155
Gaping at death, and dies while it recoils.

XXVII

And just as far as ever from the end!
Nought in the distance but the evening, nought
To point my footstep further! At the thought,
A great black bird, Apollyon's bosom-friend,[23]
Sailed past, nor beat his wide wing dragon-penned[24] 160
That brushed my cap—perchance the guide I sought.

XXVIII

For, looking up, aware I somehow grew,
'Spite of the dusk, the plain had given place
All round to mountains—with such name to grace
Mere ugly heights and heaps now stolen in view. 165
How thus they had surprised me,—solve it, you!
How to get from them was no clearer case.

XXIX

Yet half I seemed to recognize some trick
Of mischief happened to me, God knows when—
In a bad dream perhaps. Here ended, then, 170
Progress this way. When, in the very nick
Of giving up, one time more, came a click
As when a trap shuts—you're inside the den!

XXX

Burningly it came on me all at once,
This was the place! those two hills on the right, 175
Crouched like two bulls locked horn in horn in fight;
While to the left, a tall scalped mountain . . . Dunce,

[22] About one-fourth of an acre. [23] Apollyon, or "The Destroyer," according to Revelation 9:11, is the "angel of the bottomless pit." [24] Having the feathers (pens) of a dragon.

Dotard, a-dozing at the very nonce,[25]
After a life spent training for the sight!

XXXI

What in the midst lay but the Tower itself? 180
The round squat turret, blind as the fool's heart,
Built of brown stone, without a counterpart
In the whole world. The tempest's mocking elf
Points to the shipman thus the unseen shelf
He strikes on, only when the timbers start.[26] 185

XXXII

Not see? because of night perhaps?—why, day
Came back again for that! before it left,
The dying sunset kindled through a cleft:
The hills, like giants at a hunting, lay,
Chin upon hand, to see the game at bay,— 190
"Now stab and end the creature—to the heft!"

XXXIII

Not hear? when noise was everywhere! it tolled
Increasing like a bell. Names in my ears
Of all the lost adventurers my peers,—
How such a one was strong, and such was bold, 195
And such was fortunate, yet each of old
Lost, lost! one moment knelled the woe of years.

XXXIV

There they stood, ranged along the hillsides, met
To view the last of me, a living frame
For one more picture! in a sheet of flame 200
I saw them and I knew them all. And yet
Dauntless the slug-horn[27] to my lips I set,
And blew. "*Childe Roland to the Dark Tower came.*"

[25] Occasion. [26] Become loosened or forced out of place. [27] Trumpet.

WALT WHITMAN

1819–1892

STARTING FROM PAUMANOK

1

Starting from fish-shape Paumanok[1] where I was born,
Well-begotten, and rais'd by a perfect mother,
After roaming many lands, lover of populous pavements,
Dweller in Mannahatta my city, or on southern savannas,
Or a soldier camp'd or carrying my knapsack and gun, or a miner in California, 5
Or rude in my home in Dakota's woods, my diet meat, my drink from the spring,
Or withdrawn to muse and meditate in some deep recess,
Far from the clank of crowds intervals passing rapt and happy,
Aware of the fresh free giver the flowing Missouri, aware of mighty Niagara, 10
Aware of the buffalo herds grazing the plains, the hirsute and strong-breasted bull,
Of earth, rocks, Fifth-month flowers experienced, stars, rain, snow, my amaze,
Having studied the mocking-bird's tones and the flight of the mountain-hawk,
And heard at dawn the unrivall'd one, the hermit thrush from the swamp-cedars,
Solitary, singing in the West, I strike up for a New World. 15

2

Victory, union, faith, identity, time,
The indissoluble compacts, riches, mystery,
Eternal progress, the kosmos, and the modern reports.

This then is life,
Here is what has come to the surface after so many throes and convulsions. 20

How curious! how real!
Underfoot the divine soil, overhead the sun.

[1] Indian name of Long Island, New York.

See revolving the globe,
The ancestor-continents away group'd together,
The present and future continents north and south, with the isthmus
between. 25

See, vast trackless spaces,
As in a dream they change, they swiftly fill,
Countless masses debouch upon them,
They are now cover'd with the foremost people, arts, institutions, known.

See, projected through time,
For me an audience interminable. 30

With firm and regular step they wend, they never stop,
Successions of men, Americanos, a hundred millions,
One generation playing its part and passing on,
Another generation playing its part and passing on in its turn,
With faces turn'd sideways or backward towards me to listen, 35
With eyes retrospective towards me.

3

Americanos! conquerors! marches humanitarian!
Foremost! century marches! Libertad![2] masses!
For you a programme of chants.

Chants of the prairies, 40
Chants of the long-running Mississippi, and down to the Mexican sea,
Chants of Ohio, Indiana, Illinois, Iowa, Wisconsin and Minnesota,
Chants going forth from the centre from Kansas, and thence equidistant,
Shooting in pulses of fire ceaseless to vivify all.

4

Take my leaves[3] America, take them South and take them North, 45
Make welcome for them everywhere, for they are your own offspring,
Surround them East and West, for they would surround you,
And you precedents, connect lovingly with them, for they connect
lovingly with you.

I conn'd old times,
I sat studying at the feet of the great masters, 50
Now if eligible O that the great masters might return and study me.

[2] (Spanish) Liberty. [3] Poems; Whitman published his poetry in a volume entitled *Leaves of Grass.*

In the name of these States shall I scorn the antique?
Why these are the children of the antique to justify it.

5

Dead poets, philosophs, priests,
Martyrs, artists, inventors, governments long since, 55
Language-shapers on other shores,
Nations once powerful, now reduced, withdrawn, or desolate,
I dare not proceed till I respectfully credit what you have left wafted
hither,
I have perused it, own it is admirable, (moving awhile among it,)
Think nothing can ever be greater, nothing can ever deserve more than
it deserves, 60
Regarding it all intently a long while, then dismissing it,
I stand in my place with my own day here.

Here lands female and male,
Here the heir-ship and heiress-ship of the world, here the flame of materials,
Here spirituality the translatress, the openly-avow'd, 65
The ever-tending, the finalè of visible forms,
The satisfier, after due long-waiting now advancing,
Yes here comes my mistress the soul.

6

The soul,
Forever and forever—longer than soil is brown and solid—longer than
water ebbs and flows. 70

I will make the poems of materials, for I think they are to be the most
spiritual poems,
And I will make the poems of my body and of mortality,
For I think I shall then supply myself with the poems of my soul and
of immortality.

I will make a song for these States that no one State may under any
circumstances be subjected to another State,
And I will make a song that there shall be comity by day and by night
between all the States, and between any two of them, 75
And I will make a song for the ears of the President, full of weapons
with menacing points,
And behind the weapons countless dissatisfied faces;
And a song make I of the One form'd out of all,
The fang'd and glittering One whose head is over all,
Resolute warlike One including and over all, 80
(However high the head of any else that head is over all.)

I will acknowledge contemporary lands,
I will trail the whole geography of the globe and salute courteously
every city large and small,
And employments! I will put in my poems that with you is heroism
upon land and sea,
And I will report all heroism from an American point of view. 85

I will sing the song of companionship,
I will show what alone must finally compact these,
I believe these are to found their own ideal of manly love, indicating
it in me,
I will therefore let flame from me the burning fires that were threaten-
ing to consume me,
I will lift what has too long kept down those smouldering fires, 90
I will give them complete abandonment,
I will write the evangel-poem of comrades and of love,
For who but I should understand love with all its sorrow and joy?
And who but I should be the poet of comrades?

7

I am the credulous man of qualities, ages, races, 95
I advance from the people in their own spirit,
Here is what sings unrestricted faith.

Omnes![4] omnes! let others ignore what they may,
I make the poem of evil also, I commemorate that part also,
I am myself just as much evil as good, and my nation is—and I say
there is in fact no evil, 100
(Or if there is I say it is just as important to you, to the land or to me,
as any thing else.)

I too, following many and follow'd by many, inaugurate a religion, I
descend into the arena,
(It may be I am destin'd to utter the loudest cries there, the winner's
pealing shouts,
Who knows? they may rise from me yet, and soar above every thing.)

Each is not for its own sake, 105
I say the whole earth and all the stars in the sky are for religion's sake.

I say no man has ever yet been half devout enough,
None has ever yet adored or worship'd half enough,

[4] (Latin) All.

None has begun to think how divine he himself is, and how certain the future is.

I say that the real and permanent grandeur of these States must be their religion, 110
Otherwise there is no real and permanent grandeur;
(Nor character nor life worthy the name without religion,
Nor land nor man or woman without religion.)

8

What are you doing young man?
Are you so earnest, so given up to literature, science, art, amours? 115
These ostensible realities, politics, points?
Your ambition or business whatever it may be?

It is well—against such I say not a word, I am their poet also,
But behold! such swiftly subside, burnt up for religion's sake,
For not all matter is fuel to heat, impalpable flame, the essential life of the earth, 120
Any more than such are to religion.

9

What do you seek so pensive and silent?
What do you need camerado?[5]
Dear son do you think it is love?

Listen dear son—listen America, daughter or son, 125
It is a painful thing to love a man or woman to excess, and yet it satisfies, it is great,
But there is something else very great, it makes the whole coincide,
It, magnificent, beyond materials, with continuous hands sweeps and provides for all.

10

Know you, solely to drop in the earth the germs of a greater religion,
The following chants each for its kind I sing. 130

My comrade!
For you to share with me two greatnesses, and a third one rising inclusive and more resplendent,
The greatness of Love and Democracy, and the greatness of Religion.

[5] Camarado (Spanish), comrade, friend.

Melange mine own, the unseen and the seen,
Mysterious ocean where the streams empty, 135
Prophetic spirit of materials shifting and flickering around me,
Living beings, identities now doubtless near us in the air that we know not of,
Contact daily and hourly that will not release me,
These selecting, these in hints demanded of me.

Not he with a daily kiss onward from childhood kissing me, 140
Has winded and twisted around me that which holds me to him,
Any more than I am held to the heavens and all the spiritual world,
After what they have done to me, suggesting themes.

O such themes—equalities! O divine average!
Warblings under the sun, usher'd as now, or at noon, or setting, 145
Strains musical flowing through ages, now reaching hither,
I take to your reckless and composite chords, add to them, and cheerfully pass them forward.

11

As I have walk'd in Alabama my morning walk,
I have seen where the she-bird the mocking-bird sat on her nest in the briers hatching her brood.

I have seen the he-bird also, 150
I have paus'd to hear him near at hand inflating his throat and joyfully singing.

And while I paus'd it came to me that what he really sang for was not there only,
Nor for his mate nor himself only, nor all sent back by the echoes,
But subtle, clandestine, away beyond,
A charge transmitted and gift occult for those being born. 155

12

Democracy! near at hand to you a throat is now inflating itself and joyfully singing.

Ma femme![6] for the brood beyond us and of us,
For those who belong here and those to come,

[6] (French) My wife.

I exultant to be ready for them will now shake out carols stronger and haughtier than have ever yet been heard upon earth.

I will make the songs of passion to give them their way, 160
And your songs outlaw'd offenders, for I scan you with kindred eyes, and carry you with me the same as any.

I will make the true poem of riches,
To earn for the body and the mind whatever adheres and goes forward and is not dropt by death;
I will effuse egotism and show it underlying all, and I will be the bard of personality,
And I will show of male and female that either is but the equal of the other, 165
And sexual organs and acts! do you concentrate in me, for I am determin'd to tell you with courageous clear voice to prove you illustrious,
And I will show that there is no imperfection in the present, and can be none in the future,
And I will show that whatever happens to anybody it may be turn'd to beautiful results,
And I will show that nothing can happen more beautiful than death,
And I will thread a thread through my poems that time and events are compact, 170
And that all the things of the universe are perfect miracles, each as profound as any.

I will not make poems with reference to parts,
But I will make poems, songs, thoughts, with reference to ensemble,
And I will not sing with reference to a day, but with reference to all days,
And I will not make a poem nor the least part of a poem but has reference to the soul, 175
Because having look'd at the objects of the universe, I find there is no one nor any particle of one but has reference to the soul.

13

Was somebody asking to see the soul?
See, your own shape and countenance, persons, substances, beasts, the trees, the running rivers, the rocks and sands.

All hold spiritual joys and afterwards loosen them;
How can the real body ever die and be buried? 180

Of your real body and any man's or woman's real body,
Item for item it will elude the hands of the corpse-cleaners and pass to fitting spheres,
Carrying what has accrued to it from the moment of birth to the moment of death.

Not the types set up by the printer return their impression, the meaning, the main concern,
Any more than a man's substance and life or a woman's substance and life return in the body and the soul, 185
Indifferently before death and after death.

Behold, the body includes and is the meaning, the main concern, and includes and is the soul;
Whoever you are, how superb and how divine is your body, or any part of it!

14

Whoever you are, to you endless announcements!

Daughter of the lands did you wait for your poet? 190
Did you wait for one with a flowing mouth and indicative hand?

Toward the male of the States, and toward the female of the States,
Exulting words, words to Democracy's lands.

Interlink'd, food-yielding lands!
Land of coal and iron! land of gold! land of cotton, sugar, rice! 195
Land of wheat, beef, pork! land of wool and hemp! land of the apple and the grape!
Land of the pastoral plains, the grass-fields of the world! land of those sweet-air'd interminable plateaus!
Land of the herd, the garden, the healthy house of adobie!
Lands where the north-west Columbia winds, and where the south-west Colorado winds!
Land of the eastern Chesapeake! land of the Delaware! 200
Land of Ontario, Erie, Huron, Michigan!
Land of the Old Thirteen! Massachusetts land! land of Vermont and Connecticut!
Land of the ocean shores! land of sierras and peaks!
Land of boatmen and sailors! fishermen's land!
Inextricable lands! the clutch'd together! the passionate ones! 205
The side by side! the elder and younger brothers! the bony-limb'd!

The great women's land! the feminine! the experienced sisters and the inexperienced sisters!
For breath'd land! Arctic braced! Mexican breez'd! the diverse! the compact!
The Pennsylvanian! the Virginian! the double Carolinian!
O all and each well-loved by me! my intrepid nations! O I at any rate include you all with perfect love! 210
I cannot be discharged from you! not from one any sooner than another!
O death, O for all that, I am yet of you unseen this hour with irrepressible love,
Walking New England, a friend, a traveler,
Splashing my bare feet in the edge of the summer ripples on Paumanok's sands,
Crossing the prairies, dwelling again in Chicago, dwelling in every town, 215
Observing shows, births, improvements, structures, arts,
Listening to orators and oratresses in public halls,
Of and through the States as during life, each man and woman my neighbor,
The Louisianian, the Georgian, as near to me, and I as near to him and her,
The Mississippian and Arkansian yet with me, and I yet with any of them, 220
Yet upon the plains west of the spinal river,[7] yet in my house of adobie,
Yet returning eastward, yet in the Seaside State[8] or in Maryland,
Yet Kanadian[9] cheerily braving the winter, the snow and ice welcome to me,
Yet a true son either of Maine or of the Granite State,[10] or the Narragansett Bay State,[11] or the Empire State,[12]
Yet sailing to other shores to annex the same, yet welcoming every new brother, 225
Hereby applying these leaves to the new ones from the hour they unite with the old ones,
Coming among the new ones myself to be their companion and equal, coming personally to you now,
Enjoining you to acts, characters, spectacles, with me.

15

With me with firm holding, yet haste, haste on.

For your life adhere to me, 230
(I may have to be persuaded many times before I consent to give myself really to you, but what of that?
Must not Nature be persuaded many times?)

[7] The Mississippi. [8] Probably New Jersey. [9] Canadian. [10] New Hampshire. [11] Rhode Island. [12] New York.

No dainty dolce affettuoso[13] I,
Bearded, sun-burnt, gray-neck'd, forbidding, I have arrived,
To be wrestled with as I pass for the solid prizes of the universe, 235
For such I afford whoever can persevere to win them.

16

On my way a moment I pause,
Here for you! and here for America!
Still the present I raise aloft, still the future of the States I harbinge
glad and sublime,
And for the past I pronounce what the air holds of the red aborigines. 240

The red aborigines,
Leaving natural breaths, sounds of rain and winds, calls as of birds and
animals in the woods, syllabled to us for names,
Okonee, Koosa, Ottawa, Monongahela, Sauk, Natchez, Chattahoochee,
Kaqueta, Oronoco,
Wabash, Miami, Saginaw, Chippewa, Oshkosh, Walla-Walla,
Leaving such to the States they melt, they depart, charging the water
and the land with names. 245

17

Expanding and swift, henceforth,
Elements, breeds, adjustments, turbulent, quick and audacious,
A world primal again, vistas of glory incessant and branching,
A new race dominating previous ones and grander far, with new
contests,
New politics, new literatures and religions, new inventions and arts. 250

These, my voice announcing—I will sleep no more but arise,
You oceans that have been calm within me! how I feel you, fathomless, stirring, preparing unprecedented waves and storms.

18

See, steamers steaming through my poems,
See, in my poems immigrants continually coming and landing,
See, in arriere,[14] the wigwam, the trail, the hunter's hut, the flat-boat,
the maize-leaf, the claim,[15] the rude fence, and the backwoods
village, 255
See, on the one side the Western Sea and on the other the Eastern
Sea, how they advance and retreat upon my poems as upon their
own shores,

[13] (Italian) Gentle, mild, and loving person. [14] (French) Behind (looking backwards). [15] Claimed tract of land.

See, pastures and forests in my poems—see, animals wild and tame—see, beyond the Kaw,[16] countless herds of buffalo feeding on short curly grass,
See, in my poems, cities, solid, vast, inland, with paved streets, with iron and stone edifices, ceaseless vehicles, and commerce,
See, the many-cylinder'd steam printing-press—see, the electric telegraph stretching across the continent,
See, through Atlantica's depths[17] pulses American Europe reaching, pulses of Europe duly return'd, 260
See, the strong and quick locomotive as it departs, panting, blowing the steam-whistle,
See, ploughmen ploughing farms—see, miners digging mines—see, the numberless factories,
See, mechanics busy at their benches with tools—see from among them superior judges, philosophs, Presidents, emerge, drest in working dresses,
See, lounging through the shops and fields of the States, me well-belov'd, close-held by day and night,
Hear the loud echoes of my songs here—read the hints come at last. 265

19

O camerado close! O you and me at last, and us two only.
O a word to clear one's path ahead endlessly!
O something ecstatic and undemonstrable! O music wild!
O now I triumph—and you shall also;
O hand in hand—O wholesome pleasure—O one more desirer and lover! 270
O to haste firm holding—to haste, haste on with me.

WHEN LILACS LAST IN THE DOORYARD BLOOM'D

1

When lilacs last in the dooryard bloom'd,
And the great star[1] early droop'd in the western sky in the night,
I mourn'd, and yet shall mourn with ever-returning spring.

Ever-returning spring, trinity sure to me you bring,
Lilac blooming perennial and drooping star in the west, 5
And thought of him I love.

[16] The Kansas River. [17] *Atlantica,* here, is the Atlantic Ocean.

[1] The planet Venus, or the "evening star."

2

O powerful western fallen star!
O shades of night—O moody, tearful night!
O great star disappear'd—O the black murk that hides the star!
O cruel hands that hold me powerless—O helpless soul of me! 10
O harsh surrounding cloud that will not free my soul.

3

In the dooryard fronting an old farm-house near the white-wash'd
palings,
Stands the lilac-bush tall-growing with heart-shaped leaves of rich
green,
With many a pointed blossom rising delicate, with the perfume strong
I love,
With every leaf a miracle—and from this bush in the dooryard, 15
With delicate-color'd blossoms and heart-shaped leaves of rich green,
A sprig with its flower I break.

4

In the swamp in secluded recesses,
A shy and hidden bird is warbling a song.

Solitary the thrush, 20
The hermit withdrawn to himself, avoiding the settlements,
Sings by himself a song.

Song of the bleeding throat,
Death's outlet song of life, (for well dear brother I know,
If thou wast not granted to sing thou would'st surely die.) 25

5

Over the breast of the spring, the land, amid cities,
Amid lanes and through old woods, where lately the violets peep'd
from the ground spotting the gray debris,
Amid the grass in the fields each side of the lanes, passing the endless
grass,
Passing the yellow-spear'd wheat, every grain from its shroud in the
dark-brown fields uprisen,
Passing the apple-tree blows of white and pink in the orchards, 30
Carrying a corpse to where it shall rest in the grave,
Night and day journeys a coffin.

6

Coffin that passes through lanes and streets,
Through day and night with the great cloud darkening the land,
With the pomp of the inloop'd flags with the cities draped in black, 35
With the show of the States themselves as of crape-veil'd women standing,
With processions long and winding and the flambeaus of the night,
With the countless torches lit, with the silent sea of faces and the unbared heads,
With the waiting depot, the arriving coffin, and the sombre faces,
With dirges through the night, with the thousand voices rising strong and solemn, 40
With all the mournful voices of the dirges pour'd around the coffin,
The dim-lit churches and the shuddering organs—where amid these you journey,
With the tolling tolling bells' perpetual clang,
Here, coffin that slowly passes,
I give you my sprig of lilac. 45

7

(Nor for you, for one alone,
Blossoms and branches green to coffins all I bring,
For fresh as the morning, thus would I chant a song for you O sane and sacred death.

All over bouquets of roses,
O death, I cover you over with roses and early lilies, 50
But mostly and now the lilac that blooms the first,
Copious I break, I break the sprigs from the bushes,
With loaded arms I come, pouring for you,
For you and the coffins all of you O death.)

8

O western orb sailing the heaven, 55
Now I know what you must have meant as a month since I walk'd,
As I walk'd in silence the transparent shadowy night,
As I saw you had something to tell as you bent to me night after night,
As you droop'd from the sky low down as if to my side, (while the other stars all look'd on,)
As we wander'd together the solemn night, (for something I know not what kept me from sleep,) 60
As the night advanced, and I saw on the rim of the west how full you were of woe,
As I stood on the rising ground in the breeze in the cool transparent night,

As I watch'd where you pass'd and was lost in the netherward black
of the night,
As my soul in its trouble dissatisfied sank, as where you sad orb,
Concluded, dropt in the night, and was gone. 65

9

Sing on there in the swamp,
O singer bashful and tender, I hear your notes, I hear your call,
I hear, I come presently, I understand you,
But a moment I linger, for the lustrous star has detain'd me,
The star my departing comrade holds and detains me. 70

10

O how shall I warble myself for the dead one there I loved?
And how shall I deck my song for the large sweet soul that has gone?
And what shall my perfume be for the grave of him I love?

Sea-winds blown from east and west,
Blown from the Eastern sea and blown from the Western sea, till there
on the prairies meeting, 75
These and with these and the breath of my chant,
I'll perfume the grave of him I love.

11

O what shall I hang on the chamber walls?
And what shall the pictures be that I hang on the walls,
To adorn the burial-house of him I love? 80

Pictures of growing spring and farms and homes,
With the Fourth-month eve at sundown, and the gray smoke lucid and
bright,
With floods of the yellow gold of the gorgeous, indolent, sinking sun,
burning, expanding the air,
With the fresh sweet herbage under foot, and the pale green leaves of
the trees prolific,
In the distance the flowing glaze, the breast of the river, with a wind-
dapple here and there, 85
With ranging hills on the banks, with many a line against the sky, and
shadows,
And the city at hand with dwellings so dense, and stacks of chimneys,
And all the scenes of life and the workshops, and the workmen homeward returning.

12

Lo, body and soul—this land,
My own Manhattan with spires, and the sparkling and hurrying tides, and the ships, 90
The varied and ample land, the South and the North in the light, Ohio's shores and flashing Missouri,
And ever the far-spreading prairies cover'd with grass and corn.

Lo, the most excellent sun so calm and haughty,
The violet and purple morn with just-felt breezes,
The gentle soft-born measureless light, 95
The miracle spreading bathing all, the fulfill'd noon,
The coming eve delicious, the welcome night and the stars,
Over my cities shining all, enveloping man and land.

13

Sing on, sing on you gray-brown bird,
Sing from the swamps, the recesses, pour your chant from the bushes, 100
Limitless out of the dusk, out of the cedars and pines.

Sing on dearest brother, warble your reedy song,
Loud human song, with voice of uttermost woe.

O liquid and free and tender!
O wild and loose to my soul—O wondrous singer! 105
You only I hear—yet the star holds me, (but will soon depart,)
Yet the lilac with mastering odor holds me.

14

Now while I sat in the day and look'd forth,
In the close of the day with its light and the fields of spring, and the farmers preparing their crops,
In the large unconscious scenery of my land with its lakes and forests, 110
In the heavenly aerial beauty, (after the perturb'd winds and the storms,)
Under the arching heavens of the afternoon swift passing, and the voices of children and women,
The many-moving sea-tides, and I saw the ships how they sail'd,
And the summer approaching with richness, and the fields all busy with labor,
And the infinite separate houses, how they all went on, each with its meals and minutia of daily usages, 115
And the streets how their throbbings throbb'd, and the cities pent—lo, then and there,

Falling upon them all and among them all, enveloping me with the rest,
Appear'd the cloud, appear'd the long black trail,
And I knew death, its thought, and the sacred knowledge of death.

Then with the knowledge of death as walking one side of me, 120
And the thought of death close-walking the other side of me,
And I in the middle as with companions, and as holding the hands of
companions,
I fled forth to the hiding receiving night that talks not,
Down to the shores of the water, the path by the swamp in the
dimness,
To the solemn shadowy cedars and ghostly pines so still. 125

And the singer so shy to the rest receiv'd me,
The gray-brown bird I know receiv'd us comrades three,
And he sang the carol of death, and a verse for him I love.

From deep secluded recesses,
From the fragrant cedars and the ghostly pines so still, 130
Came the carol of the bird.

And the charm of the carol rapt me,
As I held as if by their hands my comrades in the night,
And the voice of my spirit tallied the song of the bird.

Come lovely and soothing death, 135
Undulate round the world, serenely arriving, arriving,
In the day, in the night, to all, to each,
Sooner or later delicate death.

Prais'd be the fathomless universe,
For life and joy, and for objects and knowledge curious, 140
And for love, sweet love—but praise! praise! praise!
For the sure-enwinding arms of cool-enfolding death.

Dark mother always gliding near with soft feet,
Have none chanted for thee a chant of fullest welcome?
Then I chant it for thee, I glorify thee above all, 145
I bring thee a song that when thou must indeed come, come
unfalteringly.

Approach strong deliveress,
When it is so, when thou hast taken them I joyously sing the dead,
Lost in the loving floating ocean of thee,
Laved in the flood of thy bliss O death. 150

From me to thee glad serenades,
Dances for thee I propose saluting thee, adornments and feastings for thee,
And the sights of the open landscape and the high-spread sky are fitting,
And life and the fields, and the huge and thoughtful night.

The night in silence under many a star, 155
The ocean shore and the husky whispering wave whose voice I know,
And the soul turning to thee O vast and well-veil'd death,
And the body gratefully nestling close to thee.

Over the tree-tops I float thee a song,
Over the rising and sinking waves, over the myriad fields and the prairies wide, 160
Over the dense-pack'd cities all and the teeming wharves and ways,
I float this carol with joy, with joy to thee O death.

15

To the tally of my soul,
Loud and strong kept up the gray-brown bird,
With pure deliberate notes spreading filling the night. 165

Loud in the pines and cedars dim,
Clear in the freshness moist and the swamp-perfume,
And I with my comrades there in the night.

While my sight that was bound in my eyes unclosed,
As to long panoramas of visions. 170

And I saw askant the armies,
I saw as in noiseless dreams hundreds of battle-flags,
Borne through the smoke of the battles and pierc'd with missiles I saw them,
And carried hither and yon through the smoke, and torn and bloody,
And at last but a few shreds left on the staffs, (and all in silence,) 175
And the staffs all splinter'd and broken.

I saw battle-corpses, myriads of them,
And the white skeletons of young men, I saw them,
I saw the debris and debris of all the slain soldiers of the war,
But I saw they were not as was thought, 180
They themselves were fully at rest, they suffer'd not,
The living remain'd and suffer'd, the mother suffer'd,
And the wife and the child and the musing comrade suffer'd,
And the armies that remain'd suffer'd.

16

Passing the visions, passing the night, 185
Passing, unloosing the hold of my comrades' hands,
Passing the song of the hermit bird and the tallying song of my soul,
Victorious song, death's outlet song, yet varying ever-altering song,
As low and wailing, yet clear the notes, rising and falling, flooding the night,
Sadly sinking and fainting, as warning and warning, and yet again bursting with joy, 190
Covering the earth and filling the spread of the heaven,
As that powerful psalm in the night I heard from recesses,
Passing, I leave thee lilac with heart-shaped leaves,
I leave thee there in the door-yard, blooming, returning with spring.

I cease from my song for thee, 195
From my gaze on thee in the west, fronting the west, communing with thee,
O comrade lustrous with silver face in the night.

Yet each to keep and all, retrievements out of the night,
The song, the wondrous chant of the gray-brown bird,
And the tallying chant, the echo arous'd in my soul, 200
With the lustrous and drooping star with the countenance full of woe,
With the holders holding my hand nearing the call of the bird,
Comrades mine and I in the midst, and their memory ever to keep, for the dead I loved so well,
For the sweetest, wisest soul of all my days and lands—and this for his dear sake,
Lilac and star and bird twined with the chant of my soul, 205
There in the fragrant pines and the cedars dusk and dim.

MATTHEW ARNOLD

1822–1888

SHAKESPEARE

Others abide[1] our question. Thou art free.
We ask and ask: Thou smilest and art still,
Out-topping knowledge. For the loftiest hill
That to the stars uncrowns his majesty,
Planting his steadfast footsteps in the sea, 5
Making the Heaven of Heavens his dwelling-place,
Spares but the cloudy border of his base
To the foil'd searching of mortality:
And thou, who didst the stars and sunbeams know,
Self-school'd, self-scann'd,[2] self-honour'd, self-secure, 10
Didst walk on Earth unguess'd at. Better so!
All pains the immortal spirit must endure,
All weakness that impairs, all griefs that bow,
Find their sole voice in that victorious brow.

MEMORIAL VERSES

April, 1850

Goethe in Weimar sleeps,[1] and Greece,
Long since, saw Byron's struggle cease.[2]
But one such death remain'd to come;
The last poetic voice is dumb.
What shall be said o'er Wordsworth's tomb? 5

When Byron's eyes were shut in death,
We bow'd our head and held our breath.
He taught us little: but our soul
Had *felt* him like the thunder's roll.

[1] Submit to, face. [2] Self-examined (introspectively).

[1] Johann Wolfgang von Goethe (1749–1832), German poet and dramatist, was buried in Weimar. [2] The English poet, Byron, died in Greece in a battle for that country's independence.

With shivering heart the strife we saw 10
Of Passion with Eternal Law;
And yet with reverential awe
We watch'd the fount of fiery life
Which serv'd for that Titanic strife.

When Goethe's death was told, we said— 15
Sunk, then, is Europe's sagest head.
Physician of the Iron Age,
Goethe has done his pilgrimage.
He took the suffering human race,
He read each wound, each weakness clear— 20
And struck his finger on the place
And said—*Thou ailest here, and here—*
He look'd on Europe's dying hour
Of fitful dream and feverish power;
His eye plung'd down the weltering strife, 25
The turmoil of expiring life;
He said—*The end is everywhere:*
Art still has truth, take refuge there.
And he was happy, if to know
Causes of things, and far below 30
His feet to see the lurid flow
Of terror, and insane distress,
And headlong fate, be happiness.

And Wordsworth!—Ah, pale Ghosts, rejoice!
For never has such soothing voice 35
Been to your shadowy world convey'd,
Since erst, at morn, some wandering shade
Heard the clear song of Orpheus come
Through Hades,[3] and the mournful gloom.
Wordsworth has gone from us—and ye, 40
Ah, may ye feel his voice as we.
He too upon a wintry clime
Had fallen—on this iron time
Of doubts, disputes, distractions, fears.
He found us when the age had bound 45
Our souls in its benumbing round;
He spoke, and loos'd our heart in tears.
He laid us as we lay at birth
On the cool flowery lap of earth;
Smiles broke from us and we had ease, 50
The hills were round us, and the breeze
Went o'er the sun-lit fields again:

[3] In Greek mythology, Orpheus, a semi-divine musician, went to Hades in an attempt to bring back Eurydice, his wife.

Our foreheads felt the wind and rain.
Our youth return'd: for there was shed
On spirits that had long been dead, 55
Spirits dried up and closely-furl'd,
The freshness of the early world.

Ah, since dark days still bring to light
Man's prudence and man's fiery might,
Time may restore us in his course 60
Goethe's sage mind and Byron's force:
But where will Europe's latter hour
Again find Wordsworth's healing power?
Others will teach us how to dare,
And against fear our breast to steel: 65
Others will strengthen us to bear—
But who, ah who, will make us feel?
The cloud of mortal destiny,
Others will front it fearlessly—
But who, like him, will put it by? 70

Keep fresh the grass upon his grave,
O Rotha![4] with thy living wave.
Sing him thy best! for few or none
Hears thy voice right, now he is gone.

TO MARGUERITE IN RETURNING A VOLUME OF THE LETTERS OF ORTIS

Yes: in the sea of life enisl'd,
With echoing straits between us thrown,
Dotting the shoreless watery wild,
We mortal millions live *alone*.
The islands feel the enclasping flow, 5
And then their endless bounds they know.

But when the moon their hollow lights,
And they are swept by balms of spring,
And in their glens, on starry nights,
The nightingales divinely sing; 10
And lovely notes, from shore to shore,
Across the sounds and channels pour;

[4] A river that flows past Grasmere churchyard, where Wordsworth is buried.

Oh then a longing like despair
Is to their farthest caverns sent;
For surely once, they feel, we were 15
Parts of a single continent.
Now round us spreads the watery plain—
Oh might our marges[1] meet again!

Who order'd, that their longing's fire
Should be, as soon as kindled, cool'd? 20
Who renders vain their deep desire?—
A God, a God their severance rul'd;
And bade betwixt their shores to be
The unplumb'd, salt, estranging sea.

THE SCHOLAR GIPSY[1]

Go, for they call you, Shepherd, from the hill;
Go, Shepherd, and untie the wattled cotes:[2]
No longer leave thy wistful flock unfed,
Nor let thy bawling fellows rack their throats,
Nor the cropp'd grasses shoot another head. 5
But when the fields are still,
And the tired men and dogs all gone to rest,
And only the white sheep are sometimes seen
Cross and recross the strips of moon-blanch'd green;
Come, Shepherd, and again renew the quest. 10

Here, where the reaper was at work of late,
In this high field's dark corner, where he leaves
His coat, his basket, and his earthen cruise,[3]

[1] Margins, boundaries.

[1] Arnold included the following passage from Glanvil's *Vanity of Dogmatizing* (1661), as a footnote to the title of this poem: "There was very lately a lad in the University of Oxford, who was by his poverty forced to leave his studies there; and at last to join himself to a company of vagabond gipsies. Among these extravagant people, by the insinuating subtilty of his carriage, he quickly got so much of their love and esteem as that they discovered to him their mystery. After he had been a pretty while will exercised in the trade, there chanced to ride by a couple of scholars, who had formerly been of his acquaintance. They quickly spied out their old friend among the gipsies; and he gave them an account of the necessity which drove him to that kind of life, and told them that the people he went with were not such impostors as they were taken for, but that they had a traditional kind of learning among them, and could do wonders by the power of imagination, their fancy binding that of others: that himself had learned much of their art, and when he had compassed the whole secret, he intended, he said, to leave their company, and give the world an account of what he had learned. [2] Pens made of poles interwoven with slender branches. [3] Cruse, that is, jar, pot.

And in the sun all morning binds the sheaves,
Then here, at noon, comes back his stores to use; 15
Here will I sit and wait,
While to my ear from uplands far away
The bleating of the folded flocks is borne,
With distant cries of reapers in the corn—
All the live murmur of a summer's day. 20

Screen'd is this nook o'er the high, half-reap'd field,
And here till sun-down, Shepherd, will I be.
Through the thick corn the scarlet poppies peep,
And round green roots and yellowing stalks I see
Pale blue convolvulus in tendrils creep: 25
And air-swept lindens yield
Their scent, and rustle down their perfum'd showers
Of bloom on the bent grass where I am laid,
And bower me from the August sun with shade;
And the eye travels down to Oxford's towers: 30

And near me on the grass lies Glanvil's book—
Come, let me read the oft-read tale again,
The story of that Oxford scholar poor
Of pregnant parts[4] and quick inventive brain,
Who, tir'd of knocking at Preferment's door, 35
One summer morn forsook
His friends, and went to learn the Gipsy lore,
And roam'd the world with that wild brotherhood,
And came, as most men deem'd, to little good,
But came to Oxford and his friends no more. 40

But once, years after, in the country lanes,
Two scholars whom at college erst he knew
Met him, and of his way of life inquir'd.
Whereat he answer'd, that the Gipsy crew,
His mates, had arts to rule as they desir'd 45
The workings of men's brains;
And they can bind them to what thoughts they will:
"And I," he said, "the secret of their art,
When fully learn'd, will to the world impart:
But it needs heaven-sent moments for this skill." 50

This said, he left them, and return'd no more,
But rumours hung about the country side
That the lost Scholar long was seen to stray,

[4] Promising characteristics.

Seen by rare glimpses, pensive and tongue-tied,
In hat of antique shape, and cloak of grey, 55
The same the Gipsies wore.
Shepherds had met him on the Hurst[5] in spring;
At some lone alehouse in the Berkshire moors,
On the warm ingle[6] bench, the smock-frock'd boors[7]
Had found him seated at their entering, 60

But, mid their drink and clatter, he would fly:
And I myself seem half to know thy looks,
And put the shepherds, Wanderer, on thy trace;
And boys who in lone wheatfields scare the rooks[8]
I ask if thou hast pass'd their quiet place; 65
Or in my boat I lie
Moor'd to the cool bank in the summer heats,
Mid wide grass meadows which the sunshine fills,
And watch the warm green-muffled Cumner hills,
And wonder if thou haunt'st their shy retreats. 70

For most, I know, thou lov'st retired ground.
Thee, at the ferry, Oxford riders blithe,
Returning home on summer nights, have met
Crossing the stripling Thames at Bab-lock-hithe,
Trailing in the cool stream thy fingers wet, 75
As the slow punt swings round:
And leaning backwards in a pensive dream,
And fostering in thy lap a heap of flowers
Pluck'd in shy fields and distant Wychwood bowers,
And thine eyes resting on the moonlit stream: 80

And then they land, and thou art seen no more.
Maidens who from the distant hamlets come
To dance around the Fyfield elm in May,
Oft through the darkening fields have seen thee roam,
Or cross a stile into the public way. 85
Oft thou hast given them store
Of flowers—the frail-leaf'd, white anemone—
Dark bluebells drench'd with dews of summer eves—
And purple orchises with spotted leaves—
But none has words she can report of thee. 90

And, above Godstow Bridge, when hay-time's here
In June, and many a scythe in sunshine flames,

[5] Bank or hillock. [6] Fireside. [7] Peasants, rustics. [8] Birds resembling crows.

Men who through those wide fields of breezy grass
Where black-wing'd swallows haunt the glittering Thames,
To bathe in the abandon'd lasher[9] pass, 95
Have often pass'd thee near
Sitting upon the river bank o'ergrown:
Mark'd thy outlandish garb, thy figure spare,
Thy dark vague eyes, and soft abstracted air;
But, when they came from bathing, thou wert gone. 100

At some lone homestead in the Cumner hills,
Where at her open door the housewife darns,
Thou hast been seen, or hanging on a gate
To watch the threshers in the mossy barns.
Children who early range these slopes and late 105
For cresses[10] from the rills,
Have known thee watching, all an April day,
The springing pastures and the feeding kine;[11]
And mark'd thee, when the stars come out and shine,
Through the long dewy grass move slow away. 110

In Autumn, on the skirts of Bagley wood,
Where most the Gipsies by the turf-edg'd way
Pitch their smok'd tents, and every bush you see
With scarlet patches tagg'd and shreds of grey,
Above the forest ground call'd Thessaly— 115
The blackbird picking food
Sees thee, nor stops his meal, nor fears at all;
So often has he known thee past him stray
Rapt, twirling in thy hand a wither'd spray,
And waiting for the spark from Heaven to fall. 120

And once, in winter, on the causeway chill
Where home through flooded fields foot-travellers go,
Have I not pass'd thee on the wooden bridge
Wrapt in thy cloak and battling with the snow,
Thy face towards Hinksey and its wintry ridge? 125
And thou hast climb'd the hill
And gain'd the white brow of the Cumner range,
Turn'd once to watch, while thick the snowflakes fall,
The line of festal light in Christ-Church hall—
Then sought thy straw in some sequester'd grange. 130

[9] A pool formed by water (of the Thames) that lashes, or rushes, over an opening in a barrier. [10] Watercress. [11] Cattle.

But what—I dream! Two hundred years are flown
Since first thy story ran through Oxford halls,
And the grave Glanvil did the tale inscribe
That thou wert wander'd from the studious walls
To learn strange arts, and join a Gipsy tribe: 135
And thou from earth art gone
Long since, and in some quiet churchyard laid;
Some country nook, where o'er thy unknown grave
Tall grasses and white flowering nettles wave—
Under a dark red-fruited yew-tree's shade. 140

—No, no, thou hast not felt the lapse of hours.
For what wears out the life of mortal men?
'Tis that from change to change their being rolls:
'Tis that repeated shocks, again, again,
Exhaust the energy of strongest souls, 145
And numb the elastic powers.
Till having us'd our nerves with bliss and teen,[12]
And tir'd upon a thousand schemes our wit,
To the just-pausing Genius we remit
Our worn-out life, and are—what we have been. 150

Thou hast not liv'd, why should'st thou perish, so?
Thou hadst *one* aim, *one* business, *one* desire:
Else wert thou long since number'd with the dead—
Else hadst thou spent, like other men, thy fire.
The generations of thy peers are fled, 155
And we ourselves shall go;
But thou possessest an immortal lot,
And we imagine thee exempt from age
And living as thou liv'st on Glanvil's page,
Because thou hadst—what we, alas, have not! 160

For early didst thou leave the world, with powers
Fresh, undiverted to the world without,
Firm to their mark, not spent on other things;
Free from the sick fatigue, the languid doubt,
Which much to have tried, in much been baffled, brings. 165
O Life unlike to ours!
Who fluctuate idly without term[13] or scope,
Of whom each strives, nor knows for what he strives,
And each half lives a hundred different lives;
Who wait like thee, but not, like thee, in hope. 170

[12] Suffering. [13] Limit (in time).

Thou waitest for the spark from Heaven: and we,
Vague half-believers of our casual creeds,
Who never deeply felt, nor clearly will'd,
Whose insight never has borne fruit in deeds,
Whose weak resolves never have been fulfill'd; 175
For whom each year we see
Breeds new beginnings, disappointments new;
Who hesitate and falter life away,
And lose to-morrow the ground won to-day—
Ah, do not we, Wanderer, await it too? 180

Yes, we await it, but it still delays,
And then we suffer; and amongst us One,[14]
Who most has suffer'd, takes dejectedly
His seat upon the intellectual throne;
And all his store of sad experience he 185
Lays bare of wretched days;
Tells us his misery's birth and growth and signs,
And how the dying spark of hope was fed,
And how the breast was sooth'd, and how the head,
And all his hourly varied anodynes. 190

This for our wisest: and we others pine,
And wish the long unhappy dream would end,
And waive all claim to bliss, and try to bear,
With close-lipp'd Patience for our only friend,
Sad Patience, too near neighbour to Despair: 195
But none has hope like thine.
Thou through the fields and through the woods dost stray,
Roaming the country side, a truant boy,
Nursing thy project in unclouded joy,
And every doubt long blown by time away. 200

O born in days when wits were fresh and clear,
And life ran gaily as the sparkling Thames;
Before this strange disease of modern life,
With its sick hurry, its divided aims,
Its heads o'ertax'd, its palsied hearts, was rife— 205
Fly hence, our contact fear!
Still fly, plunge deeper in the bowering wood!
Averse, as Dido did with gesture stern

[14] Probably Goethe.

From her false friend's approach in Hades turn,[15]
Wave us away, and keep thy solitude. 210

Still nursing the unconquerable hope,
Still clutching the inviolable shade,
With a free onward impulse brushing through,
By night, the silver'd branches of the glade—
Far on the forest skirts, where none pursue, 215
On some mild pastoral slope
Emerge, and resting on the moonlit pales,[16]
Freshen thy flowers, as in former years,
With dew, or listen with enchanted ears,
From the dark dingles,[17] to the nightingales. 220

But fly our paths, our feverish contact fly!
For strong the infection of our mental strife,
Which, though it gives no bliss, yet spoils for rest;
And we should win thee from thy own fair life,
Like us distracted, and like us unblest. 225
Soon, soon thy cheer would die,
Thy hopes grow timorous, and unfix'd thy powers,
And thy clear aims be cross and shifting made:
And then thy glad perennial youth would fade,
Fade, and grow old at last, and die like ours. 230

Then fly our greetings, fly our speech and smiles!
—As some grave Tyrian trader, from the sea,
Descried at sunrise an emerging prow
Lifting the cool-hair'd creepers stealthily,
The fringes of a southward-facing brow 235
Among the Aegean isles;
And saw the merry Grecian coaster come,
Freighted with amber grapes, and Chian wine,
Green bursting figs, and tunnies steep'd in brine;
And knew the intruders on his ancient home, 240

The young light-hearted Masters of the waves;
And snatch'd his rudder, and shook out more sail,

[15] Early in his long journey, Aeneas, hero of Virgil's *Aeneid,* comes to Carthage whose queen, Dido, falls in love with his and offers to share her throne with him. He is strongly tempted but, knowing he has a mission to accomplish, he refuses and leaves her. Later, he makes a trip to the underworld, and there meets Dido, who had committed suicide when Aeneas left her. He begs her forgiveness and weeps at her misfortune, but she refuses to recognize him. [16] Palings. [17] Deep dells or hollows.

And day and night held on indignantly
O'er the blue Midland waters with the gale,
Betwixt the Syrtes and soft Sicily, 245
To where the Atlantic raves
Outside the Western Straits, and unbent sails
There, where down cloudy cliffs, through sheets of foam,
Shy traffickers, the dark Iberians come;
And on the beach undid his corded bales.[18] 250

GEORGE MEREDITH

1828–1909

LUCIFER IN STARLIGHT

On a starred night Prince Lucifer uprose.
Tired of his dark dominion swung the fiend
Above the rolling ball in cloud part screened,
Where sinners hugged their spectre of repose.
Poor prey to his hot fit of pride were those. 5
And now upon his western wing he leaned,
Nor his huge bulk o'er Afric's sands careened,
Now the black planet shadowed Arctic snows.
Soaring through wider zones that pricked his scars
With memory of the old revolt from Awe, 10
He reached a middle height, and at the stars,
Which are the brain of heaven, he looked, and sank.
Around the ancient track marched, rank on rank,
The army of unalterable law.

[18] Both Tyre and Iberia were great ancient civilizations that were conquered by Greece, which Arnold here likens to the "strange disease of modern life" that he would like the "scholar gypsy" to escape.

EMILY DICKINSON

1830–1886

PAPA ABOVE!

Papa above!
Regard a Mouse
O'erpowered by the Cat!
Reserve within thy kingdom
A "Mansion" for the Rat! 5

Snug in seraphic Cupboards
To nibble all the day,
While unsuspecting Cycles[1]
Wheel solemnly away!

THERE'S A CERTAIN SLANT OF LIGHT

There's a certain Slant of light,
Winter Afternoons—
That oppresses, like the Heft
Of Cathedral Tunes—

Heavenly Hurt, it gives us— 5
We can find no scar,
But internal difference,
Where the Meanings, are—

None may teach it—Any—
'Tis the Seal Despair— 10
An imperial affliction
Sent us of the Air—

When it comes, the Landscape listens—
Shadows—hold their breath—

[1] Revolutions (of planets), ages; but there is an intentional pun on "bicycles" also.

When it goes, 'tis like the Distance 15
On the look of Death—

A CLOCK STOPPED—

A Clock stopped—
Not the Mantel's—
Geneva's farthest skill
Cant put the puppet bowing—
That just now dangled still— 5

An awe come on the Trinket!
The Figures hunched, with pain—
Then quivered out of Decimals—
Into Degreeless Noon—

It will not stir for Doctor's— 10
This Pendulum of snow—
The Shopman importunes it—
While cool—concernless No—

Nods from the Gilded pointers—
Nods from the Seconds slim— 15
Decades of Arrogance between
The Dial life—
And Him—

I TASTE A LIQUOR NEVER BREWED

I taste a liquor never brewed—
From Tankards scooped in Pearl—
Not all the Frankfort Berries
Yield such an Alcohol!

Inebriate of Air—am I— 5
And Debauchee of Dew—
Reeling—thro endless summer days—
From inns of Molten Blue—

When "Landlords" turn the drunken Bee
Out of the Foxglove's door— 10

When Butterflies—renounce their "drams"—
I shall but drink the more!

Till Seraphs swing their snowy Hats—
And Saints—to windows run—
To see the little Tippler 15
From Manzanilla come!

BECAUSE I COULD NOT STOP FOR DEATH

Because I could not stop for Death—
He kindly stopped for me—
The Carriage held but just Ourselves—
And Immortality.

We slowly drove—He knew no haste 5
And I had put away
My labor and my leisure too,
For His Civility—

We passed the School, where Children strove
At Recess—in the Ring— 10
We passed the Fields of Gazing Grain—
We passed the Setting Sun—

Or rather—He passed Us—
The Dews drew quivering and chill—
For only Gossamer, my Gown— 15
My Tippet[1]—only Tulle—

We paused before a House that seemed
A Swelling of the Ground—
The Roof was scarcely visible—
The Cornice—in the Ground— 20

Since then—'tis Centuries—and yet
Feels shorter than the Day
I first surmised the Horses Heads
Were toward Eternity—

[1] Shoulder cape.

I'VE SEEN A DYING EYE

I've seen a Dying Eye
Run round and round a Room—
In search of Something—as it seemed—
Then Cloudier become—
And then—obscure with Fog— 5
And then—be soldered down
Without disclosing what it be
'Twere blessed to have seen—

A NARROW FELLOW IN THE GRASS

A narrow Fellow in the Grass
Occasionally rides—
You may have met Him—did you not
His notice sudden is—

The Grass divides as with a Comb— 5
A spotted shaft is seen—
And then it closes at your feet
And opens further on—

He likes a Boggy Acre—
A Floor too cool for Corn— 10
But when a Boy and Barefoot—
I more than once at Noon
Have passed I thought a Whip Lash
Unbraiding in the Sun
When stooping to secure it 15
It wrinkled, and was gone—

Several of Nature's People
I know, and they know me—
I feel for them a transport
Of cordiality— 20

But never met this Fellow
Attended, or alone
Without a tighter breathing
And Zero at the Bone—

"HEAVENLY FATHER"—TAKE TO THEE

"Heavenly Father"—take to thee
The supreme iniquity
Fashioned by thy candid Hand
In a moment contraband—
Though to trust us—seem to us 5
More respectful—"We are Dust"—
We apologize to thee
For thine own Duplicity—

'TWAS LATER WHEN THE SUMMER WENT

'Twas later when the summer went
Than when the Cricket came—
And yet we knew that gentle Clock
Meant nought but Going Home—
'Twas sooner when the Cricket went 5
Than when the Winter came
Yet that pathetic Pendulum
Keeps esoteric Time

ALGERNON CHARLES SWINBURNE

1837–1909

BEFORE THE BEGINNING OF YEARS

Chorus from "Atlanta in Calydon"

Before the beginning of years
    There came to the making of man
Time, with a gift of tears;
    Grief, with a glass that ran;

Pleasure, with pain for leaven; 5
    Summer, with flowers that fell;
Remembrance fallen from heaven,
    And madness risen from hell;
Strength without hands to smite,
    Love that endures for a breath; 10
Night, the shadow of light,
    And life, the shadow of death.

And the high gods took in hand
    Fire, and the falling of tears,
And a measure of sliding sand 15
    From under the feet of the years;
And froth and drift of the sea;
    And dust of the labouring earth;
And bodies of things to be
    In the houses of death and of birth; 20
And wrought with weeping and laughter,
    And fashioned with loathing and love,
With life before and after
    And death beneath and above,
For a day and a night and a morrow, 25
    That his strength might endure for a span
With travail and heavy sorrow,
    The holy spirit of man.

From the winds of the north and the south
    They gathered as unto strife; 30
They breathed upon his mouth,
    They filled his body with life;
Eyesight and speech they wrought
    For the veils of the soul therein,
A time for labour and thought, 35
    A time to serve and to sin;
They gave him light in his ways,
    And love, and a space for delight,
And beauty and length of days,
    And night, and sleep in the night. 40
His speech is a burning fire;
    With his lips he travaileth;
In his heart is a blind desire,
    In his eyes foreknowledge of death;
He weaves, and is clothed with derision; 45
    Sows, and he shall not reap;
His life is a watch or a vision
    Between a sleep and a sleep.

WHEN THE HOUNDS OF SPRING

Chorus from "Atlanta in Calydon"

When the hounds of spring are on winter's traces,
    The mother of months in meadow or plain
Fills the shadows and windy places
    With lisp of leaves and ripple of rain;
And the brown bright nightingale amorous 5
Is half assuaged for Itylus,
For the Thracian ships and the foreign faces,
    The tongueless vigil, and all the pain.[1]

Come with bows bent and with emptying of quivers,
    Maiden most perfect,[2] lady of light, 10
With a noise of winds and many rivers,
    With a clamour of waters, and with might;
Bind on thy sandals, O thou most fleet,
Over the splendour and speed of thy feet;
For the faint east quickens, the wan west shivers, 15
    Round the feet of the day and the feet of the night.

Where shall we find her, how shall we sing to her,
    Fold our hands round her knees, and cling?
O that man's heart were as fire and could spring to her,
    Fire, or the strength of the streams that spring! 20
For the stars and the winds are unto her
As raiment, as songs of the harp-player;
For the risen stars and the fallen cling to her,
    And the southwest-wind and the west-wind sing.

For winter's rains and ruins are over, 25
    And all the season of snows and sins;
The days dividing lover and lover,
    The light that loses, the night that wins;
And time remembered is grief forgotten,
And frosts are slain and flowers begotten, 30
And in green underwood and cover
    Blossom by blossom the spring begins.

[1] The allusion is to the Greek legend that Procne, wife of Theseus, king of Thrace, killed her son, Itylus, to avenge herself on her husband, and subsequently became a nightingale. Theseus had married Procne's sister, telling her that Procne, whose tongue he had cut out, was dead. [2] Artemis, Greek goddess of hunting and childbirth.

The full streams feed on flower of rushes,
Ripe grasses trammel a travelling foot,
The faint fresh flame of the young year flushes 35
From leaf to flower and flower to fruit,
And fruit and leaf are as gold and fire,
And the oat[3] is heard above the lyre,
And the hoofèd heel of a satyr crushes
The chestnut-husk at the chestnut-root. 40

And Pan by noon and Bacchus by night,[4]
Fleeter of foot than the fleet-foot kid,
Follows with dancing and fills with delight
The Maenad and the Bassarid;[5]
And soft as lips that laugh and hide 45
The laughing leaves of the trees divide,
And screen from seeing and leave in sight
The god pursuing, the maiden hid.

The ivy falls with the Bacchanal's hair[6]
Over her eyebrows hiding her eyes; 50
The wild vine slipping down leaves bare
Her bright breast shortening into sighs;
The wild vine slips with the weight of its leaves,
But the berried ivy catches and cleaves
To the limbs that glitter, the feet that scare 55
The wolf that follows, the fawn that flies.

THE GARDEN OF PROSERPINE[1]

Here, where the world is quiet;
Here, where all trouble seems
Dead winds' and spent waves' riot
In doubtful dreams of dreams;
I watch the green field growing 5
For reaping folk and sowing,
For harvest-time and mowing,
A sleepy world of streams.

[3] Oaten pipe, a rustic musical instrument. [4] Pan and Bacchus were frolicsome gods of the forest and wine, respectively. [5] The Maenads and Bassarids were women who were inspired to ecstatic frenzy by worship of Dionysus. [6] The Bacchanals were similar to Maenads and Bassarids.

[1] Persephone, the goddess of Hades; Proserpine is her Latin name.

I am tired of tears and laughter,
And men that laugh and weep, 10
Of what may come hereafter
For men that sow to reap:
I am weary of days and hours,
Blown[2] buds of barren flowers,
Desires and dreams and powers 15
And everything but sleep.

Here life has death for neighbour,
And far from eye or ear
Wan waves and wet winds labour,
Weak ships and spirits steer; 20
They drive adrift, and whither
They wot[3] not who make thither;
But no such winds blow hither,
And no such things grow here.

No growth of moor or coppice, 25
No heather-flower or vine,
But bloomless buds of poppies,
Green grapes of Proserpine.
Pale beds of blowing rushes
Where no leaf blooms or blushes 30
Save this whereout she crushes
For dead men deadly wine.

Pale, without name or number,
In fruitless fields of corn,
They bow themselves and slumber 35
All night till light is born;
And like a soul belated,
In hell and heaven unmated,
By cloud and mist abated
Comes out of darkness morn. 40

Though one were strong as seven,
He too with death shall dwell,
Nor wake with wings in heaven,
Nor weep for pains in hell;
Though one were fair as roses, 45
His beauty clouds and closes;

[2] Blossomed. [3] Know.

And well though love reposes,
    In the end it is not well.

Pale, beyond porch and portal,
    Crowned with calm leaves, she stands 50
Who gathers all things mortal
    With cold immortal hands;
Her languid lips are sweeter
Than love's who fears to greet her
To men that mix and meet her 55
    From many times and lands.

She waits for each and other,
    She waits for all men born;
Forgets the earth her mother,[4]
    The life of fruits and corn; 60
And spring and seed and swallow
Take wing for her and follow
Where summer song rings hollow
    And flowers are put to scorn.

There go the loves that wither, 65
    The old loves with wearier wings;
And all dead years draw thither,
    And all disastrous things;
Dead dreams of days forsaken,
Blind buds that snows have shaken, 70
Wild leaves that winds have taken,
    Red strays of ruined springs.

We are not sure of sorrow,
    And joy was never sure;
To-day will die to-morrow; 75
    Time stoops to no man's lure;
And love, grown faint and fretful,
With lips but half regretful
Sighs, and with eyes forgetful
    Weeps that no loves endure. 80

From too much love of living,
    From hope and fear set free,

[4] Demeter, corn goddess, was the mother of Persephone; she governed all fruits of the earth.

We thank with brief thanksgiving
Whatever gods may be
That no life lives for ever; 85
That dead men rise up never;
That even the weariest river
Winds somewhere safe to sea.

Then star nor sun shall waken,
Nor any change of light: 90
Nor sound of waters shaken,
Nor any sound or sight:
Nor wintry leaves nor vernal,
Nor days nor things diurnal;
Only the sleep eternal 95
In an eternal night.

SAPPHICS[1]

All the night sleep came not upon my eyelids,
Shed not dew, nor shook nor unclosed a feather,
Yet with lips shut close and with eyes of iron
Stood and beheld me.

Then to me so lying awake a vision 5
Came without sleep over the seas and touched me,
Softly touched mine eyelids and lips; and I too,
Full of the vision,

Saw the white implacable Aphrodite,
Saw the hair unbound and the feet unsandalled 10
Shine as fire of sunset on western waters;
Saw the reluctant

Feet, the straining plumes of the doves that drew her,
Looking always, looking with necks reverted,
Back to Lesbos, back to the hills whereunder 15
Shone Mitylene;[2]

[1] The poem is written in "Sapphic" verses, named after the Greek poetess, Sappho, who used this verse form. Sappho (born 612 B.C.), one of the most famous lyric poets of all time, was a native of Lesbos. She married and had a daughter. As a leader of young girls devoted to music, poetry, and Aphrodite (goddess of love and marriage), she often addressed poems to her followers. [2] The principal city of Lesbos, where Sappho lived.

Heard the flying feet of the Loves behind her
Make a sudden thunder upon the waters,
As the thunder flung from the strong unclosing
Wings of a great wind. 20

So the goddess fled from her place, with awful
Sound of feet and thunder of wings around her;
While behind a clamour of singing women
Severed the twilight.

Ah the singing, ah the delight, the passion! 25
All the Loves wept, listening; sick with anguish,
Stood the crowned nine Muses about Apollo;[3]
Fear was upon them,

While the tenth[4] sang wonderful things they knew not.
Ah the tenth, the Lesbian! the nine were silent, 30
None endured the sound of her song for weeping;
Laurel by laurel,

Faded all their crowns; but about her forehead,
Round her woven tresses and ashen temples
White as dead snow, paler than grass in summer, 35
Ravaged with kisses,

Shone a light of fire as a crown for ever.
Yea, almost the implacable Aphrodite
Paused, and almost wept; such a song was that song.
Yea, by her name too 40

Called her, saying, "Turn to me, O my Sappho;"
Yet she turned her face from the Loves, she saw not
Tears for laughter darken immortal eyelids,
Heard not about her

Fearful fitful wings of the doves departing, 45
Saw not how the bosom of Aphrodite
Shook with the weeping, saw not her shaken raiment,
Saw not her hands wrung;

[3] The nine Muses were goddesses of arts and sciences. Apollo, the god of light and medicine, became the most widely worshipped Greek god. [4] Sappho was often called the tenth muse.

Saw the Lesbians kissing across their smitten
Lutes with lips more sweet than the sound of lute-strings, 50
Mouth to mouth and hand upon hand, her chosen,
Fairer than all men;

Only saw the beautiful lips and fingers,
Full of songs and kisses and little whispers,
Full of music; only beheld among them 55
Soar, as a bird soars

Newly fledged, her visible song, a marvel,
Made of perfect sound and exceeding passion,
Sweetly shapen, terrible, full of thunders,
Clothed with the wind's wings. 60

Then rejoiced she, laughing with love, and scattered
Roses, awful roses of holy blossom;
Then the Loves thronged sadly with hidden faces
Round Aphrodite,

Then the Muses, stricken at heart, were silent; 65
Yea, the gods waxed pale; such a song was that song.
All reluctant, all with a fresh repulsion,
Fled from before her.

All withdrew long since, and the land was barren,
Full of fruitless women and music only. 70
Now perchance, when winds are assuaged at sunset,
Lulled at the dewfall,

By the grey sea-side, unassuaged, unheard-of,
Unbeloved, unseen in the ebb of twilight,
Ghosts of outcast women return lamenting, 75
Purged not in Lethe,[5]

Clothed about with flame and with tears, and singing
Songs that move the heart of the shaken heaven,
Songs that break the heart of the earth with pity,
Hearing, to hear them. 80

[5] The river of Hades, whose waters bring forgetfulness.

THOMAS HARDY

1840–1928

THE SUBALTERNS

I

"Poor wanderer," said the leaden sky,
    "I fain would lighten thee,
But there are laws in force on high
    Which say it must not be."

II

—"I would not freeze thee, shorn one," cried   5
    The North, "knew I but how
To warm my breath, to slack my stride;
    But I am ruled as thou."

III

—"To-morrow I attack thee, wight,"
    Said Sickness. "Yet I swear   10
I bear thy little ark no spite,
    But am bid enter there."

IV

—"Come hither, Son," I heard Death say;
    "I did not will a grave
Should end thy pilgrimage to-day,   15
    But I, too, am a slave!"

V

We smiled upon each other then,
    And life to me had less
Of that fell look it wore ere when
    They owned their passiveness.   20

WIVES IN THE SERE[1]

I

Never a careworn wife but shows,
  If a joy suffuse her,
Something beautiful to those
  Patient to peruse her,
Some one charm the world unknows 5
  Precious to a muser,
Haply what, ere years were foes,
  Moved her mate to choose her.

II

But, be it a hint of rose
  That an instant hues her, 10
Or some early light or pose
  Wherewith thought renews her—
Seen by him at full, ere woes
  Practised to abuse her—
Sparely comes it, swiftly goes, 15
  Time again subdues her.

THE LACKING SENSE

SCENE.—*A sad-coloured landscape, Waddon Vale*

I

"O Time, whence comes the Mother's moody look amid her labours,
  As of one who all unwittingly has wounded where she loves?
  Why weaves she not her world-webs to according lutes and tabors,[1]
  With nevermore this too remorseful air upon her face,
    As of angel fallen from grace?" 5

II

—"Her look is but her story: construe not its symbols keenly:
  In her wonderworks yea surely has she wounded where she loves.
The sense of ills misdealt for blisses blanks the mien most queenly,
  Self-smitings kill self-joys; and everywhere beneath the sun
    Such deeds her hands have done." 10

[1] The adjective *sere* is used as a noun; the title means "wives growing old" or "withering."

[1] Lutes and tabors in accord (with her weaving).

III

—"And how explains thy Ancient Mind her crimes upon her creatures,
These fallings from her fair beginnings, woundings where she loves,
Into her would-be perfect motions, modes, effects, and features
Admitting cramps, black humours, wan decay, and baleful blights,
Distress into delights?" 15

IV

—"Ah! knowest thou not her secret yet, her vainly veiled deficience,
Whence it comes that all unwittingly she wounds the lives she loves?
That sightless are those orbs[2] of hers?—which bar to her omniscience
Brings those fearful unfulfilments, that red ravage through her zones[3]
Whereat all creation groans. 20

V

"She whispers it in each pathetic strenuous slow endeavour,
When in mothering she unwittingly sets wounds on what she loves;
Yet her primal doom pursues her, faultful, fatal is she ever;
Though so deft and nigh to vision is her facile[4] finger-touch
That the seers marvel much. 25

VI

"Deal, then, her groping skill no scorn, no note of malediction;
Not long on thee will press the hand that hurts the lives it loves;
And while she plods dead-reckoning on, in darkness of affliction,
Assist her where thy creaturely dependence can or may,
For thou art of her clay." 30

THE DARKLING[1] THRUSH

I leant upon a coppice gate
When Frost was spectre-gray,
And Winter's dregs made desolate
The weakening eye of day.
The tangled bine-stems[2] scored the sky 5
Like strings of broken lyres,
And all mankind that haunted nigh[3]
Had sought their household fires.

[2] Eyes. [3] From astronomy, the areas in which she moves. [4] Assured, poised.

[1] In the dark. [2] Stems of woodbine. [3] Lived nearby.

The land's sharp features seemed to be
    The Century's corpse outleant,[4]
His crypt the cloudy canopy,
    The wind his death-lament.
The ancient pulse of germ and birth
    Was shrunken hard and dry,
And every spirit upon earth
    Seemed fervourless as I.

At once a voice arose among
    The bleak twigs overhead
In a full-hearted evensong
    Of joy illimited;[5]
An aged thrush, frail, gaunt, and small,
    In blast-beruffled[6] plume,
Had chosen thus to fling his soul
    Upon the growing gloom.

So little cause for carolings
    Of such ecstatic sound
Was written on terrestrial things
    Afar or nigh around,
That I could think there trembled through
    His happy good-night air
Some blessed Hope, whereof he knew
    And I was unaware.

THE VOICE

Woman much missed, how you call to me, call to me,
Saying that now you are not as you were
When you had changed from the one who was all to me.
But as at first, when our day was fair.

Can it be you that I hear? Let me view you, then,
Standing as when I drew near to the town
Where you would wait for me: yes, as I knew you then,
Even to the original air-blue gown!

Or is it only the breeze, in its listlessness
Travelling across the wet mead to me here,

[4] Outlined. [5] Unlimited. [6] Windblown.

You being ever dissolved to wan wistlessness,[1]
Heard no more again far or near?

Thus I; faltering forward,
Leaves around me falling,
Wind oozing thin through the thorn from norward,[2] 15
And the woman calling.

THE FIVE STUDENTS

The sparrow dips in his wheel-rut bath,
The sun grows passionate-eyed,
And boils the dew to smoke by the paddock-path;
As strenuously we stride,—
Five of us; dark He, fair He, dark She, fair She, I, 5
All beating by.

The air is shaken, the high-road hot,
Shadowless swoons the day,
The greens are sobered and cattle at rest; but not
We on our urgent way,— 10
Four of us; fair She, dark She, fair He, I, are there,
But one—elsewhere.

Autumn moulds the hard fruit mellow,
And forward still we press
Through moors, briar-meshed plantations, clay-pits yellow, 15
As in the spring hours—yes,
Three of us; fair He, fair She, I, as heretofore,
But—fallen one more.

The leaf drops: earthworms draw it in
At night-time noiselessly, 20
The fingers of birch and beech are skeleton-thin,
And yet on the beat are we,—
Two of us; fair She, I. But no more left to go
The track we know.

Icicles tag the church-aisle leads,[1] 25
The flag-rope gibbers hoarse,

[1] Inattentiveness. [2] Northward.

[1] Sheets of lead forming the roof.

The home-bound foot-folk wrap their snow-flaked heads,
Yet I still stalk the course—
One of us. . . . Dark and fair He, dark and fair She, gone
The rest—anon. 30

"WHO'S IN THE NEXT ROOM?"

"Who's in the next room?—who?
I seemed to see
Somebody in the dawning passing through,
Unkown to me."
"Nay: you saw nought. He passed invisibly." 5

"Who's in the next room?—who?
I seem to hear
Somebody muttering firm in a language new
That chills the ear."
"No: you catch not his tongue who has entered there." 10

"Who's in the next room?—who?
I seem to feel
His breath like a clammy draught, as if it drew
From the Polar Wheel."
"No: none who breathes at all does the door conceal." 15

"Who's in the next room?—who?
A figure wan
With a message to one in there of something due?
Shall I know him anon?"
"Yea he; and he brought such; and you'll know him anon." 20

AFTERWARDS

When the Present has latched its postern behind my tremulous stay,
And the May month flaps its glad green leaves like wings,
Delicate-filmed as new-spun silk, will the neighbours say,
"He was a man who used to notice such things"?

If it be in the dusk when, like an eyelid's soundless blink, 5
The dewfall-hawk comes crossing the shades to alight
Upon the wind-warped upland thorn, a gazer may think,
"To him this must have been a familiar sight."

If I pass during some nocturnal blackness, mothy and warm,
When the hedgehog travels furtively over the lawn, 10
One may say, "He strove that such innocent creatures should come to no harm,
But he could do little for them; and now he is gone."

If, when hearing that I have been stilled at last, they stand at the door,
Watching the full-starred heavens that winter sees,
Will this thought rise on those who will meet my face no more, 15
"He was one who had an eye for such mysteries"?

And will any say when my bell of quittance is heard in the gloom,
And a crossing breeze cuts a pause in its outrollings,
Till they rise again, as they were a new bell's boom,
"He hears it not now, but used to notice such things?" 20

GERARD MANLEY HOPKINS

1844–1889

SPRING AND FALL

To a Young Child

Márgarét, are you gríeving
Over Goldengrove unleaving?
Leáves, líke the things of man, you
With your fresh thoughts care for, can you?
Áh! ás the heart grows older 5
It will come to such sights colder
By and by, nor spare a sigh
Though worlds of wanwood leafmeal[1] lie;
And yet you wíll weep and know why.
Now no matter, child, the name: 10
Sórrow's spríngs áre the same.
Nor mouth had, no nor mind, expressed
What heart heard of, ghost guessed:
It ís the blight man was born for,
It is Margaret you mourn for. 15

[1] Words Hopkins coined to suggest faded leaves fallen to the ground.

THE WINDHOVER[1]

To Christ Our Lord

I caught this morning morning's minion,[2] king-
    dom of daylight's dauphin,[3] dapple-dawn-drawn Falcon, in his riding
    Of the rolling level underneath him steady air, and striding
High there, how he rung[4] upon the rein of a wimpling[5] wing
In his ecstasy! then off, off forth on swing, 5
    As a skate's heel sweeps smooth on a bow-bend: the hurl and gliding
    Rebuffed the big wind. My heart in hiding
Stirred for a bird,—the achieve of, the mastery of the thing!

Brute beauty and valour and act, oh, air, pride, plume here
    Buckle! AND the fire that breaks from thee then, a billion 10
Times told lovelier, more dangerous, O my chevalier!

    No wonder of it: shéer plód makes plough down sillion[6]
Shine, and blue-bleak embers, ah my dear,
    Fall, gall themselves, and gash gold-vermilion.

PIED BEAUTY

Glory be to God for dappled things—
    For skies of couple-colour as a brinded cow;
        For rose-moles all in stipple upon trout that swim;
Fresh-firecoal chestnut-falls; finches' wings;
    Landscape plotted and pieced—fold,[1] fallow, and plough; 5
        And áll trádes, their gear and tackle and trim.

All things counter, original, spare, strange;
    Whatever is fickle, freckled (who knows how?)
        With swift, slow; sweet, sour; adazzle, dim;
He fathers-forth whose beauty is past change: 10
                Praise him.

[1] A small falcon that hovers in the air against the wind. The male is bluish gray. [2] Darling, favorite. [3] Prince. [4] Coined word suggesting both *wrung* and *reined*. [5] Rippling. [6] A word coined from French *sillon,* furrow created by a plough.

[1] An undulation in the landscape.

CARRION COMFORT

Not, I'll not, carrion comfort, Despair, not feast on thee;
Not untwist—slack they may be—these last strands of man
In me ór, most weary, cry *I can no more*. I can;
Can something, hope, wish day come, not choose not to be.
But ah, but O thou terrible, why wouldst thou rude on me 5
Thy wring-world right foot rock? lay a lionlimb against me? scan
With darksome devouring eyes my bruisèd bones? and fan,
O in turns of tempest, me heaped there; me frantic to avoid thee and flee?

Why? That my chaff might fly; my grain lie, sheer and clear.
Nay in all that toil, that coil, since (seems) I kissed the rod,[1] 10
Hand rather, my heart lo! lapped strength, stole joy, would laugh, chéer.
Cheer whom though? the hero whose heaven-handling flung me, fóot tród
Me? or me that fought him? O which one? is it each one? That night, that year
Of now done darkness I wretch lay wrestling with (my God!) my God.

A. E. HOUSMAN

1859–1936

LOVELIEST OF TREES

Loveliest of trees, the cherry now
Is hung with bloom along the bough,
And stands about the woodland ride
Wearing white for Eastertide.

Now, of my threescore years and ten, 5
Twenty will not come again,
And take from seventy springs a score,
It only leaves me fifty more.

And since to look at things in bloom
Fifty springs are little room, 10

[1] Willingly submitted to punishment or correction.

About the woodlands I will go
To see the cherry hung with snow.

BE STILL, MY SOUL, BE STILL

Be still, my soul, be still; the arms you bear are brittle,
    Earth and high heaven are fixt of old and founded strong.
Think rather,—call to thought, if now you grieve a little,
    The days when we had rest, O soul, for they were long.

Men loved unkindness then, but lightless in the quarry 5
    I slept and saw not; tears fell down, I did not mourn;
Sweat ran and blood sprang out and I was never sorry:
    Then it was well with me, in days ere I was born.

Now, and I muse for why and never find the reason,
    I pace the earth, and drink the air, and feel the sun. 10
Be still, be still, my soul; it is but for a season:
    Let us endure an hour and see injustice done.

Ay, look: high heaven and earth ail from the prime foundation;
    All thoughts to rive the heart are here, and all are vain:
Horror and scorn and hate and fear and indignation— 15
    Oh why did I awake? when shall I sleep again?

RUDYARD KIPLING

1865–1936

DANNY DEEVER

"What are the bugles blowin' for?" said Files-on-Parade.
"To turn you out, to turn you out," the Colour-Sergeant said.
"What makes you look so white, so white?" said Files-on-Parade.

"I'm dreadin' what I've got to watch," the Colour-Sergeant said.
For they're hangin Danny Deaver, you can hear the Dead March play, 5
The Regiment's in 'ollow square—they're hangin' him to-day:
They've taken of his buttons off an' cut his stripes away,
An' they're hangin' Danny Deever in the mornin'.

"What makes the rear-rank breathe so 'ard?" said Files-on-Parade.
"It's bitter cold, it's bitter cold," the Colour-Sergeant said. 10
"What makes that front-rank man fall down?" said Files-on-Parade.
"A touch o' sun, a touch o' sun," the Colour-Sergeant said.
They are hangin' Danny Deever, they are marchin' of 'im round,
They 'ave 'alted Danny Deever by 'is coffin on the ground;
An' 'e'll swing in 'arf a minute for a sneakin' shootin' hound— 15
O they're hangin' Danny Deever in the mornin'!

" 'Is cot was right-'and cot to mine," said Files-on-Parade.
" 'E's sleepin' out an' far to-night," the Colour-Sergeant said.
"I've drunk 'is beer a score o' times," said Files-on-Parade.
" 'E's drinkin' bitter beer alone," the Colour-Sergeant said. 20
They are hangin' Danny Deever, you must mark 'im to 'is place,
For 'e shot a comrade sleepin'—you must look 'im in the face;
Nine 'undred of 'is county an' the Regiment's disgrace,
While they're hangin' Danny Deever in the mornin'.

"What's that so black agin the sun?" said Files-on-Parade. 25
"It's Danny fightin' 'ard for life," the Colour-Sergeant said.
"What's that that whimpers over'ead?" said Files-on-Parade.
"It's Danny's soul that's passin' now," the Colour-Sergeant said.
For they're done with Danny Deever, you can 'ear the quickstep play,
The Regiment's in column, an' they're marchin' us away; 30
Ho! the young recruits are shakin', an' they'll want their beer to-day,
After hangin' Danny Deever in the mornin'!

RECESSIONAL

God of our fathers, known of old,
Lord of our far-flung battle-line,
Beneath whose awful Hand we hold
Dominion over palm and pine—
Lord God of Hosts, be with us yet, 5
Lest we forget—lest we forget!

The tumult and the shouting dies;
 The captains and the kings depart:
Still stands Thine ancient sacrifice,
 An humble and a contrite heart. 10
Lord God of Hosts, be with us yet,
Lest we forget—lest we forget!

Far-called, our navies melt away;
 On dune and headland sinks the fire:
Lo, all our pomp of yesterday 15
 Is one with Nineveh and Tyre![1]
Judge of the Nations, spare us yet,
Lest we forget—lest we forget!

If, drunk with sight of power, we loose
 Wild tongues that have not Thee in awe, 20
Such boastings as the Gentiles[2] use,
 Or lesser breeds without the Law—
Lord God of Hosts, be with us yet,
Lest we forget—lest we forget!

For heathen heart that puts her trust 25
 In reeking tube and iron shard,
All valiant dust that builds on dust,
 And guarding, calls not Thee to guard,
For frantic boast and foolish word—
Thy mercy on Thy People, Lord! 30

WILLIAM BUTLER YEATS

1865–1939

BYZANTIUM

The unpurged images of day recede;
The Emperor's drunken soldiery are abed;
Night resonance recedes, night-walkers' song

[1] Nineveh was the last capital of the ancient Assyrian Empire and Tyre, the most important city of ancient Phoenicia. [2] Heathens, pagans, "the unchosen."

After great cathedral gong;
A starlit or a moonlit dome disdains 5
All that man is,
All mere complexities,
The fury and the mire of human veins.

Before me floats an image, man or shade,
Shade more than man, more image than a shade; 10
For Hades' bobbin bound in mummy-cloth
May unwind the winding path;
A mouth that has no moisture and no breath
Breathless mouths may summon;
I hail the superhuman; 15
I call it death-in-life and life-in-death.

Miracle, bird or golden handiwork,
More miracle than bird or handiwork,
Planted on the star-lit golden bough,
Can like the cocks of Hades crow, 20
Or, by the moon embittered, scorn aloud
In glory of changeless metal
Common bird or petal
And all complexities of mire or blood.

At midnight on the Emperor's pavement flit 25
Flames that no faggot feeds, nor steel has lit,
Nor storm disturbs, flames begotten of flame,
Where blood-begotten spirits come
And all complexities of fury leave,
Dying into a dance, 30
An agony of trance,
An agony of flame that cannot singe a sleeve.

Astraddle on the dolphin's mire and blood,
Spirit after spirit! The smithies break the flood,
The golden smithies of the Emperor! 35
Marbles of the dancing floor
Break bitter furies of complexity,
Those images that yet
Fresh images beget,
That dolphin-torn, that gong-tormented sea. 40

LEDA AND THE SWAN

A sudden blow: the great wings beating still
Above the staggering girl, her thighs caressed
By the dark webs, her nape caught in his bill,
He holds her helpless breast upon his breast.

How can those terrified vague fingers push 5
The feathered glory from her loosening thighs?
And how can body, laid in that white rush,
But feel the strange heart beating where it lies?

A shudder in the loins engenders there
The broken wall, the burning roof and tower 10
And Agamemnon dead.
Being so caught up,
So mastered by the brute blood of the air,
Did she put on his knowledge with his power
Before the indifferent beak could let her drop?

THE SECOND COMING

Turning and turning in the widening gyre
The falcon cannot hear the falconer;
Things fall apart; the centre cannot hold;
Mere anarchy is loosed upon the world,
The blood-dimmed tide is loosed, and everywhere 5
The ceremony of innocence is drowned;
The best lack all conviction, while the worst
Are full of passionate intensity.

Surely some revelation is at hand;
Surely the Second Coming is at hand. 10
The Second Coming! Hardly are those words out
When a vast image out of *Spiritus Mundi*
Troubles my sight: somewhere in sands of the desert
A shape with lion body and the head of a man,
A gaze blank and pitiless as the sun, 15
Is moving its slow thighs, while all about it
Reel shadows of the indignant desert birds.
The darkness drops again; but now I know
That twenty centuries of stony sleep
Were vexed to nightmare by a rocking cradle, 20

And what rough beast, its hour come round at last,
Slouches towards Bethlehem to be born?

A PRAYER FOR MY DAUGHTER

Once more the storm is howling, and half hid
Under this cradle-hood and coverlid
My child sleeps on. There is no obstacle
But Gregory's wood and one bare hill
Whereby the haystack- and roof-levelling wind, 5
Bred on the Atlantic, can be stayed;
And for an hour I have walked and prayed
Because of the great gloom that is in my mind.

I have walked and prayed for this young child an hour
And heard the sea-wind scream upon the tower, 10
And under the arches of the bridge, and scream
In the elms above the flooded stream;
Imagining in excited reverie
That the future years had come,
Dancing to a frenzied drum, 15
Out of the murderous innocence of the sea.

May she be granted beauty and yet not
Beauty to make a stranger's eye distraught,
Or hers before a looking-glass, for such,
Being made beautiful overmuch, 20
Consider beauty a sufficient end,
Lose natural kindness and maybe
The heart-revealing intimacy
That chooses right, and never find a friend.

Helen being chosen found life flat and dull 25
And later had much trouble from a fool,
While that great Queen, that rose out of the spray,
Being fatherless could have her way
Yet chose a bandy-leggèd smith for man.
It's certain that fine women eat 30
A crazy salad with their meat
Whereby the Horn of Plenty is undone.

In courtesy I'd have her chiefly learned;
Hearts are not had as a gift but hearts are earned

By those that are not entirely beautiful; 35
Yet many, that have played the fool
For beauty's very self, has charm made wise,
And many a poor man that has roved,
Loved and thought himself beloved,
From a glad kindness cannot take his eyes. 40

May she become a flourishing hidden tree
That all her thoughts may like the linnet be,
And have no business but dispensing round
Their magnanimities of sound,
Nor but in merriment begin a chase, 45
Nor but in merriment a quarrel.
O may she live like some green laurel
Rooted in one dear perpetual place.

My mind, because the minds that I have loved,
The sort of beauty that I have approved, 50
Prosper but little, has dried up of late,
Yet knows that to be choked with hate
May well be of all evil chances chief.
If there's no hatred in a mind
Assault and battery of the wind 55
Can never tear the linnet from the leaf.

An intellectual hatred is the worst,
So let her think opinions are accursed.
Have I not seen the loveliest woman born
Out of the mouth of Plenty's horn, 60
Because of her opinionated mind
Barter that horn and every good
By quiet natures understood
For an old bellows full of angry wind?

Considering that, all hatred driven hence, 65
The soul recovers radical innocence
And learns at last that it is self-delighting,
Self-appeasing, self-affrighting,
And that its own sweet will is Heaven's will;
She can, though every face should scowl 70
And every windy quarter howl
Or every bellows burst, be happy still.

And may her bridegroom bring her to a house
Where all's accustomed, ceremonious;

For arrogance and hatred are the wares
Peddled in the thoroughfares.
How but in custom and in ceremony
Are innocence and beauty born?
Ceremony's a name for the rich horn,
And custom for the spreading laurel tree. 80

EDWIN ARLINGTON ROBINSON

1869–1935

LUKE HAVERGAL

Go to the western gate, Luke Havergal,
There where the vines cling crimson on the wall,
And in the twilight wait for what will come.
The leaves will whisper there of her, and some,
Like flying words, will strike you as they fall; 5
But go, and if you listen she will call.
Go to the western gate, Luke Havergal—
Luke Havergal.

No, there is not a dawn in eastern skies
To rift the fiery night that's in your eyes; 10
But there, where western glooms are gathering,
The dark will end the dark, if anything:
God slays Himself with every leaf that flies,
And hell is more than half of paradise.
No, there is not a dawn in eastern skies— 15
In eastern skies.

Out of a grave I come to tell you this,
Out of a grave I come to quench the kiss
That flames upon your forehead with a glow
That blinds you to the way that you must go. 20

Yes, there is yet one way to where she is,
Bitter, but one that faith may never miss.
Out of a grave I come to tell you this—
To tell you this.

There is the western gate, Luke Havergal, 25
There are the crimson leaves upon the wall.
Go, for the winds are tearing them away—
Nor think to riddle the dead words they say,
Nor any more to feel them as they fall;
But go, and if you trust her she will call. 30
There is the western gate, Luke Havergal—
Luke Havergal.

MINIVER CHEEVY

Miniver Cheevy, child of scorn,
    Grew lean while he assailed the seasons;
He wept that he was ever born,
    And he had reasons.

Miniver loved the days of old 5
    When swords were bright and steeds were prancing.
The vision of a warrior bold
    Would set him dancing.

Miniver sighed for what was not,
    And dreamed, and rested from his labors; 10
He dreamed of Thebes and Camelot,
    And Priam's neighbors.

Miniver mourned the ripe renown
    That made so many a name so fragrant;
He mourned Romance, now on the town, 15
    And Art, a vagrant.

Miniver loved the Medici,
    Albeit he had never seen one;
He would have sinned incessantly
    Could he have been one. 20

Miniver cursed the commonplace
    And eyed a khaki suit with loathing;
He missed the mediæval grace
    Of iron clothing.

Miniver scorned the gold he sought, 25
    But sore annoyed was he without it;
Miniver thought, and thought, and thought,
    And thought about it.

Miniver Cheevy, born too late,
    Scratched his head and kept on thinking: 30
Miniver coughed, and called it fate,
    And kept on drinking.

MR. FLOOD'S PARTY

Old Eben Flood, climbing alone one night
Over the hill between the town below
And the forsaken upland hermitage
That held as much as he should ever know
On earth again of home, paused warily. 5
The road was his with not a native near;
And Eben, having leisure, said aloud,
For no man else in Tilbury Town to hear:

"Well, Mr. Flood, we have the harvest moon
Again, and we may not have many more; 10
The bird is on the wing, the poet says,
And you and I have said it here before.
Drink to the bird." He raised up to the light
The jug that he had gone so far to fill,
And answered huskily: "Well, Mr. Flood, 15
Since you propose it, I believe I will."

Alone, as if enduring to the end
A valiant armor of scarred hopes outworn,
He stood there in the middle of the road
Like Roland's ghost winding a silent horn. 20
Below him, in the town among the trees,
Where friends of other days had honored him,

A phantom salutation of the dead
Rang thinly till old Eben's eyes were dim.

Then, as a mother lays her sleeping child 25
Down tenderly, fearing it may awake,
He set the jug down slowly at his feet
With trembling care, knowing that most things break;
And only when assured that on firm earth
It stood, as the uncertain lives of men 30
Assuredly did not, he paced away,
And with his hand extended paused again:

"Well, Mr. Flood, we have not met like this
In a long time; and many a change has come
To both of us, I fear, since last it was 35
We had a drop together. Welcome home!"
Convivially returning with himself,
Again he raised the jug up to the light;
And with an acquiescent quaver said:
"Well, Mr. Flood, if you insist, I might. 40

"Only a very little, Mr. Flood—
For auld lang syne. No more, sir; that will do."
So, for the time, apparently it did,
And Eben evidently thought so too;
For soon amid the silver loneliness 45
Of night he lifted up his voice and sang,
Secure, with only two moons listening,
Until the whole harmonious landscape rang—
"For auld lang syne." The weary throat gave out,
The last word wavered; and the song being done, 50
He raised again the jug regretfully
And shook his head, and was again alone.
There was not much that was ahead of him,
And there was nothing in the town below—
Where strangers would have shut the many doors 55
That many friends had opened long ago.

WALTER DE LA MARE

1873–1956

THE LISTENERS

"Is there anybody there?" said the Traveller,
Knocking on the moonlit door;
And his horse in the silence champed the grasses
Of the forest's ferny floor:
And a bird flew up out of the turret, 5
Above the Traveller's head:
And he smote upon the door again a second time;
"Is there anybody there?" he said.
But no one descended to the Traveller;
No head from the leaf-fringed sill 10
Leaned over and looked into his grey eyes,
Where he stood perplexed and still.
But only a host of phantom listeners
That dwelt in the lone house then
Stood listening in the quiet of the moonlight 15
To that voice from the world of men:
Stood thronging the faint moonbeams on the dark stair,
That goes down to the empty hall,
Hearkening in an air stirred and shaken
By the lonely Traveller's call. 20
And he felt in his heart their strangeness,
Their stillness answering his cry,
While his horse moved, cropping the dark turf,
'Neath the starred and leafy sky;
For he suddenly smote on the door, even 25
Louder, and lifted his head:—
"Tell them I came, and no one answered,
That I kept my word," he said.
Never the least stir made the listeners,
Though every word he spake 30
Fell echoing through the shadowiness of the still house
From the one man left awake:
Ay, they heard his foot upon the stirrup,
And the sound of iron on stone,
And how the silence surged softly backward, 35
When the plunging hoofs were gone.

ROBERT FROST

1874–1963

HOME BURIAL

He saw her from the bottom of the stairs
Before she saw him. She was starting down,
Looking back over her shoulder at some fear.
She took a doubtful step and then undid it
To raise herself and look again. He spoke 5
Advancing toward her: 'What is it you see
From up there always—for I want to know.'
She turned and sank upon her skirts at that,
And her face changed from terrified to dull.
He said to gain time: 'What is it you see,' 10
Mounting until she cowered under him.
'I will find out now—you must tell me, dear.'
She, in her place, refused him any help
With the least stiffening of her neck and silence.
She let him look, sure that he wouldn't see, 15
Blind creature, and awhile he didn't see.
But at last he murmured, 'Oh,' and again, 'Oh.'

'What is it—what?' she said.

'Just that I see.'

'You don't,' she challenged. 'Tell me what it is.'

'The wonder is I didn't see at once. 20
I never noticed it from here before.
I must be wonted to it—that's the reason.
The little graveyard where my people are!
So small the window frames the whole of it.
Not so much larger than a bedroom, is it? 25
There are three stones of slate and one of marble,
Broad-shouldered little slabs there in the sunlight
On the sidehill. We haven't to mind *those*.
But I understand: it is not the stones,
But the child's mound—'

'Don't, don't, don't, don't,' she cried. 30

She withdrew shrinking from beneath his arm
That rested on the bannister, and slid downstairs;
And turned on him with such a daunting look,
He said twice over before he knew himself:
'Can't a man speak of his own child he's lost?' 35

'Not you! Oh, where's my hat? Oh, I don't need it!
I must get out of here. I must get air.
I don't know rightly whether any man can.'

'Amy! Don't go to someone else this time.
Listen to me. I won't come down the stairs.' 40
He sat and fixed his chin between his fists.
'There's something I should like to ask you, dear.'

'You don't know how to ask it.'

'Help me, then.'

Her fingers moved the latch for all reply.

'My words are nearly always an offense. 45
I don't know how to speak of anything
So as to please you. But I might be taught
I should suppose. I can't say I see how.
A man must partly give up being a man
With women-folk. We could have some arrangement 50
By which I'd bind myself to keep hands off
Anything special you're a-mind to name.
Though I don't like such things 'twixt those that love.
Two that don't love can't live together without them.
But two that do can't live together with them.' 55
She moved the latch a little. 'Don't—don't go.
Don't carry it to someone else this time.
Tell me about it if it's something human.
Let me into your grief. I'm not so much
Unlike other folks as your standing there 60
Apart would make me out. Give me my chance.
I do think, though, you overdo it a little.
What was it brought you up to think it the thing

To take your mother-loss of a first child
So inconsolably—in the face of love. 65
You'd think his memory might be satisfied—'

'There you go sneering now!'

'I'm not, I'm not!
You make me angry. I'll come down to you.
God, what a woman! And it's come to this,
A man can't speak of his own child that's dead.' 70

'You can't because you don't know how to speak.
If you had any feelings, you that dug
With your own hand—how could you?—his little grave;
I saw you from that very window there,
Making the gravel leap and leap in air, 75
Leap up, like that, like that, and land so lightly
And roll back down the mound beside the hole.
I thought, Who is that man? I didn't know you.
And I crept down the stairs and up the stairs
To look again, and still your spade kept lifting. 80
Then you came in. I heard your rumbling voice
Out in the kitchen, and I don't know why,
But I went near to see with my own eyes.
You could sit there with the stains on your shoes
Of the fresh earth from your own baby's grave 85
And talk about your everyday concerns.
You had stood the spade up against the wall
Outside there in the entry, for I saw it.'

'I shall laugh the worst laugh I ever laughed.
I'm cursed. God, if I don't believe I'm cursed. 90

'I can repeat the very words you were saying.
"Three foggy mornings and one rainy day
Will rot the best birch fence a man can build."
Think of it, talk like that at such a time!
What had how long it takes a birch to rot 95
To do with what was in the darkened parlor.
You *couldn't* care! The nearest friends can go
With anyone to death, comes so far short
They might as well not try to go at all.
No, from the time when one is sick to death, 100
One is alone, and he dies more alone.

Friends make pretense of following to the grave,
But before one is in it, their minds are turned
And making the best of their way back to life
And living people, and things they understand.   105
But the world's evil. I won't have grief so
If I can change it. Oh, I won't, I won't!'

'There, you have said it all and you feel better.
You won't go now. You're crying. Close the door.
The heart's gone out of it: why keep it up.   110
Amy! There's someone coming down the road!'

'*You*—oh, you think the talk is all. I must go—
Somewhere out of this house. How can I make you—'

'If—you—do!' She was opening the door wider.
'Where do you mean to go? First tell me that.   115
I'll follow and bring you back by force. I *will!*—'

STOPPING BY WOODS ON A SNOWY EVENING

Whose woods these are I think I know
His house is in the village though;
He will not see me stopping here
To watch his woods fill up with snow.

My little horse must think it queer   5
To stop without a farmhouse near
Between the woods and frozen lake
The darkest evening of the year.

He gives his harness bells a shake
To ask if there is some mistake.   10
The only other sound's the sweep
Of easy wind and downy flake.

The woods are lovely, dark and deep,
But I have promises to keep,

And miles to go before I sleep, 15
And miles to go before I sleep.

DESIGN

I found a dimpled spider, fat and white,
On a white heal-all, holding up a moth
Like a white piece of rigid satin cloth—
Assorted characters of death and blight
Mixed ready to begin the morning right, 5
Like the ingredients of a witches' broth—
A snow-drop spider, a flower like a froth,
And dead wings carried like a paper kite.

What had that flower to do with being white, 10
The wayside blue and innocent heal-all?
What brought the kindred spider to that height,
Then steered the white moth thither in the night?
What but design of darkness to appall?—
If design govern in a thing so small? 15

PROVIDE, PROVIDE

The witch that came (the withered hag)
To wash the steps with pail and rag,
Was once the beauty Abishag,

The picture pride of Hollywood.
Too many fall from great and good 5
For you to doubt the likelihood.

Die early and avoid the fate.
Or if predestined to die late,
Make up your mind to die in state.

Make the whole stock exchange your own! 10
If need be occupy a throne,
Where nobody can call *you* crone.

Some have relied on what they knew;
Others on being simply true.
What worked for them might work for you. 15

No memory of having starred
Atones for later disregard,
Or keeps the end from being hard.

Better to go down dignified
With boughten friendship at your side 20
Than none at all. Provide, provide!

DIRECTIVE

Back out of all this now too much for us,
Back in a time made simple by the loss
Of detail, burned, dissolved, and broken off
Like graveyard marble sculpture in the weather,
There is a house that is no more a house 5
Upon a farm that is no more a farm
And in a town that is no more a town.
The road there, if you'll let a guide direct you
Who only has at heart your getting lost,
May seem as if it should have been a quarry— 10
Great monolithic knees the former town
Long since gave up pretense of keeping covered.
And there's a story in a book about it:
Besides the wear of iron wagon wheels
The ledges show lines ruled southeast northwest, 15
The chisel work of an enormous Glacier
That braced his feet against the Arctic Pole.
You must not mind a certain coolness from him
Still said to haunt this side of Panther Mountain.
Nor need you mind the serial ordeal 20
Of being watched from forty cellar holes
As if by eye pairs out of forty firkins.
As for the woods' excitement over you
That sends light rustle rushes to their leaves,
Charge that to upstart inexperience. 25
Where were they all not twenty years ago?
They think too much of having shaded out
A few old pecker-fretted apple trees.
Make yourself up a cheering song of how
Someone's road home from work this once was, 30
Who may be just ahead of you on foot
Or creaking with a buggy load of grain.

The height of the adventure is the height
Of country where two village cultures faded
Into each other. Both of them are lost. 35
And if you're lost enough to find yourself
By now, pull in your ladder road behind you
And put a sign up CLOSED to all but me.
Then make yourself at home. The only field
Now left's no bigger than a harness gall. 40
First there's the children's house of make believe,
Some shattered dishes underneath a pine,
The playthings in the playhouse of the children.
Weep for what little things could make them glad.
Then for the house that is no more a house, 45
But only a belilaced cellar hole,
Now slowly closing like a dent in dough.
This was no playhouse but a house in earnest.
Your destination and your destiny's
A brook that was the water of the house, 50
Cold as a spring as yet so near its source,
Too lofty and original to rage.
(We know the valley streams that when aroused
Will leave their tatters hung on barb and thorn.)
I have kept hidden in the instep arch 55
Of an old cedar at the waterside
A broken drinking goblet like the Grail
Under a spell so the wrong ones can't find it,
So can't get saved, as Saint Mark says they mustn't.
(I stole the goblet from the children's playhouse.) 60
Here are your waters and your watering place.
Drink and be whole again beyond confusion.

WALLACE STEVENS

1879–1955

SUNDAY MORNING

I

Complacencies of the peignoir, and late
Coffee and oranges in a sunny chair,
And the green freedom of a cockatoo

Upon a rug mingle to dissipate
The holy hush of ancient sacrifice. 5
She dreams a little, and she feels the dark
Encroachment of that old catastrophe,
As a calm darkens among water-lights.
The pungent oranges and bright, green wings
Seem things in some procession of the dead, 10
Winding across wide water, without sound.
The day is like wide water, without sound,
Stilled for the passing of her dreaming feet
Over the seas, to silent Palestine,
Dominion of the blood and sepulchre. 15

2

Why should she give her bounty to the dead?
What is divinity if it can come
Only in silent shadows and in dreams?
Shall she not find in comforts of the sun,
In pungent fruit and bright, green wings, or else 20
In any balm or beauty of the earth,
Things to be cherished like the thought of heaven?
Divinity must live within herself:
Passions of rain, or moods in falling snow;
Grievings in loneliness, or unsubdued 25
Elations when the forest blooms; gusty
Emotions on wet roads on autumn nights;
All pleasures and all pains, remembering
The bough of summer and the winter branch.
These are the measures destined for her soul. 30

3

Jove in the clouds had his inhuman birth.
No mother suckled him, no sweet land gave
Large-mannered motions to his mythy mind.
He moved among us, as a muttering king,
Magnificent, would move among his hinds, 35
Until our blood, commingling, virginal,
With heaven, brought such requital to desire
The very hinds discerned it, in a star.
Shall our blood fail? Or shall it come to be
The blood of paradise? And shall the earth 40
Seem all of paradise that we shall know?
The sky will be much friendlier then than now,
A part of labor and a part of pain,
And next in glory to enduring love,
Not this dividing and indifferent blue. 45

4

She says, "I am content when wakened birds,
Before they fly, test the reality
Of misty fields, by their sweet questionings;
But when the birds are gone, and their warm fields
Return no more, where, then, is paradise?" 50
There is not any haunt of prophecy,
Nor any old chimera of the grave,
Neither the golden underground, nor isle
Melodious, where spirits gat them home,
Nor visionary south, nor cloudy palm 55
Remote on heaven's hill, that has endured
As April's green endures; or will endure
Like her remembrance of awakened birds,
Or her desire for June and evening, tipped
By the consummation of the swallow's wings. 60

5

She says, "But in contentment I still feel
The need of some imperishable bliss."
Death is the mother of beauty; hence from her,
Alone, shall come fulfilment to our dreams
And our desires. Although she strews the leaves 65
Of sure obliteration on our paths,
The path sick sorrow took, the many paths
Where triumph rang its brassy phrase, or love
Whispered a little out of tenderness,
She makes the willow shiver in the sun 70
For maidens who were wont to sit and gaze
Upon the grass, relinquished to their feet.
She causes boys to pile new plums and pears
On disregarded plate. The maidens taste
And stray impassioned in the littering leaves. 75

6

Is there no change of death in paradise?
Does ripe fruit never fall? Or do the boughs
Hang always heavy in that perfect sky,
Unchanging, yet so like our perishing earth,
With rivers like our own that seek for seas 80
They never find, the same receding shores
That never touch with inarticulate pang?
Why set the pear upon those river-banks
Or spice the shores with odors of the plum?
Alas, that they should wear our colors there, 85
The silken weavings of our afternoons,
And pick the strings of our insipid lutes!

Death is the mother of beauty, mystical,
Within whose burning bosom we devise
Our earthly mothers waiting, sleeplessly. 90

7

Supple and turbulent, a ring of men
Shall chant in orgy on a summer morn
Their boisterous devotion to the sun,
Not as a god, but as a god might be,
Naked among them, like a savage source. 95
Their chant shall be a chant of paradise,
Out of their blood, returning to the sky;
And in their chant shall enter, voice by voice,
The windy lake wherein their lord delights,
The trees, like serafin, and echoing hills, 100
That choir among themselves long afterward.
They shall know well the heavenly fellowship
Of men that perish and of summer morn.
And whence they came and whither they shall go
The dew upon their feet shall manifest. 105

8

She hears, upon that water without sound,
A voice that cries, "The tomb in Palestine
Is not the porch of spirits lingering.
It is the grave of Jesus, where he lay."
We live in an old chaos of the sun, 110
Or old dependency of day and night,
Or island solitude, unsponsored, free,
Of that wide water, inescapable.
Deer walk upon our mountains, and the quail
Whistle about us their spontaneous cries; 115
Sweet berries ripen in the wilderness;
And, in the isolation of the sky,
As evening, casual flocks of pigeons make
Ambiguous undulations as they sink,
Downward to darkness, on extended wings. 120

ANECDOTE OF THE JAR

I placed a jar in Tennessee,
And round it was, upon a hill.
It made the slovenly wilderness
Surround that hill.

The wilderness rose up to it,
And sprawled around, no longer wild.
The jar was round upon the ground
And tall and of a port in air. 5

It took dominion everywhere.
The jar was gray and bare. 10
It did not give of bird or bush,
Like nothing else in Tennessee.

PETER QUINCE AT THE CLAVIER

1

Just as my fingers on these keys
Make music, so the self-same sounds
On my spirit make a music too.

Music is feeling then, not sound;
And thus it is that what I feel, 5
Here in this room, desiring you,

Thinking of your blue-shadowed silk,
Is music. It is like the strain
Waked in the elders by Susanna:

Of a green evening, clear and warm, 10
She bathed in her still garden, while
The red-eyed elders, watching, felt

The basses of their being throb
In witching chords, and their thin blood
Pulse pizzicati of Hosanna. 15

2

In the green water, clear and warm,
Susanna lay.
She searched
The touch of springs,
And found 20
Concealed imaginings.
She sighed
For so much melody.

Upon the bank, she stood
In the cool 25

Of spent emotions.
She felt, among the leaves,
The dew
Of old devotions.

She walked upon the grass, 30
Still quavering.
The winds were like her maids,
On timid feet,
Fetching her woven scarves,
Yet wavering. 35

A breath upon her hand
Muted the night.
She turned—
A cymbal crashed,
And roaring horns. 40

3

Soon, with a noise like tambourines,
Came her attendant Byzantines.

They wondered why Susanna cried
Against the elders by her side:

And as they whispered, the refrain 45
Was like a willow swept by rain.

Anon their lamps' uplifted flame
Revealed Susanna and her shame.

And then the simpering Byzantines,
Fled, with a noise like tambourines. 50

4

Beauty is momentary in the mind—
The fitful tracing of a portal;
But in the flesh it is immortal.

The body dies; the body's beauty lives.
So evenings die, in their green going, 55
A wave, interminably flowing.
So gardens die, their meek breath scenting
The cowl of Winter, done repenting.
So maidens die to the auroral
Celebration of a maiden's choral. 60

Susanna's music touched the bawdy strings
Of those white elders; but, escaping,
Left only Death's ironic scraping.
Now in its immortality, it plays
On the clear viol of her memory, 65
And makes a constant sacrament of praise.

THIRTEEN WAYS OF LOOKING AT A BLACKBIRD

I

Among twenty snowy mountains,
The only moving thing
Was the eye of the blackbird.

II

I was of three minds,
Like a tree 5
In which there are three blackbirds.

III

The blackbird whirled in the autumn winds.
It was a small part of the pantomime.

IV

A man and a woman
Are one. 10
A man and a woman and a blackbird
Are one.

V

I do not know which to prefer,
The beauty of inflections
Or the beauty of innuendos, 15
The blackbird whistling
Or just after.

VI

Icicles filled the long window
With barbaric glass.
The shadow of the blackbird 20

Crossed it, to and fro.
The mood
Traced in the shadow
An indecipherable cause.

VII

O thin men of Haddam, 25
Why do you imagine golden birds?
Do you not see how the blackbird
Walks around the feet
Of the women about you?

VIII

I know noble accents 30
And lucid, inescapable rhythms;
But I know, too,
That the blackbird is involved
In what I know.

IX

When the blackbird flew out of sight, 35
It marked the edge
Of one of many circles.

X

At the sight of blackbirds
Flying in a green light,
Even the bawds of euphony 40
Would cry out sharply.

XI

He rode over Connecticut
In a glass coach.
Once, a fear pierced him,
In that he mistook 45
The shadow of his equipage
For blackbirds.

XII

The river is moving.
The blackbird must be flying.

XIII

It was evening all afternoon. 50
It was snowing
And it was going to snow.
The blackbird sat
In the cedar-limbs.

SOLDIER, THERE IS A WAR

Soldier, there is a war between the mind
And sky, between thought and day and night. It is
For that the poet is always in the sun,

Patches the moon together in his room
To his Virgilian cadences, up down, 5
Up down. It is a war that never ends.

Yet it depends on yours. The two are one.
They are a plural, a right and left, a pair,
Two parallels that meet if only in

The meeting of their shadows or that meet 10
In a book in a barrack, a letter from Malay.
But your war ends. And after it you return

With six meats and twelve wines or else without
To walk another room . . . Monsieur and comrade,
The soldier is poor without the poet's lines, 15

His petty syllabi, the sounds that stick,
Inevitably modulating, in the blood.
And war for war, each has its gallant kind.

How simply the fictive hero becomes the real;
How gladly with proper words the soldier dies, 20
If he must, or lives on the bread of faithful speech.

D. H. LAWRENCE

1885–1930

TORTOISE SHOUT

I thought he was dumb,
I said he was dumb,
Yet I've heard him cry.

First faint scream,
Out of life's unfathomable dawn, 5
Far off, so far, like a madness, under the horizon's dawning rim,
Far, far off, far scream.

Tortoise *in extremis.*

Why were we crucified into sex?
Why were we not left rounded off, and finished in ourselves, 10
As we began,
As he certainly began, so perfectly alone?

A far, was-it-audible scream,
Or did it sound on the plasm direct?

Worse than the cry of the new-born, 15
A scream,
A yell,
A shout,
A pæan,
A death-agony, 20
A birth-cry,
A submission,
All, tiny, far away, reptile under the first dawn.

War-cry, triumph, acute-delight, death-scream reptilian,
Why was the veil torn? 25
The silken shriek of the soul's torn membrane?

The male soul's membrane
Torn with a shriek half music, half horror.

Crucifixion.
Male tortoise, cleaving behind the hovel-wall of that dense female, 30
Mounted and tense, spread-eagle, out-reaching out of the shell
In tortoise-nakedness,
Long neck, and long vulnerable limbs extruded, spread-eagle over her
house-roof,
And the deep, secret, all-penetrating tail curved beneath her walls,
Reaching and gripping tense, more reaching anguish in uttermost
tension 35
Till suddenly, in the spasm of coition, tupping like a jerking leap,
and oh!
Opening its clenched face from his outstretched neck
And giving that fragile yell, that scream,
Super-audible,
From his pink, cleft, old-man's mouth, 40
Giving up the ghost,
Or screaming in Pentecost, receiving the ghost.

His scream, and his moment's subsidence,
The moment of eternal silence,
Yet unreleased, and after the moment, the sudden, startling jerk of
coition, and at once 45
The inexpressible faint yell—
And so on, till the last plasm of my body was melted back
To the primeval rudiments of life, and the secret.

So he tups, and screams
Time after time that frail, torn scream 50
After each jerk, the longish interval,
The tortoise eternity,
Age-long, reptilian persistence,
Heart-throb, slow heart-throb, persistent for the next spasm.

I remember, when I was a boy, 55
I heard the scream of a frog, which was caught with his
foot in the mouth of an up-starting snake;
I remember when I first heard bull-frogs break into sound in the spring;
I remember hearing a wild goose out of the throat of night
Cry loudly, beyond the lake of waters;
I remember the first time, out of a bush in the darkness, a nightingale's
piercing cries and gurgles startled the depths of my soul; 60
I remember the scream of a rabbit as I went through a wood
at midnight;

I remember the heifer in her heat, blorting and blorting through the
hours, persistent and irrepressible;
I remember my first terror hearing the howl of weird, amorous cats;
I remember the scream of a terrified, injured horse, the sheet-lightning,
And running away from the sound of a woman in labour, something
like an owl whooing, 65
And listening inwardly to the first bleat of a lamb,
The first wail of an infant,
And my mother singing to herself,
And the first tenor singing of the passionate throat of a young collier,
who has long since drunk himself to death,
The first elements of foreign speech 70
On wild dark lips.

And more than all these,
And less than all these,
This last,
Strange, faint coition yell 75
Of the male tortoise at extremity,
Tiny from under the very edge of the farthest far-off horizon of life.

The cross,
The wheel on which our silence first is broken,
Sex, which breaks up our integrity, our single inviolability, our deep
silence, 80
Tearing a cry from us.

Sex, which breaks us into voice, sets us calling across the deeps,
calling, calling for the complement,
Singing, and calling, and singing again, being answered, having
found.

Torn, to become whole again, after long seeking for what is lost,
The same cry from the tortoise as from Christ, the Osiris-cry of
abandonment, 85
That which is whole, torn asunder,
That which is in part, finding its whole again throughout the universe.

THE ELEPHANT IS SLOW TO MATE

The elephant, the huge old beast,
is slow to mate;
he finds a female, they show no haste,
they wait.

for the sympathy in their vast shy hearts
    slowly, slowly to rouse
as they loiter along the river-beds
    and drink and browse

and dash in panic through the brake
    of forest with the herd, 5
and sleep in massive silence, and wake
    together, without a word.

So slowly the great hot elephant hearts
    grow full of desire,
and the great beasts mate in secret at last,
    hiding their fire.

Oldest they are and the wisest of beasts
    so they know at last
how to wait for the loneliest of feasts,
    for the full repast. 10

They do not snatch, they do not tear;
    their massive blood
moves as the moon-tides, near, more near,
    till they touch in flood

SNAKE

A snake came to my water-trough
On a hot, hot day, and I in pyjamas for the heat,
To drink there.

In the deep, strange-scented shade of the great dark carobtree
I came down the steps with my pitcher 5
And must wait, must stand and wait, for there he was at the trough
    before me.

He reached down from a fissure in the earth-wall in the gloom
And trailed his yellow-brown slackness soft-bellied down, over the
    edge of the stone trough
And rested his throat upon the stone bottom,

And where the water had dripped from the tap, in a small clearness, 10
He sipped with his straight mouth,
Softly drank through his straight gums, into his slack long body,
Silently.

Someone was before me at my water-trough,
And I, like a second comer, waiting. 15
He lifted his head from his drinking, as cattle do,
And looked at me vaguely, as drinking cattle do,
And flickered his two-forked tongue from his lips, and mused a
moment,
And stooped and drank a little more,
Being earth-brown, earth-golden from the burning bowels of the earth 20
On the day of Sicilian July, with Etna smoking.

The voice of my education said to me
He must be killed,
For in Sicily the black, black snakes are innocent, the gold are
venomous.

And voices in me said, If you were a man 25
You would take a stick and break him now, and finish him off.

But must I confess how I liked him,
How glad I was he had come like a guest in quiet, to drink at my
water-trough
And depart peaceful, pacified, and thankless,
Into the burning bowels of this earth? 30

Was it cowardice, that I dared not kill him?
Was it perversity, that I longed to talk to him?
Was it humility, to feel so honoured?
I felt so honoured.

And yet those voices: 35
If you were not afraid, you would kill him!

And truly I was afraid, I was most afraid,
But even so, honoured still more
That he should seek my hospitality
From out the dark door of the secret earth. 40

He drank enough
And lifted his head, dreamily, as one who has drunken,
And flickered his tongue like a forked night on the air, so black,
Seeming to lick his lips,
And looked around like a god, unseeing, into the air, 45
And slowly turned his head,
And slowly, very slowly, as if thrice adream,
Proceeded to draw his slow length curving round
And climb again the broken bank of my wall-face.

And as he put his head into that dreadful hole, 50
And as he slowly drew up, snake-easing his shoulders, and entered
farther,
A sort of horror, a sort of protest against his withdrawing into that
horrid black hole,
Deliberately going into the blackness, and slowly drawing himself
after,
Overcame me now his back was turned.

I looked round, I put down my pitcher, 55
I picked up a clumsy log
And threw it at the water-trough with a clatter.

I think it did not hit him,
But suddenly that part of him that was left behind convulsed in
undignified haste,
Writhed like lightning, and was gone 60
Into the black hole, the earth-lipped fissure in the wall-front,
At which, in the intense still noon, I stared with fascination.

And immediately I regretted it.
I thought how paltry, how vulgar, what a mean act!
I despised myself and the voices of my accursed human education. 65

And I thought of the albatross,
And I wished he would come back, my snake.

For he seemed to me again like a king,
Like a king in exile, uncrowned in the underworld,
Now due to be crowned again. 70

And so, I missed my chance with one of the lords
Of life.

And I have something to expiate;
A pettiness.

EZRA POUND

1885–

A PACT

I make a pact with you, Walt Whitman—
I have detested you long enough.
I come to you as a grown child
Who has had a pig-headed father;
I am old enough now to make friends. 5
It was you that broke the new wood,
Now is a time for carving.
We have one sap and one root—
Let there be commerce between us.

ITE

Go, my songs, seek your praise from the young and from the intolerant,
move among the lovers of perfection alone.
Seek ever to stand in the hard Sophoclean light
And take your wounds from it gladly.

LES MILLWIN

The little Millwins attend the Russian Ballet.
The mauve and greenish souls of the little Millwins
Were seen lying along the upper seats
Like so many unused boas.

The turbulent and undisciplined host of art students— 5
The rigorous deputation from "Slade"—
Was before them.

With arms exalted, with fore-arms
Crossed in great futuristic X's, the art students
Exulted, they beheld the splendours of *Cleopatra*. 10

And the little Millwins beheld these things;
With their large and anaemic eyes they looked out upon this configuration.

Let us therefore mention the fact,
For it seems to us worthy of record.

COME MY CANTILATIONS

Come my cantilations,
Let us dump our hatreds into one bunch and be done with them,
Hot sun, clear water, fresh wind,
Let me be free of pavements,
Let me be free of the printers. 5
Let come beautiful people
Wearing raw silk of good colour,
Let come the graceful speakers,
Let come the ready of wit,
Let come the gay of manner, the insolent and the exulting. 10
We speak of burnished lakes,
Of dry air, as clear as metal.

PRAYER FOR HIS LADY'S LIFE

From Propertius, Elegiae, lib. III, 26

Here let thy clemency, Persephone, hold firm,
Do thou, Pluto, bring here no greater harshness.
So many thousand beauties are gone down to Avernus,
Ye might let one remain above with us.

With you is Iope, with you the white-gleaming Tyro, 5
With you is Europa and the shameless Pasiphae,
And all the fair from Troy and all from Achaia,
From the sundered realms, of Thebes and of aged Priamus;
And all the maidens of Rome, as many as they were,
They died and the greed of your flame consumes them. 10

Here let thy clemency, Persephone, hold firm,
Do thou, Pluto, bring here no greater harshness.
So many thousand fair are gone down to Avernus,
Ye might let one remain above with us.

MARIANNE MOORE

1887–

POETRY

I, too, dislike it: there are things that are important beyond all this fiddle.
Reading it, however, with a perfect contempt for it, one discovers in
it after all, a place for the genuine.
    Hands that can grasp, eyes
    that can dilate, hair that can rise 5
        if it must, these things are important not because a

high-sounding interpretation can be put upon them but because they are
    useful. When they become so derivative as to become unintelligible,
    the same thing may be said for all of us, that we
        do not admire what 10
        we cannot understand: the bat
            holding on upside down or in quest of something to

eat, elephants pushing, a wild horse taking a roll, a tireless wolf under
    a tree, the immovable critic twitching his skin like a horse that
                feels a flea, the base-
    ball fan, the statistician— 15
        nor is it valid
            to discriminate "against business documents and

school-books"; all these phenomena are important. One must make a
                distinction
    however: when dragged into prominence by half poets, the result
                is not poetry,

nor till the poets among us can be
"literalists of
the imagination"—above
insolence and triviality and can present

for inspection, imaginary gardens with real toads in them, shall we have
it. In the meantime, if you demand on the one hand, 25
the raw material of poetry in
all its rawness and
that which is on the other hand
genuine, then you are interested in poetry.

ELEPHANTS

Uplifted and waved until immobilized
wistaria-like, the opposing opposed
mouse-grey twined proboscises' trunk formed by two
trunks, fights itself to a spiraled inter-nosed

deadlock of dyke-enforced massiveness. It's a 5
knock-down drag-out fight that asks no quarter? Just
a pastime, as when the trunk rains on itself
the pool it siphoned up; or when—since each must

provide his forty-pound bough dinner—he broke
the leafy branches. These templars of the Tooth, 10
these matched intensities, take master care of
master tools. One, sleeping with the calm of youth,

at full length in the half dry sun-flecked stream-bed,
rests his hunting-horn-curled trunk on shallowed stone.
The sloping hollow of the sleeper's body 15
cradles the gently breathing eminence's prone

mahout, asleep like a lifeless six-foot
frog, so feather light the elephant's stiff
ear's unconscious of the crossed feet's weight. And the
defenceless human thing sleeps as sound as if 20

incised with hard wrinkles, embossed with wide ears,
invincibly tusked, made safe by magic hairs!
As if, as if, it is all ifs; we are at
much unease. But magic's masterpiece is theirs,—

Houdini's serenity quelling his fears. 25
Elephant ear-witnesses-to-be of hymns
and glorias, these ministrants all grey or
grey with white on legs or trunks, are a pilgrims'

pattern of revery not reverence,—a
religious procession without any priests, 30
the centuries-old carefullest unrehearsed
play. Blessed by Buddha's Tooth, the obedient beasts

themselves as toothed temples blessing the street, see
the white elephant carry the cushion that
carries the casket that carries the Tooth. 35
Amenable to what, matched with him, are gnat

trustees, he does not step on them as the white-
canopied blue-cushioned Tooth is augustly
and slowly returned to the shrine. Though white is
the colour of worship and of mourning, he 40

is not here to worship and he is too wise
to mourn,—a life prisoner but reconciled.
With trunk tucked up compactly—the elephant's
sign of defeat—he resisted, but is the child

of reason now. His straight trunk seems to say: when 45
what we hoped for came to nothing, we revived.
As loss could not ever alter Socrates'
tranquillity, equanimity's contrived

by the elephant. With the Socrates of
animals as with Sophocles the Bee, on whose 50
tombstone a hive was incised, sweetness tinctures
his gravity. His held up fore-leg for use

as a stair, to be climbed or descended with
the aid of his ear, expounds the brotherhood
of creatures to man the encroacher, by the 55
small word with the dot, meaning know,—the verb bud.

These knowers 'arouse the feeling that they are
allied to man' and can change roles with their trustees.

Hardship makes the soldier; then teachableness
makes him the philosopher—as Socrates, 60

prudently testing the suspicious thing, knew
the wisest is he who's not sure that he knows.
Who rides on a tiger can never dismount;
asleep on an elephant, that is repose.

THOMAS STEARNS ELIOT

1888–1965

LA FIGLIA CHE PIANGE

O quam te memorem virgo . . .

Stand on the highest pavement of the stair—
Lean on a garden urn—
Weave, weave the sunlight in your hair—
Clasp your flowers to you with a pained surprise—
Fling them to the ground and turn 5
With a fugitive resentment in your eyes:
But weave, weave the sunlight in your hair.

So I would have had him leave,
So I would have had her stand and grieve,
So he would have left 10
As the soul leaves the body torn and bruised,
As the mind deserts the body it has used.
I should find
Some way incomparably light and deft,
Some way we both should understand, 15
Simple and faithless as a smile and shake of the hand.

She turned away, but with the autumn weather
Compelled my imagination many days,
Many days and many hours:
Her hair over her arms and her arms full of flowers. 20

And I wonder how they should have been together!
I should have lost a gesture and a pose.
Sometimes these cogitations still amaze
The troubled midnight and the noon's repose.

SWEENEY AMONG THE NIGHTINGALES

Why Should I speak of the nightingale? The nightingale sings of adulterous wrong.

Apeneck Sweeney spreads his knees
Letting his arms hang down to laugh,
The zebra stripes along his jaw
Swelling to maculate giraffe.

The circles of the stormy moon 5
Slide westward to the River Plate,
Death and the Raven drift above
And Sweeney guards the hornèd gate.

Gloomy Orion and the Dog
Are veiled; and hushed the shrunken seas; 10
The person in the Spanish cape
Tries to sit on Sweeney's knees

Slips and pulls the table cloth
Overturns a coffee cup,
Reorganized upon the floor 15
She yawns and draws a stocking up;

The silent man in mocha brown
Sprawls at the window-sill and gapes;
The waiter brings in oranges,
Bananas, figs and hot-house grapes; 20

The silent vertebrate exhales,
Contracts and concentrates, withdraws;
Rachel *née* Rabinovitch
Tears at the grapes with murderous paws;

She and the lady in the cape 25
Are suspect, thought to be in league;

Therefore the man with heavy eyes
Declines the gambit, shows fatigue,

Leaves the room and reappears
Outside the window, leaning in, 30
Branches of wistaria
Circumscribe a golden grin;

The host with someone indistinct
Converses at the door apart,
The nightingales are singing near 35
The Convent of the Sacred Heart,

And sang within the bloody wood
When Agamemnon cried aloud,
And let their liquid siftings fall
To stain the stiff dishonoured shroud. 40

JOURNEY OF THE MAGI

"A cold coming we had of it,
Just the worst time of the year
For a journey, and such a long journey:
The ways deep and the weather sharp,
The very dead of winter." 5
And the camels galled, sore-footed, refractory,
Lying down in the melting snow.
There were times we regretted
The summer palaces on slopes, the terraces,
And the silken girls bringing sherbet. 10
Then the camel men cursing and grumbling
And running away, and wanting their liquor and women,
And the night-fires going out, and the lack of shelters,
And the cities hostile and the towns unfriendly
And the villages dirty and charging high prices: 15
A hard time we had of it.
At the end we preferred to travel all night,
Sleeping in snatches,
With the voices singing in our ears, saying
That this was all folly. 20

Then at dawn we came down to a temperate valley,
Wet, below the snow line, smelling of vegetation;
With a running stream and a water-mill beating the darkness,

And three trees on the low sky,
And an old white horse galloped away in the meadow. 25
Then we came to a tavern with vine-leaves over the lintel,
Six hands at an open door dicing for pieces of silver,
And feet kicking the empty wine-skins.
But there was no information, and so we continued
And arrived at evening, not a moment too soon 30
Finding the place; it was (you may say) satisfactory.

All this was a long time ago, I remember,
And I would do it again, but set down
This set down
This: were we led all that way for 35
Birth or Death? There was a Birth, certainly,
We had evidence and no doubt. I had seen birth and death,
But had thought they were different; this Birth was
Hard and bitter agony for us, like Death, our death.
We returned to our places, these Kingdoms, 40
But no longer at ease here, in the old dispensation,
With an alien people clutching their gods.
I should be glad of another death.

ANIMULA

"Issues from the hand of God, the simple soul"
To a flat world of changing lights and noise,
To light, dark, dry or damp, chilly or warm;
Moving between the legs of tables and of chairs,
Rising or falling, grasping at kisses and toys, 5
Advancing boldly, sudden to take alarm,
Retreating to the corner of arm and knee,
Eager to be reassured, taking pleasure
In the fragrant brilliance of the Christmas tree,
Pleasure in the wind, the sunlight and the sea; 10
Studies the sunlit pattern on the floor
And running stags around a silver tray;
Confounds the actual and the fanciful,
Content with playing-cards and kings and queens,
What the fairies do and what the servants say. 15
The heavy burden of the growing soul
Perplexes and offends more, day by day;
Week by week, offends and perplexes more
With the imperatives of "is and seems"
And may and may not, desire and control 20
The pain of living and the drug of dreams
Curl up the small soul in the window seat

Behind the *Encyclopædia Britannica.*
Issues from the hand of time the simple soul
Irresolute and selfish, misshapen, lame, 25
Unable to fare forward or retreat,
Fearing the warm reality, the offered good,
Denying the importunity of the blood,
Shadow of its own shadows, specter in its own gloom,
Leaving disordered papers in a dusty room; 30
Living first in the silence after the viaticum.

Pray for Guiterriez, avid of speed and power,
For Boudin, blown to pieces,
For this one who made a great fortune,
And that one who went his own way. 35
Pray for Floret, by the boarhound slain between the yew trees,
Pray for us now and at the hour of our birth.

JOHN CROWE RANSOM

1888–

HERE LIES A LADY

Here lies a lady of beauty and high degree.
Of chills and fever she died, of fever and chills,
The delight of her husband, her aunt, an infant of three,
And of medicos marveling sweetly on her ills.

For either she burned, and her confident eyes would blaze, 5
And her fingers fly in a manner to puzzle their heads—
What was she making? Why, nothing; she sat in a maze
Of old scraps of laces, snipped into curious shreds—

Or this would pass, and the light of her fire decline
Till she lay discouraged and cold, like a stalk white and blown, 10
And would not open her eyes, to kisses, to wine;
The sixth of these states was her last; the cold settled down.

Sweet ladies, long may ye bloom, and toughly I hope ye may thole,
But was she not lucky? In flowers and lace and mourning,
In love and great honor we bade God rest her soul 15
After six little spaces of chill, and six of burning.

BELLS FOR JOHN WHITESIDE'S DAUGHTER

There was such speed in her little body,
And such lightness in her footfall,
It is no wonder her brown study
Astonishes us all.

Her wars were bruited in our high window. 5
We looked among orchard trees and beyond,
Where she took arms against her shadow,
Or harried unto the pond

The lazy geese, like a snow cloud
Dripping their snow on the green grass, 10
Tricking and stopping, sleepy and proud,
Who cried in goose, Alas,

For the tireless heart within the little
Lady with rod that made them rise
From their noon apple-dreams, and scuttle 15
Goose-fashion under the skies!

But now go the bells, and we are ready;
In one house we are sternly stopped
To say we are vexed at her brown study,
Lying so primly propped. 20

BLUE GIRLS

Twirling your blue skirts, traveling the sward
Under the towers of your seminary,
Go listen to your teachers old and contrary
Without believing a word.

Tie the white fillets then about your lustrous hair
And think no more of what will come to pass
Than bluebirds that go walking on the grass
And chattering on the air. 5

Practice your beauty, blue girls, before it fail;
And I will cry with my loud lips and publish 10
Beauty which all our power shall never establish,
It is so frail.

For I could tell you a story which is true:
I know a lady with a terrible tongue,
Blear eyes fallen from blue, 15
All her perfections tarnished—and yet it is not long
Since she was lovelier than any of you.

ARCHIBALD MACLEISH

1892-

ARS POETICA

A poem should be palpable and mute
As a globed fruit

Dumb
As old medallions to the thumb

Silent as the sleeve-worn stone 5
Of casement ledges where the moss has grown—

A poem should be wordless
As the flight of birds

A poem should be motionless in time
As the moon climbs 10

Leaving, as the moon releases
Twig by twig the night-entangled trees,

Leaving, as the moon behind the winter leaves,
Memory by memory the mind—

A poem should be motionless in time 15
As the moon climbs

A poem should be equal to:
Not true

For all the history of grief
An empty doorway and a maple leaf 20

For love
The leaning grasses and two lights above the sea—

A poem should not mean
But be

THE END OF THE WORLD

Quite unexpectedly, as Vasserot
The armless ambidextrian was lighting
A match between his great and second toe,
And Ralph the lion was engaged in biting
The neck of Madame Sossman while the drum 5
Pointed, and Teeny was about to cough
In waltz-time swinging Jocko by the thumb—
Quite unexpectedly the top blew off:

And there, there overhead, there, there hung over
Those thousands of white faces, those dazed eyes, 10
There in the starless dark the poise, the hover,
There with vast wings across the cancelled skies,
There in the sudden blackness the black pall
Of nothing, nothing, nothing—nothing at all.

YOU, ANDREW MARVELL

And here face down beneath the sun,
And here upon earth's noonward height
To feel the always coming on,
The always rising of the night.

To feel creep up the curving east 5
The earthly chill of dusk and slow
Upon those under lands the vast
And ever-climbing shadow grow,

And strange at Ecbatan the trees
Take leaf by leaf the evening, strange, 10
The flooding dark about their knees,
The mountains over Persia change,

And now at Kermanshah the gate,
Dark, empty, and the withered grass,
And through the twilight now the late 15
Few travelers in the westward pass.

And Baghdad darken and the bridge
Across the silent river gone,
And through Arabia the edge
Of evening widen and steal on, 20

And deepen on Palmyra's street
The wheel rut in the ruined stone,
And Lebanon fade out and Crete
High through the clouds and overblown,

And over Sicily the air 25
Still flashing with the landward gulls,
And loom and slowly disappear
The sails above the shadowy hulls,

And Spain go under and the shore
Of Africa, the gilded sand, 30
And evening vanish and no more
The low pale light across that land,

Nor now the long light on the sea—
And here face downward in the sun
To feel how swift, how secretly, 35
The shadow of the night comes on. . . .

E. E. CUMMINGS

1894–1962

ALL IN GREEN WENT MY LOVE RIDING

All in green went my love riding
on a great horse of gold
into the silver dawn.

four lean hounds crouched low and smiling
the merry deer ran before. 5

Fleeter be they than dappled dreams
the swift sweet deer
the red rare deer.

Four red roebuck at a white water
the cruel bugle sang before. 10

Horn at hip went my love riding
riding the echo down
into the silver dawn.

four lean hounds crouched low and smiling
the level meadows ran before. 15

Softer be they than slippered sleep
the lean lithe deer
the fleet flown deer.

Four fleet does at a gold valley
the famished arrow sang before. 20

Bow at belt went my love riding
riding the mountain down
into the silver dawn.

four lean hounds crouched low and smiling
the sheer peaks ran before. 25

Paler be they than daunting death
the sleek slim deer
the tall tense deer.

Four tall stags at a green mountain
the lucky hunter sang before. 30

All in green went my love riding
on a great horse of gold
into the silver dawn.

four lean hounds crouched low and smiling
my heart fell dead before. 35

MY GIRL'S TALL WITH HARD LONG EYES

my girl's tall with hard long eyes
as she stands, with her long hard hands keeping
silence on her dress, good for sleeping
is her long hard body filled with surprise
like a white shocking wire, when she smiles 5
a hard long smile it sometimes makes
gaily go clean through me tickling aches,
and the weak noise of her eyes easily files
my impatience to an edge—my girl's tall
and taut, with thin legs just like a vine 10
that's spent all of its life on a garden-wall,
and is going to die. When we grimly go to bed
with these legs she begins to heave and twine
about me, and to kiss my face and head.

ANYONE LIVED IN A PRETTY HOW TOWN

anyone lived in a pretty how town
(and up so floating many bells down)
spring summer autumn winter
he sang his didn't he danced his did.

Women and men (both little and small) 5
cared for anyone not at all
they sowed their isn't they reaped their same
sun moon stars rain

children guessed (but only a few
and down they forgot as up they grew 10
autumn winter spring summer)
that noone loved him more by more

when by now and tree by leaf
she laughed his joy she cried his grief
bird by snow and stir by still 15
anyone's any was all to her

someones married their everyones
laughed their cryings and did their dance
(sleep wake hope and then) they
said their nevers they slept their dream 20

stars rain sun moon
(and only the snow can begin to explain
how children are apt to forget to remember
with up so floating many bells down)

one day anyone died i guess 25
(and noone stooped to kiss his face)
busy folk buried them side by side
little by little and was by was

all by all and deep by deep
and more by more they dream their sleep 30
noone and anyone earth by april
wish by spirit and if by yes.

Women and men (both dong and ding)
summer autumn winter spring
reaped their sowing and went their came 35
sun moon stars rain

i say no world

can hold a you
shall see the not
because
and why but
(who 5
stood within his steam beginning and
began to sing all
here is hands machine no

good too quick i know this 10
suit you pay
a store too
much yes what
too much o much cheap
me i work i know i say i have 15
not any
never
no vacation here

is hands is work since i am
born is good 20
but there this cheap this suit too
quick no suit there every
-thing
nothing i
say the 25
world not fit
you) he is

not (i say the world
yes any world is much
too not quite big enough to 30
hold one tiny this with
time's
more than

most how
immeasurable
anguish

pregnant one fearless
one good yes
completely kind
mindheart one true one generous child-
man
-god one eager
souldoll one
unsellable not buyable alive
one i say human being) one

goldberger

ROBERT GRAVES

1895–

WARNING TO CHILDREN

Children, if you dare to think
Of the greatness, rareness, muchness,
Fewness of this precious only
Endless world in which you say
You live, you think of things like this:
Blocks of slate enclosing dappled
Red and green, enclosing tawny
Yellow nets, enclosing white
And black acres of dominoes,
Where a neat brown paper parcel
Tempts you to untie the string.
In the parcel a small island,
On the island a large tree,
On the tree a husky fruit,
Strip the husk and pare the rind off:
In the kernel you will see

Blocks of slate enclosed by dappled
Red and green, enclosed by tawny
Yellow nets, enclosed by white
And black acres of dominoes, 20
Where the same brown paper parcel—
Children, leave the string untied!
For who dares undo the parcel
Finds himself at once inside it,
On the island, in the fruit, 25
Blocks of slate about his head,
Finds himself enclosed by dappled
Green and red, enclosed by yellow
Tawny nets, enclosed by black
And white acres of dominoes, 30
With the same brown paper parcel
Still untied upon his knee.
And, if he then should dare to think
Of the fewness, muchness, rareness,
Greatness of this endless only 35
Precious world in which he says
He lives—he then unties the string.

THE CLIMATE OF THOUGHT

The climate of thought has seldom been described.
It is no terror of Caucasian frost,
Nor yet that brooding Hindu heat
For which a loin-rag and a dish of rice
Suffice until the pestilent monsoon. 5
But, without winter, blood would run too thin;
Or, without summer, fires would burn too long.
In thought the seasons run concurrently.

Thought has a sea to gaze, not voyage on;
And hills, to rough the edge of the bland sky, 10
Not to be climbed in search of blander prospect;
Few birds, sufficient for such caterpillars
As are not fated to turn butterflies;
Few butterflies, sufficient for the flowers
That are the luxury of a full orchard; 15
Wind, sometimes, in the evening chimneys; rain
On the early morning roof, on sleepy sight;
Snow streaked upon the hilltop, feeding
The fond brook at the valley-head
That greens the valley and that parts the lips; 20

The sun, simple, like a country neighbour;
The moon, grand, not fanciful with clouds.

TO JUAN AT THE WINTER SOLSTICE

There is one story and one story only
That will prove worth your telling,
Whether as learned bard or gifted child;
To it all lines or lesser gauds belong
That startle with their shining 5
Such common stories as they stray into.

Is it of trees you tell, their months and virtues,
Or strange beasts that beset you,
Of birds that croak at you the Triple will?
Or of the Zodiac and how slow it turns 10
Below the Boreal Crown,
Prison of all true kings that ever reigned?

Water to water, ark again to ark,
From woman back to woman:
So each new victim treads unfalteringly 15
The never altered circuit of his fate,
Bringing twelve peers as witness
Both to his starry rise and starry fall.

Or is it of the Virgin's silver beauty,
All fish below the thighs? 20
She in her left hand bears a leafy quince;
When, with her right she crooks a finger smiling,
How may the King hold back?
Royally then he barters life for love.

Or of the undying snake from chaos hatched, 25
Whose coils contain the ocean,
Into whose chops with naked sword he springs,
Then in black water, tangled by the reeds,
Battles three days and nights,
To be spewed up beside her scalloped shore? 30

Much snow is falling, winds roar hollowly,
The owl hoots from the elder,

Fear in your heart cries to the loving-cup:
Sorrow to sorrow as the sparks fly upward.
The log groans and confesses 35
There is one story and one story only.

Dwell on her graciousness, dwell on her smiling,
Do not forget what flowers
The great boar trampled down in ivy time.
Her brow was creamy as the crested wave, 40
Her sea-blue eyes were wild
But nothing promised that is not performed.

HART CRANE

1899–1932

VOYAGES (II)

And yet this great wink of eternity,
Of rimless floods, unfettered leewardings,
Samite sheeted and processioned where
Her undinal vast belly moonward bends,
Laughing the wrapt inflections of our love; 5

Take this Sea whose diapason knells
On scrolls of silver snowy sentences,
The sceptred terror of whose sessions rends
As her demeanors motion well or ill,
All but the pieties of lovers' hands. 10

And onward, as bells off San Salvador
Salute the crocus lustres of the stars,
In these poinsettia meadows of her tides,—
Adagios of islands, O my Prodigal,
Complete the dark confessions her veins spell. 15

Mark how her turning shoulders wind the hours,
And hasten while her penniless rich palms

Pass superscription of bent foam and wave,—
Hasten, while they are true,—sleep, death, desire,
Close round one instant in one floating flower. 20

Bind us in time, O Seasons clear, and awe.
O minstrel galleons of Carib fire,
Bequeath us to no earthly shore until
Is answered in the vortex of our grave
The seal's wide spindrift gaze toward paradise. 25

AT MELVILLE'S TOMB

Often beneath the wave, wide from this ledge
The dice of drowned men's bones he saw bequeath
An embassy. Their numbers as he watched,
Beat on the dusty shore and were obscured.

And wrecks passed without sound of bells, 5
The calyx of death's bounty giving back
A scattered chapter, lived hieroglyph,
The portent wound in corridors of shells.

Then in the circuit calm of one vast coil,
Its lashings charmed and malice reconciled, 10
Frosted eyes there were that lifted altars;
And silent answers crept across the stars.

Compass, quadrant and sextant contrive
No farther tides . . . High in the azure steeps
Monody shall not wake the mariner. 15
This fabulous shadow only the sea keeps.

ALLEN TATE

1899–

THE MEDITERRANEAN

Quem das finem, rex magne, dolorum?

Where we went in the boat was a long bay
A slingshot wide, walled in by towering stone—
Peaked margin of antiquity's delay,
And we went there out of time's monotone:

Where we went in the black hull no light moved 5
But a gull white-winged along the feckless wave,
The breeze, unseen but fierce as a body loved,
That boat drove onward like a willing slave:

Where we went in the small ship the seaweed
Parted and gave to us the murmuring shore 10
And we made feast and in our secret need
Devoured the very plates Aeneas bore:

Where derelict you see through the low twilight
The green coast that you, thunder-tossed, would win,
Drop sail, and hastening to drink all night 15
Eat dish and bowl—to take that sweet land in!

Where we feasted and caroused on the sandless
Pebbles, affecting our day of piracy,
What prophecy of eaten plates could landless
Wanderers fulfil by the ancient sea? 20

We for that time might taste the famous age
Eternal here yet hidden from our eyes
When lust of power undid its stuffless rage;
They, in a wineskin, bore earth's paradise.

Let us lie down once more by the breathing side 25
Of Ocean, where our live forefathers sleep

As if the Known Sea still were a month wide—
Atlantis howls but is no longer steep!

What country shall we conquer, what fair land
Unman our conquest and locate our blood? 30
We've cracked the hemispheres with careless hand!
Now, from the Gates of Hercules we flood

Westward, westward till the barbarous brine
Whelms us to the tired world where tasseling corn,
Fat beans, grapes sweeter than muscadine 35
Rot on the vine: in that land were we born.

ODE TO THE CONFEDERATE DEAD

Row after row with strict impunity
The headstones yield their names to the element,
The wind whirrs without recollection;
In the riven troughs the splayed leaves
Pile up, of nature the casual sacrament 5
To the seasonal eternity of death,
Then driven by the fierce scrutiny
Of heaven to their business in the vast breath,
They sough the rumor of mortality.

Autumn is desolation in the plot 10
Of a thousand acres where these memories grow
From the inexhaustible bodies that are not
Dead, but feed the grass row after rich row:
Remember now the autumns that have gone—
Ambitious November with the humours of the year, 15
With a particular zeal for every slab,
Staining the uncomfortable angels that rot
On the slabs, a wing chipped here, an arm there:
The brute curiosity of an angel's stare
Turns you like them to stone, 20
Transforms the heaving air,
Till plunged to a heavier world below
You shift your sea-space blindly,
Heaving like the blind crab.

Dazed by the wind, only the wind 25
The leaves flying, plunge

You know who have waited by the wall
The twilit certainty of an animal;
Those midnight restitutions of the blood
You know—the immitigable pines, the smoky frieze 30
Of the sky, the sudden call; you know the rage—
The cold pool left by the mounting flood—
The rage of Zeno and Parmenides.
You who have waited for the angry resolution
Of those desires that should be yours tomorrow,
You know the unimportant shrift of death
And praise the vision
And praise the arrogant circumstance
Of those who fall
Rank upon rank, hurried beyond decision— 40
Here by the sagging gate, stopped by the wall.

Seeing, seeing only the leaves
Flying, plunge and expire

Turn your eyes to the immoderate past
Turn to the inscrutable infantry rising 45
Demons out of the earth—they will not last.
Stonewall, Stonewall, and the sunken fields of hemp,
Shiloh, Antietam, Malvern Hill, Bull Run.
Lost in that orient of the thick and fast
You will curse the setting sun. 50

Cursing only the leaves crying
Like an old man in a storm

You hear the shout—the crazy hemlocks point
With troubled fingers to the silence which
Smothers you, a mummy, in time.

The hound bitch 55
Toothless and dying, in a musty cellar
Hears the wind only.

Now that the salt of their blood
Stiffens the saltier oblivion of the sea,
Seals the malignant purity of the flood,
What shall we, who count our days and bow 60
Our heads with a commemorial woe,

In the ribboned coats of grim felicity,
What shall we say of the bones, unclean
—Their verdurous anonymity will grow—
The ragged arms, the ragged heads and eyes 65
Lost in these acres of the insane green?
The gray lean spiders come; they come and go;
In a tangle of willows without light
The singular screech-owl's bright
Invisible lyric seeds the mind 70
With the furious murmur of their chivalry.

We shall say only, the leaves
Flying, plunge and expire

We shall say only, the leaves whispering
In the improbable mist of nightfall 75
That flies on multiple wing:
Night is the beginning and the end,
And in between the ends of distraction
Waits mute speculation, the patient curse
That stones the eyes, or like the jaguar leaps 80
For his own image in a jungle pool, his victim.

What shall we say who have knowledge
Carried to the heart? Shall we take the act
To the grave? Shall we, more hopeful, set up the grave
In the house? The ravenous grave?

Leave now 85
The turnstile and the old stone wall:
The gentle serpent, green in the mulberry bush,
Riots with his tongue through the hush—
Sentinel of the grave who counts us all!

ROBERT PENN WARREN

1905–

VARIATION: ODE TO FEAR

When the dentist adjusts his drill
And leers at the molar he's going to fill,
Murmuring softly as a mother,
"Just hold tight, it'll soon be over,"
Timor mortis conturbat me. 5

When the surgeon whets his scalpel
And regards me like an apple,
And the tumor or the wart
Sings, "The best of friends must part,"
Timor mortis conturbat me. 10

When flushed with morning's genial hope
I slit the crisped envelope
And read the message too oft known,
"Your account $3.00 overdrawn,"
Timor mortis conturbat me. 15

When I wait on the railway platform
To say goodbye, and the friend's form,
Which was substantial, wavers there
Thinner than smoke upon the air,
Timor mortis conturbat me. 20

When I think that the national debt
Will blight the children we beget,
And especially blight those of our heirs
Who have the instincts of financiers,
Timor mortis conturbat me. 25

When I read in Charles A. Beard
That the Founding Fathers whom we revered
Were not above a cozy deal

And would skin a pig for the pig's squeal,
Timor mortis conturbat me. 30

And read that Milton was neurotic
And Saint Joan charmingly psychotic
And Jesus in Gethsemane
Was simply sweating from T. B.,
Timor mortis conturbat me. 35

When Focke-Wulf mounts, or Zero,
And my knees say I'm no hero
And manly marrow turns to soup
And lunch expertly loops the loop,
Timor mortis conturbat me. 40

When in the midnight's pause I mark
The breath beside me in the dark,
And know that breath's a clock, and know
That breath's the clock that's never slow,
Timor mortis conturbat me. 45

O thou, to whom the world unknown
With all its shadowy shapes is shown,
Whose foot makes no sound on the floor,
Who need no latchkey for the door
(*Timor mortis conturbat me*), 50

Who gaze from out the chic dummy's gaze,
In the display window, to amaze
The yearning matron by whom you sat
At dinner last night and in her soup spat
(*Timor mortis conturbat me*), 55

Who pinch the maiden's tenderest part
But warm no cockles of her heart,
Who snarl the horse's tail, who spill
The bucket fetched by Jack and Jill
(*Timor mortis conturbat me*), 60

Whose sleights are slier than Houdini's
And make Puck's pranks look like a ninny's
—Though you were with me *in utero,*

Your own birthday was long ago
    (*Timor mortis conturbat me*), 65

And though you fawn and follow like Fido,
You'll find other master when I go.
For I'm not the first or last of men
And so I will try to remember when
    Timor mortis conturbat me. 70

That various men in various ages
Have dispensed with heroes and with sages,
And managed without our Constitution
Or intercession and absolution
    (*Timor mortis conturbat me*), 75

And when they walked by grove or shore
Enjoyed the scene, not metaphor,
And when they got it in the gut
Took what comfort they could from a cigarette butt
    (*Timor mortis conturbat me*), 80

And though they found the going hard
Did without Jesus or the gold standard,
Or lay alone, and reaching over
Could find no hand upon the cover
    (*Timor mortis conturbat me*). 85

So when I wake I'll pat the head
Of the beast that sleeps beside the bed,
And put on my pants and vest, and go
Down to eat my breakfast, though
    Timor mortis conturbat me. 90

BEARDED OAKS

The oaks, how subtle and marine,
Bearded, and all the layered light
Above them swims; and thus the scene,
Recessed, awaits the positive night.

So, waiting, we in the grass now lie 5
Beneath the langourous tread of light:

The grasses, kelp-like, satisfy
The nameless motions of the air.

Upon the floor of light, and time,
Unmurmuring, of polyp made, 10
We rest; we are, as light withdraws,
Twin atolls on a shelf of shade.

Ages to our construction went,
Dim architecture, hour by hour:
And violence, forgot now, lent 15
The present stillness all its power.

The storm of noon above us rolled,
Of light the fury, furious gold,
The long drag troubling us, the depth:
Dark is unrocking, unrippling, still. 20

Passion and slaughter, ruth, decay
Descend, minutely whispering down,
Silted down swaying streams, to lay
Foundation for our voicelessness.

All our debate is voiceless here, 25
As all our rage, the rage of stone;
If hope is hopeless, then fearless fear,
And history is thus undone.

Our feet once wrought the hollow street
With echo when the lamps were dead 30
At windows, once our headlight glare
Disturbed the doe that, leaping, fled.

I do not love you less that now
The caged heart makes iron stroke,
Or less that all that light once gave 35
The graduate dark should now revoke.

We live in time so little time
And we learn all so painfully,
That we may spare this hour's term
To practice for eternity. 40

STANLEY KUNITZ

1905–

FOREIGN AFFAIRS

We are two countries girded for the war,
Whisking our scouts across the pricked frontier
To ravage in each other's fields, cut lines
Along the lacework of strategic nerves,
Loot stores; while here and there, 5
In ambushes that trace a valley's curves,
Stark witness to the dangerous charge we bear,
A house ignites, a train's derailed, a bridge
Blows up sky-high, and water floods the mines.
Who first attacked? Who turned the other cheek? 10
Aggression perpetrated is as soon
Denied, and insult rubbed into the injury
By cunning agents trained in these affairs,
With whom it's touch-and-go, don't-tread-on-me,
I-dare-you-to, keep-off, and kiss-my-hand. 15
Tempers could sharpen knives, and do; we live
In states provocative
Where frowning headlines scare the coffee cream
And doomsday is the eighth day of the week.

Our exit through the slammed and final door 20
Is twenty times rehearsed, but when we face
The imminence of cataclysmic rupture,
A lesser pride goes down upon its knees.
Two countries separated by desire!—
Whose diplomats speed back and forth by plane, 25
Portmanteaus stuffed with fresh apologies
Outdated by events before they land.
Negotiations wear them out: they're driven mad
Between the protocols of tears and rapture.

Locked in our fated and contiguous selves, 30
These worlds that too much agitate each other,
Interdependencies from hip to head,
Twin principalities both slave and free,
We coexist, proclaiming Peace together.

Tell me no lies! We are divided nations 35
With malcontents by thousands in our streets,
These thousands torn by inbred revolutions.
A triumph is demanded, not moral victories
Deduced from small advances, small retreats.
Are the gods of our fathers not still daemonic? 40
On the steps of the Capitol
The outraged lion of our years roars panic,
And we suffer the guilty cowardice of the will,
Gathering its bankrupt slogans up for flight
Like gold from ruined treasuries. 45
And yet, and yet, although the murmur rises,
We are what we are, and only life surprises.

FOR THE WORD IS FLESH

O ruined father dead, long sweetly rotten
Under the dial, the time-dissolving urn,
Beware a second perishing, forgotten,
Heap fallen leaves of memory to burn
On the slippery rock, the black eroding heart, 5
Before the wedged frost splits it clean apart.

The nude hand drops no sacramental flower
Of blood among the tough upthrusting weeds.
Senior, in this commemorative hour,
What shall the quick commemorate, what deeds 10
Ephemeral, what dazzling words that flare
Like rockets from the mouth to burst in air?

Of hypochondriacs that gnawed their seasons
In search of proofs, Lessius found twenty-two
Fine arguments, Tolet gave sixty reasons 15
Why souls survive. And what are they to you?
And, father, what to me, who cannot blur
The mirrored brain with fantasies of Er,

Remembering such factual spikes as pierce
The supplicating palms, and by the sea 20
Remembering the eyes, I hear the fierce
Wild cry of Jesus on the holy tree,
Yet have of you no syllable to keep,
Only the deep rock crumbling in the deep.

Observe the wisdom of the Florentine 25
Who, feeling death upon him, scribbled fast
To make revision of a deathbed scene,
Gloating that he was accurate at last.
Let sons learn from their lipless fathers how
Man enters hell without a golden bough. 30

STANLEY BURNSHAW

1906–

HISTORICAL SONG OF THEN AND NOW

Earth early and huge,
No eye dared hope to travel
The palette of its rage

Till, late, they learned to wind
Shackles into its veins, 5
Shrank it to fit a cage.

So trust contracts to fear.
The tribes give up their feuds.
All wars are now one war.

And will you indict this breed 10
That strained against a code
Where safe-and-fed was good?

Fled from its mothering wood,
It found in its hand the thought
To light up endless day, 15

Revel with sleepless eye,
Make of itself a god,
And the veins a level sun—

Now it stumbles, dwarf in the maze
That the thinking hand had spun. 20
Blind in its blaze of stone,

Whom can this breed indict
That its sun is a blast of darkness,
That light is always night?

MODES OF BELIEF

Ever since I grew cold
In heart, I always hear
Most men that I behold
Cry like a creature caught
In tones of dying will, 5
Such as their eyelids bear
With cuneiforms of fail—

Where are the young and wild
Teeming in hope of power?
Though striving lifts the bud, 10
None can achieve the flower.
Where can the bud disperse
Within? Must every man
Entomb a withered child?—

What early hearts can store 15
Of sweetness still endures
Fever of flood or drought,
Till groping up from within,
A self-bereaving curse
Masses in reefs of thought, 20
Burns and bites the blood—

POETRY: THE ART
In the Form of an Apostrophe to Whitman

I used to read your book and hear your words
Explode in me and blast new passageways
Deep in my brain, until its crowding rooms
Held more light than my head could balance. Now

That the tunnels all are cut, I pace the rooms 5
Looking for you, though certain I shall find
No more of you than you yourself could gather
Out of the pieces of self. The years have burned
The sharpness from the edges: I can fit
The pieces, but the mortar must be mixed 10
Out of our blending wills. Others have tried
And failed. I too shall fail if I forget
How thought can range beyond the last frontiers
That common sense has civilized with names.

Others who looked for you have made you say 15
Words you might have said if they were you:
Have lost you in their passion for a phrase.
The private man's infinitude defies
The singleness they look for when they strive
To sort your various colors to a scheme 20
Of thought-and-action. Desperate for pattern,
They make the key *Calamus* and they twist
Your other selves around the centerpiece,
Losing you in that love.

And others forge 25
A key of social thought that cracks apart
When words and actions contradict: *Walt Whitman,*
You said you love the common man! Where were you
When Parsons' friends were hanged? Were you asleep
Or writing more fine words about mechanics 30
And farmers?—How much cosier for you
To prate about democracy than live it—
You, its self-appointed poet!

Others,
Seeking you in your plangent celebrations
Of science and the holiness of flesh 35
And earth, end with a fierce *You too, Walt Whitman,*
You flinched, you stumbled, hankering for a "soul" . . .
The substances of sense too harsh too bitter
A truth for you to live by! Underneath
Your protest boils the soft romantic sickness 40
Of all the Shelley, Heines—bright lost leaders
We hoped were men. You were afraid of the dark:
You who had thundered "Science is true religion"
Sang the groveler's wooing song to Death
And God and Spirit! . . . Hide, at least, the image 45
Revealed: the gaudy chaos of a man
Reviling his own faith!

But who can dare
To arbitrate the depths of you that anger
Against your tranquil self? I am not certain:
I have seen the signposts of contradiction 50
Planted by men impotent to discern
The harmony beneath the subtle wholeness,
And in their self-defence erect confusion
On quiet entities. A poet's words
Are signatures of self—the many selves 55
Subsumed in one profounder sense that knows
An all-according truth: a single eye
Uncovering the countless constellations
Of heart and mind. Wherefore the syllables
Reach outward from the self in an embrace 60
Of multitudes. The poetries of speech
Are acts of thinking love; and I must find
The thought that grows the center of your passion.

And so I say to those who precontemn
The message of *Calamus* as the flowers 65
Of twisted love what Plato showed of truths
Uttered by poets. And I say to those
Who spit upon your social thought "*Respondez!*"
The human race is restive, on the watch
For some new era—some divine war— 70
Whose triumph will entrench a brave good-will
Among the common people everywhere—
The trodden multitudes for whom you clamored
A new and tender reverence.

But for those
Who sneer because you looked for lights beyond 75
The planes of sense, there is no final answer
If they deny the mind its birthright freedom
To range all worlds of thought and sense and vision.
Everything that can be believ'd is an image of truth—
The images refined to great and small 80
Will cluster into orbits of belief
And hold together as the planets hold
By kinship and denial, in one vaster
All encompassing circle. Let the sneerers
Proclaim your chief intent or keep their silence 85
Until its name is found.

It is not found,
The answer to your central search—"the problem,
The only one"—*adjust the individual*
Into your mass. For we have just begun

To fit the world to men, men to the world; 90
And we shall stumble till the single heart
Discovers all its selves and learns therefrom
How singleness and multitude can live
In valiant marriage. With your hungry hope
You pierced the shells of feeling, trumpeted 95
Into your country's ears, and flooded strength
Into the wavering hearts of men lonely
For courage to fulfill their need: to thrust
Their single faith against the massed-up wills
Of many. "Sing your self!" you told them. Listening, 100
They pledged the valors of the inward man.
And others turned from you with dull, deaf ears,
Afraid to listen, waiting to be taught
The trial-and-error way of rats in a maze . . .

A poem "is," some men believe. I say 105
A poem "is" when it has spread its root
Inside a listener's thought and grows a tree there
Strong enough to burst a room in the brain,
And bring its branch to blossom. Then the host
Forgets the verse and ponders on the mind 110
That made this seed of growth . . . as I forget
Your poem: as I strive to learn your mind,
Thinking that when I come to understand,
I may begin to touch serenities
You saw beneath the springs of pain that nourished 115
Your world that was beginning—dim, green world
Trembling with death-and-birth: divinest war.

W. H. AUDEN

1907–

MUSÉE DES BEAUX ARTS

About suffering they were never wrong,
The Old Masters: how well they understood
Its human position; how it takes place
While someone else is eating or opening a window or just walking
dully along;

How, when the aged are reverently, passionately waiting 5
For the miraculous birth, there always must be
Children who did not specially want it to happen, skating
On a pond at the edge of the wood:
They never forgot
That even the dreadful martyrdom must run its course 10
Anyhow in a corner, some untidy spot
Where the dogs go on with their doggy life and the torturer's horse
Scratches its innocent behind on a tree.

In Breughel's *Icarus*, for instance: how everything turns away
Quite leisurely from the disaster; the ploughman may 15
Have heard the splash, the forsaken cry,
But for him it was not an important failure; the sun shone
As it had to on the white legs disappearing into the green
Water; and the expensive delicate ship that must have seen
Something amazing, a boy falling out of the sky, 20
Had somewhere to get to and sailed calmly on.

IN MEMORY OF W. B. YEATS

I

He disappeared in the dead of winter:
The brooks were frozen, the airports almost deserted,
The snow disfigured the public statues;
The mercury sank in the mouth of the dying day.
O all the instruments agree 5
The day of his death was a dark cold day.

Far from his illness
The wolves ran on through the evergreen forests,
The peasant river was untempted by the fashionable quays;
By mourning tongues 10
The death of the poet was kept from his poems.

But for him it was his last afternoon as himself,
An afternoon of nurses and rumours;
The provinces of his body revolted, 15
The squares of his mind were empty,
Silence invaded the suburbs,
The current of his feeling failed: he became his admirers.

Now he is scattered among a hundred cities
And wholly given over to unfamiliar affections;
To find his happiness in another kind of wood 20

And be punished under a foreign code of conscience.
The words of a dead man
Are modified in the guts of the living.

But in the importance and noise of tomorrow
When the brokers are roaring like beasts on the floor of the Bourse, 25
And the poor have the sufferings to which they are fairly accustomed,
And each in the cell of himself is almost convinced of his freedom;
A few thousand will think of this day
As one thinks of a day when one did something slightly unusual.
O all the instruments agree 30
The day of his death was a dark cold day.

2

You were silly like us: your gift survived it all;
The parish of rich women, physical decay,
Yourself; mad Ireland hurt you into poetry.
Now Ireland has her madness and her weather still, 35
For poetry makes nothing happen: it survives
In the valley of its saying where executives
Would never want to tamper; it flows south
From ranches of isolation and the busy griefs,
Raw towns that we believe and die in; it survives, 40
A way of happening, a mouth.

3

Earth, receive an honoured guest;
William Yeats is laid to rest:
Let the Irish vessel lie
Emptied of its poetry. 45

Time that is intolerant
Of the brave and innocent,
And indifferent in a week
To a beautiful physique,

Worships language and forgives 50
Everyone by whom it lives;
Pardons cowardice, conceit,
Lays its honours at their feet.

Time that with this strange excuse
Pardoned Kipling and his views, 55
And will pardon Paul Claudel,
Pardons him for writing well.

In the nightmare of the dark
All the gods of Europe bark,

And the living nations wait, 60
Each sequestered in its hate;

Intellectual disgrace
Stares from every human face,
And the seas of pity lie
Locked and frozen in each eye. 65

Follow, poet, follow right
To the bottom of the night,
With your unconstraining voice
Still persuade us to rejoice;

With the farming of a verse 70
Make a vineyard of the curse,
Sing of human unsuccess
In a rapture of distress;

In the deserts of the heart
Let the healing fountain start, 75
In the prison of his days
Teach the free man how to praise.

THE SHIELD OF ACHILLES

She looked over his shoulder
For vines and olive trees,
Marble well-governed cities
And ships upon untamed seas,
But there on the shining metal 5
His hands had put instead
An artificial wilderness
And a sky like lead.

A plain without a feature, bare and brown,
No blade of grass, no sign of neighbourhood, 10
Nothing to eat and nowhere to sit down,
Yet, congregated on its blankness, stood
An unintelligible multitude.
A million eyes, a million boots in line,
Without expression, waiting for a sign. 15

Out of the air a voice without a face
Proved by statistics that some cause was just

In tones as dry and level as the place:
    No one was cheered and nothing was discussed;
    Column by column in a cloud of dust 20
They marched away enduring a belief
Whose logic brought them, somewhere else, to grief.

She looked over his shoulder
    For ritual pieties,
White flower-garlanded heifers, 25
    Libation and sacrifice,
But there on shining metal
    Where the altar should have been,
She saw by his flickering forge-light
    Quite another scene. 30

Barbed wire enclosed an arbitrary spot
    Where bored officials lounged (one cracked a joke)
And sentries sweated for the day was hot:
    A crowd of ordinary decent folk
    Watched from without and neither moved nor spoke 35
As three pale figures were led forth and bound
To three posts driven upright in the ground.

The mass and majesty of this world, all
    That carries weight and always weighs the same
Lay in the hands of others; they were small 40
    And could not hope for help and no help came:
    What their foes liked to do was done, their shame
Was all the worst could wish; they lost their pride
And died as men before their bodies died.

She looked over his shoulder 45
    For athletes at their games,
Men and women in a dance
    Moving their sweet limbs
Quick, quick, to music,
    But there on the shining shield 50
His hands had set no dancing-floor
    But a weed-choked field.

A ragged urchin, aimless and alone,
    Loitered about that vacancy, a bird
Flew up to safety from his well-aimed stone: 55
    That girls are raped, that two boys knife a third,
    Were axioms to him, who'd never heard

Of any world where promises were kept.
Or one could weep because another wept.

The thin-lipped armourer, 60
Hephaestos hobbled away,
Thetis of the shining breasts
Cried out in dismay
At what the god had wrought
To please her son, the strong 65
Iron-hearted man-slaying Achilles
Who would not live long.

THEODORE ROETHKE

1908–1963

FRAU BAUMAN, FRAU SCHMIDT, AND FRAU SCHWARTZE

Gone the three ancient ladies
Who creaked on the greenhouse ladders,
Reaching up white strings
To wind, to wind
The sweet-pea tendrils, the smilax, 5
Nasturtiums, the climbing
Roses, to straighten
Carnations, red
Chrysanthemums; the stiff
Stems, jointed like corn, 10
They tied and tucked,—
These nurses of nobody else.
Quicker than birds, they dipped
Up and sifted the dirt;
They sprinkled and shook; 15
They stood astride pipes,
Their skirts billowing out wide into tents,
Their hands twinkling with wet;
Like witches they flew along rows
Keeping creation at ease; 20
With a tendril for needle

They sewed up the air with a stem;
They teased out the seed that the cold kept asleep,—
All the coils, loops, and whorls.
They trellised the sun; they plotted for more than themselves. 25

I remember how they picked me up, a spindly kid,
Pinching and poking my thin ribs
Till I lay in their laps, laughing,
Weak as a whiffet;
Now, when I'm alone and cold in my bed, 30
They still hover over me,
These ancient leathery crones,
With their bandannas stiffened with sweat,
And their thorn-bitten wrists,
And their snuff-laden breath blowing lightly over me in my first sleep. 35

THE FAR FIELD

I

I dream of journeys repeatedly:
Of flying like a bat deep into a narrowing tunnel,
Of driving alone, without luggage, out a long peninsula,
The road lined with snow-laden second growth,
A fine dry snow ticking the windshield, 5
Alternate snow and sleet, no on-coming traffic,
And no lights behind, in the blurred side-mirror,
The road changing from glazed tarface to a rubble of stone,
Ending at last in a hopeless sand-rut,
Where the car stalls, 10
Churning in a snowdrift
Until the headlights darken.

II

At the field's end, in the corner missed by the mower,
Where the turf drops off into a grass-hidden culvert,
Haunt of the cat-bird, nesting-place of the field-mouse, 15
Not too far away from the ever-changing flower-dump,
Among the tin cans, tires, rusted pipes, broken machinery,—
One learned of the eternal;
And in the shrunken face of a dead rat, eaten by rain and ground-
beetles
(I found it lying among the rubble of an old coal bin) 20
And the tom-cat, caught near the pheasant-run,
Its entrails strewn over the half-grown flowers,

Blasted to death by the night watchman.
I suffered for birds, for young rabbits caught in the mower,
My grief was not excessive. 25
For to come upon warblers in early May
Was to forget time and death:
How they filled the oriole's elm, a twittering restless cloud, all one morning,
And I watched and watched till my eyes blurred from the bird shapes,—
Cape May, Blackburnian, Cerulean,— 30
Moving, elusive as fish, fearless,
Hanging, bunched like young fruit, bending the end branches,
Still for a moment,
Then pitching away in half-flight,
Lighter than finches, 35
While the wrens bickered and sang in the half-green hedgerows,
And the flicker drummed from his dead tree in the chicken-yard.

—Or to lie naked in sand,
In the silted shallows of a slow river,
Fingering a shell, 40
Thinking:
Once I was something like this, mindless,
Or perhaps with another mind, less peculiar;
Or to sink down to the hips in a mossy quagmire;
Or, with skinny knees, to sit astride a wet log, 45
Believing:
I'll return again,
As a snake or a raucous bird,
Or, with luck, as a lion.

I learned not to fear infinity, 50
The far field, the windy cliffs of forever,
The dying of time in the white light of tomorrow,
The wheel turning away from itself,
The sprawl of the wave,
The on-coming water. 55

III

The river turns on itself,
The tree retreats into its own shadow.
I feel a weightless change, a moving forward
As of water quickening before a narrowing channel
When banks converge, and the wide river whitens; 60
Or when two rivers combine, the blue glacial torrent
And the yellowish-green from the mountainy upland,—

At first a swift rippling between rocks,
Then a long running over flat stones
Before descending to the alluvial plain, 65
To the clay banks, and the wild grapes hanging from the elmtrees,
The slightly trembling water
Dropping a fine yellow silt where the sun stays;
And the crabs bask near the edge,
The weedy edge, alive with small snakes and bloodsuckers,— 70

I have come to a still, but not a deep center,
A point outside the glittering current;
My eyes stare at the bottom of a river,
At the irregular stones, iridescent sandgrains,
My mind moves in more than one place, 75
In a country half-land, half-water.

I am renewed by death, thought of my death,
The dry scent of a dying garden in September,
The wind fanning the ash of a low fire.
What I love is near at hand, 80
Always, in earth and air.

IV

The lost self changes,
Turning toward the sea,
A sea-shape turning around,—
An old man with his feet before the fire, 85
In robes of green, in garments of adieu.

A man faced with his own immensity
Wakes all the waves, all their loose wandering fire.
The murmur of the absolute, the why
Of being born fails on his naked ears. 90
His spirit moves like monumental wind
That gentles on a sunny blue plateau.
He is the end of things, the final man.

All finite things reveal infinitude:
The mountain with its singular bright shade 95
Like the blue shine on freshly frozen snow,
The after-light upon ice-burdened pines;
Odor of basswood on a mountain-slope,
A scent beloved of bees;
Silence of water above a sunken tree: 100

The pure serene of memory in one man,—
A ripple widening from a single stone
Winding around the waters of the world.

LIGHT LISTENED

O what could be more nice
Than her ways with a man?
She kissed me more than twice
Once we were left alone.
Who'd look when he could feel? 5
She'd more sides than a seal.

The close air faintly stirred.
Light deepened to a bell,
The love-beat of a bird.
She kept her body still 10
And watched the weather flow.
We live by what we do.

All's known, all, all around:
The shape of things to be;
A green thing loves the green 15
And loves the living ground.
The deep shade gathers night;
She changed with changing light.

We met to leave again
The time we broke from time; 20
A cold air brought its rain,
The singing of a stem.
She sang a final song;
Light listened when she sang.

DELMORE SCHWARTZ

1913–

IN THE NAKED BED, IN PLATO'S CAVE

In the naked bed, in Plato's cave,
Reflected headlights slowly slid the wall,
Carpenters hammered under the shaded window,
Wind troubled the window curtains all night long,
A fleet of trucks strained uphill, grinding, 5
Their freights covered, as usual.

The ceiling lightened again, the slanting diagram
Slid slowly forth.
Hearing the milkman's chop,
His striving up the stair, the bottle's chink,
I rose from bed, lit a cigarette, 10
And walked to the window. The stony street
Displayed the stillness in which buildings stand,
The street-lamp's vigil and the horse's patience.
The winter sky's pure capital
Turned me back to bed with exhausted eyes. 15

Strangeness grew in the motionless air. The loose
Film grayed. Shaking wagons, hooves' waterfalls,
Sounded far off, increasing, louder and nearer.
A car coughed, starting. Morning, softly
Melting the air, lifted the half-covered chair 20
From underseas, kindled the looking-glass,
Distinguished the dresser and the white wall.
The bird called tentatively, whistled, called,
Bubbled and whistled, so! Perplexed, still wet
With sleep, affectionate, hungry and cold. So, so, 25
O son of man, the ignorant night, the travail
Of early morning, the mystery of beginning
Again and again,
while History is unforgiven.

THE HEAVY BEAR

"the withness of the body" WHITEHEAD

The heavy bear who goes with me,
A manifold honey to smear his face,
Clumsy and lumbering here and there,
The central ton of every place,
The hungry beating brutish one 5
In love with candy, anger, and sleep,
Crazy factotum, dishevelling all,
Climbs the building, kicks the football,
Boxes his brother in the hate-ridden city.

Breathing at my side, that heavy animal, 10
That heavy bear who sleeps with me,
Howls in his sleep for a world of sugar,
A sweetness intimate as the water's clasp,
Howls in his sleep because the tight-rope
Trembles and shows the darkness beneath. 15
—The strutting show-off is terrified,
Dressed in his dress-suit, bulging his pants,
Trembles to think that his quivering meat
Must finally wince to nothing at all.

That inescapable animal walks with me, 20
Has followed me since the black womb held,
Moves where I move, distorting my gesture,
A caricature, a swollen shadow,
A stupid clown of the spirit's motive,
Perplexes and affronts with his own darkness, 25
The secret life of belly and bone,
Opaque, too near, my private, yet unknown,
Stretches to embrace the very dear
With whom I would walk without him near,
Touches her grossly, although a word 30
Would bare my heart and make me clear,
Stumbles, flounders, and strives to be fed
Dragging me with him in his mouthing care,
Amid the hundred million of his kind,
The scrimmage of appetite everywhere. 35

DYLAN THOMAS

1914–1953

THE FORCE THAT THROUGH THE GREEN FUSE DRIVES THE FLOWER

The force that through the green fuse drives the flower
Drives my green age; that blasts the roots of trees
Is my destroyer.
And I am dumb to tell the crooked rose
My youth is bent by the same wintry fever. 5

The force that drives the water through the rocks
Drives my red blood; that dries the mouthing streams
Turns mine to wax.
And I am dumb to mouth unto my veins
How at the mountain spring that same mouth sucks. 10

The hand that whirls the water in the pool
Stirs the quicksand; that ropes the blowing wind
Hauls my shroud sail.
And I am dumb to tell the hanging man
How of my clay is made the hangman's lime. 15

The lips of time leech to the fountain head;
Love drips and gathers, but the fallen blood
Shall calm her sores.
And I am dumb to tell a weather's wind
How time has ticked a heaven round the stars. 20

And I am dumb to tell the lover's tomb
How at my sheet goes the same crooked worm.

FERN HILL

Now as I was young and easy under the apple boughs
About the lilting house and happy as the grass was green,

The night above the dingle starry,
Time let me hail and climb
Golden in the heydays of his eyes, 5
And honoured among wagons I was prince of the apple towns
And once below a time I lordly had the trees and leaves
Trail with daisies and barley
Down the rivers of the windfall light.

And as I was green and carefree, famous among the barns 10
About the happy yard and singing as the farm was home,
In the sun that is young once only,
Time let me play and be
Golden in the mercy of his means,
And green and golden I was huntsman and herdsman, the calves 15
Sang to my horn, the foxes on the hills barked clear and cold,
And the sabbath rang slowly
In the pebbles of the holy streams.

All the sun long it was running, it was lovely, the hay
Fields high as the house, the tunes from the chimneys, it was air 20
And playing, lovely and watery
And fire green as grass.
And nightly under the simple stars
As I rode to sleep the owls were bearing the farm away,
All the moon long I heard, blessed among the stables, the nightjars 25
Flying with the ricks, and the horses
Flashing into the dark.

And then to awake, and the farm, like a wanderer white
With the dew, come back, the cock on his shoulder: it was all
Shining, it was Adam and maiden, 30
The sky gathered again
And the sun grew round that very day.
So it must have been after the birth of the simple light
In the first, spinning place, the spellbound horses walking warm
Out of the whinnying green stable 35
On to the fields of praise.

And honoured among foxes and pheasants by the gay house
Under the new made clouds and happy as the heart was long,
In the sun born over and over,
I ran my heedless ways, 40
My wishes raced through the house high hay
And nothing I cared, at my sky blue trades, that time allows

In all his tuneful turning so few and such morning songs
Before the children green and golden
Follow him out of grace, 45

Nothing I cared, in the lamb white days, that time would take me
Up to the swallow thronged loft by the shadow of my hand,
In the moon that is always rising,
Nor that riding to sleep
I should hear him fly with the high fields 50
And wake to the farm forever fled from the childless land.
Oh as I was young and easy in the mercy of his means,
Time held me green and dying
Though I sang in my chains like the sea.

DO NOT GO GENTLE INTO THAT GOOD NIGHT

Do not go gentle into that good night,
Old age should burn and rave at close of day;
Rage, rage against the dying of the light.

Though wise men at their end know dark is right,
Because their words had forked no lightning they 5
Do not go gentle into that good night.

Good men, the last wave by, crying how bright
Their frail deeds might have danced in a green bay,
Rage, rage against the dying of the light.

Wild men who caught and sang the sun in flight, 10
And learn, too late, they grieved it on its way,
Do not go gentle into that good night.

Grave men, near death, who see with blinding sight
Blind eyes could blaze like meteors and be gay,
Rage, rage against the dying of the light. 15

And you, my father, there on the sad height,
Curse, bless, me now with your fierce tears, I pray.
Do not go gentle into that good night.
Rage, rage against the dying of the light.

IN MY CRAFT OR SULLEN ART

In my craft or sullen art
Exercised in the still night
When only the moon rages
And the lovers lie abed
With all their griefs in their arms, 5
I labour by singing light
Not for ambition or bread
Or the strut and trade of charms
On the ivory stages
But for the common wages 10
Of their most secret heart.
Not for the proud man apart
From the raging moon I write
On these spindrift pages
Not for the towering dead 15
With their nightingales and psalms
But for the lovers, their arms
Round the griefs of the ages,
Who pay no praise or wages
Nor heed my craft or art. 20

JOHN BERRYMAN

1914–

CONVERSATION

Whether the moorings are invisible
Or gone, we said we could not tell.
But argument held one thing sure
That none of us that night could well endure:
The ship is locked with fog, no man aboard 5
Can see what he is moving toward,
There's little food, less love, no sleep,
The sea is dark and we are told it's deep.

Where is an officer who knows this coast?
If all such men long since have faced 10

Downward, one summon. Who knows how,
With what fidelity his voice heard now
Could shout directions from the ocean's floor?
Traditional characters no more
Their learnéd simple parts rehearse, 15
But bed them down at last from the time's curse.

A broken log fell out upon the hearth,
The flaming harbinger come forth
Of holocausts that night and day
Shrivel from the mind its sovereignty. 20
We watched the embers cool; those embers brought
To one man there the failing thought
Of cities stripped of knowledge, men,
Our continent a wilderness again.

These are conclusions of the night, we said; 25
And drank, and were not satisfied.
The fire died down, smoke in the air
Took the alarming postures of our fear;
The overhead horror, in the padded room
The man who cannot tell his name, 30
The guns and enemies that face
Into this delicate and dangerous place.

DREAM SONG: 14

Life, friends, is boring. We must not say so.
After all, the sky flashes, the great sea yearns,
we ourselves flash and yearn,
and moreover my mother told me as a boy
(repeatingly) 'Ever to confess you're bored 5
means you have no

Inner Resources.' I conclude now I have no
inner resources, because I am heavy bored.
Peoples bore me,
literature bores me, especially great literature, 10
Henry bores me, with his plights & gripes
as bad as achilles,

who loves people and valiant art, which bores me.
And the tranquil hills, & gin, look like a drag

and somehow a dog
has taken itself & its tail considerably away
into mountains or sea or sky, leaving
behind: me, wag. 15

DREAM SONG: 18

A Strut for Roethke

Westward, hit a low note, for a roarer lost
across the Sound but north from Bremerton,
hit a way down note.
And never cadenza again of flowers, or cost.
Him who could really do that cleared his throat 5
& staggered on.

The bluebells, pool-shallows, saluted his over-needs,
while the clouds growled, heh-heh, & snapped, & crashed.

No stunt he'll ever unflinch once more will fail
(O lucky fellow, eh Bones?)—drifted off upstairs, 10
downstairs, somewheres.
No more daily, trying to hit the head on the nail:
thirstless: without a think in his head:
back from wherever, with it said.

Hit a high long note, for a lover found 15
needing a lower into friendlier ground
to bug among worms no more
around um jungles where ah blurt 'What for?'
Weeds, too, he favoured as most men don't favour men.
The Garden Master's gone. 20

ROBERT LOWELL

1917–

THE QUAKER GRAVEYARD IN NANTUCKET

(For Warren Winslow, Dead at Sea)

Let man have dominion over the fishes of the sea and the fowls of the air and the beasts and the whole earth, and every creeping creature that moveth upon the earth.

I

A brackish reach of shoal off Madaket,—
The sea was still breaking violently and night
Had steamed into our North Atlantic Fleet,
When the drowned sailor clutched the drag-net. Light
Flashed from his matted head and marble feet, 5
He grappled at the net
With the coiled, hurdling muscles of his thighs:
The corpse was bloodless, a botch of reds and whites,
Its open, staring eyes
Were lustreless dead-lights 10
Or cabin-windows on a stranded hulk
Heavy with sand. We weight the body, close
Its eyes and heave it seaward whence it came,
Where the heel-headed dogfish barks its nose
On Ahab's void and forehead; and the name 15
Is blocked in yellow chalk.
Sailors, who pitch this portent at the sea
Where dreadnaughts shall confess
Its hell-bent deity,
When you are powerless 20
To sand-bag this Atlantic bulwark, faced
By the earth-shaker, green, unwearied, chaste
In his steel scales: ask for no Orphean lute
To pluck life back. The guns of the steeled fleet
Recoil and then repeat 25
The hoarse salute.

II

Whenever winds are moving and their breath
Heaves at the roped-in bulwarks of this pier,

The terns and sea-gulls tremble at your death
In these home waters. Sailor, can you hear 30
The Pequod's sea wings, beating landward, fall
Headlong and break on our Atlantic wall
Off 'Sconset, where the yawing S-boats splash
The bellbuoy, with ballooning spinnakers,
As the entangled, screeching mainsheet clears 35
The blocks: off Madaket, where lubbers lash
The heavy surf and throw their long lead squids
For blue-fish? Sea-gulls blink their heavy lids
Seaward. The winds' wings beat upon the stones,
Cousin, and scream for you and the caws rush 40
At the sea's throat and wring it in the slush
Of this old Quaker graveyard where the bones
Cry out in the long night for the hurt beast
Bobbing by Ahab's whaleboats in the East.

III

All you recovered from Poseidon died 45
With you, my cousin, and the harrowed brine
Is fruitless on the blue beard of the god,
Stretching beyond us to the castles in Spain,
Nantucket's westward haven. To Cape Cod
Guns, cradled on the tide, 50
Blast the eelgrass about a waterclock
Of bilge and backwash, roil the salt and sand
Lashing earth's scaffold, rock
Our warships in the hand
Of the great God, where time's contrition blues 55
Whatever it was these Quaker sailors lost
In the mad scramble of their lives. They died
When time was open-eyed,
Wooden and childish; only bones abide
There, in the nowhere, where their boats were tossed 60
Sky-high, where mariners had fabled news
Of IS, the whited monster. What it cost
Them is their secret. In the sperm-whale's slick
I see the Quakers drown and hear their cry:
"If God himself had not been on our side, 65
If God himself had not been on our side,
When the Atlantic rose against us, why,
Then it had swallowed us up quick."

IV

This is the end of the whaleroad and the whale
Who spewed Nantucket bones on the thrashed swell 70
And stirred the troubled waters to whirlpools

To send the Pequod packing off to hell:
This is the end of them, three-quarters fools,
Snatching at straws to sail
Seaward and seaward on the turntail whale, 75
Spouting out blood and water as it rolls,
Sick as a dog to these Atlantic shoals:
Clamavimus, O depths. Let the sea-gulls wail

For water, for the deep where the high tide
Mutters to its hurt self, mutters and ebbs. 80
Waves wallow in their wash, go out and out,
Leave only the death-rattle of the crabs,
The beach increasing, its enormous snout
Sucking the ocean's side.
This is the end of running on the waves; 85
We are poured out like water. Who will dance
The mast-lashed master of Leviathans
Up from this field of Quakers in their unstoned graves?

V

When the whale's viscera go and the roll
Of its corruption overruns this world 90
Beyond tree-swept Nantucket and Wood's Hole
And Martha's Vineyard, Sailor, will your sword
Whistle and fall and sink into the fat?
In the great ash-pit of Jehoshaphat
The bones cry for the blood of the white whale, 95
The fat flukes arch and whack about its ears,
The death-lance churns into the sanctuary, tears
The gun-blue swingle, heaving like a flail,
And hacks the coiling life out: it works and drags
And rips the sperm-whale's midriff into rags, 100
Gobbets of blubber spill to wind and weather,
Sailor, and gulls go round the stoven timbers
Where the morning stars sing out together
And thunder shakes the white surf and dismembers
The red flag hammered in the mast-head. Hide, 105
Our steel, Jonas Messias, in Thy side.

VI

OUR LADY OF WALSINGHAM

There once the penitents took off their shoes
And then walked barefoot the remaining mile;
And the small trees, a stream and hedgerows file
Slowly along the munching English lane, 110
Like cows to the old shrine, until you lose
Track of your dragging pain.

The stream flows down under the druid tree,
Shiloah's whirlpools gurgle and make glad
The castle of God. Sailor, you were glad 115
And whistled Sion by that stream. But see:

Our Lady, too small for her canopy,
Sits near the altar. There's no comeliness
At all or charm in that expressionless
Face with its heavy eyelids. As before, 120
This face, for centuries a memory,
Non est species, neque decor,
Expressionless, expresses God: it goes
Past castled Sion. She knows what God knows,
Not Calvary's Cross nor crib at Bethlehem 125
Now, and the world shall come to Walsingham.

VII

The empty winds are creaking and the oak
Splatters and splatters on the cenotaph,
The boughs are trembling and a gaff
Bobs on the untimely stroke 130
Of the greased wash exploding on a shoal-bell
In the old mouth of the Atlantic. It's well;
Atlantic, you are fouled with the blue sailors,
Sea-monsters, upward angel, downward fish:
Unmarried and corroding, spare of flesh 135
Mart once of supercilious, wing'd clippers,
Atlantic, where your bell-trap guts its spoil
You could cut the brackish winds with a knife
Here in Nantucket, and cast up the time
When the Lord God formed man from the sea's slime 140
And breathed into his face the breath of life,
And blue-lung'd combers lumbered to the kill.
The Lord survives the rainbow of His will.

MR. EDWARDS AND THE SPIDER

I saw the spiders marching through the air,
Swimming from tree to tree that mildewed day
In latter August when the hay
Came creaking to the barn. But where
The wind is westerly, 5
Where gnarled November makes the spiders fly
Into the apparitions of the sky,
They purpose nothing but their ease and die
Urgently beating east to sunrise and the sea;

What are we in the hands of the great God? 10
It was in vain you set up thorn and briar
In battle array against the fire
And treason crackling in your blood;
For the wild thorns grow tame
And will do nothing to oppose the flame; 15
Your lacerations tell the losing game
You play against a sickness past your cure.
How will the hands be strong? How will the heart endure?

A very little thing, a little worm,
Or hourglass-blazoned spider, it is said, 20
Can kill a tiger. Will the dead
Hold up his mirror and affirm
To the four winds the smell
And flash of his authority? It's well
If God who holds you to the pit of hell, 25
Much as one holds a spider, will destroy,
Baffle and dissipate your soul. As a small boy

On Windsor Marsh, I saw the spider die
When thrown into the bowels of fierce fire:
There's no long struggle, no desire 30
To get up on its feet and fly—
It stretches out its feet
And dies. This is the sinner's last retreat;
Yes, and no strength exerted on the heat
Then sinews the abolished will, when sick 35
And full of burning, it will whistle on a brick.

But who can plumb the sinking of that soul?
Josiah Hawley, picture yourself cast
Into a brick-kiln where the blast
Fans your quick vitals to a coal— 40
If measured by a glass,
How long would it seem burning! Let there pass
A minute, ten, ten trillion; but the blaze
Is infinite, eternal: this is death,
To die and know it. This is the Black Widow, death. 45

THE FAT MAN IN THE MIRROR
(After Werfel)

What's filling up the mirror? O, it is not I;
Hair-belly like a beaver's house? An old dog's eye?

The forenoon was blue
In the mad King's zoo
Nurse was swinging me so high, so high! 5

The bullies wrestled on the royal bowling green;
Hammers and sickles on their hoods of black sateen . . .
Sulking on my swing
The tobacco King
Sliced apples with a pen-knife for the Queen. 10

This *I*, who used to mouse about the parafined preserves,
And jammed a finger in the coffee-grinder, serves
Time before the mirror.
But this pursey terror . . .
Nurse, it is a person. *It is nerves.* 15

Where's the Queen-Mother waltzing like a top to staunch
The blood of Lewis, King of Faerie? Hip and haunch
Lard the royal grotto;
Straddling Lewis' motto,
Time, the Turk, its sickle on its paunch. 20

Nurse, Nurse, it rises on me . . . O, it starts to roll,
My apples, O, are ashes in the meerschaum bowl . . .
If you'd only come,
If you'd only come,
Darling, if . . . The apples that I stole, 25

While Nurse and I were swinging in the Old One's eye . . .
Only a fat man with his beaver on his eye,
Only a fat man,
Only a fat man
Bursts the mirror. O, it is not I! 30

JAMES DICKEY

1923–

THE FIEND

He has only to pass by a tree   moodily walking   head down
A worried accountant   not with it   and he is swarming
He is gliding up the underside light of leaves   upfloating
In a seersucker suit   passing window after window of her building.
He finds her at last, chewing gum   talking on the telephone.   5
The wind sways him softly   comfortably sighing   she must bathe
Or sleep.   She gets up, and he follows her along the branch
Into another room.   She stands there for a moment   and the teddy
    bear
On the bed feels its guts spin as she takes it by the leg and tosses
It off.   She touches one button at her throat, and rigor mortis   10
Slithers into his pockets, making everything there—keys, pen
And secret love—stand up.   He brings from those depths the knife
And flicks it open   it glints on the moon one time   carries
Through the dead walls   making a wormy static on the TV screen.
He parts the swarm of gnats that live excitedly at this perilous level   15
Parts the rarefied light high windows give out into inhabited trees
Opens his lower body to the moon.   This night the apartments are
    sinking

To ground level   burying their sleepers in the soil   burying all floors
But the one where a sullen shopgirl gets ready to take a shower,
Her hair in rigid curlers, and the rest.   When she gives up   20
Her aqua terry-cloth robe the wind quits in mid-tree   the birds
Freeze to their perches round his head   a purely human light
Comes out of a one-man oak   around her an energy field   she
    stands
Rooted   not turning to anything else   then begins to move like a
    saint
Her stressed nipples rising like things about to crawl off her   as he
    gets   25
A hold on himself.   With that clasp she changes   senses   some-
    thing

Some breath through the fragile walls   some all-seeing eye
Of God   some touch that enfolds her body   some hand come up
    out of roots

That carries her as she moves   swaying   at this rare height. She
wraps
The curtain around her and streams.   The room fades.   Then
coming   30
Forth magnificently   the window blurred from within   she moves
in a cloud
Chamber   the tree in the oak currents sailing   in clear air keep-
ing pace
With her white breathless closet—he sees her mistily part her lips
As if singing to him   come up from river-fog   almost hears her
as if
She sang alone in a cloud   its warmed light streaming into his
branches   35
Out through the gauze glass of the window.   She takes off her bath-
ing cap
The tree with him ascending   himself and the birds all moving
In darkness together   sleep crumbling the bark in their claws.
By this time he holds in his awkward, subtle limbs the limbs

Of a hundred understanding trees.   He has learned what a plant is
like   40
When it moves near a human habitation   moving closer the later it
is
Unfurling its leaves near bedrooms   still keeping its wilderness life
Twigs covering his body with only one way out   for his eyes into
inner light
Of a chosen window   living with them night after night   watch-
ing
Watching with them at times their favorite TV shows   learning—   45
Though now and then he hears a faint sound: gunshot, bombing,
Building-fall—how to read lips: the lips of laconic cowboys
Bank robbers   old and young doctors tense-faced   gesturing savagely
In wards and corridors   like reading the lips of the dead

The lips of men interrupting the program at the wrong time   50
To sell you a good used car on the Night Owl Show   men silently
reporting
The news out the window.   But the living as well, three-dimensioned,
Silent as the small gray dead, must sleep at last   must save their lives
By taking off their clothes. It is his beholding that saves them:
God help the dweller in windowless basements   the one obsessed   55
With drawing curtains this night. At three o'clock in the morning
He descends   a medium-sized shadow   while that one sleeps and
turns
In her high bed in loss   as he goes limb by limb   quietly down
The trunk with one lighted side. Ground upon which he could not
explain

His presence he walks with toes uncurled from branches, his bird-
movements 60
Dying hard. At the sidewalk he changes gains weight a solid
citizen

Once more. At apartments there is less danger from dogs, but he has
For those a super-quiet hand a hand to calm sparrows and rivers,
And watchdogs in half-tended bushes lie with him watching their
women
Undress the dog's honest eyes and the man's the same pure beast's 65
Comprehending the same essentials. Not one of these beheld would
ever give
Him a second look but he gives them all a first look that goes
On and on conferring immortality while it lasts while the sub-
urb's leaves
Hold still enough while whatever dog he has with him holds its
breath
Yet seems to thick-pant impatient as he with the indifferent men 70
Drifting in and out of the rooms or staying on, too tired to move
Reading the sports page dozing plainly unworthy for what
women want
Dwells in bushes and trees: what they want is to look outward,

To look with the light streaming into the April limbs to stand
straighter
While their husbands' lips dry out feeling that something is there 75
That could dwell in no earthly house: that in poplar trees or beneath
The warped roundabout of the clothesline in the sordid disorder
Of communal backyards some being is there in the shrubs
Sitting comfortably on a child's striped rubber ball filled with rainwater
Muffling his glasses with a small studious hand against a sudden 80
Flash of houselight from within or flash from himself a needle's
eye
Uncontrollable blaze of uncompromised being. Ah, the lingerie
Hung in the bathroom! The domestic motions of single girls living to-
gether
A plump girl girding her loins against her moon-summoned blood:
In that moon he stands the only male lit by it, covered with leaf-
shapes. 85
He coughs, and the smallest root responds and in his lust he is set
By the wind in motion. That movement can restore the green eyes
Of middle age looking renewed through the qualified light
Not quite reaching him where he stands again on the ususal branch
Of his oldest love his tie not loosened a plastic shield 90
In his breast pocket full of pencils and ballpoint pens given him by
salesmen
His hat correctly placed to shade his eyes a natural gambler's tilt

And in summer wears an eyeshade   a straw hat Caribbean style.
In some guise or other he is near them when they are weeping without
    sound
When the teen-age son has quit school   when the girl has broken
    up   95
With the basketball star   when the banker walks out on his wife.
He sees mothers counsel desperately with pulsing girls face down
On beds full of overstuffed beasts   sees men dress as women
In ante-bellum costumes with bonnets   sees doctors come, looking
    oddly
Like himself   though inside the houses   worming a medical arm   100
Up under the cringing covers   sees children put angrily to bed
Sees one told an invisible fairy story   with lips moving silently as
    his
Are also moving   the book's few pages bright. It will take years
But at last he will shed his leaves   burn his roots   give up
Invisibility   will step out   will make himself known to the one   105
He cannot see loosen her blouse   take off luxuriously   with lips
Compressed against her mouth-stain   her dress   her stockings
Her magic underwear.   To that one he will come   up frustrated
    pines
Down alleys   through window blinds   blind windows   kitchen
    doors
On summer evenings. It will be something small that sets him off: 110
Perhaps a pair of lace pants on a clothesline   gradually losing
Water to the sun   filling out in the warm light with a well-rounded
Feminine wind as he watches   having spent so many sleepless nights
Because of her   because of her hand on a shade always coming
    down
In his face   not leaving even a shadow stripped naked upon the
    brown paper   115
Waiting for her now in a green outdated car with a final declaration
Of love   pretending to read   and when she comes and takes down
Her pants, he will casually follow her in   like a door-to-door sales-
    man
The godlike movement of trees stiffening with him   the light
Of a hundred favored windows   gone wrong somewhere in his
    glasses   120
Where his knocked-off panama hat was   in his painfully vanishing
    hair.

ALLEN GINSBERG

1926–

A SUPERMARKET IN CALIFORNIA

What thoughts I have of you tonight, Walt Whitman, for I walked down the sidestreets under the trees with a headache self-conscious looking at the full moon.

In my hungry fatigue, and shopping for images, I went into the neon fruit supermarket, dreaming of your enumerations!

What peaches and what penumbras! Whole families shopping at night! Aisles full of husbands! Wives in the avocados, babies in the tomatoes!—and you, Garcia Lorca, what were you doing down by the watermelons?

I saw you, Walt Whitman, childless, lonely old grubber, poking among the meats in the refrigerator and eyeing the grocery boys.

I heard you asking questions of each: Who killed the pork chops? What price bananas? Are you my Angel? 5

I wandered in and out of the brilliant stacks of cans following you, and followed in my imagination by the store detective.

We strode down the open corridors together in our solitary fancy tasting artichokes, possessing every frozen delicacy, and never passing the cashier.

Where are we going, Walt Whitman? The doors close in an hour. Which way does your beard point tonight?

(I touch your book and dream of our odyssey in the supermarket and feel absurd.)

Will we walk all night through solitary streets? The trees add shade to shade, lights out in the houses, we'll both be lonely. 10

Will we stroll dreaming of the lost America of love past blue automobiles in driveways, home to our silent cottage?

Ah, dear father, graybeard, lonely old courage-teacher, what America did you have when Charon quit poling his ferry and you got out on a smoking bank and stood watching the boat disappear on the black waters of Lethe?

TO AUNT ROSE

Aunt Rose—now—might I see you
with your thin face and buck tooth smile and pain
                    of rheumatism—and a long black heavy shoe
                              for your bony left leg

limping down the long hall in Newark on the running carpet 5
past the black grand piano
in the day room
where the parties were
and I sang Spanish loyalist songs
in a high squeaky voice 10
(hysterical) the committee listening
while you limped around the room
collected the money—
Aunt Honey, Uncle Sam, a stranger with a cloth arm
in his pocket 15
and huge young bald head
of Abraham Lincoln Brigade

—your long sad face
your tears of sexual frustration
(what smothered sobs and bony hips 20
under the pillows of Osborne Terrace)
—the time I stood on the toilet seat naked
and you powdered my thighs with Calomine
against the poison ivy—my tender
and shamed first black curled hairs 25
what were you thinking in secret heart then
knowing me a man already—
and I an ignorant girl of family silence on the thin pedestal
of my legs in the bathroom—Museum of Newark.
Aunt Rose 30
Hitler is dead, Hitler is in Eternity; Hitler is with
Tamburlane and Emily Brontë

Though I see you walking still, a ghost on Osborne Terrace
down the long dark hall to the front door
limping a little with a pinched smile 35
in what must have been a silken
flower dress
welcoming my father, the Poet, on his visit to Newark
—see you arriving in the living room
dancing on your crippled leg 40
and clapping hands his book
had been accepted by Liveright

Hitler is dead and Liveright's gone out of business
The Attic of the Past and *Everlasting Minute* are out of print
Uncle Harry sold his last silk stocking 45
Claire quit interpretive dancing school
Buba sits a wrinkled monument in Old
Ladies Home blinking at new babies

last time I saw you was the hospital
pale skull protruding under ashen skin 50
blue veined unconscious girl
in an oxygen tent
the war in Spain has ended long ago
Aunt Rose

INDEX